HOMETOWN KID
CITY KID

A TRUE STORY OF DEMOGRAPHIC CHANGE IN A NORTHERN INNER RING SUBURB...
A WINNING BASKETBALL TEAM THAT REFLECTED THIS CHANGE...
AND MANY LONG-TIME FANS AND CITIZENS WHO
EMBRACED THE TEAM AND THE CHANGE...
REVIVING MEMORIES OF GLORY YEARS

AND A TRUE STORY OF A SMALL GROUP OF PEOPLE
WHO SAW THE CHANGES IN THE BASKETBALL PROGRAM AS A PROBLEM...
AND INFLUENCED A NEW ADMINISTRATION
TO FIRE THE COACH

HOMETOWN KID CITY KID

JIM DIMICK JR

MILL CITY PRESS

Mill City Press, Inc.
2301 Lucien Way #415
Maitland, FL 32751
407.339.4217
www.millcitypress.net

Printed in the United States of America

Paperback ISBN-13: 978-1-6628-1553-9
Ebook ISBN-13: 978-1-6628-1554-6

Prologue

I t was a clear sunny Saturday morning in March of 2009. I was at the Fred Babcock Post #555 VFW Club in Richfield, Minnesota. I was in the post's dining hall, which was on the east side of the building. Windows lined the east and south walls, and the bright sunlight of late winter was streaming in. There were tables and chairs throughout the room, and the place was about half full of patrons, all of them enjoying the hearty breakfasts that the club was known for. The room was full of the smell of coffee and the sounds of conversation and laughter.

I was the head boys' basketball coach at Richfield High School. The VFW Club and the American Legion were both generous donors to my program. My team had just finished eating, while sitting at the long tables with the white linen tablecloths. After the meal, the players left in small groups. My four senior starters had taken longer to leave. After about ten minutes they stood and slowly walked out of the club. All four young men were African-American. They all had short fade hair-cuts, no facial hair, they all were wearing well fit stylish jeans pulled up snug, classy athletic shoes, and all four were sporting Richfield High School lettermen's jackets. The jackets were made completely of leather, and the leather was colored cardinal. The only other color on the jackets was the white trim. On the left breast of each jacket was a big R. The four seniors had a very clean-cut look to them.

After talking to the manager for a few minutes, I began to walk out, retracing the steps of the four seniors. As I neared the arched door to the entryway which separated the dining room from the bar, I noticed an old white man sitting alone at the last table. He was facing me and leaning forward with his left hand on his cane. As I neared him, he raised his right hand and looked me in the eye. He appeared to be in his eighties. He was wearing a navy-blue baseball hat adorned with gold-colored letters and small military insignias. He was obviously a World War II veteran. I pointed to his hat and asked him if he fought in Europe or the Pacific.

"The Pacific. Are you the basketball coach?"

"Yes."

"Were those your players?"

"Yes."

He was still looking me directly in the eyes and nodding, "you've got a fine-looking ball club."

"Thank you."

We talked for another five minutes. He wanted to know how the team was doing, and I wanted to know about him. I asked him where he was originally from, how long he had lived in Richfield, where he had worked, and about his family. He gave me the expected answers. He had returned from the war, built a small story and a half house with the GI bill, and he had been active in the community ever since.

Turn the clock back thirty-five years. The scene would have been pretty much the same, with a few obvious differences. The coach would have been Stu Starner. The players would have all been Americans of European descent. They would have had hair flopping down to their eyebrows and even a little over their ears. The snug fitting jeans would have flared near the floor into bell bottoms, and the shoes would have been Adidas or Pumas. The R on the chest of the letter jackets would have been smaller and been framed by a Spartan emblem. These players would have also had a clean-cut look to them.

The veteran might have been wearing the same hat, but he wouldn't have been leaning on the cane. He would have known how many mortgage payments were remaining on his house. And he would have been beginning the discussion with his wife, on how many more years they should work, before a long retirement.

Turn the clock back another fifteen years. The coach would have been Gene Farrell. The players would have all been white kids with crew cuts. The hair would have been just a shadow on the sides, with the top maybe a little longer or a flat top. The jeans would have been snug from top to bottom, and the shoes might have been Converse All-Stars. The letter jackets would have been cardinal with white sleeves. Once again, these kids would have had a very clean-cut look to them.

The veteran most likely wouldn't have been at the VFW. He would have been at home in the rambler eating breakfast with his wife and children, before beginning his to-do list of Saturday morning chores and errands.

Turn the clock back another seventy-five years. The building housing the VFW Club wasn't there. Fred Babcock, the World War I veteran who it was named after wasn't born yet. The place where the building stands would have been the north wood lot of the Bartholomew farm. It would have been a timbered stand of mostly oak trees. The farmer, Riley Bartholomew may have been using the mild late winter day to harvest some firewood, and exercise his horses. The horses would have been pawing at the ground on the south facing slope looking for early season grass. And the singsong sound of the crosscut saw would have been harmonized by the spring songs of cardinals and chickadees and the drumming of downy woodpeckers.

* * *

When my 2005 Richfield basketball team advanced to state, it ended a 31-year drought of state tournament appearances. I invited two of the alums of the 1973 and 1974 teams to speak to my players. Both the 1973 and 1974 teams lost in the state finals. These were guys who graduated in a class of over 900 students. They both played three sports. They saw the number of boys playing basketball in their grade get winnowed down from 100 players in sixth grade to 30 players in ninth grade to seven or eight players as seniors.

The team was sitting in a circle in the high school gym after practice. Two fit guys in their late forties with short haircuts graying at the temples were standing in the middle. They spent about ten to fifteen minutes telling the story of their back-to-back state runs, noting the support of the students and the community, and their coach Stu Starner. They told the team to enjoy every moment, because it would go so fast. They emphasized to enjoy your buddies, because this group would rarely if ever be together again. Every eye was on them. You could have heard a pin drop.

Then one of them closed the session. I will never forget it.

"You guys don't know how lucky you are. When we played the whole team was white. We didn't have one black kid. We didn't have a kid who was born in Africa, like you," and he pointed at one of our players, who grinned. They all grinned. "We all looked the same. We all lived in the same kind of houses, the houses like you live in, and you live in, and you," and he pointed at some more kids. "We grew up in those houses. It was all that we knew."

"We didn't have any diversity. Look at you guys. You're all different colors. You are so...so lucky. You got buddies who don't look like you. We never got to experience that."

He was animated. He was sincere. He was speaking from the heart. He had attended the Richfield schools from kindergarten through his senior year. He still lived in Richfield. He spent his entire life coming home to one of two similar houses, which were two of the many small houses that were built after World War II.

* * *

I was hired as the basketball coach in the summer of 2001. The program hit rock bottom seven years earlier. My predecessor, Greg Miller, spent the next seven years rebuilding the entire program from the bottom up. I took over from Greg, reaping the benefits of the great job that he did and, with more talent, took the program to the next level. Greg went back to the suburb where he grew up, and took over the successful Robbinsdale Armstrong High School program. His new program remained solidly at that same next level. In the next nine years the successes of both programs mirrored each other.

During this sixteen-year period, the inner ring suburb of Richfield was going through a rapid demographic change. Historically Richfield had been a working-class suburb, with small homes full of large families and apartments full of young couples who had yet to buy their first house. Both the single-family homes and the apartment buildings were filled with almost all European-Americans, or white people. The apartment buildings were now transitioning to small families, many of them minorities and African-Americans. Some of the homes were also being purchased by minority couples who were starting their families.

The demographics of the schools soon reflected this change. Both coaches did everything possible to welcome the minority kids into the program. However, as the head boys' basketball coach I had a few advantages that my predecessor didn't have.

My predecessor had tried to get financial aid for kids who were on reduced and free school lunch so that they could play traveling basketball. The board of the Richfield Boys Basketball Association denied his request. He was a teacher at the high school. I was a CPA. With my business connections, I was able to independently raise the money for the financial aid. The same basketball board then approved this.

I came from coaching at a Minneapolis high school where there were after school study halls for ninth grade athletes. I had seen this succeed in Minneapolis, and I implemented this at Richfield.

For elementary and middle school students, I was able to reduce the fee for the June summer camp, and make the July 3 on 3 league free. I ran free open gyms on June and July evenings and worked with any and all kids who showed up.

I had two young rising assistant coaches who were African-American. And I had the additional advantage of being married to an African-American woman who was a product of the sixties and seventies. My wife Martha was born and raised in Milwaukee. She grew up experiencing and overcoming systemic racism in one of the most segregated cities in the north. She was quick to point out racial inequities and urged me and my coaching staff to step up and speak out.

In a few short years, the demographic change that started with Coach Miller's teams accelerated. This rapid change of the student body was soon reflected on my teams, and at all levels, and especially at the upper levels of the program. After nine years, including a three-year run of 20-win seasons with two state tournament berths, we were anticipating another three-year run of 20-win seasons. Two years after the district hired a new superintendent whose office entertained a steady parade of disgruntled parents, all homeowners and all white, I was suddenly fired.

In Minnesota, a fired high school coach has the right to an open school board hearing, followed by a vote of school board members to either reinstate the coach or keep him fired. I exercised that right. I listed the positive accomplishments of the program, both athletically and academically. More importantly, I informed the administration, the school board, and the public that if we ran the program the way that the complainers wanted us to run it, it would be a textbook case of institutional/systemic racism backed up with an argument of tokenism. Being a CPA, I supported this statement with definitions, quotes, statistics, and pie graphs. This led to a public debate on why I was fired which included Twin Cities talk show radio.

* * *

I forced the administration to publicly address an issue that I believe they discussed in private, and had done everything that they could to sweep under the carpet. They conceded to the request of these disgruntled parents, as well as a small group of people who called themselves the 'concerned-citizens'. These two groups of people, by unifying, spread their message throughout the community, and influenced many more people. The essence of the message was that I didn't care about the Richfield kids. The public spectacle that was portrayed on the radio and in the newspapers ended up being a black eye for the school administrators.

The discussion also transitioned from institutional/systemic (northern) racism, which I addressed in my speech, to overt (southern) racism which was not a subject in my speech. There were many community members who supported my teams, and who disagreed with and were surprised by the firing. These people experienced the glory years of the high school when the Richfield Spartans, with their cardinal and white uniforms, were synonymous with Lake Conference and state-wide success. Some of these people played on the championship teams. Others were parents or neighbors of kids who played on those teams. Their pride and loyalty to their community ran deep. Because they weren't at the school board hearing, they never heard my unabridged message. They had to have been confused and upset and hurt, and probably pissed off. This ended up being a black eye for their community.

I thought of the World War II vet sitting in the VFW, and the two basketball alums standing in the gym. They unquestionably did not see color, and they unquestionably welcomed diversity and competition into Richfield. And they were members of two generations of life-long Richfield residents.

I felt good that the administration's cover-up was exposed. I didn't feel good that my supporters and longtime Richfield residents were hurt. For both of these conflicting feelings, I felt the need to set the record straight. When I shared all of this with my inner circle of friends, I was told that I should write a book. This is the result.

* * *

The farmer Riley Bartholomew was no stranger to a controversy about race. As a middle-aged man in northeast Ohio, he would have followed the debates in congress over slavery and state's rights of the 1840s and 1850s. Later, as a General in the Ohio Militia, he and his troops fought alongside and under the direction of the Union Army. Some regiments of the Ohio Militia fought at the battle of Shiloh, the first major bloodbath of the western part of the war. Over 23,000 soldiers were casualties, killed, wounded, or missing. One hundred fifty years later, the debate over the war has been renewed. The debate is deeply divided on geographic lines. Mostly northerners believe that the war was about slavery, while many southerners insist that it was only about state's rights, and that it had nothing to do with slavery or race.

The debate about the Richfield boys' basketball program and my firing was also deeply divided, but along racial lines. Many Richfield white people emphatically and emotionally said, "it had absolutely nothing to do with race." I heard that other Richfield white people refused to even discuss it as a racial issue, "when it comes to race, there is nothing to discuss." They believed it was about Richfield kids losing their spots to kids that weren't Richfield kids, and they believed it was about me recruiting to Richfield these kids who weren't Richfield kids. I talked to a good friend of mine who was white and from Minneapolis. He was removed from the controversy except for following it in the papers. He had brought up the subject. He looked at me, kind of grimaced, and shook his head from side to side, "is it about race? Uh...I don't think so."

Another good friend of mine who was also white and from Minneapolis said the exact opposite, nodding his head emphatically, "there's no question if it was about race." An African-American man who worked many years for the city of Richfield looked me in the eye, pointed his finger at me, and said "what happened to you at Richfield had everything to do with race, and there is no question about that." Many other white people, and every other black person that I knew agreed with this friend. And many of them believed that it centered on one thing, the definition of a 'Richfield kid'.

This book is most certainly a story of high school basketball, youth sports, sports-parents, booster clubs, open enrollment, a northern inner ring suburb, and demographic change. Is it about race and racism? That question is for the reader to decide. Again, most certainly, there will be disagreement.

Table of Contents

Washburn

You look at where you're going and where you are and it never makes sense, but then you look at where you've been and a pattern seems to emerge.

—Robert Pirsig

I was in my office doing some accounting work on a beautiful morning in early May when the phone rang. It was Dan Pratt, the athletic director at Washburn High School.

"Can you come into the office today? We need to meet to discuss some things."

I quickly answered "Sure, what's up, Dan?"

There was a pause. "Well, it's some things that we need to discuss face to face."

There was another pause. "I'd rather not… I'd rather that you come in. When could you come in?"

I told him that I would leave my office in five minutes.

Fifteen minutes later I walked into his office. He got up to close the door. He then sat across from me and said, "Well, we're not going to renew your contract." There was another pause. I looked him in the eye and calmly said, "You're not going to renew my contract. In other words, you're firing me." After another pause, he said "Well, you're on a one-year contract from year to year and we're not going to renew it next year."

He paused, and then went on. "I don't agree with the decision, Jim. I know how hard you've worked to build the program. You were in a really tough spot, and I think that you should have been given more time. But the decision has been made."

"Well, if you didn't make the decision, then who did?"

"You know who my bosses are."

"Well Dan, I think that I deserve to be told why I've been fired."

For the next five minutes we discussed the high school, the basketball program, the city conference, and what it would take to turn the basketball program around. I then walked out of his office, up the stairs, and walked into the principal's office. His secretary said that he was out for the day. I left him a short note to call me. I called three times the next week and told his secretary to tell him to call me. He never did.

* * *

On the drive over to the high school, my intuition told me what was coming. For the last four months, I saw the signs. I was the head basketball coach at Washburn for three years, and I was on the hot seat the last winter. I learned that once you realize that you are on the hot seat, you develop a sixth sense that notices things. The first sign was our record. We finished 3-21. The principal, who was the third new principal in three years, attended five or six games the last half of the season. Normally a principal only attends a couple of games all year. One of the assistant principals, also in his first year, observed practices early in the year, and we spoke at these practices. He said that he was really impressed with my drills, and the way that I ran a practice. In January he stopped coming to practices. Two sets of parents who openly did not like each other began conversing at games. Underlying everything, we had junior and senior classes with the worst talent in the city, a couple of vocal sets of parents who thought these kids were talented, and one of whom had been good friends for a number of years with the new principal.

As a few days went by, it began to sink in. At first, I was embarrassed and humiliated. Over the years, I remembered discussing the subject of high school coach firings with my friends and other coaches. I always said that if you are a really good coach, the players know it, and they tell their parents. Their parents tell other people, and the word gets out in the community. In addition, the administrators and other coaches all know who the really good coaches are, and the word spreads. A good coach never gets fired. Now I was a fired coach. I would be getting a lot of phone calls from my coaching colleagues and friends. My record at Washburn in three years was 17-51. It would be in the paper. With my big ego, I was not looking forward to it.

* * *

I was asked to apply for the Washburn job in October of 1998 by an alumnus who was active in the community. Historically, Washburn was a traditional power in most sports on the south side of the city. Along with Southwest, it was located near the chain of lakes in the more affluent southwest quadrant. Before it closed in 1982, Central to the south of downtown was another traditional power. When Central closed, its students were split between Washburn and Roosevelt. Central had encompassed the south side black neighborhood. For many years, the only three high schools in the state with African-Americans had been Central and North in Minneapolis, and Central in St Paul. By the time that I interviewed for the job, almost the entire conference was made up of black basketball players.

I called my friend Dave Buss to get his opinion. Dave was a retired college coach. He coached at UW-Green Bay, and Long Beach State. At Green Bay, two of his teams were Division II national runners-up. He finished his coaching career at St Olaf, the Division III college that I attended. I knew him from being an assistant in the same conference at the University of St Thomas. He was the best basketball coach I ever coached against, and we became good friends. After I explained the situation to him, he said "you know it's funny that you called. A couple of years ago I got a similar phone call from a former player of mine at Green Bay. He had just been hired at Vincent High School in Milwaukee. Your situation sounds exactly like his. If you can get the good players to attend your high school and get them to play your defense, you'll start winning, and the whole thing will snowball. You'll attract kids to the school, and you'll have a lot of fun with this."

Two weeks later I was sitting in an office in the old high school with the athletic director Gary Stenerson, the principal Debra Brooks-Golden, and a parent. I was asked if I could build a feeder program from the top down. I was also asked what my expectations were regarding off the court behavior of the players. A week later I was hired, three weeks prior to the start of the season.

The former coach, Louis Boone was at Washburn for twenty years. The high point of his tenure was winning the state title in 1994. The past two seasons the team had sunk to the bottom half of the conference standings. His son Adam was the returning point guard. Adam was the varsity point guard since his eighth-grade year, and was selected All-City as a sophomore. He transferred to Minnetonka, an affluent second ring suburban school to the west.

Like the other six Minneapolis public schools, the program that I inherited lacked the financial resources of the neighboring private and suburban schools. There were two coaches coaching two teams, a varsity and a B squad. The B squad was made up of sophomores and freshmen. There was no ninth-grade team. There was no support staff to help with the non-coaching administrative duties. The varsity practiced after school, and the junior varsity practiced at 5:30 pm. There were no study halls. Because the varsity coach taught his system, and the B squad coach taught his system, there was no continuity from team to team. There was no practice gear. The team went "shirts and skins" in practice. Many of the players had academic issues. The year before, when the semester ended in the middle of January, a number of players were removed from the team due to sub-par grade point averages. There was no feeder program being run by the Washburn coaches for the kids of the Washburn area. I believed that to turn a program around, a coach needs one class with three or four players who are good students, good enough players to win the conference, and good enough to make a run at the state tournament. When we had tryouts two weeks later, it was obvious that this kind of class did not exist at Washburn.

Ninety kids from grades nine through twelve tried out for the two teams. We ended up selecting thirteen for the varsity and fifteen for the junior varsity. These kids and their parents all signed contracts which described expected behavior on the court, off the court, and in the classroom. The primary message of the contracts centered on "taking care of business"; being on time for class, turning in assignments on time, studying for tests, and being a good citizen in the hallways.

We finished fifth in the conference, after having been picked to finish last, and our overall record was 5-17. More importantly, we had installed my system. This was nothing more than the team man-to-man defense and motion offense first made popular by Bob Knight, and utilized by many of the successful college and high school programs in the country. It takes players anywhere from six weeks to a year and a half to learn how to play this way. I believed ever since I was a young coach, that it was the best way to play the game, and that it was the way to beat the good teams. By early February, our kids were starting to get it, and in six of our last ten games we had even totally shut down the other team's offense. Our B squad finished sixth out of seven teams in the conference. When one of my buddies asked me how our freshmen and sophomores were, I replied "if they make up our varsity in two years, we're in trouble". In addition, my assistant Jason Moore and I did not work well together. Two days after the season ended, we parted ways.

* * *

The next two summers I ran three weeks of "shooting camps" at three of the local parks. The camps were free of charge to any kids who showed up from grades five through nine. My goal was to identify the local kids who had talent, to establish a relationship with them, and to teach them individual offensive fundamentals at an early age. We also had individual workouts for the high school kids and any other kids who showed up two nights a week for eight weeks at Martin Luther King Park, which was in the Washburn area. We made corrections to their shooting form, and taught them the same fundamentals that we were teaching the young kids. It was obvious that we were teaching them things that they had never learned before.

We also started winter traveling teams for kids going into sixth, seventh, and eighth grades. I raised the money to finance these teams, to hire and pay a ninth-grade coach a salary equal to the junior varsity coach, and to pay our ninth-grade coach an additional $1,000 to monitor mandatory after school study halls for our freshman and sophomores.

I found a young and loyal varsity assistant in Alcindor Hollie. He grew up in an African-American family that had deep roots on the south side of the city. He had attended Washburn, and made All-City in both football and basketball. After high school, he played strong safety at the University of Minnesota-Duluth for legendary coach Jim Malosky. His goal was to someday be a head coach in the city. He was a natural teacher, and he had a gift for relating to kids. We worked together well, and we had a lot of fun.

I found another loyal volunteer assistant in Nick Puzak. Nick played on the 1976 Minneapolis Marshall-University state championship team. After graduating from Carleton College, he returned to Minneapolis and was self-employed as a realtor. I now had two solid Minneapolis guys on my staff.

Three years in a row in the spring, Alcindor and I coached an AAU team of Washburn area seventh and eighth graders. We practiced three times a week and played in weekend tournaments. We charged $20 per kid, so that nobody would be excluded due to finances. This gave us an opportunity to gain their confidence as coaches. It also enabled us to develop a relationship with the parents, and for them to see the improvement in the individuals and the team. In those three years, our records were 14-5, 19-4, and 22-3. We taught parts of our team man-to-man defense. The kids were smart and athletic. At times our defense was awesome. The kids had "bought in" and they were talking about coming to Washburn. My wife came to the games, and she was really excited. She kept saying "they'll play defense like the DeLaSalle kids someday."

I hired Jeff Sill as our ninth-grade coach and study hall supervisor. Jeff worked in the building, and was also the defensive coordinator of the football team. The football team was coached by Pete Haugen. Pete was a physical education teacher, a Washburn grad, and had been at Washburn four years. He had instituted a system of mandatory study halls. After school, the entire team attended a one-hour study hall. During this time, some kids went to classrooms to get extra help from teachers. After this one-hour time period, the team began football practice. This system had resulted in many football players improving academically and staying eligible. The City Conference had a mandatory 2.0 GPA eligibility requirement, with an appeal process for special situations. If a student didn't maintain the 2.0 GPA, he could not practice or play with the team. The key to keeping kids eligible and on track to graduate, was to get them as freshmen, teach and/or reinforce study skills, and never let them fall behind. Pete and Jeff did a great job of this. In addition, the team was also beginning to win a lot of games. Jeff was a study hall monitor and tutor for the football team, and he would now do the same for the basketball team.

In addition to Alcindor and Jeff, I had the good fortune of getting Lance Berwald as a volunteer assistant. Lance was also a graduate of Washburn. He played college ball at Nebraska and North Dakota State, and then played nine years of pro ball in Spain and Greece. After returning from Europe, I coached two years with him at DeLaSalle. He spent the last winter as the head coach of a minor league professional team in Fargo, North Dakota. He was returning to Minneapolis to work as a realtor. He was six feet nine inches tall, he played for over twenty head coaches during his career, and he was the best big man coach in the state. He had a passion for the game, and he was a player's coach. He was excited to be part of it. He kept on emphatically saying "Jim, you get your system in at Washburn, you will win."

***

As I started my second year at Washburn, I felt that we had made strides. We had two seniors returning with college talent, and two other seniors who had not been on the team my first year. We had no depth, but with this core of four good seniors, we felt that we could finish in the top half of the conference, and be a very good team by tournament time. Our lower classes were very weak.

In the fall I heard from a faculty member that he had strong reason to believe that my two good senior guards were dealing weed. I met with them after school one day at a local coffee shop. I prefaced the conversation by saying that I didn't expect them to admit to anything, but that the talk around the high school was that they were dealing weed. I didn't preach. I didn't raise my voice. I looked both of them right in the eye. They didn't say much, but I could tell that they respected my candor. I told them that I knew that there were some basketball programs in the city where players smoked weed, and got by with it; but that Washburn wasn't going to be one of those programs. I finished by telling them that I really liked both of them as people, that I really liked working with both of them, and that I saw a lot of good in both of them. They didn't say a lot and the entire conversation took less than an hour.

The season had two high points. In early January, we beat St Paul Highland Park at home. Under long-time coach Charles Portis, they won the state title the year before in Class AAA. When we played them, their record was 5-0, and they were ranked #3 in the state in Class AAA. In late February we traveled to the southeast corner of the state to play Rushford-Peterson. They were 15-0 and ranked #1 in the state in Class A. We beat them 59-52 in front of a sellout crowd. They then went on to win the state title.

Neither of our senior guards made it through the season. We finished with a 5-7 record in the city, and 9-13 overall. We played well and lost four close games against the top three teams in the city. Patrick Henry High School, from the northwest corner of the city, went on to win the state in Class AAA.

In terms of our record, the season had not met our expectations. When I talked to Coach Buss, he said "Sometimes you have to clean house and take your lumps for a couple years, before you can start winning. You did the right thing. You haven't coached your own kids yet. You're still coaching the former coach's kids. It will be totally different once you start coaching your own kids."

* * *

Going into year three, we knew it was going to be an incredible challenge. Our top three classes were all weak both in numbers and talent. The only three players with college talent were two sophomores and a freshman. We looked at our schedule and realistically agreed that we had four games with a 50% chance of winning, six games where we could maybe win one, and thirteen games that we had no chance to win. If we could win three of the winnable games, and pull two more wins out of the air, we could finish with five wins which would be a great season. The problem was, do we tell the kids this?

And unfortunately, we had some parents with no clue, who believed that the talent was there. It was a "Catch-22" situation. If we were honest with the kids, the parents would say that "we didn't believe in them." If we told the kids that they were better than they really were, the parents would ask "why aren't we winning?" When we played South, I confided this to their coach Joe Hyser. His response was "Jim, you don't have one kid who would start for anybody else in the league, and most of your kids wouldn't play at all."

I called up Coach Buss, and asked him what to do.

"Stick to your system and play the best kids regardless of grade. Are the young kids ready?"

"They're better than all but a couple of the older kids."

"Play them, you got nothing to lose. What kind of senior leadership do you have? Are the seniors realistic? Will they accept playing with the young kids? Or do they want to play with their buddies from their own grade, even if their buddies aren't any good? If they're gonna be selfish jerks about it, you got a problem."

When I told him about the potentially poisoning parents, he asked if the administration would have my back. I told him that we had a new principal and new athletic director, and that the new principal was a longtime friend of one set of poisoning parents.

"You got a problem. Do it your way, if they fire you, they fire you."

Next, I called up Dave Thorson. Dave was the coach at DeLaSalle High School. DeLaSalle was the oldest catholic high school in the city with a long and storied basketball tradition. It was located on Nicollet Island on the Mississippi river and in the shadow of downtown. Dave had been at DeLaSalle since 1995. Prior to that, he was an assistant at the University of Minnesota. He was an aggressive recruiter, a student of the game, and a great coach.

The first thing that he asked was "who can you beat?"

I answered "Roosevelt, Southwest, and maybe one non-conference game."

"Then spend all of your time preparing for those teams. Don't tell the kids that you are doing this. Scout the heck out of those teams. I'm not saying don't scout the other teams. Scout the other teams, and prepare for the other teams, but anything that the other teams do similar to the teams that you can beat, prepare for it." There was a pause. "It sounds like you're going to have to spend a lot of time on man press and zone press offense. Knowing the city coaches, I would bet that you'll see a lot of trapping, both in the full court and the half court. You're going to have to be over prepared for this, or you won't get the ball up the court."

"So, in other words, devise our game plans for Southwest and Roosevelt early in the year, and then use those game plans or game plans similar to those in every other game that we can."

"Exactly, I would have my kids defending Southwest's out of bounds plays and set plays every week. Who cares if you lose to Henry by 30 or 40? They're going to beat you by 30 for sure anyway, no matter what you do."

An old retired coaching friend of mine attended our second game. After the game he made a point of stopping me. He said "Jim, you've got two goals for this team; keep them up and keep them together. You'll be lucky to win a couple games."

The situation went from bad to worse when our sophomore point guard was expelled from school twice and I removed him from the team. After this,

I brought up two young kids to the varsity. Craig Dyer was a 5-11 freshman point guard who was athletic in a body that was still growing. Ray Brown was our best eighth grader. He was 5-10, still growing, and was going to be a great player. Although still in the awkward stage, he was a great shooter, and he always played hard. In addition, Craig and Ray were the best passers on the team.

We ended up finishing 3-21. We split with Southwest and picked up two other wins. We also played a couple of great games at Henry and North and lost. We lost in the first game of the tournament at Columbia Heights.

When the season ended, Alcindor and I began working with our 7th and 8th grade AAU team. We were blowing teams out, the kids were improving, and the kids and parents were totally buying in to our system. We had another 7th grader with great potential named William Braziel Jr. Along with Ray, I projected him to be at least 6-4 and athletic. If they both reached this height, they would eventually be scholarship players in college. We also added a 9th grade AAU team which was coached by Mark Robinson, who was a friend of Alcindor's and who played basketball at the University of Minnesota-Duluth under legendary coach Dale Race.

I was envisioning three classes in a row of "good students, good kids, and good players." When I did not get a phone call from the administration by the end of April, I figured I had survived the storm. Two weeks later I got the phone call, and I was a fired coach.

First Summer & Winter

The coach is a teacher. His subject is fundamentals... Winning
is more related to good defense than good offense.

—Jack Ramsay

On a Saturday morning two days later, I was driving into the city. I was beginning my favorite part of the commute, the fifteen-minute drive along the north shoreline of Lake Minnetonka. It was the kind of spring morning that people who live in Minnesota dream of all winter. The sky was clear and there wasn't a ripple on the water. It was the time of the year when the water was warming up after the big thaw and the crappie bite was on. Near the many small bridges connecting the bays of the huge lake there were usually people, often minorities, shore fishing for crappies.

As I rounded a long curve, I saw Ray Brown's father Bill. He was sitting on a five-gallon bucket with a line in the water. I pulled over, parked, sat on the ground next to him, and told him that I had been fired. He said that he had already heard. He was pissed and he wasn't sure where Ray was going to go to high school. He said that most of the kids from the spring team were probably going to go to South. We talked for a while about a number of things.

Before I left, I told him, "My intuition tells me that I'll coach Ray again. I don't know where or when, but I just got a feeling that someday our paths will cross again."

"Thanks coach. You know Raymond and I will never forget what you did for him."

By the middle of May the word spread through the Twin Cities basketball community that I was fired. I remember telling my wife "they won", in reference to the parents of the upperclassmen who wanted to get rid of me. Her answer was "things happen for a reason."

I spent the next two weeks working my way through the acceptance stage of the grieving process. Lance was furious. He was like the bull in the cartoon with the hot air steaming out of his ears and nostrils. As a player, he had been an intense competitor with a warrior mentality. I remember him telling me, "As a Washburn alumnus, I am livid that they did this to you after all of the hard work that you put in." Alcindor and Mark were more resigned, slowly shaking their heads with surprise. When I talked to Al, he kept on saying, "They never gave us the chance to coach our own kids."

I received a lot of phone calls from other coaches, and the question that they all asked was if I was going to coach again. I told them that I hadn't thought about it. The more people that I talked to, and the more times that I said, "No I didn't resign, I was fired", the better I felt.

* * *

One day in late May, the phone rang again in my office.

"Hello Jim. This is Jim Baker the athletic director at Richfield High School. The Richfield basketball job is open, and we'd like it if you'd apply. Greg Miller took the Armstrong job, so the job just opened up. Good bye."

A couple of days later I called up Greg Miller. Greg and I had been friends since he had taken the Richfield job. He said that he was very happy at Richfield, but that he couldn't pass up the Armstrong job. Armstrong High School was one of the largest high schools in the state. It was the more affluent of the two high schools in the Robbinsdale school district, and Greg was from Robbinsdale.

Next, I called up my assistants Lance, Alcindor, and Mark. Their reactions were all the same. They were all ready to go to Richfield. The next week Bill Brown called me. "We heard talk that you're going to get the Richfield job. If you get it coach, we're coming." Ray and his father Bill rented an apartment two blocks north of Highway 62 in south Minneapolis. They actually lived closer to Richfield High School than they did to Washburn. He also said that the principal of Washburn called him, and wanted him and Ray to tour the high school. He excitedly told me how he had said "After what you all did to Coach Dimick, we're not interested."

* * *

I interviewed for the job in the first week of June. The interview committee consisted of Baker, Lars Oakman, a long-time faculty member who had coached a number of sports, and the president of the Richfield Boys Basketball Boosters. I gave them a copy of the manual that I gave to all of my assistants. The manual stated my philosophy, and a list of drills for individual skill development and team drills. It also showed a simplified offense and defense for use by the younger teams, which would eventually help them become ready for the high school program as ninth graders. They had a list of questions that all of the finalists were asked.

Jim Baker asked his list of questions first, all relating to the basketball program. He was a southern Minnesota guy, originally from Rochester, and had taught and coached at both Albert Lea and Lake City. He was good friends with Jerry Snyder, the hall of fame coach at Lake City. Jerry won a couple of state championships with seven-foot center Randy Breuer. Breuer went on to play for the Gophers and spent over a decade in the NBA. Jerry ran a model winning program and he was one of the coaching icons in the state. I knew Jerry from working basketball camps, so I knew that I had an in with Baker. In addition, it was obvious from his comments that he knew about my track record as a coach before I was at Washburn.

Lars wanted to know how I was going to communicate with the faculty without being in the building. I told him that I was fully aware that it was a big disadvantage not being in the building. I then told them that I had been a teacher for six years in my twenties, so I knew what it was like to be a high school teacher, and that this was an advantage over a coach who had never been in the classroom. I also said that I absolutely had to have at least one assistant who was in the building. I then gave them copies of the player contracts, and sample grade reports. In addition, I could see that Lars and I saw things the same way.

The president of the Boosters only asked two questions. The first question was if I would help coach their 1st and 2nd grade winter program. I answered yes, but that I might not always be there, and if I wasn't there, one of my assistants would be.

He then stated that often times kids from Minneapolis view Richfield as a district that they can transfer to in high school, and because our team isn't as good, they can come in and play right away. He wanted to know what my opinion was on playing these kids. I told him that the new kids would be at a disadvantage because they wouldn't know my system. On the other hand, they might be better basketball players. It would depend upon how good they were, how fast they learned my system, and how good the other kids were. "This is high school basketball and public education. I am going to put the best team on the floor and play the kids that playing together make the best team."

I then made a point without being asked a question. I told them about my little brother John who played basketball through his junior year in Northfield. I said that he was in their feeder program beginning in elementary school. I told them that he learned a lot of basketball and had a lot of fun, and that now he plays on a men's league team, he loves it, and he's still improving. I then said that the purpose of the feeder program isn't only to produce varsity players, and that we need to give kids who never play on the varsity a positive experience which they can use the rest of their lives.

Jim Baker then asked one last question.

"How are you going to get the black and white parents together?"

"I don't know... After being at DeLaSalle and Washburn, I've thought about that question a lot, and I've talked about it a lot with other coaches, and nobody seems to have the answer. Getting the black and white kids together is easy, but the getting the parents together is a whole different challenge." Jim then agreed with me, and said that after his two years working at Richfield, he was still trying to think of ways of how to get the black and white parents to come together, and he hadn't found any easy answers. Like many of the other inner ring suburbs, the percentage of minority students was increasing every year.

The last week in June, Baker called to tell me that the job was mine if I wanted it. I drove over to the high school and we talked in his office with the door open. He showed me the contract and asked me if I had any questions.

"If a member of the faculty decides next year that they want the head basketball job, or if a new faculty member is hired who wants the head basketball job, am I out?"

"No. I would never do that to you, and there is nothing in the teacher's contract that says that I have to do that. You're my coach."

We then talked about the high school, and many of the common coaching friends that we had in southern Minnesota. A lot of the stories were funny, and one funny story about one character led to another funny story. We talked for over an hour, and a number of coaches and faculty members walked in and I began meeting them. Lars sat down and joined the conversation for fifteen minutes. It was obvious that these coaches all looked up to Jim Baker, and that he had done a great job of uniting them. This was the exact opposite of Washburn. I walked outside hearing Martha's voice in my ear, "things happen for a reason."

***

In June the *Minneapolis StarTribune* published an article authored by Michael Rand which covered the top two thirds of one page in the sports section. A four-inch by seven-inch color photo of Dave DeWitt standing in the high school gym overlooked the article.

A season of job insecurity
Centennial boys' basketball coach Dave DeWitt led his team to a conference title and into the section final last winter-and his contract was not renewed. Other successful coaches also have met similar fates

Unlike tenured high school teaching positions, which offer long-term job security, coaching appointments are subject to non-renewal at the end of each season. The decision often boils down to a judgment call by a small number of people and doesn't require specific evidence for the conclusion. Coaches say they are vulnerable to losing a position they have poured their lives into without understanding why it happened...

...Two other boys' basketball coaches, Minneapolis Washburn's Jim Dimick and New London-Spicer's Bob Knutson, faced similar situations this year...

..."Coaches don't really have any recourse," said DeWitt, who also teaches physical education at Centennial. "You have letters of assignment, one-year contracts, and there doesn't have to be any rhyme or reason for things to happen. I'm certainly not the first coach to be dismissed, and I won't be the last."...

...Tom Critchley, executive director of the Minnesota Basketball Coaches Association, said the way coaches are judged has changed. "We're finding that coaches who have demonstrated success are being let go. That's a major change from when I first started," Critchley said. "Building a program means nothing. You have to please a certain populace."

...DeWitt said that (John) Christiansen (the superintendent) gave him four reasons for being let go: temper control, lack of interpersonal skills to deal with parents, lack of community support, and the need to move the program in a new direction...

...Christiansen declined to discuss specifics of the matter, citing Section 13.43 of the Minnesota Data Practices Act, which protects personnel data. School board members directed questions to Christiansen when contacted...

"That's why the Centennial thing is so disturbing,", he (Critchley) said. "The coaches on our executive board are appalled by this. (DeWitt) is very respected among his peers, not only for his coaching ability but his leadership ability. With the pressure that's put-on coaches today, I don't think the way they're treated is fair," Critchley said. "It's just another example of what's happening out there. It's sad." [1]

Two days after the firing was announced 80 community members began a letter-writing campaign, and ten days later the school board met and unanimously supported the superintendent's recommendation of firing DeWitt. The meeting was attended by an estimated 350 people, and it was estimated that almost all of the people were supporters of DeWitt.

DeWitt spent 16 years at Centennial. He built the program from the ground up, working with the young kids in the summer. A half a dozen years later, when a couple of talented classes came through the pipeline, the Cougars showed up in the state rankings. They were in a tough section, with long time perennial power Mounds View and legendary coach Ziggy Kauls. The past two seasons the Cougars had a record of 39-13. DeWitt's last team had won the conference title with a record of 22-5.

DeWitt played for two more renowned coaches in high school and college. His high school mentor was Ed Prohofsky at Marshall-University High in Minneapolis. In college he played for Don Meyer at Hamline. Meyer finished a 38-year college coaching career by being inducted into the Naismith Basketball Hall of Fame. He spent 24 years at Lipscomb University in Tennessee where he was a big influence on a young coach named Pat Summit. He produced numerous books and videos which taught coaches how to teach players. When I was an assistant at DeLaSalle, Dave Thorson scouted a team that was playing Centennial. I asked Dave about Centennial. He said, "watching DeWitt's team is like watching a Don Meyer instructional video. Their fundamentals are perfect, individual fundamentals, team fundamentals, everything."

A week later I asked my Dad what he thought of the article.

"There had to have been some parents who knew the superintendent and were pissed off about playing time. There had to have been. But firing DeWitt is like firing the Spanish teacher, when all of the students have huge vocabularies and speak with perfect grammar. I wonder how many superintendents would do that."

* * *

The first week in July the *Richfield Sun Current* ran an article across the top of the sports page.

RHS names Dimick to lead boys' hoops program

...Dimick began coaching in 1976, serving as head boys' basketball and assistant football coach at LeSueur High School. He left there in 1981, and had stints as a college assistant coach at Macalester and St. Thomas. He was an assistant coach at DeLaSalle High School in Minneapolis before taking over at Washburn three years ago...He started at LeSueur fresh out of college, and in his six years at LeSueur, the team won three District 13 championships.

During his time at St. Thomas, Dimick was in charge of the defense under head coach Steve Fritz. "It was a good experience there, we had five conference championships during the seven years I was there," Dimick said. "We were blessed with some good athletes, and that's where I gained my reputation as a man-to-man defensive coach." He said that's the kind of defense he would like his Spartan teams to play. "I'm very much a man-to-man defensive coach. If we have the athletes, that's how I want to play."

Dimick said that Miller has left him with a good program. "It's going to be great coming into a program that doesn't have to be rebuilt," said Dimick. "Greg's invested seven years into this. We'll be retaining the assistants who are in place, and I'll be bringing two assistants with me from Washburn, Lance Berwald and Alcindor Hollie." But the new coach added..."Greg Miller has done a heck of a job building the program...I'm thrilled to be able to just pick up where he left off," Dimick said. "Philosophically, he and I are very close, both offensively and defensively. I don't plan on making a lot of changes." [2]

***

The next thing to do at Richfield was to make sure that the summer program was still up and running. The following Monday morning I walked into the Richfield gym to see about fifty boys being coached through drills by Kelly Liebfried and Matt Mullenbach. Kelly and Matt were assistant coaches under Miller. Kelly was a social studies teacher in the middle school and Matt was a math teacher in the high school. The camp consisted of one week of skills, drills, and contests. The morning session was for boys who had completed grades three through five, and the afternoon session was for boys who had completed grades six through eight. About forty boys were enrolled in the afternoon session. The second half of the summer feeder program was a three-on-three league. This began after the fourth of July and ran for three weeks. The boys would show up for two hours each day and play games of three on three. The players were assigned to the same teams for the entire three weeks, and the teams had NBA nicknames. The first two weeks of camp was the regular season, and the last week was the playoffs.

I sent out a letter to all of the returning players in grades nine through twelve announcing open gyms three nights a week for the remainder of July. To conform to state high school league rules, I stated that these open gyms were optional.

The next Tuesday 28 high school kids showed up. I spent the first half hour working with them individually on ball handling, offensive footwork, and shooting form. Then I split them up into teams and they played 3 on 3 half court make it/take it. We then progressed to 4 on 4 half court make it/take it. The last 45 minutes they went full court 5 on 5. The first team to score five baskets won the game, and the winners stayed on the court. In all of these games, I established my rules to begin teaching ball and man movement fundamentals. Three examples are a two-dribble limit, the passer has to cut after passing, or the ball has to be passed into the post at least once every four passes. This was summer basketball in its purest form. A coach gives the players individual attention and they leave with drills and techniques to work on while they are practicing on their own. Then they play shirts and skins, defense calls fouls, offense calls violations. Because the coach doesn't have to referee, he can observe and teach. A coach has the kids long enough to "give them their homework". They then go home and do it, and more importantly, they do it correctly. The next time they come back the process is repeated, and the skill development moves to the next level. For two hours, every kid is playing constantly until the 5 on 5 games. This type of open gym format fit the age-old coaching axiom that "teams are built during the winter, and players are built during the summer."

Besides inviting the high school players, I also invited the middle school players to attend. They could run through drills, and have a chance to play in the games if we needed players.

The second night 13 kids showed up. By Thursday we only had nine kids. The next three weeks we averaged between four and eight kids per night, and it was almost always the same kids. These kids benefited from the low numbers because they got a lot of individual attention. Half a dozen other kids that were playing on summer AAU teams came every night that they could. Many of the older players spent their summer evenings playing American Legion baseball.

Later that week I had lunch with Liebfried and Mullenbach. We discussed the state of the program, the returning players, and their goals as coaches. A pressing issue that I then brought up was the returning eighth graders. This was a talented group led by three outstanding players who lived in Richfield, and the word was that all three were going to Holy Angels for high school. I had not seen any of them play. They had not attended any of the open gyms or the summer camp. They were playing on a summer AAU team coached by two of their dads.

The Academy of Holy Angels was coached by Jesse Foley. He grew up in south Minneapolis and he was an alumnus of Holy Angels. He served as the director of admissions at the catholic high school, and he had an outstanding varsity team returning. Four of his best players including his two star guards Steven King and Jason Boerboom lived in Richfield, and were products of the traveling program.

I told Kelley and Matt, "The first thing we have to do if we're going to take this program to the next level, is to stop Holy Angels from raiding our best kids. If Jesse gets our best eighth grader every year, we're coaching the leftovers. We're never going to win if we don't stop this."

One of them said, "I know that you don't want to hear this, but what you should do now is to start working on next year's eighth graders, because you aren't going to get these three kids. They're gone."

The next question that I asked pertained to the camp. "What is the demographic breakdown of the elementary and middle schools in terms of race?"

"I believe that the middle school is roughly 60% white, 20% black, and 20% other minorities. The elementary schools have similar numbers, but I believe the minority percentages are higher."

Next, I asked, "Then why aren't there any black kids in the camp? I counted over ninety kids in the camp and only four black kids. Black kids like to play basketball."

They both looked at each other. One of them shrugged his shoulders and said, "Well, their parents don't sign them up, and most of them can't afford it." The other then added, "The black kids don't attend the camp or play on the traveling teams, and the primary reason for this is most certainly money. They enter the program when they go out for the junior high school team, because it doesn't cost anything."

* * *

That evening I called up Isaiah's dad Les, the coach of the AAU team. He told me that Isaiah was indeed going to Holy Angels, and that the AAU team had two more practices before leaving for their last tournament in Dallas the next weekend. He said that I was welcome to attend practice.

The next night I walked into the Richfield High School gym. It felt strange. I remember thinking, here I am, walking into my gym, watching a couple of parents coach my kids, who were going to attend my rival's high school. The only advantage that I had, was that they had picked up Ray Brown for their last couple of tournaments, and Ray's dad Bill was at the practice.

One of the most important skills of a basketball coach is being able to project the upside of a player. The upside is a term which is used to describe the future level of his playing ability. In other words, how much will he improve in the future years? How much will he grow, how much stronger and quicker will he get, and how much will his skills improve? At the high school level, while kids are still in their adolescent years, the first question is the most important; how much will he grow?

The superstar of the team was a bruising physical inside player who stood five foot nine. He was African-American, had some facial hair and hair on his legs, and he looked facially like a twenty-year-old. It was obvious to me that he was done growing. He was what I call a "junior high super star", a kid who was bigger and more physically mature than the other kids in his early teens. In high school, other kids would pass him up in height. He would have to learn to play away from the basket, or he would never play high school basketball. With his work ethic, he could do this.

Isaiah Goodman was a very skilled point guard with a bounce in his step. He was quick, and he was going to get quicker. He could go to the hoop with either hand, and he was a good shooter who could be developed into a great shooter. He was also a charismatic leader and an excellent student. He looked to me like he might grow a couple of more inches, but be under six feet. He was the kind of kid that Richfield High School needed on the basketball team and walking the halls.

Travis was the prospect. Like Isaiah he was a light skinned African-American. He stood about five foot nine. He had very good shooting form which only needed a couple of minor adjustments. He had no facial hair and he looked facially like an eighth grader. Like the other two, his offensive footwork needed a lot of work. I thought to myself, this kid is going to end up at least 6-2, and maybe taller. He's the one who has a chance to have his college paid for.

I walked up to Les and his assistant near the end of the practice.

"Do you mind if I work with your sons and their buddy Travis for fifteen minutes after practice? I know that you said that they're all going to Holy Angels, and that's fine, but I think that I can help them with their shooting, and I'm not going to go down without a fight. Best case scenario for me, you all change your mind and decide to attend Richfield. Worst case scenario for me, they all go to Holy Angels and are better shooters."

"No problem, coach", said Les. "Take all of the time that you want."

I had them take turns shooting 12-to-15-foot jump shots facing the basket while the other two rebounded. I gave each one of them one thing to work on to improve their form. They all were receptive. After 15 minutes Travis was the only one left.

I explained to them the teaching point of "shot line". The shot line is an imaginary line on the floor connecting the shooter's dominant eye with the exact middle of the basket. If the ball is going to go into the basket, the ball has to be above the shot line throughout the shot. After the ball is released, if the shooter holds his shooting arm in the air with the wrist flopping down, he can see if his arm and wrist are above this line and in a straight line to the target. My high school coach, Jed Dommeyer, taught me to move my arm to the left or right after every shot so that my arm was then above this line. By doing this, it wouldn't correct the already released shot, but it would help the next shot. I called this "sighting the shot".

I then told Travis to focus only on "sighting the shot" for the next 20 shots. I could tell from his body language that nobody had ever taught him to sight the shot. I asked him if sighting the shot made sense, and if he was making more shots. I remember him grinning and nodding.

I then asked him "What do you aim for when you shoot? What is your target?" He thought about it. I remember him saying something to the effect that he didn't know and that he just aimed for the basket. I then explained to him how an archer aims for the exact middle of the bull's eye, and that his target is the size of a pinpoint. If the arrow misses the pinpoint by an inch, it is still inside the bull's eye. I told him that there were three schools of thought on what a shooter's target should be, the pinpoint center of the front rim, the pinpoint center of the back rim, and the pinpoint center of the middle of the basket. I asked him which one he wanted to aim for. I remember him saying the middle of the basket.

"Then aim for the exact pinpoint middle of the basket. Shoot twenty more shots and sight the shot on every shot. After each shot, make sure that your arm is in line with the exact pinpoint middle of the basket." His first shot hit the left inside of the rim and went in. I said "you were off to the left." The next shot nicked the front rim and went in. I said "you were down the middle but short." The next shot hit the back rim and bounced straight back to him. I said "you were down the middle but long." Then he swished one, but it was an inch or two beyond the exact middle of the basket. I said "you were long by an inch." After 20 shots, I said "you made 14, but you only had three perfect swishes." Do you think that you'll make more shots with a smaller target and sighting the shot?" Again, I remember him nodding and smiling, and I could tell that nobody had ever taught him these things before. I remember him shaking his head and still smiling.

Then I gave him my hard sales pitch. I finished by saying, "You know Ray Brown. He's coming to Richfield. He's going to end up being at least 6'2" and maybe taller. I think you'll be at least 6'2" too, and both of you might end up being taller than that. If we have you guys together, we'll be ranked in the top five in the state, and we'll be packing this place. Look around this gym. Imagine the stands pulled out, every seat taken, and people standing in the end zones and the corners. This town's been waiting 30 years to get back to being a basketball power and it's been waiting thirty years to get back to the state tournament. If I get you and Ray, we're gonna be back there in a hurry. I'm not going to tell you how I coach, or how good a coach I am. Ask Ray and his dad about that. He's played five years for me. All that I'll tell you is that I'm going to play the best players on the varsity, no matter what grade they're in. The kids all know who the best players are, and if you're one of the best players as a freshman or a sophomore, you won't be on the sophomore team or the junior varsity playing for one of my assistants, you'll be on the varsity playing for me."

The next night they practiced again. One section of bleachers was pulled out and some parents were watching practice. Some mothers were sitting at one end. I walked up, introduced myself, and sat down near them.

"I understand that you are probably going to have your sons attend Holy Angels. Is that true?"

I remember them all saying yes.

"Is that a done deal?"

I remember them nodding.

"If you don't mind me asking, why do you want your sons to attend Holy Angels instead of Richfield?"

I remember one saying after a pause, "He thinks that there's a better chance to win over there."

"Well, I think that we're going to win a lot of games here, and your sons could be a part of that. I would like to meet with you, your husbands and your son to talk about it one time. I'm not going to bug you, or call you up repeatedly. I'd just like to sit down one time, away from here, to discuss it. Then I won't talk to you again, and you can make your decision."

I remember both of them saying that they would think about it.

The next day I set up a meeting with Lance and Jamar Hardy. Jamar had been the traveling coach for these kids for a couple of years. I met him the night before when he was also at practice. Jamar was a Richfield alum in his mid-twenties. In addition to coaching in the traveling program, he was also an assistant coach at the junior high. He was one of the first African-Americans to play basketball at Richfield. He had a passion for the game, was full of enthusiasm, and said that he wanted to learn how to coach man to man defense from me. It was clear to me that our best bet for salvaging these three kids was to name him ninth grade coach. I told Jamar that I wanted him to be the ninth-grade coach, and his first job was to get these three kids.

Two nights later, Lance, Jamar, and I were sitting in a living room talking to the parents of one of these boys. They lived in a typical Richfield house.

The meeting didn't last long. The message that I gave them was brief and to the point.

I told them that I was philosophically opposed to recruiting eighth graders. I also told them that we intended on taking the high school basketball program to the next level, and that in order to do that, we needed all of the Richfield kids who were the best players and the best students to attend Richfield High School.

"Selfishly, what's in it for us is that we want to coach the best kids. We want to win. However, we also believe that it would be best for your son. If I didn't believe that it was best for your son to play for me, I wouldn't be sitting here trying to get you to change your mind."

I promised them two things; their son would reach his potential as a student, and that he would learn more basketball than he would at any other high school. I told them that I could give them as many references as they wanted. I could give them names and phone numbers of coaches or parents of kids who had played for me. I also told them that in my opinion, if I had had the chance to work with their son and to get to know them, that we wouldn't be meeting right now. They would've decided long ago to attend Richfield. After some additional conversation, and a few questions and answers, we left. I then told Jamar that it was up to him to close the deal.

The next day Jamar called me. When the conversation ended, I was confident that the young man was coming to Richfield. I told Jamar that we had to be ready for Holy Angels to come back after him again, when they got wind of this. Then I asked Jamar about the other young men. I remember him saying that the other sets of parents weren't going to change their minds and that they didn't want to meet with us.

***

The next Sunday evening I attended my first meeting of the Richfield Boys Basketball Boosters. They met on a Sunday night, once every month at Davanni's Pizza in Richfield. The board had seven members. Its purpose as stated in its by-laws was to "promote, develop and support Richfield boys' basketball in grades 3-12, through moral, physical and financial support." It oversaw the winter feeder program which was not under the auspices of the school district.

There were three parts to this. First and second graders attended skill and contest sessions on Saturday mornings in January and February. These were coached by the high school coach and some high school players. Third and fourth graders played in a house league two nights a week. For this the kids were split into teams and were coached by parents. Fifth through eighth graders tried out for the traveling team in their grade. These four teams played against teams from other towns and school districts. They were coached by college kids or young adults who were not parents. In addition, there was a house league for fifth and sixth graders who did not make the traveling team in their grade. These programs were open to any student who lived in Richfield or attended school in Richfield. All three parts of the program required a fee to be paid by the parents; $30 for the first and second grade program, $65 for the house league, $175 for the fifth-grade traveling, and $225 for the sixth through eighth grade traveling. Each board member was responsible for managing one part of the program. This entailed a lot of work for some parts of the program.

The president was in his last year. His two sons had graduated two and three years earlier. They had been two of the best players on Greg Miller's best team. His family had never lived in Richfield. They lived in Bloomington. Their sons had attended Blessed Trinity Elementary in Richfield, and because of this they were eligible to play on the traveling teams from fifth through eighth grade. I remember him telling me at a later date, that they decided to open enroll their sons at Richfield, rather than have them attend Kennedy High School. Kennedy was the less affluent of the two Bloomington high schools, and they lived in the Kennedy area.

Jim Noonan ran the traveling program, and he had three sons in the program; a junior, an eighth grader, and a second grader. Bob and Denise Pulford were in charge of public relations and fund-raising. Their son was going to be a sophomore.

The treasurer's oldest son had graduated the year before, and his younger son was going to be a junior. Another man was in charge of the third through sixth grade house league. His wife was also on the board and was the secretary. They also had two sons in the program, one was a junior, and one was a freshman. Running the house league was a huge time commitment.

Another person ran the winter tournament. He had one son that had recently graduated and another son who was going to be a junior. The tournament was always the second weekend of December and it was a big money maker for the organization. There was another member who was a new member and director-at-large whose son was going to be a freshman. As the head coach of the high school team, I was also a board member.

Basketball boards or booster clubs like this one formed in Minnesota in the eighties with the rise of winter traveling teams. As these community-based programs rose in prominence, they replaced a portion of the school-based programs which had been in place for years. There was no way that the high school coach could oversee and coach these teams, and the school districts couldn't afford it, so parent volunteer help was needed. Each basketball board or booster club in each community, had its own relationship to the school-based program and the high school basketball team. Parents volunteered their time to coach, raise money, work at concession stands, and perform other duties. In addition, they paid fees for their sons to participate. The obvious inherent problem was that some parents expected that their sons to be granted playing time because of the time and money that they had contributed. As in the case of the president, if the sons of the parents who worked the hardest were the best players, it was easy. This was never always the case.

Twenty-five years earlier, I had been a young basketball coach in LeSueur, a small town in southern Minnesota. During that time, a parent had approached me to form a booster club. He was a former coach, a great guy, he meant well, and he had two kids in the program. When I told my athletic director and mentor Bruce Frank about this, Bruce's quick response was "Don't do it. The next thing they'll be doing is telling you who to play and how to coach."

Greg Miller inherited the program in the summer of 1991. He spent a lot of time working with these board members. It was inevitable that they were going to develop friendships. Knowing Greg, I knew that he was going to do it his way, which meant that they didn't always get their way with him. However, because of the friendships, they probably had his ear. They weren't going to have my ear.

In a conversation with Greg before taking the job, he told me about a promising sophomore named DeRail Moore who moved to Richfield from Gary, Indiana, as a ninth grader. I asked Greg if this was a common occurrence, a kid moving in during middle school or high school. His reply was that it was a phenomenon that was just starting and that it was going to happen a lot more in the future. I got the feeling that the Armstrong job opened up at the right time for Greg, in terms of preserving his friendships with the board members.

Greg had also depended on the board to pay for a number of things for the high school program. I was going to work with them, but I didn't want them to ever get the idea that I was dependent on them, and I didn't feel comfortable asking them for money. I decided early on to request money for as few things as possible, only for the same things that Greg had requested money for, and only for the same things every year. I had a big advantage here over most high school coaches. Because of my business connections, I was easily able to raise my own money.

* * *

A week later, Lance and I met with Ray Brown and his dad Bill at their apartment. Because we knew them so well, the conversation was mostly small talk about the history of Richfield High School and about basketball. They had already completed all of the paperwork necessary to open enroll under The Choice is Yours Program and were accepted.

We didn't want to let down our guard. We knew that they were invited to and toured both Holy Angels and Cretin-Derham Hall, and that they would most likely qualify for a full scholarship, or close to it, at both of these schools. In addition, a lot of his buddies who had planned on attending Washburn were now going to South. These kids were working him hard to go to South. We told them to keep recruiting Travis. Unfortunately, this is what high school sports had evolved into. Eighth graders chose high schools based upon where they thought they could win, and where their buddies were going to high school.

After we left, I told Lance, "I look forward to the day when we aren't doing this. If we do our job and work hard with the young kids in Richfield when they're coming up, they won't even be thinking about attending another high school."

"I agree with you, but not totally. You're always going to have that assistant from Holy Angels, or that alum from Cretin, telling our best player that he should attend their school. Then the same guy tells one of their kid's parents to tell our kid's parents the same thing. And they have full rides and a great education. For the public-school coach, it sucks, but that's the way it is."

"And you have to be especially vigilant of your best kid and his parents, without showing favoritism. They only go after your best kid."

"And if they get him, the other kids think about going too."

* * *

Later in July the returning varsity players played in a weekend tournament. This was organized by a couple of parents. Each of the players paid their share of the entry fee, they wore the high school practice jerseys, and they played four games against other high school teams. Sixteen juniors and seniors showed up for this, and I coached them. Many of these kids were the same kids who had decided to not attend the open gyms, and they were all program kids. These same kids played in the Metro Summer League in June. Returning seniors, juniors, and some sophomores played in the varsity division. Returning sophomores and some freshman played in the JV division. Both leagues consisted of ten games total.

On the drive home I did the math. During the weekend, we played four 40-minute games. On the average, each player played half a game, or 20 minutes. If a player played in two weekend tournaments and the summer league, they would end up playing half of 18 games. This would result in 360 minutes of 5 on 5 playing time, or six hours. This was the same amount of playing time that they would get in three to four nights of open gyms, and I was going to have 21 nights of open gyms spread out over seven weeks every summer. Of course, in the open gyms the kids didn't wear Richfield colors or play against other schools. They were either shirts or skins and they called their own fouls. And at the open gyms the stands weren't full of parents and the kids did a lot of drills and small group work. And the open gyms weren't limited to those who could pay the fee. They were free to whoever showed up.

I called Lance's cell phone and he picked up. After discussing the games and kids, I addressed the open gym subject. Lance's response was immediate and emphatic, in typical Lance fashion.

"Jim, this is the reason why the Europeans are passing us up. They don't spend their summers playing 5 on 5. They do small group drills and they work on fundamentals. Do they play 5 on 5? Yes, but it is after they have done their drill work. I played there. I saw this with my own eyes. I am convinced of this. This is why they are passing us up, and this is why you see so many of them, who aren't any more athletic than the American white kids, making it in the NBA."

* * *

The morning after Labor Day the phone rang in my office. It was a Richfield teacher and it was the first day of school. "Travis Brown is walking our halls with a handful of books. I don't know how you did it, but I commend you, for however you did it."

"I take it that his two buddies aren't there."

"No. I have not seen either of them, and two of the other kids told me that Isaiah Goodman is at Holy Angels. Of course, the big talk is that Ray Brown is here."

* * *

On a Friday night early in September I attended my first Richfield high school football game. The teams were running through their warm-ups and Jim Baker and I were standing near the end zone and talking. A number of people came by who were residents and fans. An elderly white man in his seventies walked up to Jim, and I was introduced to Leroy "Oz" Mullerleile. He was wearing the school color of cardinal from his baseball hat to his coaching shoes. He was very genial and we talked for about ten minutes about Richfield, his background, and the upcoming basketball season. I remember him saying that he was a long-time resident of Richfield, and that he was originally from a small town in southern Minnesota near Mankato. I also remember him saying that he was Richfield's number one fan, and that he attended almost all of the high school and youth sporting events. A longtime friend of mine and Richfield alum named Pat Elliott had asked me in July if I had met Oz yet. When I said no, he answered "You will," and he started laughing. Oz also had the reputation for being very outspoken and for writing letters to the editor of the *Richfield Sun Current*.

* * *

The tryouts for the winter fifth through eighth grade traveling teams were held on two Saturdays in October. It was my responsibility to conduct the tryouts and pick the teams. The coach of the traveling team was also at the tryout, and I always employed one of my assistants. As a consensus, we three picked the team. Each tryout lasted one hour.

Each team was limited to 10 players, and boys could not 'play up'. In other words, if a seventh grader was very skilled and advanced, and if he was clearly better than the older boys, he could not play on the eighth-grade team. He had to play with the boys in his grade. The boys in each grade had played together in the house league in third and fourth grade, and had attended the summer camp together. They all knew who the best players were in their grade. The fifth and sixth graders who did not make the traveling team, were relegated to have to play in the fifth and sixth grade house league. The skill level and competition in the house league was significantly lower. The seventh and eighth graders who did not make the traveling team, could still play on the middle school team. The middle school teams did not cut any players, and played a limited schedule of 12 games. If one grade had over 20 players who tried out, and if their skill level was sufficient, it was the policy of the board to have two traveling teams in that grade, an A and a B team. This was the first time that most of these boys had tried out for a team which had limited roster spots and was forced to make cuts. These kids wanted to wear the Richfield colors and play on weekends against teams from other communities. This was a very big deal for the kids who were on the bubble, and it was very stressful for their parents.

The tryouts went as planned. Fifteen to 20 boys tried out in each grade. I told the other two coaches to mentally separate the kids into three groups, the kids who obviously should make the team, the obvious cuts, and the kids who were on the bubble. We then focused on watching the kids who were on the bubble, and we matched them up against each other as much as possible in the drills. If two kids who were on the bubble were fairly evenly matched, and if we knew which kid had worked the hardest in the off season, we kept this kid. We knew these kids from the summer camp and three on three league, and we knew which kids had been in the gym and improved.

When the second Saturday of tryouts was completed, we had four teams of ten players each. Alcindor helped me with the tryouts, and we both agreed that the top two eighth graders had to play on the high school freshman team, Jordan Noonan and Duane Hardy. According to state high school league rules, eighth graders could play on both the eighth-grade traveling team and the ninth-grade high school team, as long as they didn't play in a sophomore (B squad) game. Moving them up to the ninth-grade team meant that they would not play on the middle school eighth grade team. They were better players than all but the top few ninth graders and they were both excellent students. I wanted to coach them at the high school practices, and I wanted them to play, bond, and win with the older kids. It would also give me and my staff more chances to interact with their parents. Because my high school practices were open to parents, their parents would probably see us teach, and they would see their son's improvement. This would increase the probability that they would attend Richfield High School. I was going to leave no openings for Holy Angels or any other opposing high school program to come in and recruit my best eighth graders. I did not want to ever again have to be sitting in a living room talking to the parents of an eighth grader, trying to recruit their son to their public high school, as I had done three months earlier.

***

During the fall we had coaches' meetings once a month. I felt good about the staff that I had picked. I had four paid assistants which was a big improvement over Washburn where I only had one.

Lance was going to be my right-hand man and varsity assistant, even though he was a volunteer and unpaid. He would be the offensive coordinator.

I retained Kelly Liebfried and Matt Mullenbach from the previous staff. Kelly was to be the junior varsity coach. He would be with me during practices and he would coach the junior varsity during games. The kids who were part of the varsity team but didn't get a lot of playing time in varsity games played in the junior varsity games. Matt would be the assistant ninth grade coach. In addition, Matt was to oversee the academic program, which was a big responsibility. This involved monitoring grade reports, and communicating with faculty. We were going to implement the mandatory study hall system that I had learned from Pete Haugen at Washburn. The study halls were to be in Matt's classroom. Both he and I would be monitoring them.

Alcindor was the sophomore coach and Jamar was the head ninth grade coach. Mark Robinson was the eighth-grade traveling coach. In addition, Matt Shock, who was the administrative assistant to Jim Baker, was to be a volunteer assistant to Alcindor on the sophomore team.

We were to begin every practice in the big gym with all of the kids grades from freshman to seniors doing fundamental drills. After thirty minutes we split into two gyms for defensive drills. By organizing the staff in this way, when the players were split into two gyms for defensive drills, I could be in charge of one gym and Alcindor could be in charge of the other. Kelly could learn my defensive drills while working under me. In the same way Jamar and the two Matt's could learn the drills while working under Alcindor. Mark Robinson already knew the defense having played at Minnesota-Duluth for Coach Dale Race. We were not only putting in a new system with the players, we were also putting in a new system with four coaches.

* * *

The first week of the season is always full of stress, and it's a difficult week for a coaching staff. This is because the staff has to evaluate talent, choose the team, and make cuts. Nobody likes telling a teenager that he hasn't made the team. This is especially difficult for a coach in his first season at a school. This is because the coach has seen many of the kids play only a few hours of basketball. In my first year at Richfield this was compounded by a number of other factors.

There were eight returning seniors. There were 14 juniors who were going to try out for the team. All were program kids. As this class rose through the feeder program, there were two traveling teams in their grade. During their sophomore year, three had played varsity, and the other eleven had played on the junior varsity or sophomore team. I knew that we were going to have to cut at least ten of these juniors and seniors.

There were a handful of sophomores who were improving rapidly, primarily because they had attended the open gyms and they were still growing. The freshman class was the most talented and deepest class. I projected that many of the sophomores and freshman were going to improve rapidly over the winter, and would pass up the upperclassmen.

On every game night, there were four games. The freshman game began at 3:45, which was followed by the sophomore (B squad) game at 5:00. This was followed by the junior varsity (JV) game at 6:30, and the varsity game at 8:00. Under state high school league rules, a player could play five quarters per night. It was my philosophy to keep the teams fluid, both in practice sessions and in games. Many of the kids would play five quarters per night. For example, a kid could play three quarters in the ninth-grade game and two quarters in the sophomore game, two quarters in the sophomore game and three quarters in the JV game, or two quarters in the JV game and three quarters in the varsity game. If a ninth grader passed up the older kids, he could be removed from the ninth-grade games, and begin playing sophomore and JV games. In this way, no player ever thought that he had it made. In addition, players from different grades were constantly interacting.

***

After one week of practice, we hosted a four-team scrimmage. As the host team, we always played in the main gym while the other two teams played in the smaller gym. When our first game started, Matt Mullenbach needed to run downstairs to the locker room to retrieve something. As he reentered the gym our point guard Jamar Taylor was dribbling the ball up the court and an elderly white man was standing in the doorway. The man stopped Matt, glared at him, and quickly and loudly said "Who's this kid? Where'd he come from?"

"He's a senior and he was in the high school last year, but he wasn't eligible to play." As Matt walked away, the man was shaking his head in disgust.

***

On the last Friday night before Christmas vacation, we played Holy Angels at home. The game between the cross-town rivals was always played on this night, and it always drew a big crowd. In addition to parents and townspeople, it served as a reunion night for recent graduates returning from college.

Holy Angels was undefeated and ranked in the top ten in the state in Class AAA. This was Jesse Foley's fourth year as a head coach, and this was his best team. I had scouted them three times. We played our best game of the young season. Going into the fourth quarter, we were trailing 42-41. With five minutes to go they made an 8-2 run, hit their free throws and beat us 65-56. I was very proud of how our kids had played. Because four of the kids on the Holy Angels roster came all of the way up through the Richfield feeder program, it was an intense emotional game for both teams. Three of these four kids combined to score 43 of the 65 points for Holy Angels. I told my assistants after the game, "They're beating us in our own gym with our own kids."

***

The first time around the conference our record was 2-6, and three of our losses were by 20 points. We struggled both offensively and defensively, as the kids were adapting to a new system.

In the middle of January, we played Tartan at home on a Tuesday night. I replaced one of the seniors in the starting lineup with Scott Jenkins, who was a junior. Scott played well in his first start and the senior didn't score a point. Prior to this the senior had started every game.

That Friday we hosted Mahtomedi at home. During the junior varsity game, I saw one of the senior parents motion the seniors together at one end of the gym and he was animatedly talking to them. I walked over and asked him what he was doing. When he answered that he was helping the kids get ready to play, I told him that I was the coach, he was a parent, and that I didn't need his help coaching, and that I didn't need him talking to a group of players before games. When he started to debate me, I told him that he needed to know that if I saw him doing it again, his son would not play at all. He stormed off. As I turned to walk back towards the locker room, I passed Oz who was approaching me. He stopped, glared at me, stuck his chin in the air, and slowly shook his head in a disapproving manner.

In the second half of the game, I substituted a player for the same senior. The senior player walked to the end of the bench and sat there staring straight ahead and ignoring his teammates. He didn't get up for either of the last two time-outs. After the game I took a vote of my assistants on whether or not I should cut him. It was unanimous. The next morning before practice I called the player into the coach's office, told him to hand me his practice jersey, and said that he was cut. He didn't say a word and left. Richfield's number one fan then stopped coming to the varsity games.

A week later I told another senior and program kid that I was going to reduce his playing time from 10-15 minutes a game to none, except for possible mop up minutes. A week later he quit. For both seniors, I had seen signs that they were hearing a different message at home about who should be playing and what their roles should be.

Our playing rotation had finally settled into three seniors, five juniors, and the freshman Ray Brown. The seniors were Jamar Taylor, the African-American guard from Minneapolis, Erik Abramson, a 6-6 program kid, and Kenny Uko, a 6-5 African kid who had moved to Richfield in high school. The second time around the conference every game but one was close, and our record was 3-5. As we headed into our first tournament game, we were 8-16.

***

One day late in the winter a man wandered into practice and was slowly pacing the sidelines and looking around the gym. I was busy teaching, but I did notice that he wasn't really watching us practice. When one of my assistants was talking, I approached him. When I was within a few steps of him, he stopped and turned to look at me. I was about to ask him if I could help him, and to tell him that our practices were closed. Based upon his response I was maybe going to ask him to leave. I could tell by the look on his face that he was expecting all of this.

As I was about to speak, I realized that this guy looked like Stu Starner, who had been the Richfield coach in the 70s. I hesitated, and then slowly asked, "are...you... Stu Starner?"

He broke into a quiet laugh, nodded, and said "yes". I introduced myself. He knew me from having worked with me at the Jim Dutcher basketball camps. I then told him that I was the head coach. There was a short silence. Then he lit up, and forcefully said "this is great. This is great that you're the coach at Richfield. You got some good young kids?"

"Yes, we do."

We talked for ten minutes, before he said that he was only in town for the weekend and that he had to leave. I asked him if he would talk to the team, and he answered that he'd love to, but that he didn't have time.

As he walked out of the gym, a strong feeling came over me. It was my intuition speaking to me. It was telling me that I was in the right place, and that there was a reason why I was at Richfield, and the reason was bigger than me. This was one of the moments that made a tough first year well worth it.

***

We were seeded fifth and opened the tournament at Minneapolis Edison. If we could win that game, we would have a shot at the city champion and defending state champion Patrick Henry. Edison was good. On the day of the game, one of our good juniors was kicked out of a class. Because this exact issue and the consequences were specifically spelled out in the basketball contracts, he didn't play in the game that night. The game was close from start to finish as neither team could establish a lead. We played well. They won the game 65-60 in the last two minutes.

It was not an easy season. The rift between the seniors and the underclassmen didn't disappear until the two senior guards were gone. As Coach Buss said, sometimes it takes a season to get your system in. We only had a few games late in the year where our defense totally shut down the opposition.

There were nine juniors, and as the season wound down, it was obvious that not all of them bought into spending a lot of practice time doing man to man defensive drills. As ninth graders they played mostly an aggressive 1-3-1 zone and a 1-3-1 half court trap. This is different than the 1-3-1 match-up zone that some coaches used in the seventies and eighties to defend the lane area and basket. With a 1-3-1 trap, there are often two defenders pressuring the ball. The aggressive 1-3-1 teaches kids away from the ball to primarily watch the ball and to gamble, going for steals. The lower the level of basketball, the more effective this defense is. It can work really well at the middle school level, and it can be absolutely devastating at the grade school level. At the high school level, some teams will play it as a secondary defense and at the college level one rarely sees it. Many youth coaches are in love with the 1-3-1 zone trap because it is so easy to teach. And many of these same youth coaches don't know how to teach man-to-man defense. And the young kids don't learn any of the man to man to man defensive fundamentals that they will need to succeed at higher levels of basketball.

If a coach prepares his team for a 1-3-1 trap by working against it with half an hour of progressive drills for four days, his team will cut it up. This defense isn't going to work as a primary defense against a well-coached high school team. The offensive team will shoot lay-ups and wide-open jump shots. As ninth graders, the juniors won with this defense. One of my favorite quotes on basketball defense;

> "The coach is a teacher. His subject is fundamentals...
> Winning is more related to good defense than to good offense.
> -Jack Ramsay [3]

Almost all championship teams play the team man to man defense which I learned from Bob Knight in the seventies. I was committed to teaching the fundamentals of man-to-man defense. We weren't going to win playing 1-3-1.

In addition, different kids in this class were improving at different rates. One player was a 5-11 power forward, a fullback/linebacker in football, and a great rebounder for his size. He was biracial and African-American. He had been done growing for at least a couple years. All of the others were white. Vrieze was a 5-10 guard and three sport athlete who always played hard. Dreifke at 6-2 was a gamer, a great defender, and an excellent shooter. He made All Conference. All three played varsity as sophomores. Nelson and Jenkins, who hadn't played varsity as sophomores were passing them up. Nelson had grown to 6-4 and had developed a great first step, and Jenkins was becoming a great shooter who learned how to get open in our motion offense. Four other juniors sat on the bench and played junior varsity. Josh Noonan was 6-2, developing into an excellent shooter and still growing. All except Dreifke were program kids. Dreifke lived in Richfield his entire life, but he attended Bloomington Lutheran, a K-8 school in Bloomington and he first entered the program as a ninth grader.

The good news was that the junior varsity team finished 15-6, and the sophomore team finished 17-6. As the young kids improved, we moved them up to the older teams, and they were passing up most of these juniors. By the end of the season two sophomores and two freshmen were playing two quarters sophomore and three quarters junior varsity, and this had a lot to do with the winning records. Kris Pulford was a sophomore guard and program kid still growing at 6-1 who was developing into another excellent shooter. DeRail Moore, was now 6-3, and rapidly getting better. As I had projected, Travis Brown was now 6-1 and still growing and rapidly improving. We also had a 5-9 freshman point guard named Ernest Harris who had moved into Richfield from Kansas City. He had top level Division I quickness and a great pull up jump shot off of the dribble. He did not play in games until after Christmas because he was flunking classes. He was saved by our study halls. In eight ninth grade football games, he scored over twenty touchdowns. Had he started the season with good grades, and had he been in our program for a year to learn our system, he would have been my starting point guard on the varsity from day one. These four kids all suited up varsity for the tournament. The juniors were definitely looking over their shoulders at them.

In late February on a Friday night the coaching staff was together in a restaurant after a game. I knew that the young kids were now better than some of the kids who were getting the varsity playing minutes. As was my practice, before saying this, I asked for the opinions of my assistants.

"OK, I have to ask all of you a question, and I want your individual independent opinions. If it was November, and we were starting the season right now, who would be our top seven players? Now I don't want you to pick your seven players based upon potential. In other words, don't pick who you think will be the top seven players three months from now in February. It's November right now, and who are the top seven players right now."

The consensus ended up being eight players; Harris at point guard, Moore at power forward, Uko at center, with Jenkins, the Browns, Dreifke, and Nelson playing anywhere. There was some discussion on including another of the juniors in the group, which centered on whether or not we thought that he'd want to play with the young kids. In the end he wasn't included. The eight players were one senior, three juniors, one sophomore, and three freshmen. This was the consensus of my assistants.

I then said, "We can't make this change now, with two weeks to go until the tournament. There's no way." They all agreed.

Richfield

I n 1805, soon after sending Meriwether Lewis, William Clark, and the Corps of Discovery to the Pacific Ocean to explore the lands acquired with the Louisiana Purchase, Thomas Jefferson sent out two more expeditions. William Dunbar's U.S. Army expedition headed south into the Arkansas territory, and Zebulon Pike's party went north. The goal of Pike's party was to establish a military post at the confluence of the Mississippi and St Pierre (Minnesota) Rivers. In September 1805 Pike met with a band of Dakota warriors at the site and a treaty was signed, granting the government a small piece of land on top of the bluff on the northwest corner of the confluence.

In 1824 the building of Fort Snelling was completed. The natural cliff of blond limestone, over a hundred feet tall, sits on this point and the fort and its walls rose above the top of the headland. If one stands on the bluff today and looks to the southwest, the broad Minnesota valley fades in the distance. It is almost two miles wide, a mixture of bottom land forest, marshes, and shallow lakes. The river slightly meanders through the middle of the bottoms. If one looks to the north, one sees the Mississippi spilling down the only canyon in its 2,300-mile course. The view is limited to maybe a mile. The limestone walls of the canyon are steep and covered with trees and vines. Two miles upstream on the west side, Minnehaha Creek plunges over the rock to complete its journey from Lake Minnetonka 15 miles to the west. The bottom of the canyon is narrow with shores on both sides wide enough to set up a canoe campsite, but not without being observed by the viewer on the bluff. To the east one can see the merger of the rivers flowing downstream to St Paul. The valley width narrows to less than a mile. During an era when these two rivers were the major highways of transportation, this was arguably the most critical and strategic piece of real estate in the territory.

By the 1850s three European American settlements existed near the confluence of the two big rivers. Seven miles to the north at the head of the canyon was St Anthony Falls. Next to the falls, were standing the first buildings of Minneapolis. Downstream from the falls, the nearest stretch of flat land next to the river and above the flood plain was thirteen miles away. This bench of land was on the north side of the river and overlooked an island and a floodplain to the south. On this bench St Paul was beginning to take shape. The third settlement was the fort.

When the Jeffersonian grid was platted in 1858, the township on the west side of the fort was named Richfield, for its rich black soil. The land was oak savanna, a type of lightly forested grassland, with oak the dominant and old growth type of tree. In Minnesota, oak savanna is the transition land between the big woods to the east and the tall grass prairie to the west. For early settlers from New England, this type of land provided both good soil for crops and firewood for fuel. The land that sat atop the cliffs was 150 feet above the rivers, and flat with a handful of shallow lakes and swamps. The township abutted the Fort, and in the 1820s a small trading post outside the fort was surrounded by European American settlers.

This level land to the west of the fort became a small farming community. After the Civil War, a Union General named Riley Bartholomew arrived from Ohio. He established a farm and homestead on the eastern shore of Wood Lake. Wood Lake is five miles due west of the fort, and at 150 acres, the largest lake or pond in Richfield. Bartholomew later became the Justice of the Peace for the village and a Minnesota State Senator.

The Bartholomew family was soon joined by other retired Civil War officers from the fort who also established small farms. In 1879 the township built a town hall. Early residents were from the northern tier states to the east, as well as German peasants, and potato famine Irish. The next wave of immigrants came mostly from the Scandinavian countries of Sweden, Norway, and Denmark.

In the first half of the twentieth century, Richfield became known for its vegetable selling truck farmers who supplied the residents of Minneapolis with fresh produce. There were also small dairy farms. It remained agricultural as the homes from Minneapolis kept creeping closer and closer. In 1950, a village form of government was adopted, with a mayor, a council, and a city manager.

With the invention of the airplane, the flat land next to Fort Snelling was a natural place to land a plane. After World War I, the military built a small airport with grass runways. In 1921 it was named Wold-Chamberlain Field after two fighter pilots from the Great War. As air travel increased, the airport began building asphalt runways and appropriating land from the township/village of Richfield. The airport took 240 acres in 1940, 327 acres in 1941, and 30 acres in 1942. The airport was renamed Minneapolis-St Paul International Airport in 1994. In 1996 the airport took more land.

After World War II, residential housing development overtook the farms. Small developers purchased single blocks at a time and built half a dozen ramblers at once. The lots were 60 feet to 75 feet wide and 130 feet to 140 feet deep. Most of the houses were one and a half stories, and some were one story or two stories. And most were 800 to 1,000 square feet. Finishing the basement would often increase the living space to 1,600 square feet. Many of the starter homes were financed with the GI bill. One of these GIs was Chuck Lindberg, who as a Marine Corps Corporal, was one of the soldiers who raised the first of two flags on Mount Suribachi during the battle of Iwo Jima.

Interspersed among the homes were many parks with playgrounds, baseball fields, basketball courts, and hockey rinks. Many of the new residents had jobs at the airport and the Ford plant on the east side of the river in St Paul. According to a February 11, 2008 article in the *StarTribune*, entitled 'Richfield, the state's oldest suburb', Jim Fogarty of the Minnesota Historical Society is quoted to say,

"People bought them (the houses) and put in grass. When they paid for the house, they built a garage. And when that was paid for, they built the iconic breezeway in between." [4]

Because the topography of the land in Richfield is so flat, the city blocks formed a rectangular grid of streets running either north/south or east/west. Some of the houses on the choice lots on the west side of the town were a little bigger than the other houses, but for the most part all of the lots and houses were the same size. In the fifties, sixties, and seventies, most of these homes were filled by a large family of four or more kids

People migrate to the suburbs like spokes on a wheel. When all of these ramblers were built, most of the young parents had grown up in south Minneapolis or in southern Minnesota. And some were from Iowa or Nebraska. The Minneapolis transplants migrated to the south, in a straight line away from the center of the city. Many were Scandinavian, being descendants of the Swedes and Norwegians who settled the south side of Minneapolis in the last half of the nineteenth century. The other large group of transplants found jobs in Minneapolis after growing up on the farms or in the small towns to the south. They also migrated in straight lines from their home towns toward Minneapolis, and settled in the affordable suburb in between both places. For both groups of migrants, living in Richfield minimized both the commute to work and the commute to the grandparents.

The population grew from 3,800 in 1940 to 17,500 in 1950 to 31,800 in 1954. The population peaked in 1970 at 47,000 and fell to 38,000 in 1980. The 2010 population of 35,000 includes people who live in the 10,000 single family homes that were built in the 1940s and 1950s.

Residents who grew up in the early years of the building boom have told me that it was almost like living in a small town, where one's parents knew most of the people.

During the 1960s and the early 1970s, apartment buildings began going up. By 2010, these buildings housed 5,000 apartments. In the same *StarTribune* article, Macalester College geography Professor David Lanegran is quoted,

"What makes Richfield interesting now is the degree to which they're trying to preserve their original dream. They're not being gentrified. They're still holding out as a family-based homeowner community...Richfield, to a remarkable extent, has been able to preserve the dream as being a great place for middle-income people to raise a family." [5]

The house that Riley Bartholomew and his wife Fanny built in 1852 still stands on a small rise on the east side of Lyndale Avenue. Like many of the front yards in Richfield, it is shaded by oak trees, descendants of the trees of the old oak savanna. An open-air porch with small wood columns and a wood floor faces to the west. The couple must have spent countless evenings relaxing on the porch after a hard day of work, watching the sun set over the lake. The old farmhouse now houses the Richfield Historical Society, and the old south pasture is the practice field for the high school football team.

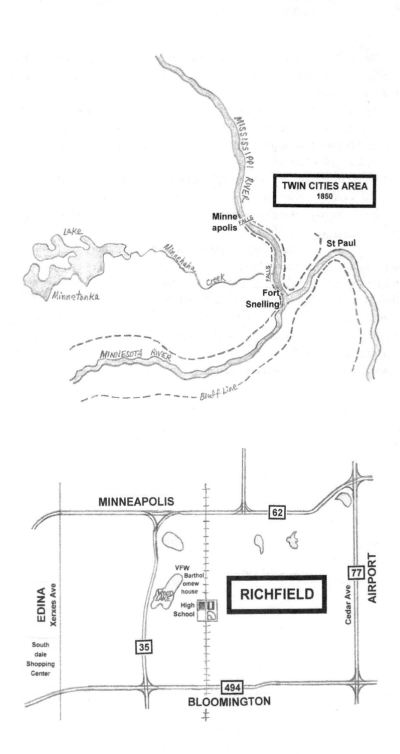

Second Summer
& Winter

If everybody likes you, you probably aren't doing your job.
—Al Berkvam

One of the things that I really liked about Richfield was that I always felt welcome at the high school. If I walked the halls, the teachers and support staff went out of their way to greet me. I was always called "Coach" or "Coach Dimick". During the off season, I made it a point to stop by the high school and walk the halls at least every other week.

On a morning in late April, I was at the high school, and Jim Baker motioned me into his office and shut the door. He shared with me that he received about half a dozen phone calls from the junior parents. Every one of the phone calls was about the same subject, and had the same message. They wanted to know which players were going to get the playing time the next winter. They all made the points that their son had come all the way up through the program, their kid had been playing with the same kids since third grade, and that these kids had all been waiting for their chance to play as seniors. They wanted to be assured that this would be the case.

As Jim talked, he rolled his eyes, shook his head, and chuckled. He told me that he told all of them that the coach would play the best players, and that it was the coach's job to decide who the best players were.

He then directed them to his brochure entitled "Parent/Coach Communication". Every parent had received one at the beginning of the season. The pamphlet included a list of "appropriate concerns to discuss with coaches." This list was

1) treatment of your child, mentally and physically
2) ways to help your child improve
3) concerns about your child's behavior.

The pamphlet also included a list of "issues not appropriate to discuss with coaches." This list was four topics;

1) playing time

2) team strategy
3) play calling
4) other student-athletes.

The pamphlet also showed a chain of command, and who a parent was to complain to. The parent was to first go directly to the coach before contacting the AD, and after talking to the AD, the parent was to then go to the principal before going to the superintendent.

Jim told me that he asked each of these parents if they had any complaints about how their son was being treated, or any questions about how their son could improve. He then repeated that he was not going to discuss playing time or who was going to play with any parents. This was up to the coach.

Two weeks later, Jim called me back to his office. He showed me a list of written complaints that these junior parents sent to him. As was protocol, these were also shared with the principal and the superintendent.

Coaches had said swear words while coaching.

Players were not dressed appropriately on game nights.

Players did not stand at attention for the national anthem.

***

Alcindor and I went to work organizing a Richfield spring eighth grade AAU team. I made up flyer's that were mailed to all of the parents of the kids that played on the seventh and eighth grade traveling team, and the seventh and eighth grade junior high teams. The flyer's explained the pertinent facts about the team. The team would be open to all seventh and eighth grade boys at the Richfield Middle School. There would be no cuts. Participation time in practice would be equal, but playing time in games would not be equal. We would practice twice a week. If the practice times conflicted with spring sports, players were expected to attend their spring sport practices. We would play in four tournaments over six weeks. Alcindor would be the head coach and I would assist him.

I also went to the middle school and talked to the physical education teacher Jeff Etienne, and two of the middle school coaches Greg Von Ruden and Steve Hemming. I asked them who the talented kids were and I talked to these kids. I got their home telephone numbers and I called their parents. I made it a point to call the parents of the top two or three kids in both seventh and eighth grade. I knew if we could get these kids to play on the team, we could get the other kids.

We established the practice times so that they would not conflict with practices for spring sports. A lot of the kids played baseball or ran track. It was the philosophy of the athletic department to encourage kids to play multiple sports, and we didn't want to discourage this. The reality of the situation though, was that the kids who were serious about basketball all played spring AAU basketball. If these kids weren't playing for us, they would be playing for someone else.

This was all part of the modern-day high school recruiting process. Often times a parent of a talented player would recruit a team of all-stars from a number of schools and communities. This parent would also be the coach, often assisted by another parent. Because of the team's talent level, they would overpower less talented teams. The kids and parents would bond, and the parents would discuss which high schools their sons were going to attend. Sometimes, the parent-coach would also act as a deal maker with interested high school coaches. I wasn't going to let anybody but my assistants and me coach my young kids and sway their decision-making process about high schools. I wanted to win, and in order to win at Richfield, I had to have the best players who lived in Richfield attending Richfield High School. And we would help them excel both athletically and academically, move on to college, and some day graduate. I believed that my staff could do this as well or better than any other coaching staff. So, it was a win-win situation. Getting the best players in town to attend the public high school would help us win, and help them succeed in life. The bottom line was, I was protecting my turf, and my turf was Richfield.

The top two eighth graders Jordan Noonan and Dwayne Hardy played, and they both played on other AAU teams. The purpose of this team was twofold. First of all, we wanted to teach our system hands on. Secondly, we didn't want someone else coaching them and recruiting them away from Richfield. When the kids saw how much they improved and won playing under us, they and their parents would be sold on attending Richfield and playing for us. Because our opposing coaches were often parents or low-level AAU coaches, it was very easy to out-coach them.

We ended up with a nucleus of about ten kids. We finished 15-2. I also learned this spring that the Noonans were great backers of the entire program, and that they understood the modern-day playing field of high school basketball. I saw Jim at the board meetings, but this team gave me some opportunities to talk to him one on one. He and his wife Jean were at every game, often picking up and dropping off other kids who didn't have rides. Jim was a straight shooter, and saw a lot of things the way that I saw them. However, because they were parents, I was cautious about what I said to them, and how I worded things.

* * *

In May, I went over to the middle school and the intermediate school to hand out flyer's advertising the summer camp and the three-on-three league to the boys in grades three through eight. I found out when these kids had their lunch hour, and with the help of teachers, I identified the best players and athletes in each grade. I personally talked to and handed out flyers to all of these kids, as well as every other kid who showed any interest. The flyer's advertised the dates and times and the cost of $50 per student. I stressed to every group of kids that I talked to, that they shouldn't worry about the money, saying "don't worry about the money, just come to the camp, and start playing, and we'll worry about the money later".

In every lunch room that I walked into, the white kids, the black kids, and the Hispanic kids sat at separate tables. I asked one of the teachers if the lunch rooms were always this segregated, and his response with a sigh was an emphatic "yes".

When I handed out the flyers to the white kids, they were enthused, and I heard comments like "oh yeah, I'll be there", or "if it's not the same time as baseball". The only question in their minds was if they wanted to attend or not.

When I went to the table where the Hispanic kids sat, I found out that they had no interest in basketball. When I asked them if they played soccer, they all smiled, nodded, and said yes.

When I approached the table where the black kids sat, the first thing that I always heard was "how much does it cost?" or "I can't." When I said "what do you mean you can't?" they'd shake their heads and say "we don't have the money". I then asked for the phone number of their parents. In the evening I called up the parents, explained the situation to them, and told them that the only thing that mattered right now was that their son was at camp the first day. I again used what was to be the standard line of the coaching staff, "show up and play, we'll worry about the money later." I made it clear to them that we wanted their son at our camp.

When the summer camp began in June the number of kids attending was about the same as the previous summer. About ninety kids attended the camp and about thirty kids were at the three-on-three league every day. However, the number of African-American students increased dramatically, now comprising about one fourth of the enrollment.

I changed the structure of the three-on- three league by not having assigned teams with NBA nicknames. The teams changed every day. In this way, if a kid missed a week to go live with his grandparents in a small town in southern Minnesota, or in a large town like Memphis, Tennessee, he could attend the weeks that he was in town. Also, if a kid moved into Richfield in July and missed the first week, he could attend the remaining weeks. I also increased the number of weeks from three to four.

The second Monday morning in July I and one of my assistants were in the gym getting things set up for the three-on-three league. Three African-American kids who we had never seen before walked into the gym bouncing a ball. I asked them their names and what grade they were in. They were going into fifth, sixth, and seventh grade.

I then asked them "where do you live?"

One of them responded "well, my brother and I live in Richfield, and our cousin lives in Minneapolis."

"Where do you go to school?"

"Last year we went to a school in Minneapolis, but next year, we're coming to Richfield."

"So, you just moved to Richfield this summer."

"Yeah, but our cousin still lives in Minneapolis."

"How did you hear about the camp?"

"From a friend of ours who lives in the same building as us."

I then told them what I told all of the kids. This camp is for kids who live in Richfield, and because you two guys live in Richfield, we want you here. I then looked directly at the cousin, "since you're their cousin and you're staying with them right now, we want you here too, and any time that you're staying over at their place, if they're coming over here, you come with them."

This was the first time that a new kid walked into the gym, sought me out, and told me that he had just moved to Richfield. When a new face, almost always a black one, showed up at the gym, it was the story that I eventually came to expect.

***

After school was out in June, I resumed the open gyms three nights every week. We averaged fifteen to twenty players per night, not including middle school kids. Within a week, the kids were used to the routine of beginning the two-hour sessions with individual drills, progressing to three on three, four on four, and finishing with full court five on five.

The players who played AAU or legion baseball attended on the nights when they didn't have a practice or game. The same core of kids that never missed the summer before, again never missed. It was gratifying to see the improvement in the kids who showed up and bought into the hard work. It was obvious that they were practicing the fundamentals on their own time. The returning junior who was a great rebounder for his 5-11 height, did not attend one open gym.

The gyms also attracted half a dozen kids who because of grades and a shortage of academic credits, were never eligible to play on the high school teams. All attended Richfield High School. All were African-American. The previous winter I saw them at the games. They were coach-able and they worked their butts off. They were very receptive to me changing their shooting form. It was obvious that they had a lot of fun, and they often made it a point to thank me for working with them. A couple of them had little brothers who because of my efforts were now included in the summer program. They accepted the fact that they would never play high school basketball. When they competed against the kids who did play high school basketball, they never backed down or thought that they weren't as good. This is a major difference between a metro basketball program and an out-state basketball program. Out in the small towns, the kids who don't play organized basketball don't consider themselves basketball players. These kids considered themselves basketball players, and they thought they had as much game as the kids wearing the uniforms on Friday nights.

In addition to this, the junior parents organized a couple of weekend tournaments for their sons, one of which I coached. All nine of the returning juniors showed up for these games. They wore the Richfield colors, played against other schools, with a scoreboard and referees, and with many of their parents sitting in the stands and cheering. The parents pooled their money to pay the entry fee. They hadn't invited any of the sophomores or freshman to play. Fortunately, both of these tournaments were on weekends when our outstanding freshman and sophomores were out of town playing in national AAU tournaments. This conveniently postponed the time bomb of the older kids versus younger kids playing time controversy.

***

Going into our second year at Richfield, I remembered what Coach Buss told me, saying that sometimes it takes a year to get your system in, and that it takes kids anywhere from six weeks to a year and a half to learn team man to man defense. Some kids pick it up quicker than others because of a high basketball IQ. And a high basketball IQ does not always equate with a high classroom IQ. In addition, a player learns much faster if many of his teammates already know the defense. This is what is known as a coach 'having his system in'.

I played for a great high school coach in Northfield named Jed Dommeyer. Jed came out of the small town of Slayton in the southwest corner of the state. After high school he served in the military and grew into his body. He attended the University of Minnesota and played for the Gophers, before being drafted by the Cincinnati Royals of the NBA. His assistant was Don Hill, who was also our head football coach. They were a demanding pair on defense, and we played full court man to man. They drilled four concepts into us, pressure the ball, front/bump cutters in the lane, talk, and box out.

In college I played two years for Bob Gelle, who also was an ex-Gopher. He had meticulous scouting reports diagramming the patterns and listing individual tendencies of every opponent. I was one of the scout squad players, running the plays of our upcoming opponents, and imitating a certain player. When we went into a game, we were always prepared.

In my senior year at St Olaf, I was a student assistant coach to Rich Decker at Kenyon High School. One year after college, I found myself as the head basketball coach and top assistant football coach at LeSueur, on the Minnesota River in southern Minnesota. The head football coach was Bruce Frank. Bruce spent 30 years there, and when he retired, he was second in the state in career wins. He was a World War II fighter pilot, and he coached with a no-nonsense military style. He had an uncanny knack for knowing which kids to place at which positions, and he overstressed the fundamentals of blocking and tackling. As the game evolved, he changed his offense and defense with it. His play calling and halftime adjustments were incredible. Bruce had the kind of respect that was passed down from older players to younger players, and neighborhood to neighborhood. The players knew that they would never be out coached.

LeSueur had a great basketball tradition, but under the one class system, they had been in a tough spot. Historically, District 13 was a basketball hotbed. It had been made up of 14 schools. St Peter with a non-college student population of 6,000 to 7,000 was the biggest town. Seven of the eight towns of the Minnesota River Conference with populations ranging from 1,500 to 3,300 were also in the District, as well as six other schools. In the 40 years of the one class system, St Peter won 10 district titles, and the Minnesota River schools won 28 titles. New Prague won it 7 times in the 50s and Montgomery won it 4 times in the 60s.

The District 13 champion advanced to the Region 4 tournament, which was basically a large school event. New Prague won the Region back-to-back in 1955 and 1956 with future Gopher great 6-7 Ron Johnson. These two New Prague teams were the only District 13 teams to ever get to state under the one class system.

LeSueur won the district three times, in 1933, 1939, and 1949. The 1949 team was led by an anomaly at that time, a 6-3, point guard named Donald Distel. The Giants were handily defeated the next game by eventual state champion St Paul Humboldt and their 6-8 center Jim Fritsche. The Giants had a number of very good teams the next twenty-some years, and advanced to the District finals a number of times, but couldn't get out the district. LeSueur had basketball tradition. When I was hired in 1975 there was nothing for me to rebuild. In my first year I inherited a very good team with good size. We went 20-4, won the District 13 championship, and all four of our losses were to teams that went to state. However, this was now the new two class system, and the district tournament was easier to win than it had been for years. It wasn't the same historical District 13. After the season Bruce Frank told me, "you got out-coached twice, the first time you played New Prague, and against Mankato Wilson in the regions."

The dean of the conference coaches was Merv Sheplee at New Prague, and they played great team man to man defense. After we played them, I asked him where he got his defense and he replied, "Bob Knight's book." We lost in the Region tournament to Mankato Wilson, coached by Gene Biewen. They ran a freewheeling and disciplined offense, with very few set plays, with every player constantly looking to take the ball to the basket. Because their offense was unpredictable, they were difficult to defend. They lost in the state finals in overtime to Minneapolis Marshall-University. I learned from this that I wanted to coach an offense with very few set plays, where the kids were taught to play on their own, and to take what the defense gives them. This was consistent with what my high school football coach Don Hill taught us, 'we take what the defense gives us'. That spring I heard Lute Olson talk at a coaching clinic about motion offense, saying that your kids can run the offense all summer when they are playing 3 on 3 and 4 on 4. The following fall Coach Biewen spoke at a coaching clinic about his offense. After he spoke, I approached him and asked him if there was a book that explained his offense. He answered, "Bob Knight's book calls it a motion offense. We've always called it pass and cut."

I worked at the Jim Dutcher basketball camp and picked the brains of the other high school coaches. I established a summer basketball camp and began working with the young kids. I stressed correct shooting form, ball handling, and offensive footwork. My last two years at LeSueur we had two more great seasons with two more District 13 titles. We drew big crowds all winter, and when the tournament approached, they became sellouts. Those winters were as fun on the basketball court as any others that I'd ever experienced. I was replaced by Tim Dittberner, who took the program to the next level with his teams advancing to state in 1985, 1986, and 1988. The 1986 team finished 26-2 and won the Class A state title, and the 1988 team also finished 26-2. The two losses in 1988 were to Rocori, the state champion in Class AA, and DeLaSalle the state champion in Class A.

Late in the season, on parent's night, we always had a shooting contest at halftime. Seven spots were marked around the perimeter 15 feet from the basket. Every parent, mother and father, took seven shots. In 1980 one father made all seven shots. Yes, seven for seven, followed by a standing ovation. He was a farmer with a heated machine shop that had a cement floor and a basket. He told me after the game that he had been practicing for two weeks, and then he burst out laughing. His son Gary was an All-Conference guard. The farmer's name was Donald Distel.

Two years later I was attending Macalester College in St Paul, working toward an accounting degree and the assistant coach to Keith Erickson. Besides being a rookie college coach, Keith looked like he was about 20 years old. I think he shaved twice a week. Here we were, two guys seven and eight years out of college coaching at the D3 collegiate level. Macalester was a member of the Minnesota Intercollegiate Athletic Conference, or the MIAC. It was the smallest school in the conference and it had the highest academic standards in the conference. We played man to man defense and experimented with switching screens. Our Macalester teams surprised everybody by finishing in the middle of the conference, playing stingy defense, and pulling off upsets against the top teams.

A couple years later, I was hired at St Thomas College by the head coach Steve Fritz. A year later he made me his defensive coordinator and he made Bill McKee his offensive coordinator. Like Macalester, St Thomas was in the MIAC. The difference was that St Thomas had the largest enrollment, and usually the best athletes. Coach Fritz was a free thinker and innovator. We were soon playing a defense predicated on denying the pass to the top of the key or high post area, dead fronting the post with back side help, and switching the ball reversal screen. We had a lot of kids between 6-2 and 6-6 who were interchangeable on defense, and they fit this defensive system. We began dominating the conference, and we became known for our man-to-man defense. Twenty years later, after an almost unbroken string of conference titles and tournament runs, the Tommies under Coach Fritz won the national title.

One year I drove to Bloomington, Indiana to attend Bob Knight's three-day coaching clinic. Five hundred coaches sat in Assembly Hall while Coach Knight spoke and answered questions. He said many things that reinforced my beliefs. I had read every one of his books. During the question-and-answer session, I asked him two questions. I asked him if he thought it was easier to switch screens against pattern (set offense) teams or motion teams. I expected him to say pattern teams. He said that he saw no difference, and he went on to clarify this. I then asked him if he thought all kids should be taught to switch screens, or if some kids played more to their strengths when their defensive roles were simpler and they didn't have to switch screens. He answered that some kids should not switch screens. He believed that some kids could do it, and that some kids couldn't do it. Once again, he clearly explained his experiences and reasoning. Coach Knight also said many other things that I brought home with me. I remember him saying that the most important offensive quality of a big man is to be able to catch the ball. He talked about fundamentals that are overlooked, and that are extremely important, such as passing and catching, and the shot fake-drive. I remember him emphatically saying that he would take quickness over size any day. He said that when a team plays man to man the defense picks the match ups, and when a team plays zone the offense picks the match ups. He said that the greater the defensive talent, the larger the area of the court that the defensive team can defend.

I next assisted Dave Thorson at DeLaSalle, who had formerly assisted Clem Haskins at Minnesota. Dave was beginning to get quick kids who were between 5-10 and 6-3, who could pressure the ball and front the post. Like at St Thomas, we had interchangeable parts. In my second year with Dave, we advanced to the state finals in Class 2A. The next year we won the state title, and they won it again the following year when I was at Washburn. Once again, I had worked under a great coach who was a student of the game. Coach Thorson believed that with the right talent, this defense would work at the DI collegiate level. I once had supper with Bill McKee and his friends Dennis Fitzpatrick and Rick Majerus. Majerus at the time was the coach at Utah. I asked Rick if he thought dead fronting the post would work in DI. His answer was quick and concise, "no, because they'll throw the ball at the basket and dunk the fucking thing."

I spoke at coaching clinics, primarily explaining the lead up drills that we used to teach our man-to-man defense. My philosophy was to work on the motion offense during the summer at the open gyms. The kids could run the offense playing 3 on 3, 4 on 4, and 5 on 5. We could then spend the winter working mostly on the team man to man defense. Like Coach Buss said, sometimes it takes a year to get your system in. We were getting closer, but we weren't there yet.

***

At the board meeting in August, I was prepared to tell the board members of my plan to provide financial aid for low-income kids to play on traveling teams. Before taking the job, I asked Greg Miller if such a program of financial aid existed. He replied that the board declined his request to establish such a program, and that the emphatic opinion of a couple of the leading board members was, "if they can't pay, they can't play". One of the long-time board members told me, "they can play in the house league and on the middle school team". This opinion ended up being the position of the board.

The reality of the situation was that if these kids were the best players, they didn't want to play in the house league against kids from Richfield who weren't good enough to make the traveling team. They also didn't want to play only on a middle school team that had 20 players, a six-week season, and played only 12 games. They wanted to play on a traveling team which played 30 to 40 games against other traveling teams. If they couldn't play for Richfield, their parents would find them a team that did provide financial aid. Two teams in Minneapolis were nonprofit organizations which were affordable for these kids and their parents. Both relied on donations to fund their programs, and to reduce the cost of participation. On the north side the Minneapolis Hustlers were coached by North High grads, and they steered the best kids to North. On the south side were the Urban Stars. These teams were often the best teams in their grade levels, and they won a lot of games and a lot of tournaments. If a Richfield kid played for the Urban Stars, he would play against Richfield in a tournament, and his team would win by 20 or 30 points. He would tell his parents that he didn't want to go to Richfield because Richfield sucks. He would bond with the other kids on the Urban Stars, and follow them to a different high school. When I pointed out such a player to the board president, he shrugged his shoulders, sighed, and said "well, he decided to go to a different high school".

My wife Martha is African-American and grew up in Milwaukee. When I discussed this with her, she had a clear loud answer, "that's how they exclude us, Jim…that's how they exclude us… and then they include one or two of us, and they say, 'see, it isn't about race.'" She was nodding her head. "We grew up with that in Milwaukee."

When I proposed the idea at the next board meeting, I was quickly told that we couldn't do it, because we didn't want to be the ones deciding which kids got financial aid and which kids didn't. I countered that financial aid would only be available to kids who were on free or reduced school lunch. They would have to apply for it by filling out a form, and we could then verify it with the middle school that they were on free or reduced school lunch. This would be the only criteria for qualifying for it. I explained that the parents of all boys who qualified would be required to pay $50. The financial aid amount would be the participation fee less $50. For example, if a boy was an eighth grader, and the fee was $225, the financial aid amount would be $175. In this way all boys who qualified would receive the same exact amount of aid. There was a long silence.

The president then said that it was a great idea, but that the board couldn't afford it. The parents of the kids who were paying would be financing the kids who received financial aid. These parents wouldn't like this. I responded that I would raise all of the money. I said that I would contact individual donors who would each sponsor a kid. If we had ten kids who were on financial aid, and this resulted in the board needing $1,800, I would personally find ten donors and raise the money. In this way, the other parents would not be financing anything. There was another long silence.

Then Jim Noonan spoke up, saying that he thought that it was a great idea. He said that it made the qualification process simple, and the money was entirely out of the hands of the board. He added that Coach Dimick picks the team at tryouts, and it's up to Coach Dimick to raise the needed amount of money. He went on to say that his youngest son Jared was a fourth grader, and assuming that Jared was good enough to play traveling basketball, Jared knows who the best players are in his grade, and Jared's going to want to have the best players in his grade on his traveling team. Bob Pulford quickly agreed, saying that the traveling teams are supposed to be for the best players, and if financial aid helps us get the best players playing traveling, we should be for it. The other board members were again silent.

I spoke up again, saying that the goal of the traveling program should be to have the best players in Richfield playing on the traveling teams; that some of the best kids shouldn't be excluded because of money; that I wanted the best kids playing traveling for Richfield, and that I wanted the best kids eventually playing for me at Richfield High School.

There was another long silence. Finally, the president spoke, stating that if I could raise the money, he thought it was a great idea. As was customary, he asked everybody if they agreed. One by one, they went around the table and every board member agreed.

In late October the traveling tryouts were held on consecutive Saturdays. Financial aid forms were available for the parents at the registration table. When the eighth graders began their tryout at noon, three African-American kids were in the gym. It was immediately obvious that they were three of the five best players on the team. It would be their first year in the program. The year before, this grade of players struggled to win games. In the end, 12 boys who were on financial aid made the four traveling teams, and it was the first year of playing in the program for each one of them. All but one of them was African-American. The racial make-up of the traveling teams was now 26 white kids and 14 black kids.

* * *

In early November, Lance and I drove to Lawrence, Kansas to watch the Jayhawks practice and meet with the KU coaching staff. Lance's daughter was attending the University and Lance watched them practice on earlier trips. He was lobbying me to use their fast break, talking about how quickly they got the ball inbounds and how hard all five players ran the floor. He thought that it would work and be a really fun way to play the game. Big time college coaches that are successful with a certain style of play have a big influence on the high school coaches in their area. Roy Williams at the University of Kansas and his up-tempo running style was no exception. Most of the high school teams in Kansas ran the Jayhawk fast break. In the upper Midwest, the emphasis was more on ball control due to the influence of the Wisconsin coaches Dick Bennett and Bo Ryan.

We sat in the Phog Allen Fieldhouse three days in a row, watching practice and picking the brains of the Kansas coaching staff. The Kansas staff had a handful of drills which they used to teach their fast break. All of the drills had all of the players involved and moving all of the time. They defined the 'head man' pass as the pass that one player makes to a teammate who is up-court or 'ahead' of the man with the ball. It is a pass where both the passer and the receiver are on the run when the pass is made, and the passer has to hit the moving target. If completed, it usually ends in a lay-up. With their drills, every player on the team was executing this pass every day, along with shooting and rebounding while on the run.

We came home committed to playing this kind of transition game. As we learned later, there were two main advantages of the Kansas fast break. One was that teams had to work on getting back on defense, especially their big guys. This hurt their offensive rebounding. Secondly, it made it very difficult to press us, because we got the ball inbounds so quickly. I was not going to change my rule of taking only high percentage shots. We were now going to sometimes get these shots a lot earlier in the offensive possession. Thanks to Lance's persistence, this was one of the best coaching moves that we made at Richfield, and along with our pressure man to man defense, the 'headman pass' became one of the trademarks for which Richfield basketball was known.

**

Tryouts began the third week in November. We had practice plans for the high school tryouts that I had refined over the years. Because we knew this year was going to be controversial, I was especially diligent about documenting everything. I knew that our methods were going to be questioned in every possible way. Jim Baker reviewed the paperwork.

Tryouts lasted three days. After the first day we made the obvious cuts, the kids who had no business trying out. After the second day, we made another round of cuts. The difficult cuts would be made after the third day. We might even go a fourth day for the last few kids if necessary. For example, if we couldn't decide which two kids out of four were to get the last two spots on the roster, we gave the remaining four kids one more day. Throughout the process, we were totally upfront with the kids and told them where they stood.

We spoke with each player individually when we cut him. The player sat in a chair facing a semicircle of coaches also sitting in chairs. I did the talking. Every player heard somewhat the same message. The message was that we had better players, and that he wasn't one of the best players. I also always told them that if they loved basketball, they should keep playing, at whatever level. Most kids never questioned things when they were cut. The kids know who the best players are. Some kids broke into tears. It wasn't fun. We also encouraged them to keep practicing and to try out next year. Although this was a long shot, it was possible. I would have liked to explain to each player more specifically why he didn't make the team, by citing parts of his game that needed improvement, or talking about his attitude or work ethic. Unfortunately, in today's climate of parent-coach relations, a coach can't mention these things. It opens the door for debate with the parent over the coach's judgment and decision. The debate will accomplish nothing.

The entire coaching staff met after tryouts every day to discuss the entire list of kids trying out. I always relied on the input of everybody, and I always asked for their opinion on a player before sharing my opinion.

It was my philosophy to get the kids in shape and to include seven players in the rotation. Numbers eight and nine might be in the rotation and play, but they would play limited minutes. Our job in the selection of the varsity team was to pick the best 12 to 13 players in the top four grades. In order for an underclassman to make the team, he had to be in the top 13. An underclassman could play the entire junior varsity game, and then sit on the bench for the varsity game, and play in one of the four quarters.

In order for a senior to make the team, he had to be projected to be in the playing rotation, which meant that he had to be in the top eight. If we kept a senior on the team, and he wasn't in the top eight, he wouldn't play. And oftentimes, the parents of "junior high superstars" sent the message to their son that the only thing that has changed since junior high is the coach. Thus, the reason why they don't score as many points, get as many rebounds, or get as much playing time as they did in junior high is the fault of the coach. The son then believes this, and this ends up being a cancer that can spread through the team, as well as spreading through the parents sitting in the stands. As all experienced coaches will attest, a "blamer" parent, combined with a "junior high superstar" son, is often an irresolvable problem for a coach. Eventually these kids quit, and the coach ends up dealing with the controversy in mid-season. I was going to make the cuts, deal with the storm head on, and be done with it.

Some years a coach can have that one exceptional senior who doesn't play, is happy to be sitting on the bench, and because of his work ethic and leadership, can help a team. Before cutting a senior, a coaching staff always discusses whether or not the senior fits this profile.

In the back of my mind, I always remembered a quote from Bob Knight. He emphatically made the point that the best team isn't always the best five individual players. The best team is the five players who playing together make the best team. My philosophy extended this quote to the entire roster. The best team isn't always the best twelve individual players. The best team is the twelve players who practicing and playing together make the best team, and my goal was to select the best team. A critical factor in the achievement of this goal was of course which seniors to keep and cut. John Wooden once listed five qualities of a championship team; playing together, playing hard, fundamentals, X's and O's (strategy), and conditioning. I believe that if a team doesn't play hard and play together, the other three qualities are a moot point, because the team will never win.

We all agreed that there were three seniors and three underclassmen that were going to be in the rotation and play major minutes. Derek Dreifke, Darren Nelson, and Scott Jenkins were the seniors. Nelson and Dreifke were both improved and grew another inch, and both were a step quicker. Nelson was playing above the rim. I tweaked Jenkins already great shooting form, and he bought into it. He was going to be an elite spot up three-point shooter. Ray Brown and Travis Brown grew to 6-4 and 6-2 and were on track with our Division I expectations for them. They both had great summers from the drill work of the open gyms and from playing a national AAU schedule. DeRail Moore spent the entire off-season lifting weights and playing every day. He was 6-3 and clearly our best rebounder. The young point guard Ernest Harris moved back to Kansas City which opened up some minutes on the perimeter.

This left one to three spots in the rotation that were up for grabs. In addition, we saw three other underclassmen that were going to compete for playing time; Alex Tilman and Kris Pulford on the perimeter, and Xavier Crawford inside. Xavier and his brother Octavius were sophomore fraternal twins who moved back to Richfield after moving away before middle school. Both were lacking in the fundamentals, but Xavier was 6-9, rail thin, and when he was finished growing, he was going to be athletic. Octavius was 6-4 and better built. The six remaining returning seniors were competing against these underclassmen for one to three spots of playing time.

Josh Noonan had a great summer, and did everything that we asked of him. We saw him as maybe our seventh or eighth man, and maybe not playing. Like Jenkins, he could shoot it, and he was now over 6-2. He was the late bloomer of his class. Of course, if we kept him, the critics would say that the only reason that he made the team was because his dad was on the board. All of this was discussed. The staff was unanimous in keeping him.

Wade Vrieze was a Legion baseball player who did everything that we asked of him over the summer that didn't conflict with baseball. We saw him as maybe our eighth man, or maybe not playing at all. He was the kind of kid that we could put in a game for two or three minutes, and maybe this would be all of his playing time for the game. The question was, would he buy into this role? We decided to tell him where he stood, and ask him if he would be happy with this role.

Four other seniors had not improved. I saw from observing some fall league games that these four were not hiding their resentment of the young kids. If we kept these four, it would be a time bomb waiting to explode. This was discussed by the entire staff, and after the discussion, I clearly remember the staff agreeing unanimously to cut three of these players. The last one was a very difficult decision. He did everything that we asked of him over the summer. He was definitely in the top twelve. The question was would he be happy if he didn't play at all? When I told him that he did not make the team, he broke down sobbing. After he left the room, the staff sat in silence.

Finally, Lance broke the long silence, "Jim, you made the right decision. He never would've been happy."

***

The next morning when the AD Jim Baker arrived at his office, he had over 20 voice mails. He spent the entire day on the phone. Overnight the senior parents had quickly organized a telephone campaign. The phone of the principal was also ringing off the hook. The superintendent and some school board members also were receiving phone calls. Some of the parents of kids who were cut the year before were also involved. Paul Rekewey was the principal. He decided that these parents had the right to be heard as a group. He told them that he would meet them in the high school cafeteria at seven o'clock that night. The meeting was open to the public. Jim told me that he didn't want me or any of the coaching staff at the meeting. He and Rekewey would listen to and deal with the parents. Over 90 people showed up for the meeting. To say that the discussion was spirited and emotional was an understatement. These people were livid.

One parent said that after coming all the way up through the program, these seniors deserved their chance to play together on the varsity. One parent said that because the seniors played together as a group all the way up, they all knew how to play with each other. One parent said that the school needed a coach who was a member of the community and who knew the kids.

One person asked "how can they cut their leading rebounder?" I had prepped Baker for this question. I gave him a copy of last year's statistics, with the names and numbers of the leading rebounders circled. He answered that he had a copy of last year's statistics, and that we didn't cut the leading rebounder. In spite of this, the complaint that we cut our leading rebounder continued to circulate around the community.

One of the 'concerned citizens' with no sons in the program stood up and emphatically stated "I represent Richfield's moral majority". He complained that kids who lived their entire lives in Richfield were being cut. He then referenced the one African-American senior that was cut and stated "now Dimick's even cutting the Richfield black kids". Jim Baker's response was that open enrollment kids had equal rights to kids who lived in Richfield.

They demanded that I be fired, and that a new coach be chosen who was a faculty member. After Jim Baker said that Jim Dimick was his coach, they demanded that tryouts be held again, because the first round of tryouts had been unfair. They proposed that an independent committee be chosen to be at this second round of tryouts to evaluate and to pick the team. After this committee picked the team, then the present coaching staff would coach the team. Jim Baker's response was that the coach picks the team. This meeting was the first attempt to get me fired, by the self-named group of 'concerned-citizens'.

***

The team had a great practice on Friday, and we scrimmaged well on Saturday. As is always the case, eliminating the divisive attitudes energized the team. Every kid who sat on the bench was happy to be there and was pulling for the team. The following Monday would give me my chance to respond to the complaints of the Thursday night meeting. The annual preseason parent's meeting would be at the high school at six o'clock. In attendance would be all of the parents of the boys who made the varsity, junior varsity, sophomore, or freshman teams. It would also be attended by the members of the basketball board. I would be able to get on my soapbox.

Monday morning when the physical education teachers entered the gym to get set up for class, they noticed graffiti written on the basketball backboards and the walls. Most of the writing was circles and swirls. Scrawled across both backboards was "FUCK YOU DIMICK". The graffiti wasn't written in spray paint. It was written in human feces. Someone or some people had gained access to the building without showing a sign of forced entry, and had written all of these things with their own shit. The custodians worked hard and had it cleaned up in time for the first hour class.

***

The Monday of the second week of basketball season was a busy day. After school was practice. This was followed by the parent's meeting which was followed by "Meet the Spartans". "Meet the Spartans" was a community event which was in its eighth year. The bleachers on one side of the gym were pulled out. The players and parents of every team in Richfield from first grade through twelfth grade were invited, as well as fans. All of the youth players received pennants and felt tipped pens. The varsity team was introduced. This was followed by a full court shooting drill, a three-point shooting contest, and a dunk contest. After the contests the youth players brought their pennants to the varsity players who autographed them. Many of the parents took photos. It was organized by the basketball board and it was a great promotion for the entire program.

The parent's meeting was held in a double sized classroom. The floor was filled with desks and fold-out chairs. In the front of the room was a podium. When the meeting started at six o'clock all of the seats were taken, with people standing against both side walls, and people standing three-deep by the back wall. A few other people showed up to support me, including Dave Thorson and Ben Johnson. Ben played at DeLaSalle when I was an assistant there, and he was a starting guard at the University of Minnesota. I will paraphrase my speech.

I drew on the chalkboard the number 160. I told them that a basketball game lasts 32 minutes and that five players play at a time and that 5 x 32 = 160. I told them that I wasn't at the meeting on Thursday night, but that I knew that the meeting was about one thing. It was about playing time. I then went on. "160 divided by 8 is 20, and that 160 divided by 7 is 23. My assistants and I are going to decide who the top seven or eight players are and these kids will get the playing time. Among these kids, the playing time isn't going to be equal. Some might play over 30 minutes a game and some might play less than 20 minutes a game. If a ninth or tenth player plays in a game, it probably won't be for a lot of minutes, and it will directly reduce the minutes of one of the other players. During the season, some kids might pass up other kids and who is in the top seven might change.

I then wrote Bob Knight's name and quote on the board. "The best team isn't always the best five players. The best team is the five players who playing together make the best team." I then said "I'm going to allot the playing time based upon this quote and based upon which kids make up the best team right now. I'm not going to base it on which grade a kid is in now, or on which kids were the best players in sixth grade, or on which team a kid played on in sixth grade. This is public education, and this is a public high school, and every student who attends this high school and who earns the right to tryout with academics and with citizenship has a right to be on this team and to compete for playing time."

I then wrote the name of one of my high school coaches on the blackboard, "Al Berkvam". Above his name I wrote another quote, "If everyone likes you, you probably aren't doing your job." I then explained that I knew that everybody would not agree with who I play, and that everybody would not like me. I then went on to refute some allegations from the Thursday meeting. "Some people want a member of the faculty to be the head coach. They got me on that one. I'm not going to quit my job and become a teacher again. Some people want the coach to be someone who lives in Richfield. They got me on that one too. My wife and I aren't going to sell our house and move to Richfield. Some people want a program of entitlement, where we pick the team and allocate the playing time based upon who's been here the longest. I'm not doing it that way."

Lance spoke next, and he was a great speaker. He started by saying "I played basketball seventeen years. I played four years in high school at Washburn. I played four years in college, one at Nebraska and three at North Dakota State. And I played nine years in the pros in Spain and Greece. In Europe alone I played for over twenty different coaches. When I came back to the cities from Europe, I coached two years at DeLaSalle with two of the coaches in this room that you're looking at". He then paused and pointed at Dave Thorson and me. "And out of all those coaches, the best two coaches that I've ever been around are right here, Jim Dimick and Dave Thorson. If I didn't think Jim Dimick was a great coach, I wouldn't be volunteering as his assistant." After five minutes he finished by saying "you don't have any idea how lucky you are to have a coach of his caliber at this high school. And you have a group of parents trying to run him out. I can't believe it." He finished by saying "Let us coach. You will see the results. Just let us coach."

Dave Thorson spoke last for another five minutes. He was also a great speaker, and he was always loud and theatrical. "I can feel the energy in this room. I not only hear it. I can feel it. We can all feel it. I am so glad that I was asked to be here." He then cranked up the volume. "What do you want? What do you want, Richfield? You want to have your top two players go to Holy Angels every year so that the average kids can play and you can maybe win ten games? You want the seniors to play every year so that the good sophomores go somewhere else…where they know they can play as sophomores?" He started laughing, "Is that what you want? You want the program to be so bad that no good players ever want to open enroll here? Is that what you want? If that's what you want, then don't complain and don't blame the coach when you don't win. If you want guaranteed playing time for certain kids, that's fine… and you'll never have to worry about open enrollment kids, and you'll never win. But then don't blame the coach for the win/loss record. Because once you start winning, and once the word gets out that these guys can coach, kids are going to start showing up. It's one or the other."

I closed by telling them that all I want to do is to coach my team. "The team has been picked. We need to move on. All that I want to do now is to be allowed to coach my team, with no interference from parents. We need to put aside our disagreements, and to agree to disagree on some things. We need to all come together as a united group, players, coaches, and parents." I paused, "white parents, black parents, gay parents, and straight parents, we need to all come together to support these kids. At the end of the season, if you all don't want me to be the coach, go tell Jim Baker to fire me, but give me this season to prove myself. That's all that I ask."

At the end of the meeting, we handed out the contracts for the players to sign. The contracts summarized the term "taking care of business"; be on time, hand in assignments, study for tests, be a good citizen in the halls. We didn't discuss one part of them. Upstairs the gym was filled up with people waiting to "Meet the Spartans".

* * *

The next morning, I got a phone call from Jim Baker. He said he heard that the meeting went really well and to stop in before practice. When I walked into his office and sat down, he looked at me and smiled. Then he rolled his eyes, and said "Well… I heard about the meeting," and he burst out laughing. "I heard that I missed a church revival. And I heard you brought in some big hitters." We then spent fifteen minutes rehashing the situation. He was elated with how it all turned out. He said that I got the last word in to the community through the remaining parents, and that now they knew how I was going to run the program. He added that every coach doesn't run their program the same way, and that the community was going to have to accept how I was going to run the program.

When he got done, I said, "Jim, these pissed off people aren't going to go away. They're just going to wait, regroup, and come at me again. We both know that. Am I on the hot seat?"

"Yup, you're on the hot seat. And they're going to complain about any possible thing that they can think of to get you fired. You've been through this before. You know what you should do and not do and say and not say. Be sure your assistants know too."

The opinion page of the next issue of the *Richfield Sun Current* included a letter.

RHS football is back in style

To the editor:

I extend my congratulations to Kyle Inforzato, Richfield High School football coach, his staff and the players for a very entertaining and successful season.

*Led by Coach Inforzato, the program took another big step forward by win-
ning the section and qualifying for the state tournament…In only two years,
he has restored pride and a winning environment to Richfield football…Coach
Inforzato's fundamental principle of giving every senior an opportunity to finish
out their high school career is especially gratifying, refreshing, and important in
rebuilding and maintaining a healthy athletic program. It is a sign of respect and
humanness that every coach should exemplify when dealing with young people.*

*This is in complete contrast to the boys basketball program, in which sev-
eral seniors have been cut or otherwise terminated during the past two seasons.*

*Strangely and sadly, RHS administrators condone this unprecedented phi-
losophy. Our football players are very fortunate that Coach Inforzato does not
allow this to happen in their program…*

Oz Mullerleile

Richfield [6]

* * *

We opened the season playing a good St Paul Humboldt team at home. Jim
Baker stopped me in the hallway during the B squad game and said that if there
were any incidents, he would handle them. He didn't want me or my assistants
to be involved in any way. As people were entering the gym it was obvious
that it was going to be another good Richfield crowd. The wooden bleacher
seats were 16 rows deep and ran from baseline to baseline on both sides of
the court. The Richfield students sat directly across from the teams and they
filled up the front rows of the middle area. The most vocal ones sat in the first
row and often jumped up to applaud exciting plays. The game started at 7:30,
and by 7:10 the students had filled up the bottom half of the bleachers from
free throw line to free throw line. Then the chants began, and I have changed
the names to keep them anonymous. "Put in Cleaver….put in Cleaver….put in
Cleaver." This was followed by "put in Haskell…put in Haskell." By the time Jim
Baker was standing in front of them they were chanting "put in Rutherford….
put in Rutherford….put in Rutherford." They were chanting for me to put in the
seniors that I had cut. These were interspersed with an occasional solo "Fuck
you Dimick." It quickly stopped when Jim talked to them and pointed to the
door. A big part of the student section, most likely made up of seniors, was
clearly hoping that we would lose.

We played well and at halftime we led 35-33. At the end of the third quarter
the game was tied 47-47. Early in the fourth quarter Dreifke and Jenkins hit
back-to-back threes which opened up an 8-point lead. We controlled the ball

down the stretch and hit free throws to win 73-67. The underclassmen contributed heavily. Travis Brown finished with 23 points and DeRail Moore had 12 rebounds. Due to a strained knee, Ray Brown did not play. It was an opening game win that we definitely needed.

Later that week I was at the high school walking down a hallway, and I saw a long-time teacher walking towards me from the opposite direction. Except for the two of us, the long hallway was empty. When we were twenty feet apart, she got on one knee, raised both arms into the air, and began bowing up and down, like a knave before a king. She was saying "you are my hero…you are my hero." I stopped and she stood up. She then began talking. She looked me in the eye and pointed her finger at me.

"What you did took a lot of guts and you gained immediate respect from the entire faculty…immediate respect…huge respect. A couple of those kids that you cut have been problems off and on in class from day one, and we all totally understand why you cut them. We all get it. You are our hero, and I want you to know that."

***

We played inconsistently the next eight weeks. Holy Angels defeated us at their place 77-68 after we had been ahead 53-52 after three quarters. This was disappointing since I felt that the teams were even. We then played our best game yet of the year and upset a very good Edina team 94-80 in their gym. Two weeks later we played well at home and lost to Tartan 68-67. This would have been a signature win for us, and it was the second year in a row that they beat us by a bucket at our place.

At the end of January, we were 5-9. On defense we were not consistently shutting teams down. We didn't have the overall quickness to apply hard ball pressure without getting beat off of the dribble, and we weren't scoring many points off of turnovers. Our opponents were running their offense in their comfort zone, and we didn't have the look of a well-coached defensive team.

***

The biggest game of the year was St Thomas Academy at home on the second Tuesday of February. They were 19-0 and ranked #1 in the state in Class 3A. They had three D1 recruits in 6-7 Dan Fitzgerald, 6-8 Isaac Rosefelt, and 6-0 Lorenzo Bellard, and a veteran team. They were also an excellent man to man defensive team which always played within their capabilities and rarely beat themselves. They had beaten us at their place in early January 96-74.

Without telling the kids, we had been gearing our practices towards them whenever possible. Our defensive drills always stressed four fundamentals; ball pressure, jump to the pass, front the cutter, and box out. We stressed these fundamentals against different combinations of ball movement and man movement; or passes, cuts, and screens. For the past month any cuts or screens that our upcoming opponents used, that were also used by St Thomas Academy, were worked on repeatedly. Going into the Tuesday game, I felt that we were as prepared as we could be.

The gym filled up early. The student section was the biggest it had been since the opening game. In the previous home games, we rarely heard the chants for the seniors that we had cut. I believed that many of the dissenters stopped coming to the games. However, on this night, they were all there. I think that they figured we were going to get killed and they wanted to watch it. It was a big crowd.

Things went our way from the start. We hit four of our first five shots, and jumped out to an 8-0 lead. Their coach Mike Sjoberg called time out. They came out of the time out and ran a double screen set play for a shot at the top of the key. Our kids switched the screen and denied the pass to the shooter. Their players were realizing that their set plays weren't going to work, and they were playing with a new sense of urgency. Our kids were also realizing this, and were playing with confidence. At the end of the first quarter, we lead 19-14, and at halftime we were ahead 30-28. They couldn't break the game open. After three quarters we were up 47-46. From this point on, it was a one possession game.

In games like this, when the clock winds down to under three minutes, the pressure and the adrenaline rush is intoxicating. The challenge as a coach is to have your options predetermined and to stay in the moment and think clearly. With a little over a minute to go they had the ball and we were up one. They missed, we got the rebound, moved the ball up court, and we spread our offense to the sidelines. With 16 seconds to go they fouled Scott Jenkins, our best free throw shooter. Both free throws rimmed in and out.

St Thomas now had the ball with one last chance to win. They pushed the ball up court and called time out with 14 seconds left. As the kids were running to the bench, I stood up and said to my assistants, "Well, we can play them all tough and try to not give them a shot or we can double off of one kid and then we pick who shoots. Plus, if we double, we're not fronting Rosefelt, so he doesn't beat us on a put back." Lance and Alcindor both said "we pick who shoots." My intuition told me that they were going to go inside to Rosefelt.

In the huddle I told Ray to stay home on Fitzgerald (play him hot), and I told DeRail to guard Rosefelt from behind and force him off of the block. I told Dreifke to totally back off of his man (play him cold) and front Rosefelt. I said that we were going to make Dreifke's man shoot the ball, then we all box out, we get the rebound, and we celebrate.

Sometimes your time outs go as planned. Sometimes they don't. This one went as planned. In the end the St Thomas kid with the ball kept looking into the post, hesitated, and then shot. It hit the back rim and went high in the air in the middle of the lane. DeRail, with Rosefelt on his butt, was in perfect position to go get it. He elevated, his long arms reached up, and snatched the ball and ripped it to his chest with his elbows out. As the horn sounded, he was mobbed by his teammates. The stands emptied, and it was a mad celebration in the middle of the court. It was our first signature win. The headline in the next day's high school section of the *Minneapolis Star Tribune* sports page was *"Two No.1s find upsets on the road"*[7]

I got a call from Jim Baker the next morning at my office. As almost always, he was upbeat and laughing. "Well, are you basking in the glory? I hope you are, 'cause you should be." We rehashed the game and laughed more. Before he hung up, he said, "and oh, by the way, congratulations, you're off the hot seat."

* * *

The best thing about the St Thomas game, was that our kids experienced shutting down a team's set plays, and seeing how that can change a game. The entire team now believed in our defense, which was a turning point for the program. The words of Dave Buss rang true in my ears, "sometimes it takes a year to get your system in". In the case of our defense, it took a year and a half. We began shutting teams down game after game. From a coach's perspective of watching all five defenders on the court at one time, we had finally achieved the look of a well-coached defensive team.

We had another signature win in Eau Claire, Wisconsin, on the second to the last Saturday of the regular season. We scheduled this game as a fun trip for the kids and a chance to play a quality team in front of a big crowd on the road. We chartered a coach bus for the one-and-a-half-hour ride, and after the game the team would eat at a buffet style restaurant in Eau Claire. The basketball board paid for the coach bus and the meal.

Eau Claire Memorial had a program steeped in tradition. Until Wisconsin adopted classes in basketball in 1971-72, Eau Claire was the biggest school in the northwest area of the state, and they made 32 two trips to the one class state tournament. Since 1972 they made an additional nine trips. Their gymnasium was built in the 1950s and as you entered it you could feel the history. Dick Bennett coached there before moving on to UW-Stevens Point and eventually Wisconsin. The current Memorial coach, Trevor Kohlhepp, was an assistant under one of Bennett's former assistants. They played tough man to man defense, and they ran the same blockers-and-movers offense that the Badgers did, with constant screens and cuts, and absolutely no pattern to it. They were ranked #6 in Wisconsin in the biggest class and their record was 16-2. They were big and physical and good.

With under a minute to go in the first quarter we were down 24-19, they had the ball, and they elected to go for one shot. After just seven minutes, it was obvious to me that we were not going to shut down their offense. They methodically worked the ball and at six seconds got a good shot from the far wing. The rebound went long. DeRail grabbed it and fired an outlet pass to Travis Brown in front of our bench. Travis sprint dribbled up the sideline in front of the scorer's table. After he crossed half court, he took one more dribble, lifted his right knee in the air as if he was shooting a lay-up, and launched a shot with a perfect follow through that swished in. Had the Eau Claire kid hit the open shot, we would have been down eight going into the second quarter. Instead, we were down only two.

We traded baskets for the next two quarters, and after three quarters we were ahead 61-60. Every time that they would begin to pull away, we would hit a three pointer, or make three shots in a row. Then in the fourth quarter they missed shots on four consecutive possessions. Derrick Dreifke made two free throws to put us up five, our biggest lead of the game. We diamond (1-2-1-1) zone pressed after the second make. While trapping the ball handler after the inbounds pass, Ray Brown deflected the ball up in the air, grabbed it, and dribbled hard at the basket for the open layup. Then he suddenly jump-stopped and fired a crosscourt pass to Jenkins. Scott was on the arc squared up to the basket with his knees bent and his hands at his chest giving Ray the target. The pass hit Scott right in the hands, and he went straight up and drilled the wide open three, hitting nothing but net. We were up eight. They called time out. Our bench emptied as our players ran off the floor. I looked at the clock and there was 4:46 to go in the game. Everyone in the huddle could feel the collective adrenalin rush. We were close to pulling off a very unlikely road win.

They kept making runs at us, and got our lead back down to three. To slow them down, Josh Noonan hit shots on consecutive possessions, and Darrin Nelson had a steal and open court hard dunk. They got the lead down to one twice in the last minute. We made thirteen consecutive free throws to win

86-79. Their coach was quoted in the *Eau Claire Leader-Telegram* the next day as saying *"they just shot the lights out."* [8] If we had played them in an NBA seven game series, they would have won 4-0 or 4-1. We didn't out coach them. We just hit a lot of shots and they missed a lot of shots. They ran into us on our best game of the season, and we were improving fast.

* * *

In Minnesota there were four classes in basketball, 4A, 3A, 2A, and 1A. The four-class system was adopted for the 1996-97 school year. In Class 3A the two metropolitan sections closest to Minneapolis and St Paul were traditionally the toughest. They were made up of most of the city schools in both cities, the Catholic schools, and some inner ring suburban schools. In our section was the Minneapolis city champion Patrick Henry and St Thomas. After we defeated St Thomas in February, Patrick Henry replaced them as the #1 ranked team in 3A, and they finished the season ranked #1. The winner of our section almost always made a run deep into the state tournament.

The last week of the season we lost at #3 seed Hill-Murray 74-66 and we beat #4 seed Henry Sibley at home 78-77. In the opening tournament game at Sibley, we played three players man to man, while our other two players played a 1-1 zone. DeRail played the bottom of the zone, and the other man was at the free throw line. They never got into their offense. We led 41-23 at halftime and won 77-62. This was the only time in my coaching career that I every used this defense.

Two days later the Saturday semifinals were played as a double header at North High in Minneapolis. It was us and Patrick Henry in the first game and St Thomas against Roosevelt in the second game. Henry was coached by Larry McKenzie. He coached his son Lawrence all the way up through the Minneapolis Hustlers youth program. When Lawrence was in middle school, Larry became an assistant at Henry, and he brought Lawrence and many of his buddies to Henry, much to the chagrin of the other Hustler coaches who were North alumni. Henry was the state runners-up in 1998. Larry became the head coach in 1999 and took them to four consecutive state tournaments, winning the past three. All of this changed the traditional power structure of the city conference. Now both schools on the north side of downtown and west of the Mississippi river were very good. North was located in the historically black and Jewish neighborhood on the near (close to downtown) north side. Henry was located two miles further north, in what had once been a neighborhood of working-class whites. Both teams were predominantly if not all black. North played in class 4A. Henry played in class 3A. Larry was in the Henry gym working hard with his kids every summer on fundamentals. They played an aggressive full court man to man defense, along with a 1-2-2 half court trap. The 1-2-2 half court trap is very similar to a 1-3-1 half court trap. If a team wasn't acclimated to this type of ball pressure, Henry could score points in flurries.

The first half went very well for us. We were more patient than usual on offense, passing up the good shots for the very good shots. We were playing our "pack" man to man defense, keeping all five defenders in or near the paint, forcing them to shoot from the outside. We knew who their worst shooters were, and we were sagging off them (playing them "cold") and helping on the others. Every time one of their best players got the ball (who we were playing "hot"), we forced him to his weak hand side, and we had a helper waiting. Our two years of defensive drills were paying off and our kids were playing defense with confidence. We had no missed box outs. They were only getting one shot, and they couldn't put together a run. They were a little out of their comfort zone.

With four minutes to go in the second quarter, Larry called time out. The next time down the court they were in their 1-2-2 trap. We burned it for six straight points to take the lead. They went back to man to man. With two minutes to go in the half we had the ball with a 40-38 lead. We went for one shot and missed.

The second half couldn't have gone better for Henry. In the first four minutes they scored eight points off of steals. I called two time-outs. Then with an eight point lead they relaxed more on offense and started hitting shots. Midway through the fourth quarter with a 12-point lead Larry had his kids spread out on offense. When we went out to pressure them, they took us off of the dribble. They were very good at driving and dishing for open shots, and then chasing the rebound against a defense that was scrambling to box out. They were now in control of the game. The final score was 91-77.

Henry went on to beat St Thomas in the section finals 59-52. The Patriots then marched to their fourth consecutive 3A state championship defeating Totino Grace 76-55, Red Wing 59-54, and Sauk Rapids-Rice in the state finals 69-55. Their north side rival North won the 4A title. The Minneapolis City Conference had swept the top two classes. In Wisconsin, after losing to us, Eau Claire Memorial put together a five-game win streak that took them to the state semi-finals in Division I where they lost to Appleton West 58-44.

* * *

When the season was done, I and my coaching staff felt great about how we finished and where the program was at. Our system was in and the kids believed in it. And the parents and kids saw how we were going to do things. The final records of our teams were varsity 13-13, JV 16-6, sophomores 14-10, and ninth grade 15-7. After going 3-5 the first round of the conference we finished in fourth place with a record of 9-7. We returned three talented classes in a row. I expected to win 20 games each of the next two years, and be ranked in the top ten in the state.

Lake Conference

A s the cities of Minneapolis and St. Paul grew during the last half of the
nineteenth century, public high schools were built to supply the demand
of the growing population. By 1900 Minneapolis had five public high schools;
Central (1857), East (1867), Logan (1888), South (1892), and North (1896).
By 1925 the city added six more high schools; University (1908), West (1909),
Vocational (1916), Edison (1922), Roosevelt (1922), and Washburn (1925).

The city was bordered by nine townships/villages; St. Anthony, Columbia
Heights, Brooklyn Center, Robbinsdale, Golden Valley, St Louis Park, Edina,
Morningside, and Richfield. In 1900, only one of these municipalities had built
their own high school, St. Louis Park in 1898. Almost 40 years later, the next
of the municipalities on the west side of the Mississippi to build a high school
was Robbinsdale in 1936. This land flanking Minneapolis to the north, west,
and south was mostly small farms. Until the townships/villages built their own
high schools, many of these farm kids attended the Minneapolis high schools.

When Minnesota was first settled by European Americans, the earliest
towns were founded along the rivers. When the railroads replaced the steam-
boats as the primary mode of transportation, a second wave of towns grew up
along the railroad lines. The railroad lines emanated out from the Twin Cities
in all directions, again like spokes on a wheel. New towns grew along the lines,
either at the interval of water stops, or more ideally, where the tracks intersected water. On the northwest side of Minneapolis, Robbinsdale was the first
town on the railroad tracks which headed on to Fargo, North Dakota. Another
set of tracks stretched almost straight west and skirted the north edge of Lake
Minnetonka. Wayzata grew up on the north shore of the lake. At the western
end of the big lake the town of Mound sprouted. A third rail line headed west
southwest from the city, and the small town of Hopkins grew up on this line
near Minnehaha Creek. Further to the west and on the same line were the
towns of Deephaven and Excelsior, which were also on the south shore of
Lake Minnetonka. By the 1920s Wayzata, Mound, Hopkins, Deephaven, and
Excelsior all had small public high schools.

After World War II, the spaces between the railroad towns and Minneapolis
transitioned from small farms to houses, and the forms of government made

the switch from township boards to city councils. This happened in Richfield and all of the other townships that bordered both Minneapolis and St. Paul. These cities soon wanted their own high schools, and they built them. Edina and Richfield built high schools in 1950 and 1955. When these and other high schools were built, the borders of the school districts didn't always exactly match the borders of the cities. The school district borders were probably platted more to maximize the efficiency of the student bus routes. This inconsistency remains true to this day. Some of the school districts encompass most of one city, and parts of other cities. The Hopkins and Robbinsdale districts both include seven cities. Students who live in the city of Plymouth attend four different high schools. Many of the business districts of these cities at one time had their own Chamber of Commerce. And after World War II, many of the cities founded their own American Legion, VFW Club, other fraternal organizations, and their own youth sports programs. As a result, some high schools had two, three, or four separate feeder programs for some of their sports. And some feeder programs fed more than one high school.

The Lake Conference was formed in 1932 with the charter members being Hopkins, Excelsior, Mound, St. Louis Park, Wayzata, and University High in Minneapolis. With three of the six schools lying on the shores of Lake Minnetonka, one can presume it was named after this huge lake. Excelsior and Deephaven consolidated in 1952 to form Minnetonka High School. Robbinsdale, Edina-Morningside, and Richfield joined in 1936, 1950, and 1955. Bloomington joined in 1957. Robbinsdale, St Louis Park, and Richfield, were all working class suburbs which shared a border with Minneapolis. Edina was the affluent inner ring suburb, sandwiched between Richfield and St Louis Park. Minnetonka, Wayzata, and Mound became affluent high schools as the upper-class Minneapolitans began building homes on and around the large lake.

One hundred years later, all of these communities are considered suburbs. The old railroad towns are considered suburbs, and the former farmland townships are considered suburbs. However, when it comes to an old main street business district, there are two types of suburbs. If one drives down the old main street of any one of these old railroad town suburbs today, there is a feeling of being in a small town in outstate Minnesota, with one-, two-, or three-story brick buildings on both sides of main street, and the railroad tracks not far away. For example, Hopkins has a number of business districts, but there is definitely only one 'downtown Hopkins'. The old farmland township suburbs all have more than one business district, but none of them have a one-hundred-year-old main street. If one drives through the business districts of these suburbs today, one definitely gets the feeling architecturally of being in a suburb, and not in a small town.

The place where both types of suburbs feel the same is on their borders. When one drives west out of downtown Robbinsdale, the only way to know you are leaving Robbinsdale is when you see the sign for Crystal, which is the next suburb. The residential neighborhoods on both sides of the border look the same. One crosses the border when one crosses a street, and without the city signs, the borders are indiscernible.

By the 1950s and 1960s, in the Lake Conference, the old railroad town high schools were Hopkins, Minnetonka, Mound, Robbinsdale, and Wayzata. The farmland township high schools were Bloomington, Edina-Morningside, Richfield, and St Louis Park. On the east side of the Mississippi River, the same situation developed in the St Paul Suburban Conference. The old railroad/river town high schools were Anoka, Hastings, North St Paul, South St Paul, Stillwater, and White Bear Lake. The younger farmland township high schools were Alexander Ramsey, Columbia Heights, Mounds View, and West St Paul Sibley.

During the 1950s and 1960s, both conferences were more or less dominated athletically by the largest high schools of the old railroad/river towns. These schools didn't win every title, but they were much more likely to finish in the top half of the conference. Two such high schools in the Lake were Hopkins and Robbinsdale. In the St Paul Suburban these high schools were Anoka, South St Paul, and White Bear Lake. This could be because the schools were founded years earlier, or it could be because they had more of a small-town identity. With this small-town identity, there probably was a stronger sense of community pride. The kids of these railroad/river towns were probably more likely to grow up attending the Friday night games with their parents. And for young kids, this gives rise to dreaming of someday playing for the local high school. And it results in more kids working hard to achieve these dreams, and more kids trying out for the teams.

The two exceptions to this rule were the high schools in Edina and Richfield. In athletics, both were dominating at the conference and the state level. Edina is located next to the southwest corner of Minneapolis and one of the most affluent neighborhoods in Minneapolis, with its chain of lakes. Compared to the other suburbs, the lots are bigger, the houses are bigger, and the residents make more money. There is very little if any low-income public housing. With this affluence there is a high level of parental involvement with children, and a greater percentage of students playing sports. When one drives across the southern part of Edina from west to east, suddenly the lots and the houses are smaller. Based upon these two features, there is a clear line of demarcation. When the driver sees this, the driver has entered Richfield.

Like all of the suburbs, Richfield has a number of business districts. Lyndale Avenue and Cedar Avenue are the old wagon trails emanating from Minneapolis, and early on they had areas with storefronts. As the houses were built, Penn Avenue, Nicollet Avenue, and Portland Avenue also became north/south thoroughfares with businesses. In later years malls were built on the east/west roadways of 66th Street and on the north frontage road of Interstate 494. Richfield now has at least half a dozen business districts, depending on how you define them. It doesn't have an old downtown. All of the business districts have a suburban feel to them.

However, when it comes to borders, Richfield is different from all of the other suburbs. On the map the city forms a rectangle, two miles north to south and almost four miles east to west. All four borders are distinct, and you can't miss them. On the north the city is bordered by Highway 62, which is a freeway with entrance and exit ramps. To the north of Highway 62 is Minneapolis. On the south side the border is another freeway, Interstate 494. On the opposite side of I-494 is Bloomington. The border on the east is Cedar Avenue which is also Highway 77, and past this freeway sits a few residential neighborhoods, the airport, the old fort, and the river. These three borders are not residential streets that one can simply walk across. They are barriers. The only border that is a residential street is Xerxes Avenue on the west, which separates Richfield from Edina, and the school district border is two blocks west of Xerxes. These few blocks of small houses are located in the city of Edina and the school district of Richfield. To the west of these little houses is the half mile wide Southdale shopping center, beyond which sit the bigger houses of Edina. The shopping mall is another barrier.

These borders make Richfield and its school district somewhat unique. Except for the few blocks of Edina, the Richfield school district encompasses only one city. It has one Chamber of Commerce, one American Legion, and one VFW club. These organizations and others like them support one youth sports program for each sport. And they support the only high school in town, which sits in almost the exact middle of the rectangle. This is the home of the Richfield Spartans, whose sports history is deeply intertwined with the history of the Lake Conference. And for the longtime residents, the old Lake Conference is a big part of their sports identity and their pride.

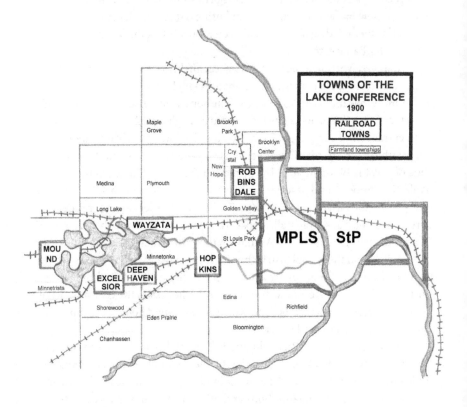

TOWNS OF THE
LAKE CONFERENCE
1900

RAILROAD
TOWNS

Farmland townships

Maple Grove

Brooklyn Park

Brooklyn Center

Crystal

New Hope

ROB BINS DALE

Medina

Plymouth

Golden Valley

Long Lake

WAYZATA

St Louis Park

MPLS

StP

MOU ND

Minnetonka

HOP KINS

Minnetrista

EXCEL SIOR

DEEP HAVEN

Shorewood

Edina

Richfield

Eden Prairie

Bloomington

Chanhassen

Third Summer

It's a sad thing not to have friends, but it is even sadder not to have enemies.

—Che Guevara

Alcindor and I again went to work the next spring on our 8th grade AAU team. We built upon what we had done the year before. Our middle school coaches Greg Von Ruden and Steve Hemming helped us by monitoring grades and classroom behavior of the kids for any possible problems. The eighth graders as a traveling team were our weakest class in the entire program. Until their eighth-grade winter, they had never won ten games in a season playing in class B winter tournaments. They now had six new African-American kids playing with them. Three had played the previous winter because of financial aid, and three more joined the spring team. All six lived in Richfield. The team finished 13-5 and the kids had fun.

Many of our returning freshman, sophomores, and juniors were playing spring AAU ball. Six were playing for elite programs, such as the Howard Pulley program. The only ones that weren't playing AAU were the three sport athletes who were now playing baseball.

***

I was at the high school one morning in May talking to Jim Baker in his office. At one point he shut the door, rolled his eyes, smiled, and said "we gotta talk about something."

He told me that Barb Devlin, the superintendent called him to her office. She had received some phone calls complaining about the way that I was running the program. She told Jim that it wasn't parents who had called, but people who called themselves 'concerned citizens.' She was told a couple of things by these 'concerned citizens.' They said that I didn't care about the Richfield kids, that I was only concerned about bringing in city kids, and that if I was the basketball coach, the Richfield kids would be excluded from the program. They reiterated to her that "Dimick doesn't care about the Richfield kids" and "we just want what's best for the Richfield kids." One of them also told her that "Dimick's team doesn't play Richfield basketball", and that as a twenty-year fan, "I want to watch Richfield basketball." Because Barb was a woman who had never been involved in athletics, she then asked Jim to explain all of this to her.

Now I rolled my eyes, shook my head, smiled, and said "when is this going to end?"

He said, "You got nothing to worry about, I explained it all to her."

"Well, if they're calling her, they're calling the school board members too."

"I know. Just watch your back and keep doing what you're doing."

"What if they convince her that I have to go, and she tells you to fire me"?

"Then I'll tell her she can find a new AD. The day that they tell me who I have to fire is the day that I resign."

I then asked "who is it?"

"She wouldn't tell me, but I know who it is. He named two men. They've always sought me out to talk, and they aren't talking to me anymore, and that's just fine. As far as I'm concerned, they're doing me a favor. You think I give a shit what those two guys think?" As usual, he then broke out laughing.

As I drove home, I was of course thinking, how does one differentiate between a Richfield kid and a city kid? And what is Richfield basketball? This was a watershed moment in my time at Richfield. I realized that what I was doing involved a lot more than just basketball, and that I might have a story to tell. From this day forward if I heard a quote that I didn't want to forget, I wrote it down and saved it.

The next time that we had a coach's meeting I opened the meeting with a discussion of some of the complaints that were circling around the community. My sources had informed me of a few of them. One source told me that if he heard it said once, he'd heard it said many times, 'well, Dimick will just bring in a black kid from Minneapolis…' Another common complaint was the question 'why does Richfield need study halls? Richfield never needed study halls before.' The loyalty of the coaching staff to the community was also being questioned, 'Dimick's not loyal to the Richfield kids. I then told them about my conversation with Baker. There was a mixed reaction of both knowing and disbelief.

Lance, the warrior who thrives on battle, was instantly pissed off, and said in only so many terms that it was racism. "Jim, if this isn't out and out racism, what is it? Who are the Richfield kids? The kids that I donate my nights working with in the summer aren't Richfield kids? And what the hell kind of basketball are we playing if it isn't Richfield basketball? What do they want us to do, play all seniors and walk the ball up the floor and win five games?"

Because Jamar had attended high school in the nineties as one of the first African-Americans to play for Richfield, he had a unique perspective. I remember him saying that he really liked coaching at Richfield, but that in some ways he wasn't that surprised.

The reaction of two other assistants, who both worked at the high school, was a combination of mild surprise and extreme disappointment. One said that there was no doubt that this was racism, but also said that it was a small group, adding that they are closet racists.

Alcindor just shook his head and said, "What is this, Mississippi? Why don't they just wear their cloaks and hoods to the games? I'm serious. They should at least admit what they are. In Mississippi they don't call us city kids, they use a different word."

Before the meeting broke up, we all agreed on a number of things. We were doing the right thing, and we were just going to work all that much harder. We couldn't do anything that would give the complainers anything to complain about. I reemphasized loyalty, telling them that we all had to have each other's backs. "The number one quality of an assistant is to be loyal to the head coach. If we have any disagreements, which we will, we discuss them here, and with nobody else."

I then began thinking about this idea of Richfield kids and city kids. I examined our rosters. In grades five through eight there were about 40 kids playing traveling basketball. All but one lived in Richfield. Because of financial aid, 12 kids were playing for the first time, and 11 of them were black.

In grades nine through twelve there were 4 open enrollment kids out of 28 kids. These four grades also included 6 kids who lived in Richfield but had never played on the traveling teams. All 6 kids were African-American and lived in the apartment buildings. Except for Ray, all 10 kids had enrolled at Richfield before I had even met them or their parents. Some of these kids were at risk academically and because of the study halls, they made the ninth-grade team, and were succeeding in the classroom.

So out of these 68 kids, 63 lived in Richfield. The 5 who didn't live in Richfield were all The Choice is Yours students, a program of voluntary integration, negotiated between the NAACP and the suburban school districts, as an alternative to forced bussing to and from Minneapolis to Richfield. The only one who didn't live in Richfield and was at Richfield because of the new coaching staff was Ray. The other varsity player who did live in Richfield and was at Richfield because of the new coaching staff was Travis.

* * *

A week later I got a call from Mullenbach. One of the kids had told him that DeRail was thinking about transferring to Henry. Two nights later Lance, Alcindor, and I were sitting in DeRail's living room with his mom Janice. They lived in one of the big apartment complexes on the south side of Richfield. He said that he had a cousin at Henry, and that his cousin was saying that it would be easier to win at Henry. I said to DeRail "you want to win, don't you?"

"Yeah, coach."

"DeRail, we all want to win. I want to win. Lance wants to win. Alcindor wants to win. Your mom wants to win. We totally understand that you want to win." I paused. "DeRail, there is no doubt in our minds. We're going to win at Richfield. Don't you think we're gonna win at Richfield? Look at the guys we got, all of your buddies, who you've been working so hard with."

Lance then took over. He finished by saying, "DeRail, if someone's telling you that we're not going to win, they have no clue what they are talking about."

"You're right coach. I never said that I was going to go to Henry. I was just talking to my cousin."

When Janice got her chance to talk, she was animated and the volume in the room went up a couple of notches. She finished by saying "you aren't going anywhere, son. After all these men have done for you, you aren't going anywhere." She looked at me. "He's staying at Richfield, coach. You have nothing to worry about."

Alcindor talked next. Then we all talked about the team, DeRail's academic work ethic, his boyhood in Gary, Indiana, the family move to Richfield prior to ninth grade, and other subjects. After we left, Lance, Alcindor, and myself all agreed that it couldn't have gone better. We also agreed that in today's climate of frequent transfers, it was necessary.

***

Mullenbach and Schock ran the summer camp. I showed up and taught. I also employed all four of the middle school coaches at the camp; Greg Von Ruden, Steve Hemming, Jarod Knodel, and Jason Meyer. All were teachers at the middle school. These six coaches worked with my lesson plans and fundamental drills for a full week. This was a win-win situation for everybody. They did a great job, gained the experience of doing it, and had some summer income. At the end of the camp, the middle school coaches all thanked me, saying that they had learned a lot and were going to incorporate the drills into their practices.

Every camper received a basketball in Richfield colors with the Richfield logo. With a magic marker, I wrote the name of every camper onto his basketball, and I traced his shooting grip over his fingers. I had gotten the idea for this when I had seen an instructional shooting basketball with the shooting grip on the basketball. We also taught the ball handling drills of Forrest Larson and the footwork drills of Terry Kunze.

Terry Kunze was a retired coach in the Twin Cities. I first heard him speak at the Jim Dutcher Basketball Camp in the summer of 1976, when he was an assistant coach with the Gophers. He taught the coaches how to teach a player offensive footwork while facing the basket. He used tape and chalk to mark on the floor where each foot was to be placed while executing each move. He had names for each foot and step; the jab step, the crossover step, and so forth. He was meticulous to detail in showing where and how to grip the ball, and how to position the upper body and even the head. His drills had a perfect progression of difficulty. The last part of his presentation was a one-on-one game where he played against the best high school players in camp, and after he scored, he would go through each move slowly and explain the move again. As a 6-4 guard in high school, Terry's Duluth Central team won the 1961 state championship. He then played at Minnesota with NBA greats Archie Clark and Lou Hudson and was All Big-Ten. He went on to play in Europe and with the Minnesota Muskies in the ABA.

We reduced the fee of the one-week camp to $20 for kids who were on reduced or free school lunch. We also reduced the cost of the 3 on 3 league from $50 to $20 for all kids. Similar to the previous summer, it was open to any kids who walked in the gym door on any given day, and it again ran for four weeks during July. Mullenbach was the coach, assisted by two varsity players. He worked with the kids on fundamentals for half an hour, and then he split the kids up and they played full court 3 on 3. Because the sessions were held in the small side gyms at the high school, the games were played crosswise on the courts. The kids shot at side baskets, with two games being played simultaneously in one gym. The games were running time with the scoreboard on. The kids played shirts and skins and the teams were different every day. Every time that I showed up, I saw a gym full of sweaty kids having a lot of fun.

***

The numbers at our open gyms increased dramatically. The core of our players in grades nine through twelve never missed, unless they had an AAU practice. On a bad night we would have 15 players, and on a good night we would have over 30. Lance was there working with the big kids. We did this for seven weeks in June and July. The kids were improving dramatically, and they were totally together. Like the summer before, a handful of the middle school kids attended the camp or the 3 on 3 leagues during the day, and then came to the open gyms and ran through the drills with the high school kids in the evening.

As a high school basketball coach who had 20 years earlier coached out state, I was used to watching players improve every year as they progressed from elementary school to middle school to high school. Each year they grew, matured physically, and worked at their game. Based upon these three factors, a coach could predict their continued improvement from year to year. I was now seeing how these phenomena had changed. A player could gain what used to be a whole year's worth of improvement during an off season. This was possible because of the strength programs, the many AAU games, and the chance to work on fundamentals with their high school coaches at open gyms. The kids were playing basketball almost every day year-round.

It was especially gratifying to sit back at the end of the open gyms and watch the kids run our offense, while playing 3 on 3, 4 on 4, and 5 on 5. They were learning to take what the defense gave them, and pass, cut, drive and dish while reading the defense. There were three offenses that I liked which read the defense and took what the defense gave them; John Wooden's 2-1-2 high post offense, Tex Winter's triangle offense, and Bo Ryan's swing offense. But it wasn't as easy to adapt these offenses to one's talent, as Coach Buss had taught me to do with motion. And although these offenses always maintained good spacing, they couldn't be practiced as easily 3 on 3 or 4 on 4. I was willing to give up the guaranteed spacing in return for repetitions in the summer.

Sometimes the parents would stop in and watch. Jim and Jean Noonan were two of these, and all of their sons were gym rats. They were always very positive, often saying what a great thing that the open gyms were. Jean was from Magnolia, a town of 400 people in extreme southwest Minnesota. This area was a basketball hotbed. She was one of the few women who couldn't play sports in high school because there were no programs, but then played in college, when women's programs were just beginning. She played basketball at the University of Minnesota-Morris where she met Jim, who was a football star. He was a graduate of Washburn. She was a born and raised Norwegian farm girl, and he was a born and raised Irish city kid. It was becoming evident to me, that they wanted their kids to be playing with the best players, and that they wanted to win. In other words, when it came to the turmoil regarding city kids, Richfield kids, and playing time, they 'got it'.

* * *

The last weekend in July, the returning varsity and JV players traveled to northern Minnesota to play in a tournament. Lance, Alcindor, and I each drove a vehicle. We rented a van, which the basketball board paid for. We played Thursday night in Brainerd, Friday afternoon in Staples, and Saturday at a tournament in Bemidji. We stayed at Lance's cabin which was west of Nevis. While at the cabin, Alcindor and some of the kids fished, and Friday night they fried fish. We could feel the excitement and energy of the team all weekend. The discord of the first two years was now old history. The kids had a blast.

All of the kids got a lot of playing time in all different combinations of lineups. For the big games, and to start every game, we played the best kids. We went undefeated and we were never challenged. The weight program and the big man drills were paying off for DeRail. He was now just under 6-4 with a huge wingspan. He had a nice short-range jumper with a high shooting pocket and release, combined with a great face up first step to the basket. He was hitting open threes off of the pass. He was finishing offensive rebounds by going up off of two legs and two hand hard dunking the ball. He was a solid D2 recruit. The area junior college coaches were all over him. People had been saying that we were going to have a 'big two' on this team in Travis and Ray. We had a 'big three.' On the trip, we heard this opinion echoed from all of the opposing coaches. In addition, the other players were playing year-round, and their improvement showed. We were going to have a difficult time deciding who should play. It was a good problem to have, and a problem that I hadn't had in a long time. I couldn't wait.

Glory Days

Richfield high school opened in the fall of 1954. The first year there were no seniors. The first graduating class was in the spring of 1956. Frederick L. Johnson wrote in his excellent book 'Richfield, Minnesota's Oldest Suburb',

Upon its opening in fall 1954, Richfield High School became a unifying source in the still-growing and disparate community. Nearly all of its students previously attended Minneapolis high schools-east Richfield residents had attended Roosevelt and west Richfield residents traveled to Washburn.[9]

According to a June 17th, 2007 column by Patrick Reusse in the *StarTribune*,

...Richfield opened its high school in the fall of 1954. Gene Olive was the baseball and hockey coach. Bob Collison was the football coach. Gene Farrell coached basketball...

...The coaches found themselves with a stable of tremendous athletes almost from the beginning.[10]

* * *

Beginning in the fall of 1954, Bob Collison's first five football teams finished near the middle of the Lake Conference. Then beginning in 1960, the Spartans won more games than they lost for the next 15 years, with an average record of 7-2. They won outright or shared six Lake Conference titles.

Football coaches know that football is a numbers game. The coaches with the most kids from which to choose their lineup, often have the best team. The graduating class of 1957 had a little less than 200 students. The senior class size grew to over 400 in 1960, to over 800 in 1965, and to over 900 for a few years in the late 1960s and early 1970s. As the number of students increased, the school district needed to erect more and more buildings. At its peak the district had eight public elementary schools, three catholic K-8 schools, and two public junior high schools, East and West.

All 13 of these schools had a tackle football team, and Collison's staff incorporated their system into every team. Boys all over town were running a version of the high school offense and defense. They were learning the Spartan cadence, numbering system for holes, and basic plays, beginning in fourth

grade. Youth coaches were teaching the fundamentals of blocking and tackling with the same drills that the high school coaches used. From the 150 boys
who began the program as fourth graders, about 30 players would emerge and
enter the high school program as sophomores.

The 1963 team finished the fall rated #1 in the state by *Minneapolis Tribune*
sportswriter Ted Peterson. Because this was still in the era before playoffs, they
were considered the mythical state champions. The Lake Conference had to be
deemed one of the toughest football conferences in the state, because Edina
was named mythical state champions in 1957, 1965, 1966, and 1969, as was
Robbinsdale in both 1958 and 1960. The 1963 University of Minnesota Rose
Bowl Champions had a roster of 48 players, and 11 of them were from the
Lake Conference.

As enrollments changed, the Lake Conference changed. Robbinsdale
split into two and then three high schools when Cooper opened in 1964
and Armstrong opened in 1970. Edina was divided into two high schools in
1973, East and West. The Richfield administrators discussed adding another
high school in the 1970s but after looking at elementary school enrollment,
decided against it. As the enrollments of other outer ring suburban high
schools outgrew their conference rivals, they joined the Lake. By 1973 the
conference had grown from 9 to 15 schools with two divisions, the Lake Red
and Lake Blue.

In 1970 Collison became the athletic director and in 1974 Dick Walker
replaced him as coach. The athletic department hired Bud Bjornaraa as one
of the first full time high school strength coaches in Minnesota, and a state-
of-the-art weight room followed. Walker won six more Lake titles in a 17-year
run. Six of his teams advanced to the state's final eight in the playoff system
that began in 1972, and two of his teams reached the state finals. His average
season record was 9-3.

All team sports were big in Richfield, but football was different. There were
no cuts. Before the growth of soccer as a fall sport, almost all of the best athletes were on the same team, the football team. And the football field on the
east side of the high school drew big crowds from the beginning. The showdown games had standing room only crowds. The field was oriented north to
south. The 'Minneapolis Northfield & Southern' railroad tracks ran parallel
to the field on the west side, between the field and the high school. Eventually,
aluminum bleachers stood on both sides of the field, supported by steel girders
and a cement foundation. A few rows of wooden bleachers were also added in
the end zones for big games. As a testament to this era these elevated bleachers
are still standing. On the home (west) side they extend from goal line to goal

line and they are 14 rows deep. On the visitors (east) side they are also 14 rows deep and they extend from 35-yard line to 35-yard line.

It isn't difficult to picture a Friday night. Residents would have parked their cars in the school parking lot, and after that was full, the nearby residential streets. Other residents would have simply walked from their homes. They would have joined the west end of the long line of people standing on the sidewalk next to the school. They may have heard the unmistakable sound of cleats striking pavement as a full team of football players strode by. At the east end of the line, they would have crossed the single set of railroad tracks to the ticket booth by the cyclone fence. After walking through the gate, they would have descended the small slope to the field level.

With the concession stand on their left, the sounds and the smell of hot popcorn would have filled the air. Adults would have been standing in small groups, sharing handshakes and hugs, catching up on the local hearsay, and laughing. Junior high and grade school boys would have either been with their parents or playing in groups beyond the goal posts, all dreaming of when it would be their turn to put on the cardinal jerseys and run on to the field. Both sets of stands would be slowly filling up with people placing blankets and pads on the aluminum seats. The home crowd might later see the full moon rising over the cottonwood trees behind the east bleachers, or hear a flock of geese honking high overhead flying south down the Mississippi flyway. After a hard week of work, neighbors and friends would be celebrating the beginning of the weekend. As one old football coach once said, "nothing brings a community together like a Friday night football game." And the Spartans were good. They were really good. And they played in the Lake Conference. And the Lake Conference was really good. Its elite players would go on to become Minnesota Gophers. Friday night lights were as good as it gets anywhere in the state, the Upper Midwest, and the country.

***

Like football, hockey is a game of numbers, and the outdoor rinks that were built in the 1950s were full of kids. Every one of the city parks had a rink, and next to each rink was a warming house. After school each day, kids flocked to the nearby rink. In grade school they entered the feeder program, and worked their way up through the levels of youth hockey; Squirts, Peewees, Bantams, and Midgets. When they became sophomores, they tried out for the first time in the high school program. The number of kids playing hockey was over 400 at all levels for many years in the 50s, 60s, and 70s. Sophomore tryouts often had over 40 players. According to a January 31, 2016 article by Dennis Brackin in the *StarTribune*,

Richfield's many outdoor skating rinks were once packed with youngsters dreaming of someday playing high school hockey for the hometown Spartans. Those youngsters, many playing nightly under the lights, would build a legacy of success...[11]

Former NHL player Darby Hendrickson who graduated in 1991 is quoted in the same article to say, *"It's the core of where you grew up. There were so many good players...my biggest goal was to make the high school varsity team. I always felt, if you could make the high school varsity team in the town you grew up in, it would be a great run."* [12]

The high school team began playing its home games at the outdoor rink at the high school. In 1971, the city built its own arena at Portland Avenue and 66th Street. It sits due north of the American Legion. It seats 1,400 fans and has the capacity for another 500 standing fans. Games were played on Thursday, Friday, and Saturday nights. Many of the games sold out, and it became another gathering spot for the community.

The state high school hockey tournament began in the winter of 1945. Compared to basketball which had almost 500 schools fielding teams, only about 100 high schools had hockey teams. Almost all of these schools were in the metro area or the northwoods. For the first 24 years the tournament was dominated by the northern schools, who won 20 state championships. Iron Range Conference schools accounted for 13 of those titles. The other four titles were all won by St. Paul Johnson.

The same *StarTribune* article states,

There were many epic region battles with Edina for a spot in the eight-team (state) tourney at old Met Center-the Spartans reached the region title game nine times between 1957 and 1971-games that often attracted as many fans as the state tourney final. [13]

Under coach Gene Olive, Richfield won these region title games in 1962, 1963, and 1964. In 1962, the Spartans lost in the opening round 4-0 to eventual state champion International Falls. In 1963, they again lost in the opening round, this time to Roseau 2-1. In 1964 Richfield advanced to the semifinals before losing again to eventual champion International Falls 3-2.

Twelve years later under coach Larry Hendrickson in 1976, the Spartans were back at state. Richfield opened the tournament with a 4-3 victory over Mounds View. In the Friday night semifinals, the Spartans beat Bemidji 5-3, followed by Grand Rapids taking out private school Hill-Murray 7-4.

The Saturday night final was played in front of a sell-out crowd of 16,199 fans at the St. Paul Civic Center. As in 1963 and 1964, Richfield came up one goal short against a team from up north. With Rapids leading 4-3 late in the third period, future Olympian Steve Christoff stick-handled the puck deep into one side of the Grand Rapids zone. He then fired a beautiful shot back across the crease to the opposite bottom corner of the net. Rapids goalie and future Gopher Jim Jetland, who was in perfect position on Christoff's side of the goal, made an even more beautiful save by kicking his skate out and back to the far side. The puck deflected off of the skate blade and into the boards, to complete one of the epic plays in tournament history. It was two beautiful plays by two great players in the span of a split second.

Thomas remained the head coach and McCoy was involved in the program for the next 21 years. The outdoor rinks of the city produced four NHL players; Steve Christoff, Brett Hauer, Darby Hendrickson, and Damian Rhodes. Christoff also played on the Miracle on Ice 1980 gold medal-winning Olympic team.

As stated in the *StarTribune* article,

He (Christoff) traces his success to those Richfield outdoor rinks-he didn't have an indoor practice until high school..."There was a warming house, and it was always crowded. Just a lot of kids playing hockey." [14]

* * *

Baseball was the sport where Richfield had the most success at the state level. One big reason for this was the Richfield Little League. The program began in the 1950s, and participation levels grew exponentially. It was soon divided into two divisions, east and west, with playoffs in late summer. At its peak it included 1,200 boys playing baseball at 20 parks in the city, with over 20 teams at each grade level. Many boys spent their entire day at the park, starting with pick-up games in the morning. In the evening parents were sitting in the small bleachers behind the backstops. A 1950's edition of Look Magazine ran a photo of a Little League Baseball scene in Richfield. The article stated that Richfield had more boys playing Little League Baseball than any other community in the country. The natural progression after Little League was to try out for the VFW team, and then the American Legion team. And all of these kids tried out for the high school teams. Out of the 250 boys who were Little Leaguers in sixth grade, probably 10 would have their names on the high school roster as seniors.

From 1959 to 1966, Gene Olive's teams won seven conference titles. After finishing fourth in the Lake, his 1962 team was the first to get to state, and they won it. Their final record was 17-4. Three years later in 1965 they won it again. That spring they ran the table and finished 25-0.

When Olive became principal, his assistant Jim Hare replaced him. In the next nine years, Hare's teams won five more conference titles. The 1967 team advanced to the state semifinal losing to eventual state champion Hastings 4-2 and left-handed pitcher Dan Carey, who many consider to be the best pitching prospect ever to come out of Minnesota. Hare's next state tournament team was in 1971, and they won it finishing 24-1. And they repeated as state champions in 1972 at 19-4.

Hare's assistant Bryan Kispert was the next head coach, and he kept the post for 26 seasons. His teams won more conference titles. Then, as the enrollment began to decline, the program lost its dominance, but it was still competitive.

For over 40 years George Karnas was with the American Legion team. As a coach, his teams matched the success of the high school program, advancing to state nine times in a row, and winning it twice. The 1973 team advanced to the American Legion World Series in Lewiston, Idaho.

Once again, Johnson wrote in his book,

Richfield High baseball teams became Minnesota's best during the 1960s. Dick Siebert, legendary University of Minnesota baseball coach, started calling the Spartans his 'farm club.' A number of Gopher standouts came from the Richfield program…These titles also came at a time when only one team could win top Minnesota high school honors. [15]

The undefeated 1965 team featured a pitching staff with four aces; left handers Al Payne and Larry Peterson, and right handers Greg Wasick and Dave Cosgrove. That same year LeSueur won the District 13 championship before losing to state runner-up St Paul Humboldt in the opening game of Region 4. Another Minnesota River Conference school, Norwood-Young America, won Region 3 and the consolation title at state. The total enrollment of the entire Minnesota River Conference senior classes in 1965 was less than 800 students. The 1965 graduating class for Richfield was over 800 students. Richfield High School had the most players, their players had a great work ethic, and they had great coaches. And as all coaches know, when these three factors are combined, you win championships.

The high school team played its home games at the field to the southeast of the high school, and to the south of the football field. Home plate was in the southwest corner. The same gradual 10-foot slope that people descended to the football field, formed a small L shaped bowl down both baselines. The railroad tracks were above the third baseline and parallel to it. Above and behind the first baseline was 72nd Street. The distance from the foul lines to the beginning of the slope was about 40 feet. A four-foot-high cyclone fence at the bottom of the slope separated the field from the fans. The outfield was ringed by a seven-foot-high cyclone fence with distances of 324 feet down the lines, 362 feet in the alleys and 381 feet to dead center. A clean warning track ringed both the outfield fence and the fences that ran down the lines. Beyond the fence in left field was the football end zone. A small grove of trees was beyond right field. At first wooden bleachers, and later aluminum stands sat behind the backstop and home plate. The slightly elevated aluminum stands had back rests and railings, with a small concession stand and cement patio behind them.

Many fans brought blankets and sat on the grassy slope. Others set lawn chairs on the level area above the slope. Even others stood behind them next to the tracks or the street. For big games even more fans stood down the foul lines. Behind the street and tracks were houses. A neighbor sitting on their patio could see a foul ball land in their garden, or hear the crack of the bat. Dugouts and lights were eventually added and games were played at night. The park couldn't match the ballparks of the out state small towns, with their roofed grandstands, sign covered outfield fences, and concession stands. There were no shade trees bordering the field, and with this no escape from the sun during a mid-summer legion game. But with the ball field's suburban feel, it was intimate. And as all of the umpires knew, the fans were right on top of the game. And players and coaches at all levels kept the field in immaculate condition. Once the program started winning, the field had tradition. And the tradition grew, and then it grew some more. An old coach once said, "Tradition isn't what you take with you, it's what you leave in the program for the next generation of players." The simple and well-manicured field at the corner of Pleasant Avenue and 72nd Street embodied that statement.

* * *

Richfield experienced success in other sports which had so many youth vying for the few select spots on the high school roster. When girls' sports began in the mid-1970s, the gymnastic team quickly won a state title in 1975. And all of this success was the result of the geography, the economics, and the administration.

Richfield may have been the only urban high school in the entire country with clearly defined borders. No family grew up with the kids across the street attending a different public high school. On the south side of Minneapolis, the kids on the north side of 36th Street attended South and the kids on the south side of the street attended Roosevelt. Near unincorporated Rush River in southern Minnesota, the farm kids on one side of a dirt road attended LeSueur, and the kids on the other side went to Arlington.

Richfield also had to have been one of the few towns in the country with almost all of the houses so similar in style, lot size, and square footage. In the small towns, some students were the children of main street business owners, and some students were the children of laborers. Other students were farm kids. These three groups of students all grew up on different sized lots and in different sized houses. New Ulm was settled in the 1850s by socialists from Germany, with all residential lots the same exact size and equally sized parks spaced uniformly across the city. These nineteenth century Germans would have approved of the city grid in Richfield that was created by capitalism, and which contributed to the collective underdog mentality and incredible work ethic.

And probably most importantly, Richfield had some brilliant administrators, who hired some great young coaches, and then gave them the freedom to coach. This first generation of coaches, built the youth programs, and they were students of the game. The combination of these three factors surely unified and accelerated the community support.

According to the January 31, 2016 article in the *StarTribune*, former Burnsville hockey coach Tom Osiecki is quoted,

"In the 1960s, they (Richfield) were the elite, probably the finest all-around program in all sports in the state. They were incredible in basketball, certainly hockey was good, and football and baseball were unbelievable..."

The article also states,

Former longtime principal Dick Maas called youth sports "huge" during his years at the school. "It was a big piece of the community. The parents were largely blue-collar and had a very powerful work ethic, and that was passed on to the kids. It was very much part of their life.

Jake McCoy who was involved in the hockey program for 50 years as a head coach or assistant, called Richfield's players "tough kids. You played Richfield, and you knew you had been in a game."

The city's residents embraced a team whose toughness and work ethic matched that of the community. [16]

According to the June 17th, 2007 column by Patrick Reusse in the StarTribune,

The houses filled the Richfield neighborhoods after World War II. One small bathroom, three small bedrooms and a confined kitchen in which Mom could make her hot dishes.

"It seemed like we all grew up in the same house," Bob Brown said. "You look back and it was crowded, but who knew? In the fall, winter and spring, we were at school. And in the summer, we were at the baseball fields by 8 in the morning."...

... "Richfield's first group of great athletes-they were our heroes," Brown said. "Bill Davis and Bob Sadek...they were gods. We all played harder in the summer, dreaming that we could be like them."

Ruesse then wrote;

I've been running into this early generation of Richfield athletes for a couple of decades and have been impressed by how true they are to their teammates, to their school and to their community. [17]

Third Winter

Sometimes the shots go in...sometimes they don't.
—*Bun Fortier*

When football practice started the second week of August Dwayne Hardy was a no show. He didn't attend the open gyms the last two weeks of July. We were thrilled that he made the Howard Pulley AAU 16 under team, and that he had a great summer. The only problem was that he connected with some of the players on the team from North, and he transferred there. This was a major blow to the program. Dwayne was a great kid, an excellent student, and from a great supporting family. His father grew up in Chicago, and moved to Minneapolis as an adult. He and Dwayne's stepmother had just purchased a house in Richfield. I projected Dwayne to be a Division 2 or low major Division 1 prospect.

Transfers had become commonplace in Minnesota high school basketball in recent years, and it was a hot subject. As with open enrollment, it was discussed in the papers, and many people saw it as a growing problem. The state high school league was trying to address the problem and correct it. Kids were transferring at any time during high school, after their freshman, sophomore, or junior year. Most often, the transferring student went to a school that some of his summer teammates attended. During summer AAU games, parents of kids from different high schools would sit together at games. They would become friends, discussing all kinds of subjects. One of the subjects that were certainly discussed was the basketball programs at their high schools, including the coaches, their son's playing time and role, and how the team would be the next winter. Kids go where they think they can win, and many transfers were from what parents perceived as poorer teams to better teams. Other parents believed that by transferring, their son would get more college exposure, and a more lucrative scholarship offer. I believe that this was an inevitable outcome in the evolution of summer AAU basketball.

Whenever a coach loses a good kid, he looks back, and asks himself what he could have done differently. We could have had Dwayne suit up for the varsity games, but he would not have been able to play five full quarters per night. The one thing that I never understood was how they could have over-looked the improvement that Dwayne made in the two years in our program. I had improved his shooting form, and he developed great one on one moves, both facing the basket and with his back to it. He bought in and worked his butt off, often with his dad sitting in the gym watching. At any rate, we failed to protect our own turf.

***

A week later I got a phone call from Jim Baker. "Did you hear about DeRail?"
"No."
"He blew out his knee."
My heart sank. It was the third week of football practice. DeRail played tight end. After a play, there was a pile on his side of the line and he couldn't get up. He was carried off on a stretcher. A couple of days later we got the prognosis. He completely tore one of the ligaments in one of his knees. He would be on crutches for six weeks, and then be rehabilitating it for ten to twelve weeks. He would miss the entire football season and he probably wouldn't be back for basketball until January. No one knew when he would be back to full strength.

The next week Lance, Alcindor, Baker, and I met DeRail at Baker's office. We had a good talk with him. Lance shared a number of stories about guys that he had played with over the years who went through the exact same thing, and bounced back to have great careers. As always, we were dead honest with him. This was definitely going to affect his senior year. He probably wouldn't be his old self until tournament time. It didn't have to affect his college career. I told him that if it was going to happen, we would want it to happen now. Tournament time was seven months away. After how hard he worked, and all of the strides that he made, it was heartbreaking to see him hobbling around on crutches.

***

There was turnover on the basketball board over the summer, with four members resigning, including the president. There was concern among the remaining board members to find enough people to replace them. About a half dozen parents found their way to a board meeting. After attending one or two meetings, they decided to not commit to being a full-time member. A couple of these parents were African Americans. The board members were always very welcoming to every new person. At one meeting, Jim Noonan talked about how great it would be if we could get some black parents on the board. His reasoning was that the teams and the community were becoming more diverse and we needed the board to reflect this. He then looked at everybody and said, "it isn't like it used to be. Richfield is changing. We are becoming more like a city school." All of the other members quickly agreed, but no black parents ever joined the board. Three parents did commit to becoming board members. One had a son who was a ninth grader, and two had sons who were sixth graders.

At traveling tryouts, a month later two board member's sons made the sixth-grade traveling team. The sixth-grade class was weak, and at this stage they were not two of the better players in the class. Another board member's son would most likely make the sophomore team in another weak class. The new president's son did not attend one open gym over the summer. Needless to say, his son was a long shot to make the varsity as a junior. I remember telling my wife after one board meeting, that I was going to retire before the sixth graders were juniors. The board member dads were both great guys, and I didn't want to have to be the one to decide whether or not to keep or cut their sons. For better or worse, except for Jim Noonan, we now had a basketball board full of parents of mediocre players.

* * *

Jill Johnson was promoted from Assistant Principal to Principal over the summer. She played basketball at D2 Mankato State in college, and she was a big backer of athletics. Whenever I saw her, she was always very supportive of the program. Jason Wenschlag was hired to replace her as Assistant Principal. Jason was in his mid-thirties, 6-11, and fit. He played basketball at Minneapolis Roosevelt and North Dakota State. Because of this, he had a connection to Lance through NDSU circles. He was also a great supporter of what we were doing, and he sometimes worked with our big kids. It was encouraging to now have two administrators who 'got it' in terms of open enrollment, and who enjoyed being in the gym.

At our coaches meeting in late September, I told the staff that I was going to rearrange the coaching positions. The previous winter, Lance was the varsity assistant and offensive coordinator. Kelly Liebfried resigned as the junior varsity coach. I made Alcindor the junior varsity coach, Jamar the sophomore coach, and Matt Mullenbach the ninth-grade coach. Matt Schock would assist both the sophomores and freshman. Rearranging their positions did not affect their pay, and all received the same salary. Lance of course received no pay.

The first 30 minutes of practice all of the teams were in the big gym working on individual fundamentals. I could watch all of the kids and all of the coaches, and the older kids interacted with the younger kids in the drills. This also built camaraderie between the classes. They were all constantly moving and nobody was standing around. Then we split up into two gyms, the upper teams in the big gym and the lower teams in the small gym.

When we split into two gyms, I needed Alcindor with both the sophomores and freshman to teach our man-to-man defense. The previous two winters Jamar had struggled coaching our man-to-man defense. The ninth graders had not met my expectations in their learning of our defensive system. This had to change. Alcindor with the two Matt's assisting him in the other gym would guarantee that our ninth graders were improving as fast as possible. And I wanted Jamar with me so that I could help him improve as a coach. I communicated these reasons to the staff.

* * *

When tryouts began in November, all of the controversy and uproar of the previous year was an old memory. Nine seniors made the team. Kris Pulford, Alex Tillman, and Jawaun Bowman would all begin the season in the playing rotation. Bryson Scott, Cory Hanley, and Peter Rykhus would compete for playing time off of the bench. Two other seniors who we had cut the year before also made the team. Mitch McGuire was a program kid and Chris Brinson was an open enrollment student from south Minneapolis. Both attended every open gym. Both would play scout squad and be senior leaders from the bench, and both were thrilled with their roles. The ninth senior was DeRail Moore, who was working hard rehabbing his knee.

We also kept 10 juniors. Ray Brown, Travis Brown, and Xavier Crawford would be in the playing rotation. Mike Windler, Adam Smith, Octavius Crawford, Nate Poke, Dusty Hinz, Dennis Robinson, Dennis Luke would all play scout squad and junior varsity. The only sophomore to make the team was Jordan Noonan, who would play one half junior varsity, and would be in the playing rotation on the varsity. We only had four sophomores and our ninth-grade class was also thin. We needed the 20 players to fill out our game night rosters.

Although there were no tough decisions deciding who to keep or cut in the top three grades, the ninth-grade situation was different. It was my third year, and I was beginning to see a pattern. The boys trying out as freshman didn't just consist of the program kids. There were a few non-program kids who played on the 8th grade AAU team the previous spring. And there were usually a couple other kids who moved into the community over the summer and attended the camp, 3 on 3 league, and/or open gyms. And there were always half a dozen new faces that we had never seen before. These were kids who either moved into the apartment buildings late in the summer, or open enrolled from south Minneapolis. Almost all of these new faces were black faces, and most lived in Richfield.

From this pool of new faces, there were also usually four to six players that were good enough basketball players to make the 9th grade team, but didn't have the grades. We told them that they were on the team and that they would attend the study halls and practices. We also told them that they could not suit up for or play in any games until their grades improved. They had to eliminate all of the F's, and show sufficient progress with the D's that there was a pattern of improvement. Coach Mullenbach also communicated with all of their teachers, discussing their work ethic and attitude. We saw in our first two years that about half of these kids improved their grades enough to eventually play in games. The other half didn't make it. These kids were almost always kids of color from low socioeconomic backgrounds. We never cut a player to make room for one of these players. However, these academic success stories eventually made it even more difficult for the program kids to earn playing time.

The ninth-grade cuts were always the most heart wrenching for a coaching staff. For the kid who was cut, it was the end of a dream. Shooting baskets in the drive way or at the park would never be the same. For the Richfield ninth graders who came up through the program, the top of the hill was getting smaller, and there were more kids trying to get there.

* * *

After the first week of the season and the cuts, we went to work on our man-to-man defensive drills and our team defense. We now had the size and quickness to be able to defend the entire half court, as well as pick the ball up full court. Our basic man to man defense was what we called 'spread', because our defense was spread across the entire half court. We forced the ball away from the middle of the court, denied perimeter passes, and dead fronted the post. The opposite of this was our 'pack' defense, which defended the area from the three-point line in to the basket. In 'pack' we forced the ball to the left or right, whichever was the weakest hand of the offensive player. The perimeter defenders that were one pass away from the ball, backed off their men towards the ball, to be ready to help on the drive. We played behind the post and doubled down if he got the ball.

We had four defensive adjustments that we could implement to slightly modify either defense

1) Defender on the ball force the ball to the baseline, middle, left, or right
2) Defender off the ball on the perimeter play his man hot, warm, or cold
3) Defender on the post dead front or play behind
4) Defenders off the ball don't switch or switch the ball reversal pass

If a defender played his man hot, the defender didn't help off of his man. This was how we guarded the great three-point shooters. If a defender off of the ball played his man cold, he would sag off of his man and help on the drive or the post. If a defender played his man warm, he would be playing our basic defense.

When I spoke at coaching clinics on how to teach this defense, I discussed what I called defensive assignments, which I borrowed from football. The first priority on defense is to keep the ball out of the lane, or the 'sweet spot' as Lance called it. There were three ways in which the offense could get the ball into the lane, they could dribble it in, pass it in, or shoot the ball and get the rebound. Defenders were assigned specific help out responsibilities such as baseline drive, middle drive, and lob pass. Every time that the ball was passed or players made cuts, the defensive assignments changed. The challenge to the coach was to use lead up drills that slowly added more ball and man movement to them, until they simulated game conditions. This was consistent with the part to whole teaching method of Coach Knight. The drills began 1 on 1, 2 on 2, or 3 on 3, with limited man and ball movement. We utilized a lot of 4 on 4 drills with moderate ball and man movement and specific types of cuts and screens. The 4 on 4 drills simulated the screens and cuts of our upcoming opponents. We also used drills which were tougher than game conditions, including five offensive players against four defenders.

After three years, the kids knew the defense, the adjustments, and the drills. We could cover a lot of defense in a short time at practice. And all of the drills were dual purpose drills, which once again, I heard Coach Knight talk about 20 years earlier. The kids who were on offense in the drills were practicing offensive fundamentals. Even though we called them defensive drills, they were also offensive drills.

We also could play a 2-3 zone or a 1-3-1 zone. We never practiced these defenses, except when practicing 5 on 5 against them. The kids knew all of the zone shifts from playing AAU, and we could play either one as a spread defense or a pack defense. I had only two rules in our zone defense. The person guarding the ball had to yell 'I got ball', and the person guarding the post had to yell 'I got post'. If I didn't hear these words constantly being called out, we were done playing zone, and the kids knew this. And every player had to be executing all of our fundamentals all of the time in terms of stance, jumping to the pass, fronting cutters, talking, and boxing out. Even without ever breaking down a zone defense or practicing it, we could play a pretty good zone. And I was a believer in Coach Buss' idea of sometimes going to a zone until the offense hits a three pointer, or scores two possessions in a row. Going into the season, I expected that we would play some zone in three or four out of the 30 games.

* * *

We began the season by easily winning at St Paul Humboldt before playing Minneapolis South at home. Joe Hyser, the coach at South was now in his eighth year. He had elevated the program at South to a perennial first division finisher in the City, and the program was attracting talented players. When the gym began to fill during pregame warm-ups, it was obvious it was going to be a big crowd. For the first time, the people in the stands weren't limited to the typical Richfield residents and opposing parents and students. The crowd included folks from the city. It included players from other high schools sporting their school colors. The crowd also included a lot of people from the overall Twin City basketball community. These were the kind of fans who scanned the schedules of all the metro area basketball teams and went to the big games. Two of the leaders of this community were sitting in the first row, Renee Pulley and Kwame McDonald. Rene was the man behind the elite Howard Pulley AAU program, and Kwame was a writer from the 'Minnesota Spokesman-Recorder", the weekly black newspaper of the Twin Cities. Both were city guys, ex-players, and well known in the Twin City basketball community. This was the first of many home games that would have this kind of atmosphere.

We trailed 46-35 at the half, and 64-56 after three quarters. Early in the fourth quarter Xavier Crawford blocked two shots and converted two putbacks to close the gap. With three minutes left in the game, the score was tied. Our defense came up with three big stops, and we hit six consecutive free throws to win 84-80. It was a total team effort. There was the feeling that we had made a statement.

Three days later we were to host Holy Angels at home. Jesse Foley had another good team. They were 2-0 and picked to contend for the Missota Conference title. It would be another huge crowd. Their best player was Isaiah

Goodman. They shot the ball well the first quarter and we didn't. At the quarter break we were down 20-11. We closed it to 29-26 at the half. After the half our offense began clicking and they cooled off. We outscored them 26-14 to lead 52-43 going into the fourth quarter. The final score was 76-60. For the first time, we heard the chant of "we own Richfield" coming from our student section and not theirs. Ray finished with 24 points, Travis with 12, and point guard Alex Tillman had a breakout game with 15. Isaiah had 24 for Holy Angels. We followed that up by winning at St Paul Harding 73-67. We were heading into Christmas 4-0 and ranked #1 in the state in Class 3A.

Next on the schedule was the Edina Christmas tournament. Edina was coached by Tom Connell, and they were one of the few teams in Minnesota that ran Pete Carril's Princeton offense, and they ran it very well. Once again, we trailed by eight points early in the game. We could never close this gap, and they returned the upset that we gave them the previous year, defeating us 60-47. They had a good team, but they weren't as good as us, and it stung. We won the consolation game 84-60. With the exception of the last game, we started slow in every game and trailed by at least eight points in the first four minutes. As a coaching staff we tried to put our finger on it, and we couldn't.

* * *

The conference season began in earnest in January. We won our first four games easily over South St Paul, Mahtomedi, Henry Sibley, and Simley. We were bigger and quicker than these teams, and with our superior athleticism, we were defending the entire court. Our players were getting very good at switching both the ball reversal screen and the ball screen. We were able to pressure the ball, deny the passing lanes, front the post, and take many teams out of their offense. They were running their offense ten feet farther away from the basket than they were accustomed to, and there was always the threat of a five second count.

One of the most enjoyable aspects of coaching basketball for me was being able to sit back during a game and let the kids play, knowing that they understood our offensive and defensive philosophy. When the ball was in play, I rarely yelled at them. The one exception was if the gym was empty and the crowd was quiet. In this situation while we were on defense, I could call out screens or defensive assignments, 'you got lob Scott', or 'your switch Josh'. When we had the ball, I didn't yell anything. My high school coach Jed Dommeyer never screamed at us who to pass the ball to, and I would have hated it if he had. Red Auerbach wrote in his book *Let Me Tell You a Story: A Lifetime in the Game*,

I see these guys standing up there screaming and hollering on every single play. Now, if they really need to do that, then their team can't be any good. If you've coached guys right in practice, they don't need you up directing them on every play. So why do they do it?...If you've done your job getting your team ready, you should sit down awhile and watch them play...Phil Jackson's not up on every play pointing to where the next pass should go...If your guys don't know where to throw the ball or who they're guarding or where they're supposed to be on defense once the game starts, you're in trouble. [18]

The kids knew our four defensive adjustments, and they sometimes suggested making them. With Mullenbach, Schock, and Alcindor doing a thorough job of scouting we rarely got beat on set plays or out of bounds plays. We were getting five or six easy baskets most games off of turnovers, and we were doing it without getting into foul trouble.

* * *

It was now evident that four of the top teams in the metro area were in our conference, and would be battling us for the conference championship; St Thomas Academy, Tartan, and Hill-Murray. We were ranked #3 in Class 3A and Tartan was ranked #3 in Class 4A. The next Friday we traveled to St Thomas. In front of another big crowd, we trailed 50-44 going into the fourth quarter. They maintained a 4-to-6 point lead and then converted 8 of 9 free throws to beat us 68-59.

The next day we beat Brainerd at home by 30. The following Tuesday we were to host Hill-Murray. Although we had been preparing for them for a month without telling the kids, we only had one day of practice to put it all together. They were coached by Chris Gargaro. Chris stood about 6-8 and he played against Lance in the Salvation Army Pro-Am summer league, which was the best summer league in the Twin Cities. His dad and uncle played against my dad and uncles in northwest Wisconsin. Over the years Chris' teams were the most successful at getting the ball into the post against our defense. They were employing schemes using ball screens leading to post ups, before many of the colleges and pros were doing the same thing. They were fundamentally sound and always well prepared. He had three-year starters in his 6-8 son Ryan who being recruited by some D1 colleges, and combo guard Travis Whipple who was being recruited by the top level D2s.

In another close game they led 45-41 going into the fourth quarter. With 1:28 left we had the ball and trailed 57-49. In the next three possessions Ray had two rebounds and a steal, and he drilled three consecutive three pointers. The last one was a thirty-footer that he swished from in front of our bench with ten seconds left to tie the game. In overtime we got the tip, Chris Pulford hit a jumper and we went on to win 72-67. After the game Chris looked at me and sighed, and said "Ray just took over the game at the end." We had defeated Hill-Murray for the first time.

We then beat a good North St Paul team at home on Friday 68-61 to run our record to 12-2. Tartan would be coming to our place the following Tuesday tied with us for the conference lead. They were the only remaining team in the conference that we had never beaten.

Tartan was coached by Mark Klingsporn who was in his twelfth year. Tartan was located in Oakdale and was the younger of the two high schools in the North St Paul-Maplewood-Oakdale school district. The older high school was located in North St Paul, which was settled in the late 1800's where the railroad line from St Paul intersected the shore of a small lake. The district encompassed the inner ring suburbs on the east side and northeast corner of St Paul, North St Paul being the northern school, and Tartan being the southern school.

North St Paul was a basketball power from the 1950s to the late 1970s under the direction of Hal Norgard. His assistant was Fred Schmiesing, who played for the legendary Joe Hutton at Hamline. When the school district split into two high schools in 1971, Fred took the job at Tartan. Mark played for him, and then attended UW-River Falls, before returning to Tartan as his assistant. Besides being a student of the game, he was one of the first high school coaches to become actively involved in summer AAU basketball. Every October he administered a one-day clinic in the Tartan gym with on-court demonstrations. He won his first state title in 2000. His teams went to the state tournament the past six years, and a large number of his players went on to play college basketball. In recent years, the program began to have minority kids. Like Richfield, most moved into the apartment buildings, and some open enrolled from St Paul. Along with this came the inevitable whispers of recruiting.

On paper, this was his most talented team. His posts were Eric Coleman, a 6-6 power forward who signed early with Northern Iowa, and Urule Igbavboa, a 6-8 junior and another D1 recruit. They had two excellent guards in Zack Ryan and Kwadzo Ahelegbe. Ahelegbe, who was in his second year as a starter as a sophomore, was another D1 recruit. Ryan was a great three sport athlete. The previous year they advanced to the semifinals of Class 4A where they lost to Osseo 48-46. The St Paul Pioneer Press ranked them #1 in Class 4A to start the season.

The game was close from start to finish. Tartan was ahead 16-13 after the first quarter, 31-29 at the half, and 46-44 at the end of the third quarter. From the opening tip both teams dug in with their man-to-man defense. Late in the game we were down by four when Jawaun Bowman converted a steal into a layup. Then Kris Pulford drilled back-to-back threes from the corner. This small run sent the game into overtime. In the overtime Travis scored on three consecutive possessions on a runner off of the fast break, a put back, and a free throw line jumper. Then it again came down to the last possession, Tartan with the ball, and us ahead 66-64. Their point guard Kwadzo Ahelegbe drove the middle into a tangle of bodies and fell down as the clock ran out. Mark thought it was a foul, I thought it was a no call. The referees agreed with me and ran off the court without blowing their whistles.

* * *

We began the second round of conference play by handily beating South St Paul and Mahtomedi. Next, we went to Henry Sibley. They were improving fast and had added a precocious 6-8, 220-pound freshman to their lineup named Trevor Mbakwe. We dodged a bullet when we beat them 81-73 in overtime. We followed that up with an easy win over Simley.

Heading into the second half of February, I felt that we were on course with our projected improvement. Our fast break wasn't nearly as effective as the year before. The opposing coaches had seen it for a year, and they were ready for it. Our transition defense and half-court defense were where I wanted them to be. Offensively, we were still turning the ball over too much. Our playing rotation settled into a top seven of seniors Alex Tillman, Kris Pulford, and Jawaun Bowman; juniors Ray Brown, Travis Brown, and Xavier Crawford; and sophomore Jordan Noonan. DeRail Moore was wearing a big knee brace, favoring his leg, and didn't have anything close to his former explosiveness.

We were looking ahead to the tournament. As Mullenbach scouted each upcoming conference opponent, he always watched them against St Thomas or Hill-Murray. In this way he was always scouting two potential tournament teams. We both watched Holy Angels. The top four teams in the section were going to be these three teams along with us, and the team that went to state was going to have to defeat two of the other three. We scouted the teams that we knew we might play at state, accumulating videos and scouting reports. If one of the second division teams in our conference ran the same set play as Holy Angels or Red Wing, we spent extra time defending that set play. We were thinking a month ahead, while at the same time preparing for the next opponent.

We defeated another good Eau Claire Memorial team at our place on a late February Saturday afternoon 88-76 before another big crowd. The following Tuesday we avenged the loss to St Thomas at home in front of a capacity crowd. We led 59-39 after three quarters and finished with a 76-68 win. Seniors Jawaun Bowman and Alex Tillman both sparked runs and finished with 15 and 12 points. The atmosphere in the school and the gym had changed. We were filling the gym and winning. Everyone on the team could feel it.

With a conference record of 12-1, we had a two-game lead on both Tartan and St Thomas at 10-3. They were followed by North St Paul and Hill-Murray with records of 9-4 and 8-5. We were to finish out the regular season on the road at Hill-Murray, North St Paul, and Tartan. We won at Hill-Murray on Friday 62-54 in a game that was closer than the score. A win at North St Paul the following Tuesday would clinch an outright conference title for us. We had won 10 in a row, our overall record was 20-2, and we were now again ranked #1 in Class 3A.

The section seeding meeting was the Saturday morning before the last week of the season. As expected, we were seeded #1 followed by St Thomas, Hill-Murray, and Holy Angels. There was a big drop off in the quality of the teams between #4 and #5. To win the section, we would have to beat Holy Angels in the semifinals and St Thomas or Hill-Murray in the finals. Mullenbach would scout Holy Angels twice the last week of the season.

* * *

North St Paul had a good team. They had a very good young coach in Jamie Thompson. We had split with them both of our first two years, and they had defeated both St Thomas and Tartan at home. We wanted to get them down early, take control of the game, and not let them play with confidence. When the game started the exact opposite happened. They hit their first three shots to open up a 7-0 lead. I called time out and chewed out the kids for not being ready to play, pointing out three defensive breakdowns. We played them even the rest of the half. In the third quarter our defense slowed them down and we hit shots to take a 46-45 lead. With under a minute left and the score tied 70-70 both teams had open looks and missed. They beat us in overtime 82-81.

On Friday night the gym at Tartan there was a tournament atmosphere. They had an unusual gym in that there was thirty feet between the baselines and the end walls. Twenty rows of wooden bleachers ran the length of the court on both sides. Behind the top row was a railing and an open area where people stood and watched the game. The fans entered the gym from this open area behind the railing and walked down to their seats. Their public address system was superb and it played the same songs as the NBA teams at every break. When the starting lineups were announced the lights were turned off and a spotlight followed the players.

When the game began, it was obvious that their game plan was to get the ball inside to their posts. They slowly inched away from us to close out the first quarter with a 24-13 advantage. We failed to make a run and the halftime score was 45-28.

At the half I told the kids that we weren't playing poorly. We were playing well against a great team that was playing their A game. They weren't going to shoot that well the entire game. If we started hitting shots, we'd make a run. It was going to take a couple of runs to get back in the game, but we could do it. We made a run early in the third quarter to cut the lead to ten points. They called time out and answered the run. The game was played evenly until the last four minutes when they spread the court. They hit free throws to finish with an 81-57 victory. We were co-champions with them, but they made a statement.

After the game in the locker room, I was very positive. I opened by saying that we got our butts kicked, and that this was very humbling. We got out played and out coached, and this loss is on every one of us in this room. I said that they might be the 4A state champions and they beat us in their gym in their best played game of the year. I said that we had to learn from this, stay up and most importantly stay together. I added that if we win the section two weeks from tonight this game will be an old memory. I then asked them what they thought and a lot of them spoke and said good things. I closed by asking them if they were ready to go to work tomorrow morning, followed by a resounding 'yes'.

***

The next day we had a good practice preparing for the #8 seed South St Paul. We had three days to get ready for them, and at the same time, we were prepping for the other three teams in the section. We also spent more time in practice doing shooting drills. The opening round games were played at the home court of the higher seeded team. We jumped out to a big lead, and led

47-22 at the half. Late in the third quarter we emptied the bench and the final score was 85-49. We knew that it might be the last time the reserves would get to play, and it was the last home game for the seniors. After the game as I shook the hands with their coach Reed Siegling, he said "win the whole thing, Jim, there's no reason why you can't". I asked him "what do I tell them?"

"One game at a time and be the aggressor. Play to beat the other team. Don't play not to lose."

* * *

Holy Angels defeated St Paul Humboldt 59-50 in their quarterfinal game. The semifinals were played at Tartan. Our game was at 8pm following the St Thomas versus Hill-Murray game. We had three more days to get ready for them. I expected their coach Jesse Foley to throw something new at us. He knew who Mullenbach was, and like most coaches, he was always aware of who was scouting his team at which games. In anticipation of this, we also practiced against different types of zones, including a box and one, and triangle and two. Holy Angels finished the regular season with an overall record of 16-9, and a third-place finish in the Missota Conference behind Shakopee and Red Wing. Red Wing was ranked in the top three all winter in Class 3A. Because it was a rivalry game, one could always throw out the season records and expect it to be close. I expected a dog fight.

* * *

The first quarter went well. They struggled against our defense and we built up a 14-8 lead. The second quarter was similar, except that we went ice cold. We entered the locker room at halftime with a 23-21 lead. We contained Isaiah Goodman quite well. We made one defensive adjustment, talked about what we had to do better on offense, and went back out to shoot.

The third quarter was similar to the first. Our defensive game plan was working, and we stretched out another lead of 41-32 to close out the quarter. One more run would blow it open. The opposite happened. We spent the first four minutes trading possessions. We again went ice cold, missing five good shots in a row. With two minutes to go in the game we had the ball and a 54-50 lead and we again missed a good shot. They hit two shots in a row, and then a long three to tie the game. I called time out. Their players and fans were going crazy. There was a hush on our side of the court. There was 1:26 to play.

We diagrammed one of our set plays to get the ball to Travis on a curl cut. If that wasn't there, we were going to run offense and take the first good shot. I closed the time out by reminding the kids "we knew we'd have to win a game like this in the tournament. We've been practicing end of game situations all year. If they make or miss, when we get the ball, if we don't have much time, we push it for a good shot, and we crash the boards like crazy. If we have time, we call time out in front of our bench."

The set play didn't work. After working the ball, Ray missed a ten-foot jumper. They got the rebound, and Isaiah walked the ball up court and set them up into their offense. Their fans were all on their feet. They worked the ball patiently. With less than fifteen seconds to go in the game he drove the middle from the right wing and hit a twelve-foot runner. We pushed the ball up court and called time out in front of our bench with seven seconds to go in the game. We ran a set play that we had practiced many times to get Ray an open jumper at the top of the key. It worked, and as he went up for the open three, he was fouled. There were two seconds to go in the game. If he makes three free throws, we win the game. If he makes two, we go into overtime. The first one hit the inside of the back rim, bounced up, hit the front rim, the back rim again, and bounced out. He swished the second one. Jesse called a full time out.

I was very positive in the huddle. I sat them down, smiled and said "all right, we knew we'd be here. This is why we practice all summer in the open gyms, to be able to be in situations like this. Ray, you hit the free throw, and we blow them out of here in overtime. After he makes it, we don't foul. We let them pass the ball in, in the back court. No long passes. Make sure we're matched up." As both teams broke the huddle, Alex was asking everybody who they had. Ray was a great free throw shooter, and he had always been a gamer, playing his best under pressure.

The free throw hit just over the front rim, hit the back rim, started to settle on the back rim next to the basket, and then rolled off to the right side. The Holy Angels player blocked out perfectly, went up, grabbed the rebound, leaned forward and spread his elbows. The buzzer went off and his teammates mobbed him. Their bench emptied. It was pandemonium in their stands.

Our kids shook their hands and walked off the court. My assistants and I gathered outside the locker room. I told them that only I would talk, and that they could talk tomorrow. I then walked into the Tartan locker room for the second time in two weeks to face a losing team. Sitting on the wooden benches, all the heads were down. There was silence except for the sound of some kids quietly crying. Most of them had tears in their eyes.

"This is going to be one of the toughest losses you guys will ever have. This is going to really hurt, and we're all going to have to live with it. I don't want anybody to analyze what they did and blame themselves. One play doesn't win or lose a game. This is part of tournament basketball. If it didn't hurt so much when you lost, it wouldn't feel so good when you win. This breaks my heart for you seniors. You guys have done everything that we've asked. You don't get another chance."

I was then interrupted by a noise from the neighboring locker room. We all sat there in silence listening to the cheer of "Ho-ly An-gels, Ho-ly An-gels, Ho-ly An-gels" being shouted at the top of their lungs by the Holy Angels players. They were celebrating, and they had every right to.

I then told the kids "if you think you feel bad right now, wait until you wake up tomorrow. We'll meet tomorrow after school in the locker room to hand in our gear."

Back out on the court I met my wife and my parents. To put it lightly, it was somber. I remember telling my Dad "you can say all you want, but losing to Holy Angels wrecks the season. Yeah, we finished 21-5 and we tied for the conference title, but whenever we look back, we're always going to end up thinking about this game and thinking, yeah....but we lost to Holy Angels."

He answered "It's gonna be a long spring. In two months, you'll be up in the Boundary Waters. Focus on that. You've got a lot to be thankful for. And don't forget, you've got a lot of kids coming back, and use it with them as a motivation for next year."

"I really hurt for the seniors. They're a great group of kids. They don't get another chance."

"I know. That's part of coaching."

I always was concerned about my Dad. He would probably take this loss harder than anybody in our family, including me.

* * *

Holy Angels won the section with a 53-51 overtime win over Hill-Murray. They defeated Spring Lake Park 45-40 in the first game of the state tournament before losing to Red Wing 56-52. Red Wing lost to Mankato West in the state finals 50-42. It was especially uncomfortable watching the state championship game, knowing that we would have been difficult match ups for both teams. Tartan advanced to the state quarterfinals in Class 4A before losing to Burnsville 56-52. Burnsville then defeated Lakeville 62-46 and lost to Chaska in the state finals 71-57. Travis, Ray, and Alex Tillman were named to the All-Conference team.

The team banquet was held the Sunday night after the state tournament. It felt both like a wake and a wedding. The mood of the seniors was thankful, and sad that it was about to end. The attitude of the underclassman was that they couldn't wait until next year. In my speech, I talked about enjoying the journey and not focusing on the destination. The seniors had a great journey, winning more games in high school than they ever expected to while in junior high. I told them that sometimes a program needs to experience a setback like we did before climbing to the next level. I told the seniors that they were the first class under my watch to put the program back on the map, and that they would be missed. When the banquet ended, Chris Brinson's mother approached. Her son played hardly any varsity minutes, and no minutes on the junior varsity. His role was to be purely a scout squad player and a senior leader from the bench. She extended her hand, gave me a huge smile, and said, "thank you so much coach, you made my son's senior year."

I remember once listening to Al McGuire discussing his 1977 NCAA championship team at Marquette. He said that he figured he had seven teams at Marquette that were as good or better than the 1977 team, but three things went the right way for the 1977 team. He then went on to say that he believed that to win the whole thing these three things had to happen; nobody can get hurt, other teams have to defeat the teams that are difficult match ups for you, and the last second shot has to go your way. In retrospect, for us, two of these things didn't happen, DeRail got hurt, and the last second shot rimmed out. We knew we would reload and be better the next season. Hopefully the following winter these three things would go our way.

Fourth Summer

One of the things that I really enjoyed about coaching was the challenge of building.

—Duane Baglien

It was as long spring. I wasn't looking forward to seeing any of my good friends after our abrupt exit in the tournament. My friends were all very supportive, philosophical and optimistic. As the spring wore on, I realized it was all part of the sports grieving process. When we began our 8th grade spring team practices the first week in April, it was invigorating to get back in the gym and work with some eager kids. Because we had so many interested kids, we also played a 7th grade schedule. Both teams had great records and the kids had fun. I met with Jim Baker the same week to discuss the program. He was totally supportive and upbeat. Most of our returning players were busy trying out for spring and summer AAU teams.

In late April I ate lunch with Howie Bunce who was the commander of the Richfield VFW. He was a former city council member, the former chairman of the chamber of commerce, and a 30-year Richfield car salesman. The next week I lunched with George Karnas who was the commander of the Richfield American Legion. George was also the former chairman of the chamber of commerce, and the former school board chairman. He retired from a career working in administration at the airport. George was also the longtime coach of the American Legion baseball team. His teams won numerous District championships and had gone to the American Legion World Series. Some people called George 'the Red Godfather'.

Both Howie and George settled in Richfield in the fifties, raised their families, and chased the American Dream. Like other members of their generation, their kids were the baby-boomers who filled the school system in the sixties and seventies. They had a lifetime worth of friends in Richfield. I was totally aware that they had heard the complaints of the people who wanted me fired. I met with them to raise money for the summer basketball camp. I also explained to them how the demographics of the players in the program had changed, and how this affected the financing of the summer camp and

3 on 3 league. In addition to raising money, I made sure that they heard my side of the story.

"It isn't like when your sons were playing little league and all of the parents were white and sat together in the stands and were neighbors. A lot of the parents are black and they live in the apartment buildings. And I want these kids in the basketball program." I then said that in order to make sure that these low-income Richfield kids were not excluded from the summer basketball program, we had to reduce the participation fees and solicit donations. I also told them that I was not being paid a penny for the time that I donated at any of the summer activities.

They were both very understanding and supportive. I remember Howie thanking me for contacting him and saying that he was very glad that we had met. I remember George telling me that it was a great thing that I was doing, and adding that he wished that they could get the black kids playing baseball. Both organizations donated generously. Combined it was enough money to pay for all of the camp T shirts and a four-year supply of camp basketballs.

* * *

The Division I coaching staffs were out in full force after Ray and Travis. Iowa State and Wisconsin had been in contact with Ray since his sophomore year. Iowa State was selling him on their up-tempo full court pressing game. Bo Ryan was beginning his third year at Wisconsin, and he felt that Ray was a perfect fit for their 'swing offense', because he could both shoot threes and post up. Bo also told me that Ray would already know their team defense on the first day of practice. Minnesota and other top-level Division I coaches were also at the high school. Bradley was selling him hard on being a big fish in a small pond.

In the same way, a wave of mid-major Division I coaches were recruiting Travis. Northern Iowa, Wyoming, Valparaiso, and Wisconsin-Green Bay had been recruiting him since his sophomore year. We had long time connections with both the Northern Iowa and Green Bay coaching staffs, and both schools told him that he would know their team defense when he stepped on campus.

Xavier was also getting visits from some low major coaches who always talked about his potential. Late in the spring Mullenbach told me that he heard Xavier was transferring to Mount Zion Christian Academy, a prep school in Durham, North Carolina. The prep school coaches probably told him and his folks that his best chance of improving his basketball skills was to transfer to their school. When I called his mother, she confirmed that he was transferring.

I wished her and Xavier the best. His brother Octavius continued to be a regular both in the gym and in the weight room.

***

By the middle of May I was in the midst of a long-awaited canoe trip to northern Minnesota. It was an annual spring trip, as was our annual fall trip. Our party usually consisted of four to six guys out of a pool of eight guys. This year, because of conflicts and family activities, it was just me and my little brother John.

The Boundary Waters Canoe Area Wilderness (BWCAW) and the Quetico Provincial Park are adjoining parks located on the Canadian border in northeast Minnesota. Together they cover over 4,600 square miles made up of over 1,600 lakes set in the boreal forest. The lakes are spring fed and are connected by rivers, streams, rapids, and waterfalls. In geological terms the land is part of the Canadian shield, a slab of granite which covers most of Canada. The Laurentian divide is located in the parks, which separates the Lake Superior/Atlantic Ocean watershed from the Rainy River/Hudson Bay watershed. The parks were set aside in 1964 with strict rules limiting motorized transport. On some of the lakes on the edges of the BWCAW motorboats are permitted. In the interior of the parks the only methods of transportation are by canoe in the summer and by cross country ski, snow shoe, or dog sled in the winter. All of the lakes are connected by portage trails and have designated campsites. For almost two hundred and fifty years the songs of the French voyageurs were heard on these lakes, as they transported furs from the interior of the continent to Montreal, before the furs crossed the ocean to London and Paris. Being in the BWCAW or the Quetico is the closest that one of us can come to experiencing what being on our continent would have been like four hundred years ago.

This year's trip took us on the Falls Chain, a succession of seven spectacular waterfalls between Saganaga Lake at the western end of the Gunflint Trail, and Kawnipi Lake in the heart of the Quetico. On the last day of our trip, we were traveling to the east along the south shore of Saganaga. Our car sat five miles distant at the end of a bay. It was late afternoon and we were tired. We had broken camp and begun paddling and portaging at daybreak.

As we entered a narrow channel, we noticed an occupied campsite on the neighboring island. A fire was smoldering and two middle aged guys were napping in lawn chairs. Above the campsite were tarps. Along the shore a motorboat was pulled up and anchored. Two fishing poles were standing in the brush with lines extending into the water. At the other end of the lines were bobbers. One of the guys saw us and yelled "hey, you guys want a cup of coffee?"

I looked at John and he said "sure". We paddled over, beached the canoe, got out and stretched our legs. Then we walked up the granite slope and settled into some comfortable chairs. After comparing trips and talking fishing for about five minutes, a man in his seventies appeared out of the woods. He saw us, walked over, stood in front of us, and introduced himself. John stood up to shake his hand when he said matter-of-factly, "don't shake my hand, I was just back at the shitter." He then began somewhat dominating the conversation with stories of his experiences over the years while camping at this campsite. I could tell from the body language of the two younger guys that they had heard the stories more than once. They were good stories.

One of the guys had a green baseball hat on with a Philadelphia Phillies style P. I asked him where the hat was from. He answered "Proctor". Proctor was a small town just west of Duluth. He then said that he was a teacher and a coach in Proctor. When I asked him what teams he coached, his answer included the ninth-grade boys basketball team. I then told him that I was the head boys basketball coach at Richfield.

As is customary with coaches, he then asked "How you gonna be next year?"

"We're hoping to win the whole thing. We were 21-5 last year, and we have our two best kids back, and we have some good young kids to replace the seniors that we lost."

A couple of minutes later, after a pause in the conversation, he blurted out "Rich Decker got fired."

"What? Rich Decker got fired? He's one of the best coaches in the state."

"I know."

I then told him that I had been a student assistant coach under Rich Decker when he was at Kenyon in 1975 when I was a senior in college. I asked him if Rich had recently done anything like hit a player or get kicked out of a bunch of games. I knew that he probably hadn't, because his behavior had always been exemplary.

"No. He didn't do anything. He just got fired."

***

Rich Decker was the coach at Lourdes high school in Rochester. Rochester was a city of 100,000 people in southeast Minnesota and the home of the world-famous Mayo Clinic. There were four high schools in Rochester. Three were public and Lourdes was catholic. Rich was the coach at Lourdes for twenty years compiling a record of 322-146, which equates to an average yearly record of 16-7. Before coming to Lourdes, he was at Kenyon and Faribault Bethlehem Academy where he was just as successful. He had a large coaching tree of ex-players that were high school coaches. He was a complete student of the game, attending every clinic and buying the recent books and videos. His teams were always meticulously prepared and they played great fundamental basketball. In addition to being a Viet Nam veteran, he was regarded by his teaching peers as one of the best history teachers in the state. In 2003 he was inducted into the Minnesota Basketball Coaches Hall of Fame. He was the kind of coach that all of the younger coaches looked up to with admiration and respect.

In an article in the *Faribault Daily News* sports editor Bruce Strand wrote that *Jerry Snyder, retired coach from Lake City said that Rich was one of the best and most competent coaches that he had ever faced, "I haven't a clue why they would let him go. It's not because the guy can't coach. That's for sure."* Also quoted in the article was *Franz Boelter of Faribault Bethlehem Academy who had known Rich for twenty-seven years, saying "Rich was highly regarded as both a teacher and a coach."* Paul Christian wrote in the *Rochester Post-Bulletin* that *Decker speculated that he may have disturbed some parents with his style as an old-style demanding coach not afraid to criticize a student or athlete who "is not hustling on the court, or is being disrespectful in the classroom."* Decker added *"That's one of the main differences between coaching today and back a few years ago. Some parents believe their son or daughter can do no wrong. That wasn't always the case."* [19]

The word in the coaching circles was that one of the families behind the firing was a huge financial donor to the high school. Most certainly, this family and their allies presented the school with a list of complaints. Behind the complaints, the real reason was also most certainly playing time, or disciplinary actions by Rich that affected playing time.

According to the *Faribault Daily News, "the school disclosed no reasons for its actions, to the public or the coach, citing school policy and the right-to-privacy act."* [20] Because a coach was an 'at will employee', a school administration was not legally required to give a coach a reason why he had been fired. In this case the Lourdes administration merely informed Rich that for the upcoming school year his contract would not be renewed. Like Dave DeWitt three years earlier, there was no procedure or forum at which Rich could defend himself against these undisclosed reasons. The firings of Dave DeWitt at Centennial and Rich Decker at Rochester Lourdes would prove to be two big turning points in Minnesota high school sports.

* * *

The school year ended the first week of June. The following Wednesday I met with a student from Prior Lake and his parents in Jim Baker's office. Bill Bauman had just finished his junior year at Prior Lake and he and his parents, Todd and Beverly, had made the decision to transfer. They had attended one or two of our home games late in the season. In May they contacted Jim Baker and requested a meeting with Jim and myself. Lance was also there.

Bill was one of the players that Lance worked with the previous summer. Lance had been teaching his big man skills to a number of high school and college big men every summer since he returned from playing in Europe. His first summer back in the states, he was a coach in the Howard Pulley AAU program. Through his connections with AAU coaches, high school coaches, and the parents of other players, these kids and their parents were referred to him. He worked with many future D1 players like Nick Horvath, Michael Bauer, Joel Pryzbilla, and Bryce Webster. He worked with Cole Aldrich who was headed to Kansas. He also worked with many players who weren't as talented. His reputation grew from this. Over the past few years, Lance coached over forty players in this fashion. The Baumans were referred to Lance by the parents of player who praised Lance for how much their son had improved from his workouts. They sought him out to help their son improve.

At no time did Lance ever try to recruit these kids to Richfield, either directly or subtly. In fact, Lance made it a point to discuss upfront the subject of transferring before he agreed to work with them. Besides telling them that he was not trying to recruit them, he told them that he wanted them to stay at their own school. He also told them what other people would be saying about the whole situation. Lance was a very direct and a very blunt person. He always wanted everyone to know what everyone else was thinking, parents included. There was no saying one thing and winking while you said it.

Before meeting with the Baumans, I discussed the situation with Jim Baker and the principal Jill Johnson. What I was told was that a student had a legal right to open enroll at a public school. We could not tell him that we would not play him just because he was an open enrollment senior transfer. We agreed that we had to tell him that we would play the best kids. I had never seen Bill play.

This wasn't the first time that this happened in my time at Richfield, and it wasn't the first time that I had these discussions with Baker and Johnson. Almost exactly a year earlier, I was sitting in Baker's office with a talented point guard from Minneapolis and his father. This student was going to be a junior. I remember telling them all of the same things that I was going to tell the Baumans.

The meeting opened with the Baumans asking a few questions about how Bill would be treated at Richfield if he transferred. They were all good questions that any parent would ask, and they were not demands or searches for guarantees. They said that the basketball reason for why Bill was transferring was because they were extremely disappointed with Bill's improvement. They said that they heard a lot of good things about our coaching staff from the parents of kids that they had met at AAU games. The one basketball question that they asked was whether or not Bill would be given a fair chance to earn playing time. I answered that I was going to play the best players, but that if two players were fairly even, the boy who was not the transfer was going to get the first shot at playing time.

I also told them about our definition of "taking care of business", be on time to class, hand in assignments, study for tests, and be a good citizen in the hallways. Their answer was that because Bill was an excellent student and had never been in trouble, this would not be an issue. I talked about attitude, work ethic, and accepting one's role. The answer that I was given was that Bill knew that his role would change if he transferred, and that he was also giving up a captaincy that he would have had at Prior Lake. I asked Bill how long he had been in the Prior Lake school system. His answer was since kindergarten. I then told them my story of getting married for the first time in my early forties, and that one of my groomsmen was the quarterback of my high school football team. I asked them if they had thought about how this would affect his class reunions for the rest of his life. In short, I told them that this involved a lot more than just basketball. Lance reiterated what I said, talked about his high school experience and life-long buddies at Washburn, and asked them if this was really what they wanted to do. Bill answered that they had talked about all of these things.

Then I gave them a short history of my three years at Richfield. I told them that a lot of Richfield people were not going to welcome them, and that some would probably be outright rude to them. They said that they were aware of all of this. They added that Bill had already decided to leave Prior Lake, and that it was just a question of which high school he was going to attend. They had already visited Holy Angels, Burnsville, and Shakopee. The entire meeting lasted twenty minutes.

After they left, I leaned back in my chair and looked at Jim Baker. We were both thinking about the same things, open enrollment, transfers, AAU teams, and how high school sports had changed. I remember discussing that this was a much better situation than we were in three summers ago. At that time, I was trying to convince parents of players who lived in Richfield to stay in Richfield. Now I was meeting with parents of players who didn't live in Richfield and wanted to come to Richfield. We both agreed that once we started winning, to some degree this would happen. However, this was the first kid that wasn't coming from Minneapolis. They weren't looking at a change from a poorer academic environment in the city, to a better academic environment in an inner ring suburb. This transfer was purely about basketball.

The next day I telephoned Dave Samuelson who was the coach at Prior Lake. He didn't pick up. I left him a message to call me. In the brief message I told him that my athletic director and I met with Todd, Beverly, and Bill Bauman at Richfield High School the day before. He never called back. The next week I received a call from the Prior Lake athletic director. She made her displeasure with the situation very clear. At the same time that the Baumans were visiting three high schools, Bill's Prior Lake classmate Jerod Ewing and his parents, were also visiting high schools. Like Bill, Jerod was a returning starter. One of the schools that they visited was Shakopee, which bordered Prior Lake to the west.

* * *

As the summer began, I was beginning my fourth year at Richfield. I felt good about the state of the summer program. However, I was surprised to see that the number of students enrolled in the summer camp decreased to less than 60 boys. The decrease was entirely in the number of white kids. The number of black kids increased. The enrollment in the 3 on 3 league remained the same, with between 30 and 40 boys playing every day.

When I arrived to the first night of open gym, there were over 20 kids waiting for me to open the doors. We continued to have these kinds of numbers at the open gyms the rest of the summer, not including the handful of middle school kids who were also there almost every night.

Later in the summer we took our trip to northern Minnesota. We went undefeated. The chemistry changed significantly without last year's seniors. As expected, Dustin Dreifke and Jordan Noonan stepped in at point guard and shooting guard. Adam Smith was a program kid who had grown to 6-5, and had passed up others in his grade. Bill Bauman totally accepted his role and always played hard. Travis and Ray were both an inch taller and a step quicker. I was starting to think that we would be better at every position.

In early August I was at a big party at a farm in southern Minnesota. I ran into two old friends from my coaching days in LeSueur, along with their wives. The two friends were brothers, and along with a third brother, they were all great point guards over an eight-year span at LeSueur. They played on some very good teams around the end of the era of the one class basketball tournament. Like a lot of top-level small-town teams, they never got to the state tournament. Both couples had children who were also very good athletes and playing on both high school and AAU teams. One couple lived in the western part of the state, and the other couple lived in the western suburbs. Both couples were totally aware of the current environment of high school athletics in Minnesota.

The older brother and his wife were closely connected to a Richfield couple who had roots in Belle Plaine. From my previous interaction with these Richfield parents, I was aware of this connection. Belle Plaine was fifteen miles downstream on the Minnesota River from LeSueur. Both schools were traditional rivals in Class 2A basketball. The Richfield couple had a son in the basketball program. He was going to be a sophomore. He was 5-11 and he was done growing. He was the best football player in his class and a marginal basketball player. He was the kind of kid who would be a starting fullback/linebacker in football at Belle Plaine, and a starting power forward in basketball at Belle Plaine. At Richfield, he would still be a stud football player, but during basketball season, he would most likely be leading cheers in the stands with paint on his face. He was a great kid who played on our spring eighth grade AAU team, and he always played his butt off, leading the team in floor burns. He was the kind of kid that every coach loves to coach. I had gotten to know his parents when he played on this team. From this limited contact, I saw them as great people, a couple who were not blamer parents, and a couple who didn't have an inflated opinion of their son's abilities.

We were standing in the shade of a grove of trees sipping beverages with the smell of barbecued chicken in the air. I hadn't seen these two guys in a couple of years, and as is normal in these situations, we were catching up and laughing a lot. Inevitably the conversation turned to basketball. During a pause in the conversation one of the wives abruptly asked me "do you recruit?" Everyone's smiles got wider and they all looked at me. I looked at her, smiled, and answered "I recruit the Richfield kids, and I recruit them hard." One of the husbands immediately followed with "good answer...goooood answer!" and he burst out laughing. And I followed that with "and if kids from the outside want to come in, I don't turn 'em away. Do I recruit outside kids? No, but if they want to come in, I don't turn 'em away."

What I had learned was that people who think that you recruit, are never going to believe you when you tell them that you don't recruit. There was no point in trying to defend yourself. They were never going to believe you. From what I heard in the basketball community, Ken Novak at Hopkins, Dave Thorson at DeLaSalle, and Mark Klingsporn at Tartan were considered the biggest recruiters in the metro area. In my opinion, they were the three best coaches in the metropolitan area. I didn't think that this was a coincidence. When I told Dave Thorson I now had the reputation as a recruiter, he said "wear it like a badge of honor. That means you've made it as a coach."

* * *

When school began in September, the presence of Bill Bauman walking the halls created a buzz of conversation in the community. He wasn't the only transfer creating the buzz. Two of the best senior football players were absent from the halls. Dylan Miller and Billy Owens had both open enrolled and transferred to my home town of Northfield. Northfield had a great senior class and was a heavy favorite to win their section and make a run deep into the state football playoffs. They had a deep and talented senior class which Dylan and Billy made deeper and more talented. They were car-pooling and making the forty-five-minute drive together every day.

In late September I was back in the Boundary Waters for the fall canoe trip. I was with two of my old buddies from LeSueur, Dick Moriarty and Dave Woodruff. Rounding out the group was Pat Woodruff, Dave's son. We break-fasted in the town of Grand Marais on Lake Superior. As we left the restaurant it was overcast and about sixty degrees. The big lake was fairly calm with half foot waves slowly rolling to the shore.

As we drove to the northwest on the Gunflint Trail it began to drizzle. We unloaded the gear and paddled and portaged through the first two lakes. It wasn't windy, and with the proper gear, experienced canoe campers know that traveling on a calm rainy day is not difficult or uncomfortable. We all had rain gear on from head to toe, and our packs were waterproof. I was paddling our canoe astern and Dick was in the bow. By the end of the second portage the rain picked up along with a light west wind. We were now sloshing through ankle deep puddles.

The next lake was Tuscarora Lake, a lake that was a mile and a half long and was oriented from west to east, with islands and bays on both sides. About halfway up the lake the rain turned to a downpour and we were facing a head-wind with one-foot waves. We brought the canoes together in the lee of a small island. When Dick said "you know we could pull over to a campsite, set up the tarp, and cook some hot soup", we all agreed that it was a great idea. We looked at our maps and saw that there was a campsite a little further on the north side. In five minutes, the campsite was in view but it was occupied. Four guys were standing under a tarp and waved to us.

In front of us was a small island just big enough for two or three small trees. The island was covered with small boulders. We landed the canoes and set up the tarp. We got the one burner stove going and in ten minutes the soup was boiling. We each sat on a boulder. We were now out of the rain slurping down hot soup with cheese and crackers. When we were about done the rain began to let up and the sun broke through the clouds. I happened to look down and saw a perfect eagle feather sticking up between some boulders. I stood, picked it up, and showed it to the other guys. Dave said "That's supposed to be a sign of good luck. Better keep it." When we finished eating and packed up, I stuck it into my pack. Three hours later we were sitting around a campfire on an island on Crooked Lake. We were warm and dry and watched the sun set.

1960 Basketball Team

U nder Coach Gene Farrell, the boys' basketball team posted records of 2-15, 8-13, 11-9, and 5-15 the first four years of the high school. In the fifth year, he returned the nucleus of a team that lost many close games, and finished strong the year before. The senior class of 1960 was talented, deep and late developing. The best player was two sport star Bill Davis who also pitched and played first base in baseball. After growing two inches over the summer, he was all of 6-6 and athletic. He was being recruited by the University of Minnesota for both basketball and baseball. The three other returning starters were also offered scholarships by the Gophers in other sports; Bob Werness (6-1), and Denny Johnson (6-2) in baseball, and Mac Lutz (6-4) in tennis. Hopes were high heading into the winter. Richfield was one of the preseason favorites to win the Lake, and this was a year that the Lake was considered to be loaded.

A columnist at the *Minneapolis Tribune* wrote,

Make no bones about it-the Lake Conference is the Big Ten of basketball and football. While Robbinsdale, Bloomington, St Louis Park and Richfield have an enrollment edge, the remaining schools-Hopkins, Edina-Morningside, Minnetonka, Wayzata and Mound manage to hold their own. These nine schools comprise a vast area of population and the coaching caliber rates with the very best. [21]

***

This was the era of the one class public school, eight team state basket-ball-tournament. It was played the last weekend in March at Williams Arena on the campus of the University of Minnesota. Four games of quarterfinals were played on Thursday, semifinal games were played Friday night, and on Saturday three games were played. The consolation finals were followed by the third-place game which was followed by the finals. All three championship sessions were always sold out. Prior to the early 1950s, families sat in living rooms and listened to the tournament on the radio. With the invention of television, they watched it on stations out of the Twin Cities, Duluth, Sioux Falls, or Fargo.

Prior to the growth in popularity of the NCAA tournament, this was by far the biggest March madness in the state.

The regular season with its conference rivalries ended in late February. The districts began the next week. Two weeks of districts were followed by a week of regions, followed by the state tournament week. In the first three weeks the number of teams was whittled down from about 500 to 128 to 32 to 8. Historically, the state tournament was dominated by large schools, and the eight regions and 32 districts did not have equal numbers of teams or students. And most significantly, they did not have equal numbers of large schools.

Even in this era there were grumblings about transfers and recruiting, especially from the small schools that were located close to the big schools. An old-timer from southern Minnesota once told me that if an area small school star was averaging over twenty points per game as a sophomore or junior, his father might be offered one of the good union jobs at the meat packing plant in Austin. A similar story was told to me by Cedric Schluter, who was a four-sport letter winner at Cass Lake, Ojibwa band member, and Hall of Fame coach. He stated that if a basketball player from a reservation or a nearby town showed great promise in junior high, he might somehow end up finishing his high school years at Bemidji. The two long time coaches at these schools, Ove Berven at Austin and Bun Fortier at Bemidji, were considered by their peers to be two of the best coaches of their generation. Berven's Austin teams were renowned for improving during the season, peaking at tournament time, and winning third game match-ups against conference foes. Based on what Fortier's players have told me, he was a coach who was ahead of his time. The Lumberjacks played tenacious man to man defense with help side principles, years before Bob Knight was talking about these concepts nationwide at coaching clinics.

* * *

Shortly after the football season ended, the Spartan's basketball hopes grew even higher when a senior transfer began walking the halls of the high school. Bob Sadek moved from the Chicago area to Richfield with his father's job relocation. Sadek was an All-State Illinois quarterback at Rich High School in the South Suburban Conference, and a Big Ten football recruit. In basketball he was a 6-3, point guard. In the turn of a week, Farrell had a fifth Division 1 athlete in his starting lineup, and one who was a natural leader, a lock-down defender, and at his best in the clutch. The Spartans instantly became the conference favorite.

The first four conference games were not easy wins. Richfield defeated Wayzata 56-55, St Louis Park 54-45, Mound 63-61, and Edina 71-56. These were sandwiched around a game at Austin, in the southern part of the state.

Austin was in the Big 9 conference, which were all cities of 8,000 to 40,000 people. Seven of the nine cities were in Districts 2, 3, and 4. From 1930 to 1959, Big 9 schools were crowned Region 1 champions every year but one. The Packers historic gym was a place where they rarely lost, and they were the current Region 1 powerhouse. They had won seven out of the past nine Region 1 championships along with the 1958 state championship. Richfield opened the game with their trademark ball pressure, and their shots were dropping. Sportswriter Bill Riemerman wrote in the *Austin Herald*,

The Spartans took charge in the middle of the third quarter and won going away. [22]

When the Spartans left Austin with a decisive 75-60 win, they had made a statement.

A month into the season Richfield was rated #1 in the state with a 5-0 record. North St Paul, another inner ring suburban school was rated #2. Minneapolis North was #3, and Austin #4. The Spartans reeled off victories over Robbinsdale 81-66, and Minnetonka 52-42 to head into the Christmas break still rated #1. North St Paul at 6-0 remained #2.

January began with a home win over Hopkins 68-54, followed by a 78-73 loss at second place Bloomington before a sell-out crowd of over 3,000 fans. Next was a 63-61 win at Wayzata, and a home loss to St Louis Park 73-60. With the win, Park surpassed Bloomington for second place in the conference. Their future Hall of Fame coach, Lloyd Holm was quoted in the *Minneapolis Tribune*.

We shot extremely well… We used a switching man-to-man defense and were able to rebound well with Richfield. It was just one of those nights." [23]

Richfield bounced back to post solid victories over Mound 57-44 and Edina 71-59. They followed these up with hard fought wins at Robbinsdale 40-39, and at home against Minnetonka 57-53. They then traveled to Hopkins to best the Warriors 66-46. The last Friday night of the season Richfield convincingly avenged the loss to Bloomington 61-42. An article in the *Minneapolis Tribune* written by Bill McGrane stated,

Nearly 2,600 enthusiasts squashed into Richfield's gymnasium which was full more than an hour before game time. THE HOWLING partisan crowd was a huge help to the fired-up Spartans who jumped to a 9-0 lead. [24]

The Spartans finished with a 63-42 win over Washburn.

Lake Conference Standings (final)

Richfield	14	-	2
St Louis Pk	13	-	3
Wayzata	9	-	7
Mound	9	-	7
Edina-Morn	8	-	8
Bloomington	8	-	8
Robbinsdale	5	-	11
Minnetonka	4	-	12
Hopkins	2	-	14

The final state rankings listed four Lake teams in the top twenty; Richfield #1 (16-2), St Louis Park #2 (14-4), Bloomington #17 (10-8), and Wayzata #18 (11-7). Two Minneapolis schools were also ranked; Roosevelt #6 (11-6) and Henry #7 (14-3). Shakopee, another District 18 school and champion of the Minnesota Valley Conference was ranked #20 (16-0). North St Paul had dropped out of the top twenty with a record of 14-4. They were replaced by St Paul Suburban Conference rival South St Paul at #14 (16-2).

***

An article appeared in the *Richfield News*:
Go, Spartans...
At this writing, Richfield high school's basketball Spartans are on the brink of big things for their school and community. If they fulfill our fond expectations, they'll be right in the thick of the biggest annual athletic event in Minnesota- the state high school basketball tournament.

Win or lose, Richfield will always think a lot of these boys. They've given the name of our village on the minds of countless thousands in winning the Lake Conference championship, one of the toughest athletic titles to acquire in Minnesota. Win or lose in district, regional and state competition, Richfield is proud of these boys.

But the Spartans may well do still more for Richfield. For years now, one of Richfield's few deficiencies has been a lack of community spirit. Perhaps this is an inevitable liability in a suburb. But a winning basketball team, particularly on the levels Richfield's team has now reached, can do more to stimulate civic

pride than all the parades, dances, speeches and political campaigns of a hun-
dred years of our history. [25]

Over the course of the second half of the season Coach Farrell and his
assistant Vance Crosby had settled on a man to man defense. Each man was
responsible for shutting down his own man with no help. With the quickness of Bob Werness, Bob Sadek, and sixth man Roger Alevisos pressuring
the opponent's guards, the other team's offense was pushed to the sidelines as
the ball crossed mid court. With Davis guarding the opponent's biggest man,
teammates never needed to help on the post. They played this defense with
tenacity, and with their size and athleticism it was effective. Rival coaches
marveled at how hard they pressured the ball and how they over played the
passing lanes. And they played both hard and with discipline, only averaging
13 fouls per game.

* * *

The Minnesota State High School League (MSHSL) was founded in 1916.
In 1930 the MSHSL divided the state into eight regions and 32 districts. The
same districts and regions were used for almost all of the sports that had a
state tournament. At this time, this probably included cross country in the fall,
basketball and wrestling in the winter, and baseball and track in the spring.
Completely opposite of this, the MSHSL had no say on how schools chose their
conference affiliation. Superintendents and school boards negotiated this with
their neighboring school districts. There were about 60 conferences. Most conferences were made up of schools that were in two or three different districts.
As new high schools were built in the metro area, the conferences changed.
And as schools grew or consolidated outstate, the conferences changed. Over
the next 30 years, the MSHSL did not realign the districts, choosing to preserve the historic district rivalries. The district rivalries were often stronger
than the conference rivalries.

Each district was autonomous in organizing its own district tournament.
With this autonomy, some of the districts set up their own de facto class systems. A few of the outstate districts had four schools with enrollments that
were five to ten times larger than the dozen or so small schools. Some of these
districts had two sub-districts, an east and a west, for the dozen small schools.
Both sub-districts would play down to a winner the first week. The two winners would receive a trophy and advance to the district semi-finals. During this
same first week, the four large schools would each play one game. The second
week of the districts, the two large school winners and the two sub-district

champions would play down for the district championship. Another district had 17 schools. Eight of the schools were larger and were in the same conference. The eight larger schools played down to one winner and the nine small schools played down to one winner. The second Saturday of the districts, the large school winner and the small school winner played for the District title. Other districts set up their tournaments with some combination of these two systems. Many of these districts seeded their large schools and the top small school teams into the quarterfinals, while the remaining small schools had to win four team 'sub-districts' to gain the quarterfinals. Under this policy of 'districts rights', 17 of the 32 districts employed a de facto class system.

The other 15 districts utilized a system of pure seeding. All of the teams were seeded 1-9, or 1-15, or 1-17, depending on the number of teams in the district. Except for opening round byes for the top seeds, all teams played equal numbers of games to get to the finals. Eleven of these districts were outstate and were made up of all or almost all very small schools. The other four districts were located in the Twin Cities and consisted of many very large schools.

Insert Image 4 here

The second week of March, the district semifinals and finals were played at neutral sites. The semifinals were often a doubleheader. In the outstate districts, one year a district might have four conference champions and more than one undefeated team. The next year the #1 seed might be a team that finished in fourth place in its conference. The semifinals and finals were often a showdown game between a good large school team and an undefeated or 'one loss' small school team. The gym would be packed to a capacity of 2,000 or 3,000 long before the teams took the floor. In addition to the fans from the two competing towns, the crowd would be full of fans and players from the entire district, including the small school's conference members. They would be cheering for their conference champion. For every team, the goal was to get out of the district. No coach ever looked past the district to the region.

The four districts in the Twin Cities had a totally different atmosphere than the outstate districts. District 15 was the high schools of the St Paul City Conference, and District 17 was the schools of the Minneapolis City Conference. District 14 was the entire St Paul Suburban Conference minus one school. And District 18 was the entire Lake. These districts had the feel of a post season conference tournament. No coach would be watching a neighboring district to see if a conference rival would emerge at the regions, forcing a third game match-up. Only one Lake team was going to get out of the district. And in District 18, at least two and probably three games would be against a Lake Conference foe. The District 18 finals were played at Williams

Arena. The finals drew more than 10,000 fans. With a capacity of about 18,000 fans, the arena was almost two-thirds full. The empty seats would be on the court level deep beneath the balcony, and the top half of the balcony seating high above. Winning the Lake was one thing, with its 16-game round robin schedule. Winning District 18 was another thing, and the district champion wasn't always the conference champion. The year before Wayzata's state championship team and coach Jack Thurnblad had finished third in the Lake.

***

Richfield with its #1 seed received a first-round bye and faced rival Edina in the district quarter finals. The Hornets were defeated by the Spartans for the third time 71-54. In other quarter final games St Louis Park beat Bloomington 54-46, Minnetonka beat Shakopee 61-32, and Mound defeated Orono 54-45.

The semifinal opponent was Mound, another team that Richfield had beaten twice. The Mohawks slowed the game down from the opening tip. At the end of the first quarter Mound was ahead 10-6. By halftime Richfield regained the lead 17-15. At the end of three quarters Richfield opened up the game with a 28-18 advantage. Late in the fourth quarter Mound guard Dave Eiss hit four consecutive baskets and with under two minutes remaining the score was 34-32. Mac Lutz then converted a free throw and Bill Davis hit two short range jumpers to secure a 39-32 win.

Gene Farrell was quoted in the *Richfield News*:

"I have had the highest respect for Mound all season. We have defeated them three times this season and they fought us to the wire in each contest." [26]

St Louis Park defeated Minnetonka 47-38 in the other semifinal to set up a rubber game for the district title on Saturday night. The top two conference finishers would meet at Williams Arena. Park was riding a 14-game winning streak including the late winter win in Richfield. Again, the game was covered by the *Richfield News*:

...in a thrill packed encounter before over 12,000 fans at Williams Arena... Bill Davis hit three straight fielders and Richfield grabbed a 16-12 first period edge. At halftime Farrell's men enjoyed a temporary five point margin at 31-26... Pandemonium reigned as Oriole baskets...provided the impetus that drove Park to a 37 to 37 deadlock with only seconds remaining in the third period. [27]

Then with 1:55 to play in the period Bill Davis picked up his fourth foul. When Bob Sadek made a 27-footer at the buzzer, the period ended with the Spartans up 39-37.

The Spartans were ahead by 5 with five minutes remaining. They maintained this slim margin as the clock wound down and time ran out. The final score was 49-43. Gene Farrell's team had survived the first round of the gauntlet with three more Lake Conference wins.

* * *

Minnesota can be divided into a number of commercial regions with a larger city as the nucleus. The regional populace listens to the radio, reads the newspaper, and watches the local television station of this city. Before the internet, these cities were the primary source of news for these areas. To this day, the sports pages of the regional newspapers thoroughly cover the high school sports in the area. And the land is different in these differing regions. In the west as one is driving out of one small town, the grain elevator and water tower of the next community can be seen faintly on the flat horizon. The roads are straight. In the southeast, the terrain is more rolling and the valleys are deeper. In the lake regions of the north and center, there are more woods and the roads wind around lakes. In the northeast the horizons are forested ridges that are higher and farther in the distance.

Rochester and Mankato are the regional centers in the southeast and south-central part of the state. In the southwest, one could argue whether Worthington, Marshall, or even Sioux Falls, South Dakota is the center. In the middle of the state St Cloud is a center. In the west, Fargo-Moorhead, and Grand Forks, North Dakota are the centers. Bemidji is a center in the north. Duluth and Hibbing/Virginia are the centers in the northeast.

The six outstate regional tournaments had an atmosphere that is unparalleled in today's playoffs. Region 1 was played at the Rochester Civic Center, with its elevated floor, balcony ringing the court, and theater seats. It felt like a CBA setting. For a number of years, it was the home of the CBA Rochester Renegade. Region 7 was played at both the University of Minnesota-Duluth and the Hibbing Memorial Arena. The Hibbing arena had a removable floor, and was used for both basketball and hockey. Like the building in Rochester, it was built before World War II, and had an old time feeling of tradition. UMD had wooden bleachers on all four sides with standing room areas in the corners. Regions 2, 3 and 6 were played at the small private colleges of Gustavus and Concordia. Both schools had old multi-sport structures with an arched roof and slightly elevated floor. Large open areas on the ends were practice areas for other sports, where wooden portable bleachers were set up. Region 8 was played at the University of North Dakota in Grand Forks, which feels like a miniature Williams Arena, with an elevated floor and balcony.

The semifinals were often a doubleheader played during the week followed by the finals on Friday or Saturday. Every venue was sold out in advance. Participating schools were allotted a set number of tickets early in the week to be sold at the school. Other region schools were similarly allotted a lesser number of tickets. While standing in the layup line during pregame warm-ups, a player could look high into the crowd and see a montage of letter jackets of different colors. Over 50 previously eliminated teams would be watching him and his teammates. Radio broadcasters sat in the front row opposite the team benches with their station banners displayed. News photographers sat on the baselines. Standing room only fans were several rows deep in all possible corners, levels and areas. At halftime adults retreated to the concourse and smoked. After halftime there would be a haze of second-hand smoke floating high above the playing floor.

From 1931 to 1970, these were truly 'regional' tournaments. And they received state-wide attention. Early in the week of the regions, the *St Paul Pioneer Press* listed the starting line-ups of all 32 district champions, including the player's height and class. Bars across the state posted 32 team bracket posters, and patrons filled out brackets to win money. This was years before the era of NCAA bracketology.

And once again, the two regions in the Twin Cities felt different than the six outstate regions. Regions 4 and 5 were played at Williams Arena. Both regions matched up two metro district champions and two district champions from nearby rural districts. For Region 5 every coach and player from both the City and Lake would be in attendance. All sessions drew over 10,000 fans. The crowds were more than twice the size of those at the outstate regionals, but they lacked the intimacy of the smaller outstate venues. In Region 5, the two rural districts extended about 100 miles out from the cities. To the north District 19 included the city of St Cloud with its 32,400 people. District 20 extended to the west, and its largest town was Willmar with a population of 10,400. Out of the remaining 29 schools in these two districts, 25 were towns of less than 2,500. Willmar had a great basketball tradition, winning the District 20 title most years. And the Cardinals almost always held their own with the large metropolitan schools.

During the 1930s and 1940s, the biggest Region 5 high schools were in Minneapolis, and the District 17 champions dominated the region. From 1933 to 1947 Minneapolis schools won the region tournament 14 out of 15 years. From 1948 to 1959, with the growth of the suburban schools, the power began to shift. During this 12-year period, the City Conference won 4 region titles, and the Lake Conference won 6. Willmar won the other 2 titles. The Region 5 champion had won 6 of the last 8 state titles. If the Spartans could survive this stage of the gauntlet, they would probably have one or two easier games at state.

***

For the region tournament at Williams Arena, the pairings were determined on a three-year rotating basis. This year Districts 17 and 18 would face off in the semifinals on Friday. Richfield got a break when Minneapolis West emerged as the champion of District 17, after finishing in fifth place in the City. In the first game District 20 champion Willmar would face District 19 champion Royalton. This was Willmar's fifth consecutive trip to the regions, and the first ever for tiny Royalton. The next edition of the *Richfield News* once again included Jerry Hoffman's weekly column.

Sports Briefs

Richfield residents witnessed perhaps their greatest athletic achievement last Saturday evening when the Spartans captured the district 18 basketball championship. In the Lake conference for five short years, Richfield has parlayed terrific coaching and the will to excel, into a state power in all high school athletics...

...This Friday and quite possibly Saturday evening at Williams arena, all of us in this area will be able to contribute his part in our athletic program. Our in-person support is vitally needed to help carry our determined squad to victory. Minneapolis West provides our first-round opposition and they have been labeled as the cinderella team of the tourney. Given an outside chance to win the district 17 title Ade Nelson's athletes upset the dope completely and defeated two of the Mill City's strongest candidates for region honors, Roosevelt and Henry. Minneapolis, you can be sure will have a generous supply of fans on hand to cheer their team to victory, but I am confident that Richfield will not be outdone in the stands or on the floor come Friday evening. All of us will take full advantage of this unprecedented opportunity and express ourselves in the only way we know how, our support. [28]

After a close first quarter, Richfield held a 32-25 lead at the intermission. Richfield then steadily pulled away. The score after three periods was 51-39, and the final was 73-54. In the second game Willmar defeated Royalton 60-47. The attendance was listed as 11,500.

The final game against Willmar was similar. At the half Richfield was ahead 34-18 and after three periods the score was 54-28. With four minutes to go in the game and a 64-34 lead, Farrell emptied the bench. The final score was 66-39.

After a 16 game Lake schedule in which Richfield outscored their conference opponents by an average of 7 points a game, they won District 18 with two games that were decided late in the fourth quarter. They followed this up by walking through the region with a comfortable victory and a blowout.

***

Like the region tournaments, the state tournament pairings were set up on a rotating basis. Thursday afternoon quarterfinal games matched up Granite Falls from Region 3 (16-7) against Melrose from Region 6 (23-1), and Austin from Region 1 (16-4) against Thief River Falls from Region 8 (17-6). The evening games pitted Edgerton from Region 2 (24-0) against Chisholm from Region 7 (22-1), and North St Paul (20-4) from Region 4 against Richfield (21-2) from Region 5.

Based upon history, the evening bracket would be tougher to get through. Along with Regions 4 and 5, it included Region 7. This region included the 16 high schools on the Mesabi Iron Range. It also included the large high schools of Duluth and the other port and lumber cities on or near Lake Superior. In the past 20 years, the Region 7 champion had won 5 of the 10 state titles that were not won by Regions 4 and 5. Chisholm with a population of 7,100 was the fourth biggest town on the Iron Range and the Bluestreaks had been to state 6 times in 30 years, the most of any Region 7 school. And this year's squad had come up one victory short of running the table in the Iron Range Conference.

The afternoon bracket included three of the four regions from the western half of the state. In these four regions, about 160 of the about 250 high schools were in prairie towns of less than 1,000 people. In Regions 3, 6, and 8 combined; there were only 13 towns with populations over 5,000. In the last 15 years the overall record of Region 3 teams at state was 14-26. In Region 6, Brainerd and Crosby-Ironton out of District 24 had together won 9 of the past 15 region championships. The combined state tourney record of the other Region 6 teams in the other six years was 5-11. In Region 8, Bemidji under Bun Fortier had always competed very well at state, but this was a year when his Lumberjacks didn't make it. They had won 9 of the past 12 Region 8 titles, including the past 7 in a row, and their 9 year record at state was 12-12.

This was the year when the two metropolitan regions would meet in the first round. Richfield would face North St Paul in the fourth and final game on Thursday night. The Polars finished second in the tough St Paul Suburban

Conference behind South St Paul. They then defeated the Packers in the District 14 finals. In the regional tournament they defeated Braham 76-69, and St Paul City Champion Mechanic Arts 65-44 to advance to state. This was their second consecutive trip to state under Coach Hal Norgard. Like Richfield, they were known for playing great man to man defense. They also zone pressed almost every minute of every game. The two teams were familiar with each other, having scrimmaged at Christmas.

The growth of the St Paul Suburban Conference in many ways mirrored the growth of the Lake Conference. As the suburban schools grew, they began to compete with the St Paul schools and traditional Big 9 powerhouse Red Wing for Region 4 supremacy. Most everyone considered the Lake versus Suburban matchup winner to be the favorite to go on and win the state championship. An article in the school newspaper, *The Spartan Spotlite* quoted North St Paul principal L.C. Arns;

This will be the championship game of the tournament. They (Richfield) have a fine ball team and we'll have to do our best to beat them. [29]

Jerry Hoffman wrote in the *Richfield News*,

Norgard rates Richfield as the team to beat in the tourney...Hal further believes that if his Polars are fortunate enough to escape the Spartan threat his athletes have an excellent chance to go all the way. [30]

In a hard-fought game Richfield slowly inched away with the quarter scores being 12-8, 26-20, and 46-36. The final was 60-51. In other games Granite Falls beat Melrose by a basket 44-42, Austin handled Thief River Falls 55-41, and tiny Edgerton surprised many people when they beat Chisholm 65-54.

Norgard was quoted in the *Minneapolis Tribune* after the game,

"We got the open shot... but we simply weren't hitting. Our defense was good and so was our rebounding, but it just wasn't' our night to hit." [31]

***

Edgerton was the surprise team of the tournament and from Region 2. In the previous 30 years Mountain Lake with a population of 1,900 had won 8 Region 2 titles. Mankato from the Big 9 with a population of 24,000 won 11. In the other 11 years, 9 titles were won by towns bigger than Mountain Lake. Edgerton was the third town in 30 years with a population of less than 1,000 to get to state out of Region 2.

Located in the extreme southwest corner of the state in District 8, the high school had 94 students in the top four grades. The school had a long history of winning seasons and championships in the tiny school Tri-County

Conference, but had never gotten out of the district. Nine schools were in the Tri-County. These towns are listed with their 1960 population; Adrian (1,200), Beaver Creek (250), Edgerton (950), Jasper (850), Hills (520), Ellsworth (630), Lake Wilson (440), Chandler (390), and Magnolia (280). The four high schools from the larger towns of the Southwest Conference had won 31 of the previous 34 District 8 titles; Luverne (4,200), Pipestone (5,300), Slayton (2,500), and Worthington (8,900). Edgerton advanced to the district semi-finals and then solidly defeated two of these schools to win their first ever championship; Pipestone 66-52 and Worthington 84-65. In the opening region game at Gustavus Adolphus College, Edgerton shocked everybody with a 73-44 romp over Mankato. Mankato had finished second in the Big 9 to Austin. The Dutchmen followed this with a victory over Mountain Lake 61-55 in the finals. They were the first District 8 champion to advance to state since 1938.

Rookie coach Rich Olson was only five years older than his players. He was a product of the Iron Range town of Virginia, and fresh out of Macalester College in St Paul. He was quoted prior to the tournament in the *Minneapolis Tribune* to say,

"We've won with team balance all season, it's hard to cite a particular strength...ANY one of the boys can score, because any one of them can shoot. That means we can play for the opening rather than for the individual." [32]

The fact that all five players could shoot the ball is a testament to the Edgerton coaches who preceded Olson; Bill Standly and Ken Kielty. No matter who the coach is, high school kids don't learn how to be great shooters in one winter. Edgerton also had the best answer of any of the teams for Bill Davis in the middle. Junior center Dean Veenhof stood over 6-5 and like Davis, he was a Division I recruit who was quick and could jump. Edgerton was also the overwhelming fan favorite. The sell-out crowds had evolved over the years to cheer for the small towns from outstate, often from the prairie towns in the western part of the state.

A state tournament record crowd of 18,812 turned out for the evening session. When the Edgerton team took the floor there was a thunderous standing ovation. Less than a minute later as the Richfield team climbed the stairs and stepped on to the same elevated playing surface, the cheers suddenly turned to loud boos.

When the game began Richfield jumped out to a 10 to 3 lead. Edgerton slowly closed the gap to 14-12 at the end of one quarter. From then on, the game was close. At halftime Edgerton had the advantage 30-28. After three quarters Edgerton was ahead 44-41. Richfield appeared to have the advantage when Veenhof fouled out with 5:09 left and Edgerton leading 50-46. With 1:36

to play Davis scored to tie the game at 56-56. After a stop, Coach Farrell went for one shot. With six seconds to play he called time out, and in the huddle, he reviewed a play that his team had practiced many times and saved for this exact situation. Mac Lutz was to set a back screen for Bill Davis who would cut diagonally from the opposite elbow to the ball-side low post. The Spartans ran the play to perfection, except that while setting the screen Lutz was called for a three second violation. The Dutchmen then missed a desperation long shot and the game went into overtime.

In the overtime, Darrel Kreun of Edgerton hit two free throws with 1:28 to go to give Edgerton a 58-56 lead. Then teammate Leroy Graphenteen hit two more with 20 seconds to play. Bob Sadek then calmly drained a jump shot to cut the margin to two. Richfield had to foul again. Davis fouled Kreun who made two more free throws to extend the lead back to 4 points. Sadek then nailed two free throws for Richfield with 14 seconds remaining to make the score 62-60. Richfield had to foul again and with 6 seconds remaining Graphenteen hit one of two to make the final score 63-60.

Playing the same aggressive and disciplined man to man defense that they played all season, the Spartans were whistled for 27 fouls, 14 above and more than double their season average. After consoling his team in a locker room of sobbing players, the coaches Gene Farrell and Vance Crosby walked to the Edgerton locker room to congratulate the winners.

* * *

The next night Richfield pounded Granite Falls in the third-place game 77-50 when Davis poured in 40 points and Farrell emptied the bench. In the state championship game Edgerton controlled the game from start to finish and defeated Austin 72-60.

* * *

Sunday morning a car caravan parade began at the Curtis Hotel in downtown Minneapolis at 11am. Over a couple miles of cars honked their horns south on Portland Avenue towards Richfield. The team and coaches then filed into the high school to a packed gymnasium. A table was set up on one baseline with the trophies and a podium. The players sat in the end zone bleachers behind the table. All three other sets of bleachers were filled to capacity. Overflow parents and children completely covered the area on the gym floor.

The mayor, school board president, superintendent and coaches all spoke. It was and still is the biggest crowd ever assembled in the gym.

The following week in the *Richfield News*, Jerry Hoffman again wrote:

Sports Briefs

I believe the parade on Portland Ave last Sunday best sums up the way all Richfield feels about their high school basketball team. For nearly an hour, hundreds of cars streamed by and everyone having any association with the team must have experienced the same sensation as I.

During the tournament, Richfield played well enough to win three games and under ordinary circumstances could well have emerged as state champions. It certainly was not ordinary the way Edgerton dropped 35 of 43 attempts from the charity line. Time and again when a miss on a one and one situation would have undoubtedly turned the tide of battle in our favor, Darrel Kreun or Leroy Graphenteen displayed great clutch marksmanship. One rarely witnesses such poise, even in college basketball. True, the officiating was tight and technical and sometimes questionable, but when the chips were down this small-town team came through in a big way.

The tournament had a sour note too, however. The unsportsmanlike conduct of the thousands of fans has no place in the sporting world.

It is the first time that I have ever witnessed any crowd boo roundly, a team that was being introduced. The Richfield and Austin players will be wondering for quite some time how a sports crowd could act the way this one did. [33]

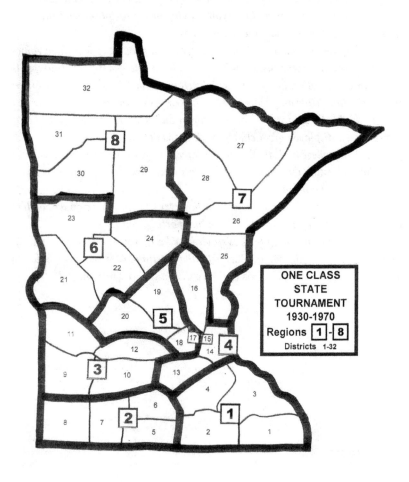

ONE CLASS
STATE
TOURNAMENT
1930-1970
Regions 1 - 8
Districts 1-32

Fourth Winter

The strength of the pack is the wolf, and the strength of the wolf is the pack.

—*Rudyard Kipling*

The second week in November was early signing day for high school seniors. Travis signed a scholarship with Northern Iowa. Ray was still undecided and did not sign. There was a signing ceremony for Travis at the high school. He was going to get his college paid for. His parents were extremely proud and they had every right to be. The next week Ray committed to Bradley.

At our coaching staff meetings in the fall, the staff was eager to get back to work. This was now our fourth winter, and the continuity of the staff was evident. Jamar Hardy had resigned which opened up another position. I moved Matt Schock from the ninth graders to the sophomores. Matt Mullenbach could then coach the ninth-grade games and go scout during the varsity games. Although we had a staff in which every assistant was an excellent scout and could X and O proficiently, Matt enjoyed it. And I liked having both Lance and Alcindor at my sides during games. We three worked well together and we had great game-time chemistry.

* * *

When tryouts began in November there were no difficult decisions when it came to cuts. From my perspective, the ideal number of players on a basketball team was 12. When I coached in the small town, I usually kept 12 or 13 players on the team. On game nights there were three games, a ninth-grade game, a B squad (sophomore) game and a varsity game. At Richfield we played four consecutive games on game nights, ninth grade, B squad (sophomore), JV (varsity reserves), and varsity, and therefore needed 14 varsity players. During practice, many of our drills were in groups of two, three, or four players. All of the players were constantly moving the entire practice until we went 5 on 5 during the last half hour. The players all received equal time in all of the drills. I had a simple substitution system to guarantee this. The players were responsible for rotating themselves in and out of the drills and the 5 on 5. The more players that we had, the fewer repetitions each player got in practice. The fewer repetitions that a player got, the slower that he and the team improved. It was simple math. At Richfield we usually kept 14 or 15 players on the team.

When we made our final cuts, we also made the cut where we had a 'clean break'. In other words, if we had two equal players vying for the fourteenth spot, we either cut them both or we kept them both. However, I was adamant that when it came to these end of the bench roster spots, attitude and work ethic counted heavily. If we had players with equal abilities, but one spent more time practicing in the off season, this one made the team. Similarly, if either of the boys exhibited signs of a selfish attitude, he was cut.

I told my assistants at the start of tryouts that Bill Bauman was not going to displace anybody who would have made the team, if Bill were not here. It was obvious that he was going to make the team, and that he would be competing for a starting position. We would end up with fifteen or sixteen players. I was not going to deprive any returning player a roster spot because of a senior transfer. If that meant that we had one more player at practice than most years, so be it. We discussed this as a staff. I also discussed it with Jim Baker, the assistant principal Jason Wenschlag, and the principal Jill Johnson.

We made the cuts at the end of every tryout/practice during the first week of the season. As in prior years, on the last day of the cuts each player came into the athletic office. If he didn't make the team, I told him. If he made the team, I told him what his role would be at the beginning of the season. This included both his offensive and defensive role in terms of individual style of play. It also included how many minutes of playing time he would get.

If the player didn't make the team, I told him that we had better players. If the player was an underclassman, we always told him what he had to improve on in order to make the team the next year. I also always added that he should come to the summer open gyms, and that I would work with him individually. Many kids did this. Most didn't. All of them improved from the open gyms, and all of them had more fun playing for the rest of their lives. If the player that I was cutting was a senior, I simply told him that we had better players and that was all that I told him.

If a player had exhibited signs of a selfish attitude the prior winter, then attitude was an issue and this was discussed by the coaching staff. Many coaches believe that if a player has a bad attitude as a young player, this will not change as he gets older. There was a quote that I heard at the high school more than once. "A leopard doesn't change its spots." This quote was passed down in the Richfield coaching fraternity from one of the coaches of the glory years.

I had a more open view on this. I believed that sometimes kids could change. However, when it came to a player with a selfish attitude or an unrealistic opinion of his abilities, I had zero tolerance. It was an easy cut. I would have liked to be able to tell a player that he was cut because of his attitude, and then give him examples of his prior behavior to support this. However, in today's coaching climate, a coach can't do this. This opens the door for a debate with the parent that will accomplish nothing. In addition, the parent of the player is often in denial about his or her son's attitude or abilities.

We ended up keeping eight seniors, five juniors, and three sophomores. Travis, Ray, Jordan Noonan, and Dustin Dreifke were two seniors and two juniors who were going to play major minutes. Seniors Adam Smith and Bill Bauman were also solidly in the rotation. We had a clear top six. After this there were 15 to 20 minutes of playing time to spread to the other players. The other three seniors would be competing for spots seven through nine, and these minutes. Dusty Hinz would be getting some of these minutes as the backup point guard to Dreifke. He would be playing two or three minutes at a time in this role. He was a solid 5-9, point guard who could run the offense, not turn the ball over, and play great defense. In these short increments, he could play all-out hard. The same could be said for both Mike Windler and Octavius Crawford. Mike at 6-2 and 220 and Octavius at 6-4 and 210 could give us short stints of great interior defense and rebounding. Like Dusty, they always played hard, and they would give us energy. Mike's other role was to play on the scout squad in practice.

Two other juniors who would be on the scout squad and play JV were Carl Ermisch and Ojullo Madho. Carl was a 6-1 program kid. He was a three-sport athlete, a second-generation Richfield athlete and a natural leader. His best sports were football and baseball. Ojullo (OJ) was a 5-9 ultra-quick Sudanese kid whose family immigrated to Minneapolis six years earlier. He first appeared to us at the ninth-grade tryouts. His role was to be in Dreifke's face every minute of every practice. The other junior was Demond Mackrell, a 6-2 wing who had been in Richfield since middle school.

Three sophomores also made the team, Steven Fischer, Santino Clay, and Dexter Jones. They would all be scout squad members and play four quarters of JV. Santino was the wild card. He was now over 6-1 and his improvement both academically and athletically was phenomenal. Standing flat footed with one arm raised in the air his fingers reached to 8'6", which is the normal reach for most guys who are 6-5. He was on the verge of pushing his way into the rotation. Because we had the luxury of not needing him, I was going to bring him along slowly.

There were three seniors on the bubble; Dennis Luke, Nate Poke, and Dennis Robinson. Dennis Robinson was an African American who open enrolled from south Minneapolis as a kindergartner, but never played traveling or attended the camps. He grew to 6-1, and improved every year. Dennis Luke was a 6-1 Ugandan immigrant whose family lived in Richfield. He also never played in the traveling program. Nate Poke was a biracial African-American and a program kid. He was 5-9 and stopped growing in middle school, and had not improved as much as the other two. All three had great attitudes and attended every possible open gym. I ranked Robinson as the best player followed by Luke and then Poke. I saw the cleanest break between Robinson and Luke. We kept Dennis Robinson.

A week later I sat the entire team down on the gym floor in a circle. I told each of them what their roles were, in front of all of their teammates. I saved Bill Bauman for last. I discussed his presence on the team. I told them that if they didn't believe in open enrollment, that this was fine. I told them that Bill chose to be here and that given the open enrollment laws, he had every right to be here. And I told them that I knew that some of them would be thinking that he took a roster spot away from someone else. I told them that this wasn't true. I told them that we had 16 players on the roster. I told them that if Bill wasn't here, we'd have 15 kids sitting here right now. I told them that he would be taking playing time away from some of them, but he was not taking a roster spot from anybody. I asked them if anybody had a problem with this. I asked them if anybody had a problem with accepting their role. Then I said "what is said here, stays here." I repeated to them John Wooden's first two qualities of a championship team, play together and play hard. It wasn't the last time that they heard "what is said here stays here" during the rest of the season. Then I used the old Viking analogy of a long boat leaving the harbor. You have to have either both feet on the boat or both feet on the dock. You can't have one foot on each. If you have one foot on the boat and one foot on the dock, now is the time to get back on the dock. I then went around the circle and asked each player if he was on board. Every one of them said "I'm on board."

* * *

We opened the season two weeks later with back-to-back games at South on Friday and against Braham on Saturday at Becker, Minnesota in the Tip-Off Classic. Joe Hyser had another good team at South, and after playing them for two years we now had a rivalry. Braham was the defending 2A state champions and they had all five starters back. We spent two weeks preparing for both games.

We beat South 68-51, pulling away in the second half. Before the game I was interviewed by Patrick Ruesse of the *StarTribune*. The *StarTribune* was the daily newspaper in Minneapolis. He would be at the game the following night in Becker and would cover it with a column in the Sunday morning paper.

The Tip-Off Classic was four games, two girl's games and two boy's games. We were to play in the fourth game at 8pm. All four games matched up teams that were ranked in the top five of the preseason polls. For our game, we were ranked #1 in Class 3A and Braham was ranked #1 in Class 2A. Becker was located thirty miles northwest of the Twin Cities. Forty miles to the northeast of Becker was Braham, a town of 1,500 people. Braham was coached by Bob Vaughn who had been at Braham for over twenty years. They won the Class 2A state championship the year before with a record of 31-2. Both losses were to Class 4A schools. He had Isaiah Dahlman who was a 6-7 junior and his 6-6 sophomore brother Noah. Both were DI prospects. Their maternal grandfather was John Kundla. Kundla coached both the Minneapolis Lakers and the Gophers in the forties, fifties and the sixties. Bob's 6-4 senior son Josh Vaughan was the point guard and had signed early with North Dakota State. With some talented athletes finally coming up through the pipeline, Vaughn was on the verge of riding a three-year run as a perennial power. This success also attracted Chris Vavra, a 6-1 guard who open enrolled from Cambridge-Isanti, the neighboring town to the south. Vavra transferred in as a junior. Bob was quoted by John Millea in the *StarTribune* as saying, *"That was a huge break. He gave us quickness that we didn't have."*

Braham ran the flex offense and they ran it well, with all five players interchanging all of the positions on the floor. They kept the floor evenly spaced with four players on the perimeter and one player in the post. They also ran a number of set plays for their best players to get shots. On defense they played mostly man to man. They would also mix in a 1-3-1 half court trap with Isaiah and his long wing span guarding the ball on the top of the zone. We had them well scouted from their state tournament run the previous winter.

I heard Bob Knight say many things that stuck with me as a coach. One of those things was comparing man and zone defenses. He said that if a coach plays man to man, the defense picks the match-ups, and that if a coach plays zone, the offense picks the match-ups. In other words, with man to man, the defensive coach decides who guards who. I had extended this premise to a switching man to man defense. The more screens that a man-to-man defense switches, the more opportunities there are for the offensive coach to pick the match ups. Our standard way of defending the flex was to switch the down screens, and they ran a lot of down screens.

Going into the Braham game, we were concerned about this. We wanted Ray guarding Isaiah Dahlman all of the time. They played against each other during the summer, and Ray wanted to guard him. Similarly, we liked the idea of having one player always guarding Noah Dahlman, which would be Bill, Adam, or Octavius. We talked about changing our defense to have three players switch screens, except for the two players guarding the Dahlman brothers. We needed three or four days of practice time to work on it, and we decided against it. If we didn't switch any screens, they would keep swinging the ball and shooting free throw area jump shots off of the pass. I wasn't going to let them do this. We were going to switch their down screens and all of our players would be guarding both Isaiah and Noah at different times.

By the end of the 6pm game, one side of the gym was almost solid Braham fans. The game was close from start to finish. Neither team could build a lead of over 6 points. Every time that we scored two quick baskets in a row, Bob Vaughn called a time out. Late in the first half they tried their 1-3-1 zone and we scored easily against it. They tried all of their set plays and none of them worked.

Then in the fourth quarter Vaughn had them run their flex offense until Ray was switched off of Isaiah. Isaiah would then dribble to the paint, elevate, and shoot jump shots over our shorter defender. He hit three big baskets in this way in the last eight minutes of the game. We were unable to cut the margin to less than 4 points. With under three minutes to go in the game they went to their delay offense and we couldn't force a turnover. They hit free throws to walk away with a 72-63 victory. Noah killed us on the boards, scoring 8 points off of put backs.

After the game there was a melancholy feeling of disappointment and missed opportunity. This game was for bragging rights. Braham was the heavy favorite to repeat as the 2A state champs, and they had beaten one of the best 3A teams. It was a bitter pill to swallow. I told the kids, "you guys didn't lose this game, I did. We were in the wrong defense." I then explained to them the defense that we should have been in. I looked at Ray. "You should've been guarding Isaiah the entire game, Ray. You weren't. That was my fault. The good news is that we're going to learn from this. We're going to practice having one defender not switch screens so that we have this defense late in the season if we need it."

After the game I stopped Bob in the concourse and we talked. I told him that he did a great job and commended him for isolating Isaiah on our smaller defenders. He said that his kids executed it better than he thought they would because very few teams defend them this way, adding that they see zones game after game. I asked him what we could do different to keep Noah off of the boards. He laughed and answered, "nothing, he's just one of those kids who's a natural offensive rebounder. He's been like that since grade school and he was probably born that way."

The next day we were the subject of a column in the Sunday edition of the *StarTribune* by Patrick Reusse. Reusse was a Minnesota native who had spent his entire writing career at various papers in the state.

Patrick Reusse: Revived Richfield Team aims high

...The Spartans were the Twin Cities' first suburban sports powerhouse, predating Edina for that distinction in the 1950s. Richfield still was an all-sports force in 1973, when Mike Karnas graduated with 900 other seniors "A year ago, my son graduated with a class of 300", he said.

The Spartans lost to Edgerton in the semifinals of the 1960 one-class boys' basketball state tournament. They were back in 1973 and 1974, losing Class AA finals to Anoka and then Bemidji. Thirty years later Richfield expected to make its fourth appearance, this time in Class 3A. The Spartans were upset 48-47 by Holy Angels, their crosstown rival, in the section semifinals last March...For now there's the getting–to-state quest to occupy the Browns and their teammates...(and winning it) a feat the Spartans never accomplished, even in their athletic heyday...

The athletic glory has been infrequent in recent times, but Mike Karnas' passion for his alma mater has remained. Jay Herman and Dick Hughes are Richfield residents (although not graduates). They have become Karnas' posse at Spartans events for years—through mediocrity and often less than that "We had a basketball run in the mid-'90s where we must have been 2-and-200," said Karnas, exaggerating to help put in perspective what not has happened with boy's basketball at Richfield.

Travis Brown is a Richfield kid. Ray Brown followed coach Jim Dimick Jr. from Minneapolis Washburn. Dimick was fired there through the efforts – surprise! – of a group of disgruntled parents. Dimick was 9-14 and 13-13 with young teams in his first two Richfield years, then the Spartans burst to 21-5 last season. There were nine seniors on that team, but the main weapons were the Browns. Longtime residents, young families and old-line loyalists filled the 1,750 fan capacity of the Richfield gym seven times in 11 home games in the winter of 2003-04...

Richfield opened its schedule with a 68-51 victory over South on Friday... on Saturday night the Spartans were whipped 72-63 by defending Class 2A champion Braham in the Tip-Off Classic at Becker High School. Braham has its entire club back from last season, and it showed…"It's crazy how things have changed in Richfield since I was a freshman," Ray Brown said. "There weren't many people at our games back then. Now there is a whole lot of people cheering for us every game." [34]

I wasn't totally happy with the article. I didn't think that the verb 'whipped' was appropriate, given that the game was close until they hit free throws at the end. I was more disappointed with Reusse putting in the paper Mike Karnas' quote about the mid-90s, and its inadvertent criticism of Greg Miller. Knowing Karnas as well as I do, I am certain that if the writer would have reread the quote to Mike and then asked Mike if he wanted the quote in the paper, Mike would have said no. From 1990 to 1995 the Richfield high school boys' basketball team recorded six consecutive losing seasons with an average record of 5-18 under Jeff Etienne, which is most likely the years to which Mike was referring.

***

The next week we won at St Paul Harding 74-41 on Tuesday. On Friday we would go to Holy Angels for the annual rivalry game and capacity crowd. We played well the first half but missed shots and were down 29-24 at the intermission. In the second half the shots started dropping and we pulled away to win 68-36. With under five minutes to go in the game we were up by over 20 points and we emptied the bench. Ray and Isaiah Goodman led both teams in scoring with 24 points each.

After the game I quieted the kids down, and told them to look at the floor for a minute of silence. I told them that I wanted them to try to remember exactly how they felt last March when we lost to Holy Angels in the tournament. After the minute I said, "think about last year's seniors. They don't get another chance. Think of all the open gyms that you guys have spent together working for this. You get another chance. But every time that you think about this game, follow the thought through back to last March and think about that game. This game means nothing."

We played well defeating South St Paul and Mahtomedi the next two games. Our playing rotation didn't change. Bill Bauman had picked up our system quickly. In less than a month, he was playing great position defense, setting good screens, and rebounding. He ran the court hard, talked on defense, and he never missed a box out. He had accepted his role completely. The majority of the minutes were going to our top six. Dusty Hinz and Octavius Crawford were giving us limited minutes off of the bench, but playing with energy.

Surprisingly, I began to see signs in the behavior of Dennis Robinson that he was not totally on board. I confronted him, described these specific behaviors, and told him that I didn't want to cut him, but if I continued to see them, he would be cut. They continued, so Alcindor and I met with him and told him that he was no longer on the team. We also told him that this should not change his academic goals and hopes in any way. I added that I totally believed in him, praised his work ethic, and that I believed that all of his dreams would come true. Basketball just was no longer going to be part of them. During the whole time that I was talking he was nodding in agreement. In the end he looked me in the eye, and said "thanks for everything coach."

* * *

We were heading into the Christmas break ranked #3 in Class 3A with a record of 6-1. From our conference Tartan was ranked #6 in Class 4A and St Thomas was ranked #6 in Class 3A. The other top ranked teams in Class 3A were Mankato West, Mankato East, Rocori, and Shakopee. We were beginning to think ahead, scouting these ranked teams and working on the common parts of game plans that we would need to beat any of them. We also were monitoring our list of goals of the execution of certain fundamentals, such as missed box outs, dumb fouls, not talking enough on defense, etc. I would adapt our practice plans to continue the improvement in these specific areas, which I believed would result in a steady overall rate of improvement of the team.

Our next game was at Eau Claire Memorial the Thursday before New Year's. Dustin Dreifke's family scheduled a surgery which required stitches to his face, and he would not play. We would not be the same team without him. I decided to move Jordan Noonan to point guard, and to give Santino Clay twenty minutes in the rotation.

We began burying Eau Claire right from the start. At the end of the half, we lead 48-14. It was that kind of game where everything went our way. The final was 92-39. In his 20 minutes of playing time Santino had 6 points and 7 rebounds. He took 4 shots, all of which were elevated jumpers in the lane or put backs. He had 2 steals in our half-court defense, both the result of being in perfect position away from the ball. In all three areas of the game; offense, defense, and transition, he totally fit in with the flow of the other players.

Ten minutes after the game, the coaching staff stood and talked in the hallway. Then Lance said "Jim" and he looked at me. He said very slowly, very softly, and very emphatically, "Santino's…gotta…play." I knew that this was coming. I looked at the other assistants and said "what do you guys think?"

One assistant quickly responded, "He's been playing our defense for two years now Jim, and he totally understands it, plus he gives us another long defender who can ball pressure like crazy without getting beat off the dribble." I looked at Alcindor. He was nodding and laughing, "he's ready Jim…he's ready. He's like another Ray or Travis in the making. He can create on both ends of the court." I looked at the last assistant. He was nodding too. "He's gotta play. He's been just dominating in the last two JV games."

I then spoke. "Well, we're gonna have a problem."

They all looked at me. I said "Dusty. He's not gonna play at all. Every minute that Dusty has been getting now goes to Santino, and when Dreifke rests, Jordan plays point guard. I agree with all of you guys. Santino's gotta play, but we now have a clear top five on the perimeter. We'll play Santino either two quarters JV and three quarters varsity, or one quarter JV and four quarters varsity. Dusty is now 100% scout squad. I'm telling Dusty before practice Monday, and I'm telling the whole team after practice."

The next Monday before practice Alcindor and I met with Dusty. I told Dusty that his role had changed and that he was not in the playing rotation at all, and that Santino was now in the top seven. His only role was to be the point guard on the scout squad. I emphasized that this was a very important role. I also repeated what I was always telling the scout squad players, which was that he could really help the team in this role. I also told him that I knew it wasn't going to be easy for him. As I always did in these situations, I then told him that if he couldn't accept this new role with a good attitude, it was better that he quit, and that I would totally understand.

I then asked him, "can you accept this, Dusty? Do you still want to be on the team?"

He looked me in the eye and said, "I wanna be on the team, coach. I'm on board."

* * *

We resumed conference play the first week of January with a win against Henry Sibley 77-54. Henry Sibley was improving quickly under the direction of their first-year coach Tom Dosovich. We defended their big post Trevor Mbakwe by playing behind him, and rotating three defenders on him. We double-teamed him hard when he got the ball. He still scored 22 points, but it was a nice road win, plus we practiced a defensive scheme that we didn't normally use, and might need in the tournament.

Thursday night after practice Mullenbach and I drove to Mankato to watch the two high schools play, East versus West. West was the defending state champion with virtually their entire team back, and East was just as good. They were both ranked in the top five in Class 3A. They were the only two public high schools in Mankato, and their match-up was always an arch-rivalry game, even when the teams weren't good. After tonight's game, they would meet once more in February, and then they would most likely meet again in March in the section finals. If we were going to win the state, we would have to beat one of them. I saw West in the state tournament the year before, we had videos on both teams, and this would be the second time that I would see East. I stopped on the way in LeSueur to pick up my canoe buddies, Dick and Woody. My little brother John also met us there. We sat in the front row across from their benches. I liked to sit in this area because I could hear the coach's calls. Both teams ran a lot of set plays that we already had, but I wanted to verify their names for the sets. West won a game that was decided in the final minute.

The second week in January, I and my three captains, Ray, Travis, and Adam were guests of Mike Max on his WCCO radio 'Sports to the Max' show. This was a two-hour interview or round table discussion from 7pm to 9pm on a Monday night. The last half hour of the show, people called in to ask questions or comment. After practice I drove from the high school to downtown Minneapolis with the three players in my car. It was a calm night with snow gently falling as we walked the downtown streets from the car to the WCCO building. The temperature was in the twenties and the snow was beginning to accumulate.

At this same time 60 miles to the southwest, my friend Jeff (Smitty) Smith was walking across a frozen Lake Washington to his ice fishing shack. After rigging his rod, he sat down, cracked a beer, and turned on his radio which was always set to WCCO and the Sports to the Max show. When Mike Max announced my name Smitty burst out laughing.

I coached against Mike when he played for Darrell Kreun at Gaylord, and I was at LeSueur. Darrell was also the deadly shooter of the 1960 Edgerton team, and one of the best shooting coaches in the state. For many years he ran a stellar program, and Mike was one of many in a long line of great shooters. He was now established as a television and radio personality in Minnesota. Because Mike played town team baseball for Gaylord, and Smitty followed the town team down the road in Arlington, Mike also knew Smitty.

The show was a blast. The players all spoke very well. When the phone calls started up, high school kids were calling in and trying to sound serious but be funny. One kid called in and said that he was Oz Mullerliele from Richfield, and that he was Richfield's number one fan, and he praised me and the great job that I was doing. When this happened, I looked at the players and they couldn't stop laughing. Five months later in a bar in LeSueur I was laughing about the show again, when I ran into my old buddy Smitty.

* * *

The next week we played at St Thomas on Friday. St Thomas had most of their best players back from the year before. They had another D1 post in Bryce Webster. Webster was a physical 6-10 junior who was being recruited by the top-level programs. When I scouted St Thomas earlier in the season, Michigan State coach Tom Izzo was at the game. Their point guard David Hicks was a low or mid major D1 recruit. They had their usual collection of very good players to go with these two, including athletic 6-4 senior transfer Darius Redd. Mike Sjoberg had been the head coach at St Thomas since 1998, and the program was one of the best in the state. He had a veteran staff of assistants, including Tom Ihnot and Tony Yazbeck. Ihnot was the former head coach who came out of retirement to assist with their defense, and their team man to man defense was as good as any that we would see. Yazbeck was a young energetic coach who was completely dedicated to the game. He also served as one of Rene Pulley's right-hand men in the summer Howard Pulley AAU program. Not coincidentally, St Thomas was often the recipient of junior and senior transfers who were also Howard Pulley players.

The game was a dogfight from the start. At the quarter breaks the scores were 18-18, 32-31, and 48-44. The Cadets maintained their lead to the end and were rewarded with a 65-58 victory. Our three post defenders took turns guarding Webster, without the benefit of our perimeter players double teaming him. Webster finished the game with 28 points, 12 rebounds, and 7 blocked shots. We played well, but needed to play better if we were to defeat them in our next two match-ups.

* * *

After winning two more games, we played at Tartan with their #3 ranking in Class 4A and 11-1 record. Their two returning starters Urule Igbavboa and Kwadzo Ahelegbe were both a year older and a year stronger, and both had had great summers playing for Howard Pulley. As was customary, Mark Klingsporn had reloaded around them with talented younger kids. Our three-year record against Tartan was 1-5, and we had never played them close at Tartan. It was a game that the kids and the coaching staff needed to win to prove a point. At our Saturday morning practice, one could feel the extra level of intensity. By the time the game started, every seat in the gym was taken. Then the lights went off and the spotlight went on to announce the Tartan starters, and the officials ran to mid-court for the opening tip-off.

The first half was maybe our best of the year, to date. We made good decisions with the ball and our team defense looked great. At the intermission we had a lead of 30-27. We hit a couple more shots than they did in the third quarter to extend our lead to 46-39. With seven minutes to play and an 8-point lead, we went to our spread offense, looking to shoot lay-ups, free throws, and wide-open threes. On the next two possessions, Travis hit a lay-up and a three, but Tartan matched both baskets. On the next two possessions we turned the ball over on what we all thought were hard fouls by the Tartan defenders. They hit shots and narrowed the lead to one point with under a minute to go. Then one of our players was called for traveling in front of our bench. In my opinion, my kid had been hacked again, and it was a terrible call, and I jumped up with my hands in the air and let the referee know this. He immediately gave me a technical. Ahelegbe hit two free throws. We ended up losing 52-51, and the technical foul was definitely a big factor in the loss. The referee was one of the best basketball officials in the state, and as we all know, coaches and officials don't always agree, and both make mistakes. After the game when I spoke to the team in the locker room, I told the kids that I would take the blame for the loss, and that I thought that the referee made two really bad calls at the end of the game. For adjectives I used swear words including f-bombs.

In an article in the *StarTribune* by John Millea, both coaches were quoted.

Jim Dimick- *"Both teams played very intense, very physical and it came down to the last few minutes, we turned the ball over three times in a row, which really hurt. We didn't execute the fundamentals, but they have a great ballclub."*

Mark Klingsporn- *"We just kind of hung in there and made some plays. I thought Richfield played well together, with a real purpose. I thought they became very difficult to cover. I thought our kids dug in and just made some defensive stops when we needed them. And we got some turnovers too."* [35]

We had to get over the loss quickly. The Target Center Shootout was on Saturday. It was a series of five high school games beginning in the late morning followed by the Timberwolves game in the evening. It matched five of the best high school teams in Minnesota against five out of state teams. We were to play in the second game against Sioux City East from Iowa. We spent the next two practices preparing mostly for Sioux City East as well as our Friday opponent

South St Paul. We won easily at South St Paul and we rested our top players for most of the second half.

Sioux City East had a record of 13-0 and they were ranked #2 in the large school class in Iowa. They had two Division 1 recruits in 6-3 guard Dan Bohall and 6-5 swing-man Roman Gentry, a recent transfer from Sioux City West. Our top players played against their top players in summer games. Bohall signed early with Iowa. Because we now had kids who had been playing our defense for four years, I let them choose the match ups. Ray and Travis wanted to guard Gentry and Bohall. When Ray or Travis was not in the game, Santino would be on one of them.

This was our first game at the Target Center. When I was an assistant at DeLaSalle we played two years in a row at the Target Center in the state tournament, and it had a whole different feel than any high school gym. The teams entered the playing area by walking through a tunnel entrance from the end of the court. They then walked about fifty feet before stepping up half a foot to the elevated floor. The court itself was 94 feet long compared to the standard high school court which was 84 feet long. As with NBA arenas, there was a long scorer's table which ran from free throw line to free throw line. Both teams sat between the free throw line and the base line. The folding chairs were padded, the lights were brighter, and the public address system was louder. The spectator's seats were also padded with armrests. The first row was right behind the team and there was a steep pitch to each successive row. The result was that when the coach stood up, he was very close to and looking eye level to the spectators in the first few rows. These spectators can also hear what is being said on the bench and during time outs. When I walked on the floor and turned to the crowd, I was looking directly at my family and my canoe buddies.

We fell behind early, but battled back, and at halftime we were up 39-33. We remained in the lead the entire second half. With less than two minutes to play and a 3-point lead, we went to our spread offense on the big court. Travis hit three free throws and Ray blocked two shots and we had a hard fought 67-64 victory.

It ended up being what I called a 'one run' game. It was a closely fought game between two even teams. We made one six-point run, combined with playing great defense, to win the game. We preached this concept to our kids constantly. The key was to play great defense, so that our opponent couldn't counter our run with a run of their own. It was also a game where many players stepped up and made big plays. Jordan scored 15 points by hitting 3 out of 7 three pointers. Santino had 9 points and 7 rebounds. Octavius Crawford scored on two fast break put backs after sprinting down the floor. We also got hard aggressive minutes from Adam Smith.

In other games Duluth East beat Randolph, Wisconsin 42-40, St Thomas lost to Sioux Falls Roosevelt 56-55, Braham defeated Compton Centennial of California 64-52; and Tartan lost to Madison Memorial of Wisconsin 59-50.

* * *

The following Friday we rolled to a 104-82 victory over Henry Sibley in front of another big home town crowd. There was an intuitive group feeling of being rewarded for all of our hard work. The kids were having fun, and the crowd was loud and into the game.

Late in the game I emptied the bench. During the second quarter, Lance walked towards the middle of the bench and he told Mike and Dusty to get the bench into the game by cheering. Dusty rolled his eyes at Lance. Mike immediately got the bench going. At halftime Lance went off on Mike and Dusty. The message was that their roles were to be scout squad leaders and senior leaders on the bench, and that both of them knew that. The message was laced with profanity including f-bombs. The entire message lasted less than twenty seconds.

After the game Lance approached me with Bill Bauman. Lance said, "Jim, we got a problem." Then he turned to Bill, "ok Bill, tell coach what you just told me." Bill said that when he came out of the game and he got to the bench, he said to the scout squad guys, "let's go Mike, let's go Dusty." Dusty responded, "take your fucking ass back to Prior Lake."

I called an immediate team meeting. I opened it up by telling the team "we got a problem, and we're going to deal with it head on." Then I wrote on the chalk board in capital letters "PLAY HARD-PLAY TOGETHER", the first two qualities of John Wooden's five qualities of a championship team. I reminded them of that. I then told them that if we were not together, nothing else mattered. We weren't going to win. I then said that if a player tells a teammate to fuck off when he's going into the game, we aren't playing together. I then said, "Bill Bauman is here, and we discussed this in November, and you all told me at that time that you were on board, and you wanted to be on the team. Now if anybody has changed their mind and they don't want to be on the team anymore, that's fine. You can leave right now. But if you have a complaint, or if something is bugging you, it's really important that you speak up now. Nothing that you say will be held against you."

Lance then described how Bill came in here with a perfect attitude, that he's never said one bad thing to anybody, that he's totally accepted his role, and that he's done everything that we asked of him. "He's here. Get over it."

There was a long silence. I then looked at Dusty and said, "Dusty, you want to say something? Now is the time. Speak your mind. We aren't going to agree on everything. I know that. Get it off your chest." Dusty said that he didn't think that it was fair that Bill was here. He said that he never sat on the bench before on any teams, and that he was frustrated. Mike Windler then raised his hand and said that he agreed with Dusty in believing that it wasn't fair. He added that he wanted to be on the team and would do whatever it took to help us get a state championship. He then looked directly at Bill and told Bill that he had no animosity towards him and that he liked him, but he just didn't like the situation. Octavius said that he agreed with Mike, also emphasizing to Bill that he liked him as a teammate. All of the other players defended Bill. Bill just said that he was going to keep working as hard as anybody.

Alcindor told them that he thought that they were lucky to have a coach who told everybody what their roles were. He said that he had been on teams where half the team didn't know what their roles were and that the roles changed every week. He added that that they were lucky to have a coach that wanted to listen to them, saying that some coaches didn't want to hear what the players were thinking.

I ended up going all the way around the room again, asking every player and every coach if they had anything so say. Every player said "I'm on board and I want to be here." I then added, "well, if I see any signs that anybody isn't on board, as you know, I reserve the right to cut anybody at any time." Lance spoke up again, "We are a family. Families have arguments. They work things out inside the family, and what is said stays in the family. If this was simmering, it was good that it came out, but now we have to agree to disagree, and then accept what coach says, and move on."

I then told them the old principal of separating your problems into the problems that you can control and the problems that you can't control. "If something is bugging you, ask yourself if it is something that you can control or if it is something that you can't control. If you can control it and change it, go to work on it. If it's something that you can't control, accept it, and accept the fact that it's going to bug you and move on. I control the playing time. You guys control your attitude and your effort. Accept the playing time and don't worry about it. Focus on your attitude and effort."

An old coach once told me that when a disgruntled senior, sits on the bench, he gains more power and becomes more of a problem as the season progresses. The reason for this is because late in the season he has less to lose. Early in the season he still has hopes of getting playing time. Many old coaches believed that was why you had to get rid of them early by cutting them. After the meeting the coaching staff discussed this topic again. We discussed cutting Dusty. Except for this one incident, his behavior had been exemplary. And when I talked to him one on one, he always spoke with candor and straight-forwardness. And he played hard every minute of every practice. He only had one speed.

We had no time to dwell on this, because we had another big Saturday afternoon game the next day against St Paul Johnson.

* * *

Johnson was in first place in the St Paul City Conference, and was ranked #7 in Class 4A with a record of 16-4. They were led by their coach Vern Simmons. Vern was African-American and recently retired from the St Paul police department. He was now the school security officer and head basketball coach. He grew up in Michigan City, Indiana, and attended Morningside College in Sioux City, Iowa where he played point guard.

Johnson was one of the oldest high schools in St Paul and was located a mile northeast of downtown. At one time the school was a long-time hockey power in a working-class white neighborhood. As the demographics changed, fewer kids were playing hockey and more kids were playing basketball. They made the Class 4A state tournament the year before, and they returned all five starters. This was the first basketball state tournament appearance for the school in eighty years. Vern's roster was loaded with size and speed. He instilled a system of constant full court man to man defense with intense ball pressure. He made almost all of his practice drills full court, including transitioning both from defense to offense or offense to defense. With this depth, he employed a nine or ten-man rotation. This would be another big crowd with a lot of fans from all over the cities.

The game was close from start to finish with many lead changes. With under twenty seconds to play we were ahead 83-82, they had the ball, and Vern called time out. They ran a set play to set up a shot off of a double screen. Jordan switched the screen and denied the pass to the shooter. The man with the ball scrambled to get open off of the dribble. Travis was all over him without fouling. A desperation shot was launched that hit the back rim and caromed high in the air. When the ball hit the floor, the game was over.

* * *

The next week we won at Simley on Tuesday 76-47, and we had the rest of the week off with no games. I planned to use these four practices to regroup as a coaching staff and a team, as well as to prepare for St Thomas. The coaching staff refined our list of goals for improvement, which we had written in November. The list included the execution of certain fundamentals, and a list of defensive adjustments. It also included a few new set plays and out-of-bounds plays that we saved for the tournament, and which we would use in games that we knew we weren't being scouted. We then asked the kids to create their own list. I reminded both the staff and the players that after this week we were down to ten practices before the tournament. The player's list ended up being about the same as the coach's list, which I had expected. I always did this because I believed that it gave the kids ownership in the direction of the ship. Hopefully the end result would be that the team would peak at tournament time. With the exception of the previous winter, my teams were known for doing this.

I also took time to remind the kids that this was a special time and that they needed to enjoy every moment and every day. In front of the entire team, I told the kids that we knew some of them were going to go on and play college ball, and that this might be the most fun team that they ever played on. I also told the scout squad in front of the entire team, that they were vitally important to our mission, and that their contribution was huge. As a head coach in today's environment, one never knew what these kids were hearing at home or from classmates. Keeping the team up and together had to be constantly worked on in subtle and different ways.

* * *

When I arrived for our Wednesday practice, the gym was still divided by the partition and the baskets were not down. The gym had a partition which hung on a track from baseline wall to baseline wall. The track was attached to the ceiling and it was powered by electricity. When it was not in use, it folded up like an accordion on the west end. When it was in use, it created a wall which divided the gym into two separate smaller gyms. The six baskets were hung from the ceiling by metal pipes which were hinged at the ceiling. Like the partition, they were winched up next to the ceiling by a steel cable when they were not in use. Many of the high school gyms that were built in the fifties had similar equipment.

In the past year, there had been problems with both the partition and the baskets getting stuck when they were being switched from one position to the other. When this happened, the janitors needed to bring in scaffolding to fix them, which would make most of the gym not usable for a day. Because of this, the only people who had access to the key which powered the electricity for the partition and the baskets were the janitors.

The physical education teachers usually had the partition out and the baskets up for the daily classes. At the end of the last hour of the school day, one janitor would come to the gym and switch the positions. We couldn't start our practice until this was done. Both the boys and the girls' basketball team used the gym for practice, alternating which team practiced early and which team practiced late. The team that practiced early had the gym from 3:00 to 5:00 and the team that practiced late had the gym from 5:00 to 7:00. At 7:00 the gyms were reserved for adult recreation or youth teams. Our practices were organized in a way that every minute of gym time was used, and our players were in constant motion from the beginning until the end. We utilized every minute of gym time in a predetermined manner.

When I entered the gym, I expected the partition to be folded up against the wall and the baskets down, or I expected to see the custodian finishing these tasks. On this day, nothing had been done. I went to look for a janitor, having no idea where one might be. When I didn't see one in either of the long hallways next to the gym, I walked into the athletic director's office and asked the secretary to have one paged. The announcement went out over the intercom, I went back to the gym, and still no janitor showed up. At 3:15 I got the varsity kids started doing drills that didn't require baskets in one half of the gym. I sent the B squad and 9th grade players and their coaches into the smaller gym. The janitor arrived at about 3:30.

I blew up at him in front of the kids and every person in the gym heard it. "It's three thirty and the baskets aren't even down yet. We've lost half an hour of practice time because you aren't doing your fucking job! Come on. Do your fucking job!" He looked at me and said calmly that he and the other custodian had been in the middle of doing something at the far end of the school and that it required two people. My response was that we only had two hours of gym time and that I expected to be able to use every minute, and I said it just as loudly as my first statement. Fifteen minutes later the partition was folded up against the wall, the baskets were down, and he walked out of the gym. He never said another word.

Half an hour later I told my assistants that I was going to go find the janitor and apologize to him, and I asked them if they could run practice. They agreed. When I found him, I said, "Can we talk?" He stopped what he was doing, turned to look at me and said "sure."

"I'm really sorry for what I said to you. I was really frustrated, but I never should have talked to you like I did. That wasn't right, and I want you to know that I know it wasn't right, and I'm apologizing. I promise you that I will never talk to you like that again."

He stuck out his hand and said "no problem, coach." We shook hands. He then said something to the effect that things happen and that he understood and that I had always treated him well. I then told him that I was going to tell the team that I had apologized to him, and that I expected them to give him the same respect that they always had. I never had another incident with him or any other custodian, and after this, we interacted as we had before, if not better. Ten minutes later I was back in the gym.

After practice I sat the entire team in a circle. I told them that I owed them an apology for how I yelled and swore at the custodian in front of them. I told them that when I left practice, I found the janitor and apologized to him. I shared the conversation of the apology and his response with them.

Then I told them that I had broken one of the most important rules that my mother had taught me, that you treat everybody the same. She taught me and my siblings that you give everyone the same interest and respect, and she lived by this. She had good friends in all of the socioeconomic classes of every town that we lived in growing up. She always praised people for their interests and passions, whether it was their new dress, their garden, their job, or their old junk car. I broke this rule. I talked to a janitor in a manner that I would never have used to talk to the principal. I shared all of these thoughts with the team. I told the team that this would never happen again, and that I expected them to give this custodian the same respect that they would give the principle, and that I most certainly would do this.

* * *

Before one of our varsity games in February I was stopped in the concourse by the father of one of my former Washburn players. He was African-American, and he lived in south Minneapolis. His son was a senior starting guard on my first team at Washburn. The son had just graduated from the U of M. The father told me that his youngest son was an eighth grader and that he wanted him at Richfield and playing for me. I told the father what I told every parent who approached me like this. I told him that he had every right to open enroll his son at Richfield and that we would treat his son no different than any other kid. I asked him if he was aware of The Choice is Yours program, and he said that he was. I also told him that some of the Richfield people weren't going to like it, and asked him if he was aware of this. His answer was that he was totally aware of it and that he could handle it just fine. I told him that if he moved to Richfield, the complainers would have nothing to complain about. He then told me that he coached his son in the Urban Stars program, and that he had a nephew who also played on the team. The nephew recently moved from the south side of Minneapolis to Bloomington, and the nephew would also probably be coming to Richfield. The nephew's name was Renard Robinson.

**

As we entered the last two weeks of the season everyone could feel the excitement building. We were to host St Thomas, Hill Murray, and Minneapolis North on Tuesday, Friday, and Saturday.

St Thomas and we were going to be seeded #1 and #2 in the section, one way or the other. If we were going to win the section, we would have to beat them. After they beat us at their place in January, this was the rematch game. If we could win, the next meeting would be the rubber match, and the game that counted. For this reason, we decided to not use our best game plan, but save some things for the tournament. I'm sure that they were doing the same. Mullenbach had been scouting our other conference opponents for a month, and he always scouted them when they played St Thomas. He had seen them play eight times. We played well and shot well, as did St Thomas. We made one more play than them as the game wound down, and the final score was 63-62 in our favor. Three days later we defeated Hill Murray76-65.

The Minneapolis North game was another 3pm game on a Saturday afternoon. Once again, the Polars were fighting Patrick Henry for the Minneapolis City Conference title. They were ranked #2 in the all-class Metro rankings with a record of 17-2. This was the first chance for our kids to play North, and a chance that they were waiting for. Adding to the anticipation was the fact that Dwayne Hardy was now a junior at North and part of their playing rotation. All of our kids really liked Dwayne, and he was their friend, but they wanted to beat him and his new team.

Bret McNeal was in his fifth year as the head coach. Bret played on one of the best North teams of all time, graduating in 1985. Both his junior and senior years the Polars finished as state runners-up, with close losses in the state finals both years to White Bear Lake. He went on to have an outstanding four-year career playing for Clem Haskins at Western Kentucky. After graduation he came back to Minneapolis, and immediately became active in the north side community. When the North job opened up in the spring of 2000, and there was no faculty member to take it, he was hired. He had on his coaching staff Ron Anderson and Reggie Perkins. Ron was a Minneapolis guy and a long-time coaching colleague of mine, who had been an assistant to Stu Starner at Montana State. Reggie was an up-and-coming Howard Pulley coach. With the natural talent from the neighborhood and an assistant at Howard Pulley, his teams were talented and deep. They won the 4A state title in 2003. This year's team was again full of players being recruited by D1 and D2 programs. Like us they played a full court man to man defense. It would be a great game.

People began filtering into the gym during the freshman game. By half-time of the junior varsity game the gym was more than half full. The Richfield fans had staked out their seats early. Besides the North fans and twin city high school basketball junkies, many high school coaches were in the stands to scout both teams for the tournament. When the game started, the gym was full and buzzing.

From the opening tip, every possession was hard fought, with both teams trading small runs. Both teams were picking up full court, playing in the passing lanes in the half court, and boxing out hard. We decided to play behind their posts. For most of the first half we kept their posts off of the block, and it worked. After one quarter we were ahead 23-17. Late in the first half Bret called time out.

Late in the half they began establishing position on the block and dumping the ball inside. After they scored three times in a row on inside feeds, Lance and Alcindor said to me, "Jim, we've gotta front the post." I answered, "I know, but I don't wanna do it now. We'll make the change at half time. I want them to spend their halftime talking about how they have to keep on going inside." As I put my head in the huddle Ray said, "coach, we wanna front the post." I then told the kids exactly what I told my assistants. We matched them two more baskets and went in at halftime ahead 46-35.

The second half we dead fronted the post and we stole the ball two out of the first three possessions, one on a direct pass to the post and one on a lob pass, before Bret called another time out. By this time, we were up 51-37. They made a run at us to close the margin to 66-56 after three quarters. Early in the fourth quarter, the ball went out of bounds in front of our bench off of a North player, and North called time out again. I made one quick point to the kids to begin the time out, and I turned it over to Lance. I stepped away, looked at the scoreboard, and took a deep breath. When I went back to the huddle, he was diagramming 'side out 2'. I took another deep breath, and quietly said to myself "oh my god".

'Side out 2' was an out of bounds play that Lance picked up while playing in Europe. Jordan Noonan was the inbounder who stood in front of our bench. Ray Brown was to stand in front of Jordan and face him. Ray would then set a down screen for Dustin Dreifke who was standing at the top of the circle. As Dustin broke for the ball, Ray would then begin to cut back to the ball side wing, before receiving a back screen from Bill Bauman at the free throw line. The play also involved Travis Brown cutting hard to the ball side corner, which totally cleared out the back side of the court. After faking the pass to Dreifke, Jordan would throw the ball at the basket where Ray was supposed to go after it, get it, and score.

When we ran the play in practice, Ray would usually catch the ball, bring it down, and go back up and score. Maybe one out of five times, he would catch the ball in the air and dunk it. Besides involving a long alley-oop pass, the play usually was close to a five second count. It was not what I would call a high percentage play. We had never run the play in a game before. Nobody knew we had it. The kids loved it. When we practiced it, they would all look at me and smile, because they knew I wasn't in love with it.

The kids ran the play flawlessly, and the North kids had no idea what was coming. Jordan threw a picture-perfect high lob pass which came down a foot in front of the rim. Ray who was wide open went up off of two legs, and met the ball when it was a foot above the basket. He spun 180 degrees to the middle of the lane, and threw down a ripping two hand dunk. The place went ballistic. My friend Dan O'Brien was sitting in the middle of the North section with his three sons. He later said, "I couldn't believe it. Even the brothers from North jumped up and were high-fiving each other."

As the game wore on North went away from their set plays and they began spacing the court and driving on our slower players. We switched to our pack defense which let them easily swing the ball, but gave us more help on their drives. During two time-outs, I preached to the kids," one tough shot and box out". With three minutes to go in the game, we went to our spread offense. Dreifke and Noonan hit 6 of 6 free throws and we ended up with an 87-76 victory.

With under a minute to go and a ten-point lead, I sat down and scanned the crowd on the other side of the gym. I saw a lot of people who were seeing these teams for the first time. I also saw a lot of high school coaches. It was a crystal-clear day outside and the light from the sinking sun low in the south-west sky was directly hitting the row of windows high on the west wall. On these late winter days this sunlight illuminated the north half of the gym and gave the gym a completely different ambiance. I leaned back in my chair in the sunlight and reflected. We were beating a great team in our own gym. When I thought of all these friends of mine in the crowd and how well we executed, it was one of the most satisfying wins of my coaching career. It was made even better a minute later. When my friend Ron Anderson shook my hand after the game, he looked me in the eye and forcefully said, "Jim, you got a great ball club."

* * *

Heading into the last week of the season we were tied for first place in the conference with Tartan. We both won on Tuesday which set up a Friday night winner take all home game for the conference title. Then both teams would move on to the section tournament with high hopes, us in Class 3A and Tartan in Class 4A.

It is customary for head coaches to meet and talk during the preliminary games. The home coach always asks the visiting coach if he needs anything for his locker room. Then the conversation turns to each other's teams and how their seasons are going. Things like common opponents, parent issues, and summer programs are discussed. Younger coaches often use older coaches as sounding boards and mentors. Late in the year, both coaches always discuss their upcoming section tournaments, especially if they are in different sections. Sometimes non-basketball subjects are covered. When we played St Thomas, Mike Sjoberg and I always spent at least ten minutes comparing last summer's Boundary Waters trips. With Mark Klingsporn and I, it was always a fun conversation, because we saw things the same way. We were both older coaches, our teams played similar styles, and our schools were located in demographically similar areas, plus he was also a Boundary Waters guy. This time when we met before the game, the mood of the conversation was almost festive. The first thing I said after shaking Mark's hand was, "this is going to be fun." He smiled and said, "I know. I know. These kinds of games don't come along every year." As we sat and caught up with each other, we had to talk loudly, because the gym was getting loud. The adrenaline rush was beginning to kick in. It always reminded me of the feeling that I got while canoeing a river, just before running a set of rapids. It was like back paddling in the calm water, but you knew the white water was coming.

When both teams hit the floor for warm ups, there wasn't an open seat. People were lined up and standing in both end-zones ten deep. It was the biggest crowd yet in my four years at Richfield. The game was just as good.

Although we didn't shoot well, we played one of our best games of the year, as did Tartan. The Titans jumped out to an early 6-point lead, and kept that margin until late in the game. With 3:35 to play, we trailed by 10 points. Then we got hot, and Ray and Travis took over. At the end of regulation Tartan had the ball and went for one shot. They got a contested running jump shot near the free throw line that rimmed in and out. Bill got the rebound and we were into overtime.

As the clock ticked down in overtime, they again had the ball but we had the lead 62-61. They ran a set play which we defended well. They backed the ball out again and started over. The clock was now under ten seconds. The ball was on the wing in front of the Tartan bench. Their 6-8 player Urule Igbavboa broke to the top of the key. Ray was guarding him and denying him the ball. Urule back cut, caught a perfect back door pass, took one dribble into the lane, and launched himself into the air. He held the ball high in his right hand as he came down and slammed down a dunk, for a 63-62 win. We got the ball in quick, fired two passes up court and missed a 40-foot runner. The Tartan fans stormed the court. As Mark and I shook hands we both said, "great game, great game…go win the state title." We could hardly hear each other.

When I got to the locker room, I told the kids that this was a tough loss. This was not what we had envisioned, finishing second in the conference. I also told them that Tartan was one of the top ten teams in the state, and losing to them twice by a basket was nothing to be ashamed of. I finished by saying, "think about two weeks from now. Two weeks from now, we could be section champs. Two weeks from now, if we're section champs, this game will be ancient history. We have to learn from it, pull together, and get back to work. Think about the open gyms. Think about how many hours you guys have spent playing basketball in the summers. This is just one game. The most fun part of the season is just beginning."

* * *

The next Monday I received a letter in my mailbox at the high school. It was in an envelope with both the senders and recipient's address handwritten. I opened it and read it. It was dated the day after the Tartan game.

February 26, 2005

Coach Dimick:

Clay and Smith instead of Noonan and Bauman. You are a coaching genius. If Brown, Brown, Dreifke, Noonan, and Bauman had played the entire game, you would have beaten Tartan by 10 points.

Dean Torgeson
7439 Lyndale Ave so

I showed it to Mike Karnas. He laughed. I told Mike that I was tempted to call Torgeson. Mike said, "you should, you should, that would be great."

My normal protocol when receiving suspicious looking letters in my school mailbox was to open them, see if they were signed, and if there was no signature, toss them in the waste basket. Jim Baker taught me this. His logic was that if you read them, you were allowing the writer to get to you.

If you didn't read them, you were taking the writer's power away. In the four years that I was at Richfield, I got about a half dozen anonymous letters. All ended up in the waste basket without being read.

I asked Mike for the phone book. I looked up the number and dialed it. He picked up right away. I said, "Dean Torgeson."

"Speaking."

"Dean, this is Jim Dimick." There was a long pause. Then I heard laughing, "So you got my letter."

"Yah, and you know what I liked about your letter? You signed your name. Most times people don't sign their name. You had the guts to sign your name. I like that."

"Well, I always sign my name. What did you think of my letter?"

"Well, yah, I want to explain the reasoning for my substitutions." I then explained our eight-man playing rotation to him, and how I divided up the minutes. I explained to him how I wanted my shooter's legs fresh at the end of the game. I said that I agreed with him that Brown, Brown, Dreifke, Noonan, and Bauman were our best five. He then asked me a couple of other questions about the team. I ended up asking him about his family, job, and how long he had lived in Richfield. He added that he had been a fan since 1970 and that his favorite player of all time was Brian Amman. At the end I made it a point to tell him to stop and shake my hand next time he was at a game.

I hung up the phone and looked at Karnas, who while sitting at his desk had heard the entire conversation. He was laughing, stood up, high fived me, and said, "That was great! You both gained a friend."

At practice I showed it to my assistants and told them about the phone call. They all laughed. For the remainder of the season, they often referred to me as 'coaching genius'.

***

The section seedings were as expected. We and St Thomas were #1 and #2 followed by #3 Holy Angels, and #4 Simley. We would open by hosting #8 Farmington in the quarterfinals the first Thursday in March. The semifinals would be a doubleheader the following Monday at Tartan, and the finals would be a single game Thursday at Tartan. All of our scouting reports were 90% finalized and written on what we saw as five teams that were clearly better than the rest. We saw these teams to be St Thomas, Mankato East, Mankato West, Rocori, and Shakopee. The final *StarTribune* Metro rankings were as follows:

1.	*Hopkins*	*25-1*	*4A*	*2*
2.	*Mpls North*	*20-3*	*4A*	*5*
3.	*Shakopee*	*24-1*	*3A*	*5*
4.	*Richfield*	*20-4*	*3A*	*3*
5.	*Eastview*	*22-4*	*4A*	*6*
6.	*Mpls Henry*	*21-5*	*4A*	*5*
7.	*Tartan*	*21-5*	*4A*	*3*
8.	*Champlin Park*	*23-3*	*4A*	*1*
9.	*Lakeville*	*20-5*	*4A*	*7*
10.	*Maple Grove*	*21-4*	*4A*	*8* [36]

The winner of our section would open up at state playing the winner of Section 7, which was located in the northeast part of the state. Matt Mullenbach would scout this section by attending both the semifinals and the finals in Duluth. If the top teams won, Rocori would play one of the Mankato's in a quarterfinal game at state. We would meet that winner in a semifinal. In the other half of the bracket, Shakopee was heavily favored to march to the finals. As I saw it, our three toughest games would be in the section finals, and the last two games of state. Of the top six teams, Mankato East had the worst draw. There were three good teams in their section and they were seeded #2. To win state they would have to win five consecutive games that could go either way, two in their section against Marshall and Mankato West, and three games at state, most likely against Rocori, us or St Thomas, and Shakopee. Mullenbach, who saw St Thomas play eleven times said to me more than once, "the best team that we are going to have to beat will be St Thomas. I see the section final game as the most difficult."

As we had been doing since Christmas, we used the first week of March practices to prepare for Farmington, Simley, St Thomas and any of these top five teams. In order to defeat St Thomas, we would have to neutralize their 6-10 post Bryce Webster. We had three post defenses ready for them, one of which they hadn't seen from us. Our game plan was to defend Farmington's post with this new defense, unless St Thomas was scouting us. If St Thomas had a scout at the game, we would not use it. We knew that Farmington and Simley would also play a 2-3 zone and some triangle and 2. We expected both Rocori and Shakopee to defend us with these defenses, so while we were preparing for Farmington, we were also preparing for both Rocori and Shakopee. We emphasized defending the out of bounds plays that St Thomas and any of these teams ran.

The last thing that a coach wants is to go into a big tournament game with one practice, or no practice, to prepare for an opponent. I believed that we had to always think one, two, or three games ahead, while at the same time preparing one game at a time.

* * *

We opened up the tournament with a 93-42 victory over Farmington at home. The semifinals would be at Tartan where we would meet Simley. They had defeated Hill-Murray 49-45. We had somewhat of a stigma about playing at Tartan. We had never won there, losing four times to Tartan and to Holy Angels the year before. Mike Karnas brought it up in the athletic office that week, mentioning that it was a tough place to play with the open areas behind the baskets. "So, it's a tough place to play, so what, go over there and play and just have fun. You win the section, you're gonna love that gym."

We struggled offensively against Simley in the first half. They were playing a good 2-3 zone defense and we were missing open shots. In the second half the shots started dropping and we made two quick runs. After they called two timeouts and the third quarter buzzer sounded, we were ahead 55-34. The final score was 64-54. In the other game St Thomas defeated Holy Angels 51-43.

* * *

The build up to the St Thomas game was everything that I expected. Some years two teams are stacked in one section and everyone anticipates the impending showdown. In Section 3, this was one of those years. The big defensive decision that we had to make was to front or play behind their center. We were going to begin the game by playing behind him and not double teaming him. The key to containing him was to keep him off of the block. Our three seniors would take turns guarding him; Bill Bauman, Adam Smith, and Octavius Crawford. All three would be giving up about 6 inches to Bryce, but all three were also physical. They had to establish position on the block, keep moving, and make him catch the ball off of the block. Our game plan was to shut down their shooters and make Bryce beat us.

At halftime we would use the old trick that I had learned from Dave Buss, of changing our defense. We would double team Bryce from the help side. If he passed the ball to the open player our perimeter defenders would rotate men. We had saved this rotation for this game. Whenever a defense relied on rotations, like the NBA teams, they were vulnerable to back cuts. Because St Thomas always spaced the perimeter perfectly with four shooters who could all bury threes, if we double teamed, they could blow open a game in a hurry. It was a case of pick your poison. Late in the game, we might even have Ray guard Bryce and dead front him, which was our basic defense. This would throw a third defense at St Thomas.

On offense we also had four new wrinkles to our set plays and out of bounds plays that we practiced and saved all year. Lance used them in a few games when we knew that nobody was scouting us.

Tuesday and Wednesday were review days on both offense and defense, with a lot of shooting. We had been preparing for this game off and on for six weeks. I was sure that it was no different in the St Thomas gym.

At three o'clock I drove over to the high school for a pep fest. The stands in the gym were full of the students and the air was electric. I stood with my assistants in the end zone area, watched the skits and we talked and laughed. Many faculty members came by to congratulate us and to wish us luck. I ended up staying and talking after the gym had emptied. I walked into the parking lot. As I approached my car, I saw a piece of paper stuck under the windshield wiper. I took it and opened it up. It was written with a pen on a piece of lined spiral notebook paper, DON'T CHOKE AGAIN EVERYBODY WILL BE WATCHING. I smiled, folded it up, and put it in my pocket. I imagined my high school coach Jed Dommeyer seeing it. He would simply burst out laughing, shake his head with his smile and bark out "go get'em Dimmer!" I went to my athletic club for a hard weight workout.

* * *

The gym filled up early. Unlike our previous games at Tartan, we now sat in the east end of the gym, where the Tartan team normally sat. Most high school gyms had a set of folding chairs for the coaches and players. At Tartan the distance between the out-of-bounds line and the first row of bleachers was minimal. Both teams sat in the bottom row of the fold out bleachers with fans sitting right behind them. Behind us the Richfield adult fans were situated. Directly across from us was the Richfield student body. The St Thomas fans were similarly aligned on the west end of the gym. Also in the crowd were players from teams that weren't playing that night, scouting coaches, and members of the Twin Cities basketball community. Many people were already standing in the large open end zone areas on both ends of the court. It was another standing room only crowd.

St Thomas won the opening tip. Both teams traded a few baskets and mostly missed shots. Then they got hot and we kept missing. I had hoped to establish a small lead early in the game and control the game. It didn't happen. After one quarter we were down 26-17. The shooting reversed itself in the second quarter and at halftime the score was 36-36.

We opened up the second half by double-teaming Webster. We ended up forcing three turnovers, with Ray blocking two of Webster's shots from the help side. Then they hit two consecutive three pointers. We quickly went back to playing them straight up, and playing behind him. We continued to trade baskets in the third quarter, and heading into the final eight minutes we were down 55-53.

Then they went on a run. I asked Lance and Alcindor if we should call time out and change our defense. Both said no. They also said it was time to start doing more set plays. I called time out with five minutes to play. I told the kids we were keeping the same defense, "no open threes, make Bryce beat us." I also told them to look to Lance on offense, and that he was going to begin calling sets. He then called one. Dreifke dribbled the ball up the court, we ran the play, and Travis drilled an open jumper off a pick by Jordan. But again, all we could do was trade stops. Webster banked in a turnaround jumper to put them up 69-61 with 3:31 on the clock. We had the ball and I called time out.

We ran another set play and Ray scored to cut the lead to 69-63. I looked up at the clock as the St Thomas point guard dribbled the ball up court. Ray was pressuring him with his butt down in his defensive stance and his nose on the ball. As the ball crossed the mid-court line, Ray did something that I never let him do, and which he hadn't done since sixth grade. He let the dribbler go around him to his left, and he reached around behind the dribbler with his right hand, and he tapped the ball towards the top of the key. Dreifke caught it and quickly threw Ray a soft pass up court which Ray caught, dribbled, and softly laid in. Just like that it was 69-65.

Mike Sjoberg, the St Thomas coach, stood up and signaled his kids to spread the court. After half a dozen passes the ball was deflected off a St Thomas player's leg out of bounds. We pushed the ball and after Ray got a nice touch at 15 feet, he drove the middle and dropped in a jump shot. We were down two. They burned 30 seconds off of the clock before getting the ball into Webster. We fouled him before he could shoot. With 30 seconds to play he missed the front end of the one and one. Dreifke pushed the ball up the court and called time out in front of our bench. After the time out we ran a set play which they defended well. We didn't force a shot and ran our offense, with every player looking to take the ball to the basket. Then with 12 seconds left, Ray again drove the middle and was fouled by point guard Sean Birr. It was Birr's fifth foul. St Thomas called time out. Ray made the first free throw. They called time out again. He missed the second free throw, and the score was 69-68. I looked up at the clock and called time out. There were 9.8 seconds left.

The time out was a review of what we practiced many times. We would line up in a man-to-man press. Jordan, Ray, and Travis would guard the three players closest to the in-bounder. They were to face guard or play between their man and the ball, in order to deny a direct inbounds pass. They would switch all screens and crossing of cutters. Bill Bauman guarded Webster near the St Thomas basket, to deny a long pass. Nobody would guard the in-bounder. Dustin Dreifke was then free to float between the free throw line and mid-court, hopefully to pick off a lob pass. When the time out ended, I looked up at the 9.8 seconds on the clock again. The thought of the eagle feather popped into my head. I felt very serene. I had never before felt so relaxed in such a moment.

Both teams lined up near the basket directly in front of our bench. Security workers stood on the sidelines in front of both student sections and were telling the students to stay off the court. The referee handed the ball to the St Thomas player and he started his count. The Cadets screened and cut and nobody was open. Twice the in-bounder began to pass and then held back. With the five second count clicking down, he threw a pass to the opposite sideline near mid court, directly in front or our student section. Dreifke darted over, caught the ball cleanly with two hands and instantly fired a pass to Ray near the top of the key. Ray took one dribble and elevated for a wide-open jumper as the gym fell silent. With his eyes focused on the rim, he began his release, and then fired another two-handed pass to his right to Travis who was streaking towards the basket. Travis caught it at the edge of the lane, went up, and cleanly laid it in. St Thomas called time out. There was a deafening roar. The clock showed 3.8 seconds. We were ahead 70-69.

We again reviewed what we had practiced many times. Now all of our defenders would be behind the free throw line. Bill would guard the in-bounder with his hands high in the air, and be ready to avoid a pick if the in-bounder ran down the baseline. Four defenders would deny all long passes and we would give them the short inbounds pass near the end line. Once again, the referee handed the ball to the St Thomas player. They ran a play to free up a cutter near mid court and nobody was open. Finally, Darius Redd ran back towards the ball and caught a pass on the far sideline. He turned, dribbled up court, and launched a shot from half court. It landed in the end zone area to the right of the backboard. I looked at the officials who were signaling game over. Behind them the entire Richfield student section was avalanching through the security line and onto the court. There was instant pandemonium in an all school on the court celebration. It was so loud I couldn't hear myself think. As I turned to the Richfield bench, I felt a hit in the chest and was almost knocked over. Somebody had tackled me and was bearhugging me. It was Martha. Her beautiful body was pressed against mine and she was laughing hysterically, "oh my Jimmy, oh my Jimmy." It was a surreal moment. Here I was hugging my wife in front of over a thousand people, with everyone screaming and cheering and high fiving. I will never forget the feeling.

I told her to stay where she was. I quickly organized the players and we walked towards the St Thomas players and coaches to shake hands. After the presentation of the trophy, the celebration lasted over half an hour. High fives and hugs were exchanged everywhere by people of all ages, accompanied by the constant sound of clicking cameras. A procession of handshakes and hugs went on and on. Jim Baker gave Martha and me a three-person hug. Staunch fans who attended lots of games like Brenda Biever, Mike Karnas, Jay Herman, and Dick Hughes all waited their turn. Mike kept repeating himself, "I told ya coach, I told ya coach." By far the biggest smile, was the smile on the face of my Dad, who sat with my brothers and their wives in the top row. As things wound down, I organized the kids for a team picture.

Ten minutes later I was standing outside the team bus. It was a mild March night. I turned on my cell phone. I called my LeSueur buddy, Dave Woodruff. He and Dick Moriarty were at the section championship game in Mankato, where East was playing West. Woody picked up right away, "East won, 50-49 in overtime." He then described the game and the finish. West finished the year 26-1. When I climbed onto the bus, I told the team. Then I sat down and quoted Al McGuire to my assistants, "if you're gonna win the whole thing, the last second shot has to go your way. This year, it went our way, and it went East's way."

After riding the team bus back to high school, I drove home to meet Martha. We were then going to meet the coaches at a Richfield restaurant. A half mile from home, I pulled into the parking lot of my swimming hole, Crescent Beach. I walked out on the ice and looked up at the stars. It was a clear night with no moon and the stars were spectacular. There was a light moist wind from the west. I could feel the power of the earth through the lake and the water and the ice. I savored the moment.

***

The next day's article in the *StarTribune* read:

"We've been talking about going to state for two years," Ray Brown said. "That has been our goal again since the beginning of the season. It is so super to finally be going."… "This is the biggest thing to happen for Richfield in a long time," Travis Brown said. "This is huge."…"If you're going to be a champion, at some point you are going to have to rally," Spartans coach Jim Dimick said. "That's what we were able to do tonight, rally". [37]

I went in to my office early. I saw both Tom Wahlberg and Gary Neubauer. Both were laughing. Gary, who watched Hopkins play the night before said, "I know you're smiling today!"

We practiced at 10am. We handed out scouting reports on Grand Rapids, and did a walk through. We were going to come right at them with our basic defense, hard ball pressure, deny perimeter passes, dead front the post, and switch the ball reversal screen. It would be a combination of quickness, length, and style that they hadn't seen. After the win on Thursday at Tartan, Mark Klingsporn talked to me. He saw Grand Rapids play in a Christmas tournament. He told me, "play your defense and you'll beat them by 15 points." Mullenbach concurred. It was a good first round match-up for us. Later in the practice, Ron Haggstrom, a writer from the *StarTribune* showed up. He was doing interviews and taking pictures.

***

The following Sunday the *StarTribune* ran the article. The headline ran across the top of the page. Beneath the headline was a photo of Ray and Travis taken at practice the previous day.

Browns co-star in a Richfield revival

His braces glistened from the gymnasium's lights. Travis Brown's smile was even larger than usual.

Ray Brown and his father were embracing each other at the end of the court. They were sharing tears of triumph and relief.

A trip to the state tournament had been two years in the making for the Browns (no relation), 31 for the city of Richfield...Richfield made its last state tournament appearance in 1974.

The scene following Richfield's thrilling 70-69 comeback victory over St Thomas Academy in the Section 3 championship epitomized the Spartans' Division I prospects. Ray Brown wears his emotions on his sleeve. Travis Brown has a constant smile, one that probably is apparent even when he's doing homework.

"Ray and Travis are alike in so many ways, but that isn't one of them," Richfield coach Jim Dimick said. Ray is more of an emotional player.".....

"We always know where each other is on the court," Travis said. "We really complement each other."

People throughout the community have come in droves to pack Richfield's gymnasium the past two seasons to watch the school's high-flying act. The tandem leaves fans gasping and wondering what the Browns might do next to top their previous acrobatic maneuver.

"Both are quick jumpers and play above the rim," Dimick said. "They are fun to watch and enjoy being around each other."

Ray is closing in on 40 dunks this season and can touch the top of the backboard square. Travis isn't far behind.

The bond the two have formed since being united four years ago-when Dimick took over as Richfield's coach after leaving Minneapolis Washburn-nearly didn't transpire. Ray transferred from Washburn to stay with his previous mentor. Travis was on the verge of attending Holy Angels.

"I was real close to going to Holy Angels," said Travis, who attended a public school in Richfield from kindergarten through eighth grade. "They are our rival. That probably wouldn't have looked too good."

Instead they joined forces, forming one of the state's most formidable athletic duos. They both average just more than 20 points and around 7 rebounds a game.

"We're a good one-two punch, but it's because of our teammates," Ray said. "They make us better. They do all the little things players don't get credit for and people don't notice."

One of which is to set continuous picks for the Browns to curl off.

"It's kind of a running joke," Travis said. "A lot of people think our teammates are only on the floor to set screens for us. We all do a good job of working together."

Much like the last Spartans basketball team that went to state in 1974. Bruce Hoffarber was the starting point guard, on a team that included Steve Bender, Brian Denman, Bruce Kottom, and Paul Meissner.

"As good as we were in the '70s, these guys are better athletes," Hoffarber said. "It's been a long time since they last went to the state tournament. They have made Richfield proud again."

Hoffarber will try to work a trip to Target Center into his busy schedule for another reason, too. His youngest son, Blake is a sophomore guard on Hopkins' state-bound team. Hoffarber's oldest son, Adam, was a member of the Royals' Class 4A championship team in 2002.

"I grew up in Richfield so I still consider that my home," Hoffarber said. "I think they'll do very well in the state tournament."

The Browns hope it's one step farther than the 1974 team. They were the Class 2A (large school) runner-up for the second consecutive year.

"We are really focused right now," Ray Brown said. "We've been on a mission all year, and winning a state championship would complete it." [38]

* * *

We would use our Monday and Tuesday practices to get ready for two games. We would meet Grand Rapids Wednesday afternoon. If we won, we would play again Thursday afternoon against either Rocori or Mankato East. If we won again, we would have a Friday practice to prepare for the finals which were on Saturday night, most likely against Shakopee. We were already well prepared for Rocori, Mankato East, and Shakopee. Grand Rapids had half a dozen set plays that we had seen before, and that were similar to the some of the set plays of the other three teams. In terms of game preparation, there was no one opponent whose style was dissimilar from the others.

We also knew we were going to see some zone, as well as a triangle and two with three players in a 1-2 zone and two players guarding Ray and Travis man to man. We saw this defense before. I called Dave Buss to ask him how to attack it, and he told me how to position our players and tweak our screening action a little. Ray and Travis would stay more on the inside, set more screens and then face up to the ball. We had practiced against this all winter. I was also confident that the other players could hit wide open shots against this defense. Jordan, Dustin, and Santino were all very good shooters and capable of hitting a bunch in a row. We were reviewing and preparing for everybody. If Shakopee got upset and didn't make it to the finals, we would deal with it. We would have seen the other team play twice, and we would have one practice to get ready for them.

When I got to the high school Monday, the halls were covered with pictures of the 1960, 1973, and 1974 teams, alongside slogans of 'one mission'.

Jim Baker was in his usual jovial mood. He told me that his AD buddies were calling and giving him crap about going to state. They were saying that it was fitting that he would have all of this extra work to do in his last year. He said, "you know, this creates a lot of work for me, don't you?" Jim was ready to retire in June.

Monday after practice Mike Karnas and Steve Bender spoke to the team. They played on the 1973 and 1974 state runner-up teams. They described what it was like thirty years earlier, and how the community got behind them. Mike had lived his entire life in Richfield. Steve was the high school coach at Rosemount. They talked about how the friendships of their team had lasted a lifetime. "You'll run into one of your teammates in ten years, and maybe you haven't seen each other, and it'll be just like you were hanging out yesterday. Nothing's changed." The final point of their message was to enjoy each other and the moment, because it was a once in a lifetime experience.

We were eager to play again on the longer NBA court at the Target Center. We practiced on Monday at Minneapolis Community College with its college length court. Jay Pivec had been coaching there for 15 years assisted by his buddy Ron Gates. Nobody worked harder at it than these guys and they were a perennial power in Minnesota D3 JUCO basketball. They had taken many inner-city kids and helped them get two-year degrees and advance on to four-year degrees. After practice I asked Jay to address the kids about how their team had made its run to the national finals in 1993. Jay, who loved to talk and always had something to say about everything, eagerly obliged.

Most of the teams would be staying in downtown Minneapolis at the same hotel. I decided to not have the team stay downtown. I wanted them eating at home, sleeping in their own beds, attending classes for a half day, and shooting at their own baskets in the RHS gym.

***

Grand Rapids won the Iron Range Conference and finished the season strong. Their overall record was 20-9. They were coached by Dan Elhard who was in his third year, and assisted by Ron Eidelbes, a retired teacher and the former head coach. They had a good mix of height, quickness, and shooters. They were a good out state Class 3A team. However, in our conference, they would have finished in fourth or fifth place.

Grand Rapids was a town of 10,000 people located on the Mississippi River 100 miles downstream from Lake Itasca. On a map, the river forms a question mark in north central Minnesota before beginning its flow to the south. The town is located on the upper right curve of the question mark. After meandering through crystal clear lakes and marshes, the current gains speed as it nears its first falls at Grand Rapids. The town sprang up around the falls as a lumber milling town, when the white pine of the northern forest was logged off to build the cities of the upper Midwest. A few miles to the northeast, is the southwest tip of the Mesabi Iron Range. As a historical member of the Iron Range Conference, Grand Rapids had a long and storied tradition in all sports, especially hockey.

***

We played at 4pm on Wednesday, which was the last of the quarterfinal games. We met for a team breakfast at the Richfield VFW club. The VFW was half a mile north of the high school, and was a community gathering spot. Plus, they had great food. Their manager, staff, and patrons always made us feel welcome. The basketball board picked up the tab for the meal. After eating, we went back to the gym to shoot.

In the first quarterfinal game Andover defeated Monticello 57-56 in overtime. Shakopee escaped an upset by Albert Lea with a 42-39 victory. After Albert Lea missed five free throws in the final five minutes, the Sabers took the lead on a lay-up with 20 seconds to play. After another Albert Lea turnover, they made two free throws with 5.6 seconds to play. Albert Lea finished the year with a record of 15-14.

As we stood outside of our locker room at the Target Center, the Mankato East players came running down the hallway and celebrating. They had just defeated Rocori and legendary coach Bob Brink 57-49. East trailed 25-19 at the half, and 38-36 after three quarters. After six lead changes in the fourth quarter, the Cougars went ahead for good with 3:26 to go. When I walked out to the arena, I saw my wife Martha, my folks, my two brothers and their families, and my college and canoe buddies sitting in the front rows.

Grand Rapids had 7 turnovers in the first quarter and we slowly pulled away. The quarter ended with us ahead 20-14. Then Jordan hit back-to-back jumpers sandwiched by baskets by Ray and Travis. They were running their offense near the sidelines, and they were out of their comfort zone. At the half we were up 42-23. After the half, they cut the lead to 44-33. We went on a mini-run and they answered it. At the end of three quarters, they were back in the game, with a score of 55-42.

Both teams traded baskets for most of the fourth quarter. With 3:01 to play and a 61-50 lead we spread the court. There was one key possession in the fourth quarter when they ran three consecutive set plays in succession and couldn't get a shot. When a player finally was open, he missed. Then Ray tipped and stole two consecutive ball reversal passes followed by dunks. With 0:55 to play and a 71-53 lead, both teams put in the substitutes. The final was 73-53, in a game that was closer than the final score.

After the teams shook hands our players ran to the corner of the arena in front of the Richfield student section and they celebrated with the student body. As I was walking toward the arched overhang to leave the arena, I was stopped by a man in his seventies who reached out to shake my hand. He quickly said, "you're doing a great job with that team Jim, boy, do you have them playing defense." It was Don Hill, my high school football coach, and assistant basketball coach. Coach Hill was a great teacher, a brilliant coach, and a great motivator. He was also a great recruiter, having recruited all of the best athletes in my hometown of Northfield to go out for football. He left teaching and coaching a few years after I graduated to become the president of the MEA (Minnesota Education Association). He followed that by becoming the long-time executive director of the NEA (National Education Association). He was one of my coaching icons. We talked for five minutes. This conversation was one of the high points of my coaching career.

In the next edition of the *Grand Rapids Herald-Review*, Ted Anderson quoted me, *"We work real hard at pressuring without fouling...and, we had some big put-back baskets."* He also quoted Rapids coach Dan Elhard, *"A lot of teams might have just rolled over and gave up. But our guys battled and boy, if a couple of those shots had rolled in, we could have had it down to six or seven points and it could have been anybody's game. But I am just proud of these guys for the way they worked right to the final whistle."* [39]

We took the team bus back to the high school after the game. Then I made copies of the Mankato East scouting reports. We did a fifteen-minute walk through of their offense and reviewed the game plan in our own gym. Then I drove home with my wife. Thursday morning would come early. The first semifinal game was at noon followed by our game at 2pm.

* * *

We had been pointing to a showdown game with one of the Mankato schools since the prior winter. Like Grand Rapids, Mankato was a river town. It was located on the Minnesota River in the middle of the southern part of the state. The city added a second public high school in the early seventies. As with many communities that split into two high schools, the end result is that one high school is more affluent than the other. East was the less affluent of the two, and included most of the minority students. These were African-Americans, West Africans, Sudanese, Hispanics, and other minorities.

East entered the game with a 24-5 record, including a 62-57 victory over Tartan in February at East. Like their rival West, they ran a double post offense with 6-7 Mitch Gossen and 6-6 Chop Tang at the two inside positions. Chop Tang was a bruising 6-6 Sudanese who was a D1 recruit, and an acquaintance of our player Ojullo Madho through the connections of their immigrant community. Gossen was a top level D2 recruit. Their physical point guard, Terrance Walton was 5-9 and quick. They also had another athletic African-American player in 6-2 wing Jesse Graves. They had more shooters to go with these players. Our players knew their players from AAU games. Their set plays included a number of high ball screens to post ups. We expected them to play us both man and zone. Our game plan on offense was to drive on Tang to force him to move his feet, and hopefully get him in foul trouble. Coach Joe Madson was in his fifth year, and he had the program humming. They would be disciplined in every way on both ends of the court.

* * *

We had another great meal at the VFW at 9:30. A number of the veterans came over to talk to the kids and wish us luck. These were retired guys who served in World War II and Korea. There were two card games in the other corner of the restaurant, which occasionally produced friendly banter and laughs. Looking at these retired vets, I couldn't imagine these kids all going off to war the summer after graduation. That's what many of these older guys did. And we were looking at the lucky ones who had made it back. I made it a point to talk about this to the team, and to remind them to always treat these guys with the utmost respect. As we filed out, there was a feeling of community that encompassed three generations. We could all feel it. They had our back.

Shakopee defeated Andover 69-51 in the first semifinal game. After trailing 31-30 at halftime, the Sabers opened up an 8-point lead early in the second half and then made 15 of 16 free throws in the fourth quarter. Andover finished the season 19-10.

* * *

Our game started slowly with both teams missing shots on their first few possessions. Then things began to go our way. Our shots started falling, and Jordan drilled a three to put us up 12-5 with 4:31 to play in the quarter. Chop Tang who was guarding Ray quickly picked up his second foul. Then on two consecutive possessions the East point guard Terrance Walton drove the middle and when our defenders helped, he dished the ball for open shots. Dreifke couldn't contain him. During the next free throw, I called Dustin over and told him to switch men with Travis. Travis kept Walton in front of him for the rest of the game. At the end of the first quarter, we were up 17-10.

Then Tang picked up his third foul. This was followed by Ray and Travis hitting jump shots in the lane on back-to-back possessions. With less than four minutes to play in the half they ran a set play that began with a post setting a ball screen at the top of the key. We practiced double teaming the ball, and rotating defenders against this play. We had saved this defense for them, and they didn't know that we had it. It was a gamble and the gamble went our way. With Travis and Bill Bauman double teaming their point guard, he passed to a teammate breaking to the top of the key. Dreifke rotated on to him. When he passed to another Cougar, Jordan picked the ball cleanly and passed to Ray. Ray then hit Travis with a bullet pass streaking towards the basket. At the end of the half, we ran a 1-4 low set play with Ray on the top of the key with the ball. He elevated over the defender and the step-back three went in to extend our lead to 42-31.

To start the third quarter, we tried a Dave Buss move of switching to a zone and staying in it until they scored two possessions in a row. We ended up staying in the 2-3 zone for the remainder of the quarter. East changed defenses to a triangle and two. Both teams had gone cold. On the last possession we went for one shot, and Ray hit Travis on a back cut for a lay-up. We were up 47-35.

We stayed in the zone for the rest of the game. As the game went on, our kids kept extending it. With Dustin and Ray on the top, they had a hard time reversing the ball quickly. With 4:37 to play in the game and a 51-42 lead, we spread the court. This was the kind of move that if it worked, the coach looks like a genius, and if it doesn't work, the coach looks like a fool. It worked. They quickly came out of their zone defense. Jordan hit a layup on another curl cut and Santino calmly sank two free throws in the last two minutes. The final score was 56-46. Ray finished with 18 points, 15 rebounds, and 4 blocks. Travis had 14 points, Jordan Noonan had 10, and Dustin Dreifke had 8.

After getting on the bus, the bus wound its way through the downtown Minneapolis rush hour traffic. It was a clear day and the March sun was high in the sky. The sun reflected off the moving metal in the city streets. It was a great feeling to sit back and savor the moment. We had beaten another great team. We were down to one more practice and one more game.

On the bus ride back to the high school, Ray and Travis asked me if Lance could direct the team through his stretching routine. It was a routine that he learned in Europe, and which the team had done before. The players would sit in pairs in a circle on the gym floor as Lance directed them through long static stretches. Lance would name the stretch and then count off a cadence of one to twenty. The entire procedure would take about fifteen minutes.

When we got to the high school the team began stretching, and I went into Jim Baker's office to make copies of the Shakopee scouting reports. We decided to not do a walk thru of their offense. When I returned to the gym, I brought the team together, talked briefly, and handed the scouting reports to the kids. Then my assistants gathered around me. Lance said "Dusty stormed out. He and I got into it. He didn't want to stretch. He began mimicking me, and then he began making fun of my daughters. I and the other kids told him to shut up, and then he starts complaining, 'why do I have to stretch, I didn't play.' I told him that we were a team, and that we were doing it as a team. He responded 'What a bunch of bullshit', and got up and stormed out. As he walked out the door, I told him 'I'm tired of your shit, go fuck yourself.' And he yelled back at me 'fuck off coach' as he walked out the door." My response was that this was the last thing that we needed right now, and that we'd talk to Baker. We were to meet Jim Baker back downtown for a meal and then we were going to go watch the 4A semifinals.

After discussing it as a group, we decided that the players should work it out before practice. The next day when Dusty entered the gym for practice he immediately went up to Lance, stuck out his hand to shake hands, and said, "Coach, no hard feelings." There was a brief team meeting without the coaches. Before practice I approached Dusty. I remember him quickly and sincerely apologizing, saying that they had worked it out and that he was ready to have a good practice so that the team could go beat Shakopee. The captains told me the same thing.

***

Shakopee was also located on the Minnesota River, 25 miles southwest of the Twin Cities. Prior to Bruce Kugath becoming coach in 1993, Shakopee was mostly a baseball town. Amateur town team baseball had always been big in Minnesota, with many small towns maintaining beautiful ballparks. Shakopee, like many of the towns in the Minnesota River valley, had this tradition. Because of Bruce, at least at the high school level, basketball was now every bit as big as baseball. He was one of the few high school coaches who spent his entire-off season coaching every team that he could at every level of his feeder program. He could be seen on the sidelines at middle school and sophomore tournament games throughout the year. He had coached these kids all of the way up.

After school we had a good practice. We reviewed our defense and our match-ups. They ran two basic offenses that many teams ran, and that we had seen before. One I called 'inside triangle' with two players occupying the blocks on both sides of the basket, and a third player at the high post. Their other offense had five players on the perimeter passing, cutting, and driving. Bruce had been running these two offenses for years, and like Bob Brink at Rocori, as the game had changed, he had adapted his offenses. They were not rigid set offenses. The players would back cut and fill the perimeter spots if the defense overplayed. They would take what we would give them and we would not be able to take them out of their offense. I expected to see the five out offense most of the game. They also had some set plays to setup their D1 prospect, Jamal Abu-Shamala. Ray would guard Jamal. He was a 6-5 wing, and was being recruited by Wisconsin, Minnesota, Iowa, and Northwestern. Bill, Adam, and Octavius would trade off on their two front line players, 6-4 senior Lenoris Drummond and 6-6 sophomore Eric Carlson. Travis would guard their point guards, primarily Brian Sammes who was a D3 recruit, and Dustin, Santino, and Jordan would match up on the other players.

We knew that they would play either a 2-3 or a 1-2-2 zone, and some triangle and 2. We knew that they would try to shorten the game, and I expected them to sacrifice some offensive rebounding to stop our fast break. They would miss very few box outs. Because they would take care of the ball, we would probably score very little on steals. Like the previous two teams, they would be disciplined. I was hoping that our pressure would wear them down. Because it's a lot easier to slow the game down than to speed it up, we expected the score to be in the forties or fifties. Besides practicing against the Shakopee defenses, and we did a lot of shooting drills.

Our kids were eager. We all felt that Shakopee had an easy route to the state finals, unlike us and the other five top teams that had to play their way through a tough bracket. We were ready to prove a point. After a week of sun, the weather turned on Friday. The clouds rolled in during the morning and when I walked out of the high school after practice, it was a dark and gray sky.

After practice, I picked up Martha at her downtown Minneapolis office and we went to the Target Center to relax and watch the Class 2A semifinal games. We ran into a number of high school coaches. Rich Decker, Keith Erickson, Steve Fritz, and Bill McKee all sought us out, and sat with us for a while. As always, when you see coaches who you used to coach with, it was fun catching up, and there were a lot of laughs. When we left the Target Center for the drive home, a late winter snow was beginning to softly fall with big flakes.

* * *

I woke up the next day to a gray and white world. There was heavy dark cloud cover, with a six-inch layer of heavy wet snow on everything. It was on the ground, on the trees, and on the telephone wires. The branches of the evergreens were sagging under its weight. It stuck to the tires of the car as I backed out of our driveway.

I rose early, went to my office to work, and then went to the gym for a work-out. In the afternoon Martha and I drove to the high school. We boarded the bus to the VFW for our pregame meal. When we walked out of the restaurant and passed the bar the patrons gave us a standing ovation. Then the bus took us to the high school for our last pregame shoot-a-round. When the bus pulled into the school parking lot a snow man was standing there with a Cardinal scarf on and holding a sign that said 'GO SPARTANS'. The feeling that I experienced in the gym was one that I had never felt as a basketball coach. Win or lose, it would be the last game of the season, and the last game with this great group of kids. The shooting session seemed no different from any other. The kids were as focused as always. When it was time to get on the bus, Alcindor and I were standing by the ball rack in the corner of the gym. The players came over one by one. The last player was Travis. As he handed me his basketball, he was shaking his head. He said, "I couldn't hit a thing. I was short on everything. My arms are really tired. I made forty-two dollars shoveling snow today." I quickly responded, "Don't even think about it. Just shoot the ball. You might have your best shooting night ever." He nodded, smiled, and answered, "OK", and he headed out the door, as Alcindor offered words of encouragement.

As I rolled the ball rack into the storage room, my heart sank. I couldn't believe it. He was going to get some wide-open shots against the Shakopee zone. This wasn't good. When I got on the bus, I turned to Lance and the other assistants and told them what he had said. I saw three expressions of disbelief.

Lance said, "what?"

I answered, "yeah, that's what he just told me."

"He shoveled snow all day?" Lance's face still had an expression of incredulity.

Nobody could believe it. The bus began chugging out of the parking lot. Then I looked out the window. The snow was melting and dripping from the oak trees.

***

The four championship games were played in the format of two double headers. In the afternoon session Russell-Tyler-Ruthton defeated Rushford-Peterson 58-55 for the 1A championship, and Braham defeated Crookston 63-39 for the 2A title. Our game would start at 6pm followed by Hopkins and Eastview facing off for the 4A title at 8pm. As the kids were in the locker room, I walked out to the arena floor. Both the Shakopee and Richfield sections were mostly full. Martha, my parents, siblings, and my buddies were sitting about ten rows up. This was Shakopee's sixth consecutive state tournament. In the middle of their fan section was a large banner declaring 'WE DON'T RECRUIT'.

After the pregame talk, the team and assistants walked to the floor. I took my time. I walked down a long tunnel, and took the right turn towards the floor. The ceiling over the tunnel was arched and 30' high as it entered the arena. The entire lower half of the arena was almost full. It was already loud. I stopped and savored the moment.

As our kids went through our defensive slide drills and two-line layups, a few people walked down to the bench to shake my hand. I was talking to two members of the 1960 team when I was interrupted by Mullenbach. "Jim, we don't have any basketballs." I turned to the alums and said, "Excuse me." Our managers forgot to bring the bag of basketballs from the locker room. They had run back to the locker room to get them, but the locker room was locked. They couldn't find anybody to unlock it. I looked out on the court and our top eight players were shooting with only two basketballs. Normally they had eight basketballs. After talking to half a dozen officials and running to the locker room myself, I ran back to the court with the bag of balls and threw them to the kids. The entire debacle took five or six minutes.

Shakopee began the game in their 2-3 zone. In our first ten possessions we turned the ball over five times and we worked the ball and missed five good shots. Then Ray missed an open three, and Abu-Shamala made a three. I called time-out, we were down 11-2, and they were high-fiving. They extended their lead to 15-3 with 2:26 to play. I called time-out again. We went on a 7-0 run, came up with another defensive stop and went for one shot. Travis rebounded a missed shot and scored at the buzzer. We had closed it to 15-11.

Ray and Santino hit catch and shoot threes to ignite another little run and with 5:19 to play the score was tied 19-19. We were getting good shots against their packed in zone. They were rock solid offensively against our man-to-man defense, not forcing anything and withstanding our ball pressure. Ray drove the middle to end the half, was fouled and hit two free throws, and we trailed 29-26.

I felt good as I walked down the tunnel to the locker room. We had been in a lot of big games like this. During the halftime talk we made no adjustments. We reviewed the open areas in their zone to cut to, and talked about crashing the boards hard and needing a couple of put back baskets. I finished by telling the kids that this was another 'one run' game. We had to just keep playing our defense, and make one offensive run to get the lead. Then we could spread the court, pull them out of their zone, make our free throws and win the game. We had won a lot of games like this against other really good teams.

Early in the third quarter, Ray made a driving lay-up off a pass from Dreifke, and the score was 29-28. In the next six minutes we had two more turnovers, and we missed six more catch and shoot jumpers in a row. Then Jamal banked in a driving off balance jumper with 2:27 to play. Ray couldn't have defended him any better. It was a beautiful clutch shot over an out-stretched arm. On the next possession Eric Carlson grabbed a long rebound, and when he went back up Jordan was called for a foul. Ray took the ball with two hands and threw it down. This was a habit of his that he often did in practice and at the open gyms. However, for the first time ever, the ball slipped through his hands and it caromed high in the air, resulting in a deserved technical foul. He didn't intend to not catch the ball, and this was the only technical of his high school career. However, it didn't look this way to the crowd. The Shakopee section stood and went crazy. They had four free throws and the ball. And Ray had the first technical foul of his Richfield career, and he was in foul trouble for the first time all year. They made three of four free throws. Two possessions later we went for one shot and Dustin passed off to Bill for a lay-up. As the buzzer sounded, we trailed 38-30.

In the next two minutes Ray scored on a lay-up and a tip-in to make it a four-point game. Once again, Abu-Shamala answered with a three pointer. Two minutes later Travis drove hard and was fouled. He made one of two free throws and Abu-Shamala answered again with another driving jumper in traffic. We were again down by eight, 43-35. With 4:12 to play and a 45-35 advantage Shakopee spread the court. We got a stop and Ray hit a three. We called time out. We threw both a 1-3-1 and a 2-3 half court trap at them, but they executed well against both. We traded points from then on, with them hitting 8 of 10 free throws to defeat us 57-46. The run that we were waiting for never came. Shakopee had answered everything that we threw at them.

After the game I shook Bruce's hand and I said, "You're a great coach and you've worked really hard for this. Enjoy every minute of it." He shook my hand hard looked me directly in the eyes and said, "Thanks, Jim."

In a quirk of fate, Bill Bauman and his Prior Lake buddy Jarod Ewing had their pictures taken after the game. Had they stayed at Prior Lake for their senior season, they would have been co-captains. Instead, they played against each other in the state finals.

When I got to the locker room the kids were sitting. I looked at them and smiled, and said, "Well…I thought we were going to win it right up until the last four minutes. You guys did everything that we asked you to do. You played hard right to the end. You have nothing to hang your heads about." Ray, Jordan, Travis, and Dustin who had all shot poorly had their heads down. Some of the kids then spoke, mostly thanking each other for the great friendships and season. I then said, "We'll talk about it as a team. Monday. There's a celebration at the high school gym. This will be our last time together in the gym, and a lot of fans and parents will be there. We have to be positive."

We took the team bus back to the high school. When we walked into the gym, I saw over three hundred people, and a loud cheer and ovation began. The people were clapping and hugging the players. People told me over and over how proud they were of the team. Little kids were collecting autographs and parents were taking pictures. Within two minutes the kids were laughing and smiling and hugging each other and the fans. I was amazed at how the kids did not feel bad. It wasn't a feeling of deep disappointment. It was more a feeling that we did everything that we could, but on this night against this opponent it wasn't enough. It was a celebration of a great season. When Jill Johnson shook my hand, she told me, "thank you for what you have done for this school."

***

The article in the *StarTribune* read:

Shakopee bottles up Richfield.

Defense on Browns give Sabers their first state title

Because Shakopee coach Bruce Kugath is a realist, he wasn't about to fool himself. Richfield, with its high-flying tandem of Ray and Travis Brown, probably had better athletes than his squad did…"We knew we could do some things that maybe didn't take great athletic ability", Kugath said, "like working hard on defense and getting rebounds. That's what we said. We've just got to outwork them." "If we make one run, we're up seven or eight, we win the game," Richfield coach Jim Dimick said. "We just couldn't seem to hit two or three in a row to make that run...We haven't shot that poorly all year." [40]

We ended up shooting 6 for 28 on three pointers, and they were all unforced open threes. Our overall field goal percentage was 31% with no forced shots. We also had an uncharacteristic bad night at the free throw line, shooting 6 for 15. They had only shot 37% from the field, in spite of Abu-Shamala hitting some very tough shots. Jamal finished with 24 points and 13 rebounds.

The next week the headline in the *Richfield Sun-Current* said

Shots didn't fall for second-place Spartans

I was quoted, "*We took the same shots we've been shooting all year. They just weren't dropping. Abu-Shamala hit some big baskets when Shakopee needed them.*" [41]

Ray was the best defensive player that I ever coached, and on this night, Jamal gave him all he could handle and more.

* * *

We met as a team the next Monday after school. It was bittersweet. We all knew that this was our last time together alone as a group. The kids sat in a circle and every player and coach had their turn to talk. Mostly they talked about the friendships, the idea of 'one mission', and how they had all banded together.

I spoke last. I thanked them and praised all of them. I told them that they were one of the most fun teams that I ever coached. I told them that all fourteen of them were important. I told them that it was one of the best scout squads that I had ever coached. Then I told them that they would never get over the Shakopee game. I said that if you play sports long enough, you are always going to have some games that you never get over. When you look back, it's always going to hurt, and you're going to say to yourself that we should have never lost that game.

"You did everything that we asked of you in that game. You played hard the entire game, and nobody outworked you. You played a great defensive game, which went as planned. Shakopee probably played their best game of the year, and that's to their credit. They played great. That doesn't take anything away from what you guys did. If we shoot like that against St Thomas, we don't get to state. When you look back on the season, you can't focus on just the Shakopee game. Go on and think about the Mankato and the St Thomas games, or the Johnson, or the North or the Sioux City game, or the two great games that we had with Tartan. Then think about the hours that you spent playing in the off-season. Think about the open gyms and all of your buddies. Very few high school athletes get to experience what you guys did. It was a great journey. You are really lucky."

* * *

Two weeks later a letter to the editor was printed in the Richfield Sun-Current:

Fans made tourney day a winner
To the editor:

This team was, in so many ways, a child's dream come true. The Richfield boys' basketball team had an experience of a lifetime-winning sections and going to the state tournament. They represented our school and our community in such a positive way-all good kids, all working hard, all doing what was "team" to make for a successful season.

Most people would think that this is achieved by a combination of talented athletes, hard work and coaching, which is true in part, but you can ask any player on the RHS team of '04-05' and the MVP of the section championship game at Tartan versus St. Thomas who was our "sixth man"-the fans.

Our student body, administration and so many people of the community rallied together to give support and encouragement to our team. They didn't stop there-they followed us to the Target Center to support the team through each of the games on their quest to be state champions. This was such a force giving incentive-always encouraging the players to "give it their all."

Well, the team felt that they came up one short-runner up for Class 3A. They didn't' achieve the goal they had and they felt that they had disappointed their fans. Heads were hanging a bit low on the bus ride back to RHS, but who was there again? The fans. They were there to clap, hug, encourage and tell the players how proud they were for everything they had done. Small children getting autographs, taking pictures with all their favorite players, and just beaming with pride that these guys were taking the time to be with them. If they only knew how much of a healing process it was for the players-all of a sudden, the smiles were back and the heads weren't hanging so low. Once again it was all of you-the fans, young and old-that made the day a winner.

Thank you so much for being there for our son and all of the players. It truly meant more than you could know.

Jim and Jean Noonan
Richfield [42]

The April edition of the school newspaper, the *Spotlite*, ran two articles covering the state tournament which covered ten pages and included twenty photos. Peter William Atkins wrote:

Almost the entire school showed some support for Richfield's varsity boys' basketball squad on their State Championship run, and it wasn't even all about getting out of school early four days out of the 5-day week. Students' pep and pride for Richfield shined during a week that many wish could last a lifetime. It was a week that felt empowering, like for once everyone was on top of the world. For those five days any low test score could be shrugged off upon the overwhelming happiness emitted by every hallway and classroom gearing up for the big game...I was captivated in action of Richfield Basketball players dribbling between their legs like nothing, and forty Richfield band members having the time of their life... as I looked up into the stands of the...Richfield spectators I instantly smiled. The spirit is contagious and unbelievable. Spirit carried for 4 quarters including a charismatic dance at halftime...The stands were...painted Red and White. Fans wore whatever outrageous outfit they could think of, so long as it had Red: A formal dress, body paint, plastic gladiator gear, and more. Richfield alumni even showed up and kept themselves out of the craziness behind the hoop. Again, it was something that no one would have wanted to miss if they were there, and something no one would understand unless they were there. Pep, joy, and happiness were at its best; tenfold that seen at the semifinals. Richfield spirit somehow made pig tails, in opposite colors, and scarlet letters all over their bodies, beautiful. It was a great game, and both teams fought hard...A camera lens wept in the final minutes of the final quarter in the final game of Richfield's varsity boys' basketball...It was as if Richfield fans and players were finally exhausted from happy faces, and everything that they pumped energy into that week. The stands were silent, full of guys and girls waiting to get out of that place hoping to skip the disappointment phase and go straight to remembering a season which was nothing short of amazing...The basketball team captivated an entire school full of guys and girls that come from all across the globe, and gave hundreds of them an experience that no one can appreciate unless experienced. The entire city tips their hat to you, the Varsity Boys' Basketball Team. Thanks for a great run.

Andy Pahl wrote:

...a seemingly innocent yet highly effective cheer with which we could strike fear into the hearts of the enemy. After countless hours of brainstorming, the venerable "Richfield, what?" was born...I have honestly never in my life seen such sheer excitement and high spirits...The light rail was packed full of glowing fans on its way back to Fort Snelling that evening...Again a horde of strangely clad teenagers took over the area's rail transit system and the ride into Minneapolis

flew by...As a new member of this community I have been thoroughly impressed with the amount of care and support given by the fans and amount of dedication and energy expended by the team and its staff. Even though we didn't win the state title, I know that whenever I look back on my days spent here in Richfield, I will remember the valiant effort that brought us so close. [43]

* * *

In Class 4A, Tartan defeated Champlin Park 48-33 before falling to Hopkins 60-55 in the semifinals. Hopkins then beat Eastview 71-60 in two overtimes for the championship. It was a heartbreaker for the Eastview Lightning. At the end of the first overtime, they were ahead 58-56 and Hopkins had the ball out of bounds under the basket with 2.5 seconds remaining. After a foiled out of bounds play and a loose ball, Blake Hoffarber made a shot while sitting on the floor with his butt on the three-point line. The shot was all over the Internet.

In Iowa, Sioux City East advanced to the largest class (Class 4A) state tournament in Iowa. They lost in the semifinals to Bettendorf 63-54, and then won the third-place game over Iowa City West 58-57.

In my season summary press release, I wrote "Eight players were part of the playing rotation. Ray and Travis Brown (no relation) were selected All-Conference, All-Metro, All-State, and All-State Tournament. This would not have been possible without the unselfish team play of twelve other Spartans. Seniors Bill Bauman, Adam Smith, and Octavius Crawford played great interior defense, while setting countless screens to get the Browns open. Bauman was also selected All-Conference and All-State Tournament. Junior starters Jordan Noonan and Dustin Dreifke were selected Honorable Mention All-Conference while playing great team defense. Sophomore sixth man Santino Clay provided instant offense and defense with his quickness. Seniors Mike Windler and Dusty Hinz played spot minutes when called upon. More important than this, they led the remaining four underclassmen as captains of our scout squad. Along with juniors Carl Ermisch and Ojullo Madho, and sophomores Steven Fischer and Dexter Jones, the scout squad ran the plays of numerous opponents throughout the season. These varying individual roles were blended together under the team motto of 'one mission'.

Fifth Summer

Well...that's not right...that's not right Cappy and you know that's not right...you know that's not right.

—*Hap Dimick*

During the last week in April, I got two phone calls. One was from Coach Buss. He called to congratulate me on the season. He wanted to know about the state games and if we saw the triangle-and-two defense, and if the minor tweak in our offense worked. I told him that it worked but we missed open shots. We talked at length about the Mankato and Shakopee games. He was philosophical. His parting comment was that it was great that I got to experience a state tournament run. "I'm really glad for you, Junior, that you got to experience that. Every coach should get to experience that at least once. It's just so much fun." He was the only person in my life who ever called me Junior, and he always called me Junior.

The other phone call was from Mullenbach. He told me that the assistant principal Jason Wenschlag asked him about the day in February when I yelled and swore at the janitor. The parents of one of our players met with the principal and complained about the incident. He said that I could expect a phone call from Jill Johnson.

Jill was now in her second year as the principal and I knew that she wanted to have my back. The next day I was at the high school meeting with her and Jason. Jill began by telling me what was said to her by the parents about the incident. She then asked me if this was true and if there was anything more that she and Jason should know. I told the entire story to both of them. When I got to the part where I apologized to the janitor and the team, I could tell that they hadn't heard this. Then I told them what I said to the team about the lesson of treating all people the same. When I finished, I said "I bet these parents didn't tell you the part about me apologizing to the janitor and the team, did they?"

Jill answered, "No they didn't, and they're probably going to go to the school board with this."

Then I said "Then I'm going to the school board. The school board needs to hear the whole story." They agreed.

* * *

The sections and classes for the state tournaments were realigned every two years. When the realignments were announced in April Richfield was moved up to Class 4A. We were now in the top class, with teams that almost always had more depth and height. We were also no longer with the smaller Class 3A private schools, which often had as much if not more talent. We were placed in the section with the two largest Minneapolis schools, South and Southwest. The other five schools were all members of the Lake Conference, Apple Valley, Bloomington Kennedy, Burnsville, Eagan, and Eastview.

During the winter sports seasons Jim Baker officially announced his resignation. Everyone knew since the previous summer that this was going to be his last year. Whenever the athletic director who hired a coach resigns, it changes the stability for the coach. After the change, the coach is working for a boss who inherited him, not the boss who hired him. The coach is on new ground with the person who is in control of his job status.

Jim Baker was a great athletic director. He was selected the 2005 Minnesota Athletic Director of the Year. He was always upbeat. He was a practical joker. He unified the coaches from all sports with everything that he did including the annual barbeque that he and his wife Janet hosted every June. The coaches used him as a sounding board to make tough decisions. If it was a decision that he as the athletic director could make, he would make it known that it was his decision, which would take the heat off of the coach. Most of all he had my back. I'll never forget what he told me when I asked him what he would do if the superintendent or school board told him to fire me. "The day they tell me to fire one of my coaches is the day I resign. I'll tell them to go find a new athletic director." He would be missed. All of the coaches felt this way.

It turned out that at least I was going to have a say in who was hired as my boss. Jill Johnson asked that I be on the search committee. In May I went to the school district office to participate in three interviews of candidates. The interview committee picked Todd Olson. He was offered the job and accepted.

* * *

The first week in June Lance called me. He said "can you believe what Dusty did?" I said, "no, what did he do?"

"He wrote an article in the school newspaper ripping Bill Bauman, and us, and the program. Most of the article is bullshit, Jim. He wrote things that weren't true, and he only told half the story. And he signed other kids' names to the article that had no idea their names were going to be included. The kids are really pissed off."

"So, you've read the article."

"Yah, you can go online and read it."

Here is the article, as it was posted and circulated on the Internet at 'http:// by107fd.bay107.hotmail.msn.com:

As many people in Richfield know, last fall Bill Bauman transferred to Richfield from Prior Lake (a daily commute of about 50-60 miles round trip) to among other things, play basketball. He did, without question, contribute on the basketball court. As far as I know, Bill went to Prior Lake public schools, played basketball in Prior Lake, lived in Prior Lake, and had friends in Prior Lake his entire life. But this is not really about Bill. Rather it is about what happens when someone, as a senior athlete, decides to leave his hometown to attend school in a new district. In short, the point of this article is to: 1) give an insider's account of how Bill's (choose one of the following): a) decision b) recruitment c) parents' ambitions d) all of the above had affected several Richfield basketball seniors and, 2) raise some essential questions not only about what happened, but also about the system that allowed it to happen.

When new talent is imported, it usually causes a "domino effect." Bubble players are cut, expectant contributors (such as, Mike Windler and myself) are marginalized, and starters ultimately lose playing time. And that's exactly what happened in Richfield this season. I will limit my discussion to the domino effect on just seniors, the '05 classmates of Bill Bauman.

Nate Poke was cut; Mike Windler and I had our playing time nearly eliminated; and Adam Smith's and Octavius Crawford's minutes were reduced significantly. (Dennis Robinson was also eventually cut, but that's a different story).

Mike, Adam, Octavius, Nate, and I, in varying degrees, came all the way up through the Richfield basketball program. Most of us started playing against each other in 3rd and 4th grade in the Richfield house league, played together on the traveling teams, and in 7th and 8th grade, played on the Richfield Middle School teams. When we got to high school, Coach Dimick had just come on board, and we continued playing together on the freshman, sophomore, and junior varsity squads. So this year was our senior season and, as is typical of players who have spent so many years in the same program and community, we knew the "lay of the land." Each of us tried out for the team with a pretty good idea of how we would be asked to contribute. Although disappointing for some, we accepted our respective roles, intending to work hard and looking forward to being teammates one last time.

When the impact of the transfer (Bill) actually sunk in, our expectations clearly were disrupted. While most remained on the team, we were asked to adjust our reasonable expectations as the domino effect took its course. Mike and I (two players who not only have lived in Richfield our entire lives, but also have gone all the way through the basketball program together) ran the scout team in practice and rode the bench during games. We did get in for the occasional minute or two, but basically, we didn't play. (Personally, not getting any playing time would have been a whole a lot easier to accept if the minutes had gone to someone who had at least come up in our program.) Adam and Octavius played less and worst of all, Nate was deprived of his chance to finish his career on Varsity.

It should be noted that by the time we realized what was going on, it was too late to pursue an "open enrollment" plan of our own.

I can only speak for myself, but transferring to another school—for any reason whatsoever—was never a consideration. It was probably an unlikely option for the rest of the senior players. We're from Richfield, and being part of this community and school means a lot to us.

To add insult to injury, during half time at one of our games, we were asked, of all things, to provide "senior leadership' (from the bench, of course). The coaches proceeded to give us a "pep talk" delivered in a tirade of vulgarities and unjustified put downs because we weren't "cheering" enough. The irony of this situation is that they targeted their frustrations specifically at the three senior players who hadn't even been in the game yet, and as I recall (and unfortunately, I do) didn't get in at all. While I certainly can handle their misdirected bullying epithets, I do not think that seventeen –year-old athletes should be subjected to a steady barrage of "F-this" and "F-that" under any circumstances, much less by alleged role models. I have played enough sports to know that coaches do need to yell at their players at times. Quite frankly, however, I was embarrassed and uncomfortable enough having my family and friends watch me sit on the bench (or get in for the occasional mop up minute) without verbal abuse compounding my disappointment and shame.

This is what the Richfield coaches have created. Since Coach Dimick graduated before open enrollment, I can only guess that he doesn't have a clue as to how several of his players were made to feel. Had he himself experienced the repercussions of a senior transfer back in his basketball days at Northfield, I wonder if he would have "bought into it" like he expected us to do. (I guess he will never know.) Mike and I both considered quitting the basketball team throughout the year. Many might ask why we didn't, but we decided to ride the season out together. After nine years of Richfield basketball, eleven teams and roughly 1,500 hours of work put in, we figured we'd hang in there to the end.

To move to the broader implications of this story, certain questions need to be asked. First, was this good for Bill? In Prior Lake, he would have been a standout. In Richfield, he was at most the third wheel on a team that featured two Division 1 signers. It is possible that his prospects for playing at the next level were harmed as much as enhanced (although he did get to play at State, an unlikely outcome at Prior Lake).

Secondly, why Richfield? Hopkins—a program notorious for recruiting—and Eden Prairie are closer and have good teams. Bill, himself, suggested that he wanted to experience more "diversity." If this was true, Minneapolis Henry and North have excellent teams with top-notch academic magnet programs. If he was seeking an education, schools like Benilde and Holy Angels give a lot of financial aid to students who excel at sports.

This naturally begs the question, was he recruited? (Surely, the "mentoring" he received from Coach Berwald these past few summers wouldn't have anything to do with the notion of recruiting, now would it?) While only the coaches, Bill and his parents know for sure, there is enough talk in the hallways and locker room about the prospects of who can be lured to Richfield next year. (One only needs to look to our south and east to identify the leading candidates for next year's lineup of wanna-get imports). For anyone to claim that no contacts or discussions have ever taken place should cause even the biggest boosters to shake their heads. (Richfield has seen the other side of the coin. Last fall, two of our classmates transferred to Northfield to play football. They have since returned to Richfield.)

Finally, how are we to value community and community schools? You don't have to be number four through seven on the basketball depth chart to realize that the end result of basketball recruiting disrupts and deflates our students and, at the same time, devalues the accomplishments of our team for those who know the inside story.

When Governor Perpich devised open enrollment in 1991, his aims were education and integration. An interesting byproduct has been the significant rise of certain sports programs like Hopkins. I have also heard that this year's 5-A Football Champs, Minnetonka, had eleven or twelve transfers on the team.

Another unintended consequence has been the dashed hopes of the non-star players who bargained on seeing their effort and loyalty eventually pay off.

I have waited to publish this essay until after the season as I did not wish to create animosity among players on a team that I genuinely hoped would go all the way. It's a once in a lifetime opportunity to go to State, and whether I played or not, it was an experience I will never forget.

But now that the season is over, I would like to recommend changes in Richfield's "open enrollment" policy and your support would be appreciated. I ask you, the student body, the booster club and the community at large, what do you want in high school competition? Do you want these recruiting practices to continue, allowing the encouragement of student athlete transfers, which in turn relegates the hometown players to the bench, or are you willing to put a stop to it and allow Richfield to compete with whatever talent we have? You decide. Because it may be me and a few others getting the shaft this year, but it will be your friends, your siblings, and your classmates on the receiving end next year (and in the years to come) if we don't do something to put a stop to it.

I do want to point out that I have nothing against Bill personally. He is a decent guy and I sincerely wish the best for him. The fact remains, however, I'm from Richfield and he's from Prior Lake.

Some might say that my intent for this article is a result of "sour grapes." I really don't care. I have nothing to gain for writing this article except the knowledge that I tried to make a difference for the betterment of the players who will follow me. You guys have worked hard for your spot on the team and I want to come back and watch you play—not some recruit sliding in for State-bound hopes and/or prospective college recognition.

Someone needs to take a stand on this, so let it begin with us. I would like our school and community as a whole to discourage upper-class transfers and to encourage the use of Richfield athletes in the Richfield program. By this, I propose that all "open enrollment" transfers sit out one year before becoming eligible to play for Richfield. Then we'll know that they are coming here for the "right" reasons beyond merely plugging a perceived hole in the starting lineup.

If you agree with this, let the school administration know. Hopefully, we will have the support of the new Athletic Director. Richfield will certainly be all right, and maybe we can do something to stem the tide of imbalance between the "haves" and the "have-nots" in Minnesota high school sports. Heck, we might even get Coach Dimick to move to Richfield.

WRITTEN BY DUSTY HINZ, WITH SHARED VIEWS OF ADAM, MIKE, NATE, AND OCTAVIUS; AND WITH THE ASSISTANCE OF A FRIEND WHO WAS THE LAST PLAYER CUT FROM HIS #1 RANKED HIGH SCHOOL BASKETBALL TEAM FOLLOWING THE IIMPORTATION OF A SENIOR CENTER WHO CAME TO PLAY FOR HIS SCHOOL[44]

As the last editions of the *Spotlite* hit the hallways, Principal Jill Johnson banned the newspaper from being distributed.

* * *

The day after the article was released, Lance saw a couple of the players whose names were in the article, and they were pissed off. These were the comments that I heard from them and Dusty's other teammates:

"If he wasn't happy on scout squad, he should have quit."

"What? He's pissed off about someone swearing. What a joke."

"He's nothing but a hack. He should have been playing for a 1A team."

"He got beat out by a sophomore."

"What he really didn't like was walking into an open gym, and seeing ten point-guards working their butts off."

"Why does he think he owns a spot? Just because you're here since fourth grade, you own a spot?"

"When a good lineman transfers in to block for him, he thinks that's great. But when basketball players transfer in, he's pissed off."

When I met with my assistants, their reaction was similar:

"I'm not surprised. Entitled kids always think that it is someone else's fault when they get beat out."

"He's got nothing to complain about. He knew where he stood the entire season. When Santino beat him out, we told him where he stood. Why didn't he complain about Santino?"-Alcindor Hollie.

"The only reason he picked on Bill is because he's white. What he's really pissed off about is all of these other kids outworking him and beating him out. Look at all of the other kids we have who open enrolled or didn't play traveling, Ray, Dennis, Jawaun, Santino, and who came to all of the open gyms. Why didn't he pick on one of them?"-Lance Berwald.

The June 5th edition of the *StarTribune* ran a story.

School newspaper yanked for opinion piece

A Richfield High School student's critical essay on open enrollment and the school's basketball team was pulled from the student newspaper Friday and banned after he singled out as an example a Prior Lake student who attended Richfield...Principal Jill Johnson said she pulled the article because it was unfair to the Prior Lake student, naming him and not giving him a chance to respond in the newspaper's last issue of the school year. "Reading through the article, this is not about someone's feelings about open enrollment. This is about how this kid came into Richfield in his senior year and wrecked my basketball season," she said.

School security staff and teachers collected the article from students, taking copies from lunch tables and students' hands, and setting off a rumor mill that buzzed for the rest of the school day, according to Hinz.

Johnson said she intends to redistribute the school newspaper, the Spotlight, on Monday morning without the Hinz article included. She also told Hinz that

he will be suspended for three days if he passes out copies of the article, meaning
he would not walk in graduation ceremonies Wednesday evening...

...Richfield basketball coach Jim Dimick said Hinz lost his position on the
starting varsity team to a sophomore, not to the Prior Lake student. "The kids
we recruit real hard are the Richfield kids," said Dimick...

...The school's newspaper adviser, Bruce Wiebe, said Saturday that he agreed
with Principal Johnson's decision to pull the article even though he found it "per-
suasively written."[45]

The next week I received a voice message: "Hey Jim Dimick, Mike Karnas
calling. Say, I just had a minute here. Now that the season's done and the last
basketball's been thrown I kinda wanted to just give you an atta boy and say
how a good job I thought you did coaching. It's a tough thing and a tough
ending to some of the stuff that was going on, but boy, I just thought that
you did a great job. And what an entertaining product for a lot of people to
watch. And just good things in the future coming up here too. But anyway, I
just wanted to give you a call and tell you how much I appreciate what you did,
and I know that there's many…many…people in the community that think the
same way. And again, if there's anything that we can do for you, please let us
know. I know that we're just little fans and little people that look at things a
little differently than parents and a little differently than some of the stuff that
goes on as go through a coaching situation. But jeez, you did a great job and
if there is ever anything that I can do for you, thanks Jim."

***

After the season I looked at our talent and I felt good. We returned two
starters in Dustin Driefke and Jordan Noonan. Santino Clay would step in
at small forward as a junior and emerge as our next Division I prospect. We
would have no size in our top three classes, but if we had to go small, I was confident we could win twelve to fifteen games and be really tough by tournament
time. Most importantly, we now had kids that were working hard at basketball year-round. Did we have a program loaded with Howard Pulley Division
I players every year like Hopkins or DeLaSalle? No. We would have our ups
and downs. But I felt that a down year would still be above five hundred, and
an up year would be like the last two, ranked in the top ten.

This all changed for at least one year, before the end of June. Suddenly we
had height in our senior class. Eric Gusaas transferred in from Bloomington
Jefferson and Dwayne Hardy transferred back from Minneapolis North.

Eric was 6-9, with a medium build. He was a typical late developing Scandinavian. He was slow, not strong, and could not jump. He finally stopped growing and his strength and coordination needed to catch-up to this growth. This would probably happen when he was in college. He was Lance's neighbor. Lance worked with him in their driveway. The past two summers he attended our open gyms, so that he could participate in Lance's drills. He had great shooting form, footwork, and fundamentals. Eric came all of the way up through the Jefferson feeder program. As a junior he played mop up minutes, because he was playing behind Cole Aldrich. Cole was 6-10, a year younger, was a starter since his freshman year, and committed early to Kansas. Cole was a top-level Division I prospect. Eric was D3 at best. After Eric's junior year, he and his parents made the decision to come to Richfield, the neighboring suburb. When I called the Jefferson coach Jeff Evens to tell him all of this, he was not surprised. He said a lot of nice things about Eric and his folks.

It was a blow to our program when Dwayne transferred to Minneapolis North after his freshman year. According to the state high school league rules, a student was only allowed one transfer after he had attended one day of school as a freshman. Because Dwayne was at Richfield as a freshman, and then transferred to North, he would be ineligible to play for half a year if he transferred back to our school. However, there was an exception to this rule. The exception was if a student's parents were not married, and if the student was changing his residence from one parent to the other parent. Because Dwayne's birth mom lived on the north side, and her home was his primary residence for his sophomore and junior years, he fit this exception. Dwayne's dad and step-mom owned a house in Richfield. His dad checked with the state high school league, and verified that he would be eligible at Richfield. Since leaving our program, Dwayne lifted weights and grew to 6-5 and 220. And he had great hands and a beautiful shot. Because he played two years for us, he knew our drills and our defense. He was a solid D2 recruit.

* * *

The open gyms were as strong as ever. The older kids were committed to working hard on fundamentals, and this attitude trickled down to the younger kids. A handful of players who we had cut also attended, some of whom had little brothers coming up through the program. I liked to work on the shooting form of all of the players once a week. I now had about 40 players seeking my attention, and I made sure that every one of them got it, no matter their skill level. The core of the high school basketball team was no longer three sport athletes who spent the summer playing legion baseball.

* * *

During the second half of June, Lance called me and told me that Todd Olson had called him to schedule a meeting. Lance asked me if I knew anything about it. When I said no, Lance's response was, "Well, he's going to fire me. Why else would he want to meet with me? I'm a volunteer assistant." The next day Lance went to the athletic director's office. After the meeting he called to tell me that he was fired. Lance said that Todd spent most of the meeting talking about his own experiences, and the many difficult situations that he had been in, and that he had never once lost his temper. He added that in spite of being condescending, Todd was also very cordial and thanked him for all of the things that he had done for the program.

The next day I got a call from Jay Pivec, "How do you fire a volunteer?"

The players were in disbelief and they were really pissed off. Lance played and coached with emotion, and he was a player's coach. He took a huge load off my shoulders when he helped the kids with communications with college coaches. He drove players in his car to places like Cedar Falls, Iowa, and Thief River Falls, Minnesota to do college visits. He donated his time and money and he asked for nothing in return. And he treated all the kids with respect and interest, from the D1 recruits to the kids on the end of the bench.

As valuable as he was every day in practice and on the bench during games, my best memories of him are from the open gyms. I picture him standing under the basket putting the big kids through the paces with his twenty-minute big-man workout. With the summer heat the kids would be gassed and wringing wet. Lance would be loud, intense, and totally positive. The kids would be listening to his every word. The program lost a person who gave his heart and time to the kids for nothing in return, and Coach Pivec's question was answered.

When we took our northern trip in July, we went 7-1, playing games in Bemidji, Cass Lake, and Moorhead. The kids bonded. It was our first northern trip without Lance, and we all felt the absence of his personality and energy.

* * *

On Monday, August 15th, Dusty Hinz and his mother spoke to the school board. Sitting in the chairs behind her were the 'concerned citizens'. They told of me swearing at the janitor, and swearing about the referee after the first Tartan game. The stories of Lance swearing on two occasions were also told.

The August 25ᵗʰ edition of the *Richfield Sun-Current* ran an article on the front page, written by Seth Rowe.

Former player blows whistle on swearing
New athletic director says he is working to improve Athletic Department's culture

Richfield Public Schools officials will consider reviewing behavior guidelines for coaches, athletes, and parents, possibly including specific language that profanity is unacceptable, new Athletic Director Todd Olson said last week...

At the Aug. 15 (board) meeting, Dusty Hinz, who graduated from Richfield High School last spring, said the district needs to specify in its handbook that coaches should not use profanity if the handbook does not already do so.

Dusty Hinz said basketball coaches used obscenities during the season last year, and he passed out sheets of paper listing what he said were four specific examples.

"Using profanity to emphasize a point is never an acceptable means of expressing one's anger or frustration, particularly from a coach or anyone else affiliated with the school system," said Dusty's mother, Linda Hinz, during the meeting.

She said the use of profanity amounted to verbal abuse and asked why district officials had not responded to an earlier written complaint...

Dusty Hinz said he wrote a letter to Superintendent Barbara Devlin detailing his point of view in late June...District staff members have followed through on the complaint, Devlin told the school board...

..."Here's a real expectation," Olson said. "We expect players to conduct themselves in as professional a manner as possible and know that they're representing the school, the community, and their family but first and foremost, they're representing themselves"...

...In the next several years, Olson and (Principal) Johnson will work together to create high expectations and high standards, he said...[46]

The next edition of the *Richfield Sun-Current* ran an article on the front page, also written by Seth Rowe. The headline covered the entire top of the first page:

Basketball coach suspended, district says

...Chair John Easterwood asked (superintendent) Devlin to consult with Athletic Director Todd Olson and other administrators about the complaints and report back to the board, at which time he would respond to Dusty and Linda Hinz. The school district initiated a second investigation in response to the concerns that

Dusty raised...Mr Dimick has received a reprimand and a suspension for having engaged in profanity in the presence of student athletes and school personnel...

...Dimick said...that he believes Dusty Hinz, his parents and others who attended the meeting were more concerned about playing time than swearing. "To take...isolated incidents and use them to portray us as verbally abusive swearers is totally misleading about our coaching style, and they know this."...

...Athletic Director Olson said...he recently has heard positive comments about the coach..."The fallout is the supportive people have started voicing their opinion after decisions have been rendered. We've now got to sit back and we have to get back to the business of high school basketball...We have to pick up and grow, and we have to get better."[47]

The next week I received a letter from the Richfield school district personnel office. The letter requested that I contact their office to schedule a meeting, and it stated that Todd Olson would also be present. My first thought was the same as Lance's reaction. Well, are they going to fire me? When I told my wife, her reaction was swift and emphatic. "You hire an attorney. You agree to meet with them, and you inform them that you will have an attorney with you. They need to know that if they want to play hardball, you're going to play hardball."

The next day I called Lance. When he picked up, I said, "Well, I might be joining you in the ranks of fired coaches." I told him what was going on. We both analyzed and speculated again about the dynamics of the administration, the parents, and the concerned citizens. By the end of the conversation, we were both laughing.

The next day Todd Bauman called me. "I don't know how you guys handle it. You work your butts off and get them where they've never been before and this is the thanks that they give you. I can't believe it."

***

I hired a successful defense attorney who I had known for a couple of years. He had gone head-to-head with my wife in her role as a county prosecutor. He grew up in north Minneapolis and lived on the north side. He was an African-American whose family had been in Minneapolis for five generations. Because he attended North and excelled there as an athlete, he followed and understood the high school sports scene.

A week later I was sitting in his office in a downtown skyscraper. The sunlight was streaming in through tall windows, and he was sitting behind his desk casually dressed in a shirt and tie. After we reconnected and talked for a couple of minutes, he asked me to explain what was going on, and how he could help me.

I told him about the letter and the upcoming meeting.

He said, "Well, I've got good news and I've got bad news. The bad news is I'm expensive. I've been doing this for a long time, and I'm good at it, and I've got all of the work that I need. My hourly rates are high. The good news is that I'm very good at what I do. I will not let them do anything to you that they cannot legally do, and they will know this."

I then started to briefly explain the Richfield situation to him, telling him about how long I'd been coaching there, the past season's run to the state finals, the incident with the janitor, and the player and mother speaking to the school board. After a little more than a minute, he leaned back in his chair, put his feet on his desk, and raised his right arm in the air like a traffic cop motioning the traffic to stop. I stopped talking.

He looked out the window and said, "I think I can save us a lot of time here." He paused. "Let's just put it this way." He looked back at me, and rapidly said "You brought in a black kid and the black kid beat out the white kid."

"Yes, except there's more to it than that. The black kid had been in Richfield since third grade, I didn't bring him in. He'd never played in the feeder program. And they're blaming a kid from Prior Lake, because he's white."

"Well, I read the articles in the paper. When you read between the lines it's obvious that a lot of it's about race."

* * *

The second week of September I was sitting in the school district office with my attorney, Todd Olson, and the human resources director Craig Holje. The demeanor of Holje was very cordial. The impression that I got from him was that the only reason we were going through this was to satisfy protocol. They gave us a two-page letter with the title 'Letter of Reprimand and Suspension' addressed to me and signed by Todd. Both parties were to eventually agree on the wording of the letter, sign it, and it would be placed in my personnel file. My attorney and I reviewed the letter.

The letter stated:

...you admitted to using profanity on several occasions during the 2004-05 basketball season, and you admitted to allowing your volunteer assistant coach to use profanity on other occasions. The examples were brought to the District's attention by a former student athlete during an August 15 Board of Education meeting, and confirmed by other student athletes...

...The use of profanity by you and/or your assistant coach violates the expectations for co-curricular staff as outlined in Section V of School board Policy 651,...and the Minnesota State High School Coaches Association Code of Ethics... In addition, these incidents demonstrated a regrettable lack of control in the presence of students...

...You are hereby directed to refrain from using profanity in the presence of students...

...As a result of this unacceptable behavior, you will be suspended from the first two basketball games of the season, and will be required to participate in athletic leadership training and development. I will contact you to discuss the content and timing of this training...

...I will work closely with you prior to and throughout the season to ensure that the basketball program is conducted and operated in accordance with school board policy, in a manner that nurtures a healthy and positive relationship with student athletes and the Richfield basketball community...

My attorney said that the actions of the student were retaliatory. "The student heard coaches in football and baseball use profanity during his senior year. Why did he not go to the school board to report their use of profanity?" Todd answered that he asked the student if he had heard any coaches in any other sports use profanity, and that the student had said no. I told Todd that football and baseball coaches told me that they swore in front of the student. My attorney asked Todd if he had made any effort to verify the truth of the answer by asking the coaches or the players in the other sports. Todd answered, "no."

My attorney then discussed some questions and clarifications related to employment law, and requested that the wording of the letter be changed. He requested that the words 'several' and 'other' be changed to 'two'. They agreed to this. The sentence was then changed to read as follows;

...you admitted to using profanity on two occasions...and you admitted to allowing your volunteer assistant coach to use profanity on two other occasions.

He also requested that if my behavior continued to be exemplary, that the documents be removed from my personnel file after two years. Holje responded that he saw no problem with that. We gave them my attorney's contact information and I told them that until this was resolved, they could communicate to me through him.

Todd did communicate one time the next week with a phone call to my attorney. The attorney then told me, "Todd wants to show you who the boss is." In the conversation he quoted Todd as having said "If he doesn't want to work with me, he's got to let me know." The attorney then said "They know that you're doing a great job. There's no question of that." He then spoke very slowly and emphatically. "But from now on, coach, you can't swear. As long as you coach at Richfield, you can never swear again."

When we returned to the school district offices for the second and final meeting, everything had already been agreed to and decided. I signed the papers, and we left.

This was my first real interaction with Todd Olson. I could tell that he wasn't happy about having to deal with an attorney. That didn't bother me a bit. My first impression was that he was a great guy and I liked him. Mike Karnas had told me that Todd was a great guy, and as always, Mike was right.

Three days later I was camped with my buddies on Ashigan Lake. We were deep in the Boundary Waters. The leaves were changing. The loons were singing less, molting their feathers, and feeding heavily. They were recharging their stores of fat for the migration through Lake Michigan to the Gulf of Mexico. And I was recharging my energy and spirit.

* * *

The article in the *Spotlite and internet* progressed to a community debate in the *Sun-Current*, as evidenced by the letters to the editor.

RHS basketball coach issue raises questions

To the editor:

This letter is in response to the article appearing in the Aug. 22 issue of the Sun-Current regarding Dusty Hinz and his request for an apology from coaches for their alleged use of swear words.

As a local resident who has had a decent level of success in the athletic arena at the high school and collegiate level, and one who has seen these accusations play out before, I would suggest people look at this issue in a different light than it was portrayed in the initial article.

This space is not big enough to cover the complete topic and my thoughts regarding it. But my first question is why the athletic director and principal are responding to these allegations when they are the ones who should be bringing it to the school board's attention, not the Hinz family. My point is not that Athletic Director Todd Olson and Richfield High School Principal Jill Johnson are not doing their jobs, but rather the Hinz family jumping a "chain of command" that is probably clearly outlined in a student manual. The order of contacts for an athlete who has a complaint usually goes coach, athletic director, assistant principal or principal and finally the superintendent before going to the school board if no responses are received.

One should also consider the accuser's background with those he is accusing. This past basketball season I was able to watch the Richfield boys' basketball team play seven games. Dusty played very limited minutes in some of those games and no minutes in the others. He is also the same person who wrote a largely publicized article in the last edition of the RHS student newspaper that singled out a transfer student coming to Richfield who took playing time from local "Richfield" kids like him. Is it possible these accusations could be a backlash against the coaches?

Before you make any judgments against the coaches mentioned in the article, ask yourself if you've ever had any interaction with either of them. What do you know about Dusty? I do not know Dusty or his family.

I ask of you to look deeper into the story before thinking that RHS has an issue with coaches swearing at kids.

Blaine Joerger

Richfield [48]

Blaine Joerger had a basketball pedigree. He played for Hall of Fame coach Lynn Peterson at Staples-Motley. I had a connection with Lynn. As young high school coaches, we both worked at Gopher Coach Jim Dutcher's basketball camps. We spent time together picking the brains of older coaches. Blaine played four years on the varsity for Lynn, and in his senior year the Cardinals lost in the state finals to Minneapolis North. He attended D2 Mankato State where he was a big spoke in the wheel of four winning Maverick teams coached by Dan McCarrell.

Staples is a small town located 140 miles northwest of the cities on the railroad line to Fargo, and 30 miles west of Brainerd, which is the largest town in the area. It is a typical western Minnesota prairie town with a main street located within walking distance of the railroad tracks, and a population of 2,900. It's the kind of town where most of the families have lived there for more than one generation, most of the people are of one or two Northern European nationalities, and people are proud of how they look out for each other.

After graduating from Mankato, Blaine bought a house in Richfield. He was a financial planner in addition to being one of the best high school basketball referees in the state. On the off nights when he wasn't working a game, he would attend our games. He would usually get there early and talk to Lance, myself, or Alcindor. His brother Dave was an up-and-coming CBA coach with the Sioux Falls Skyforce. The conversations were often about strategy, team defense, and teams that he had seen on his refereeing schedule. It was high level basketball talk. Having played for two great coaches, he had basketball insight, and I always wanted to hear his opinion or critique of our team. I remember him saying that being from a small town, he was a big fan of high school sports, and that as a little kid his parents took him to many Staples-Motley games. He once said that his biggest dream as a young boy was to someday play for the home town Cardinals. I also remember him always sitting in the front row near mid court across from our bench.

Playing time is real root of complaint

To the editor:

This letter is in response to the Richfield Sun-Current's article on Richfield High School's Boys Basketball Coach, Jim Dimick that appeared in the September 15 issue.

For the record, let me make this very clear-the use of profanity by anyone in any educational institution is unacceptable. That being said, Dusty Hinz went to the Board of Education to complain about Coach Dimick's use of profanity because he and his parents, Jack and Linda Hinz, were upset about his playing time. It's that simple.

For the first time in 31 years, Coach Dimick took the Richfield boys basketball team to the State Basketball Tournament. Dusty Hinz was a member of this championship team. He was one of the returning seniors who was informed by Coach Dimick on several occasions that his role and his playing time would be limited. Dusty Hinz told Coach Dimick on each of those occasions that he was totally "on board". Apparently, he was not. However, not once during the season or, more importantly, at the time the conduct occurred, did Dusty Hinz complain about Coach Dimick's language. Instead, he waited until after the post-season celebrations and after graduation to complain to the Board of Education about two, that's right, two incidents where Coach Dimick used profanity. Coach Dimick admitted to swearing in front of the players, once in the gym and once in the locker room. However, Dusty Hinz neglected to inform the board that soon after he swore, Coach Dimick apologized to the team, sat them down, and explained to them that his conduct was unacceptable. This was important information the board could have used during its consideration of this matter.

Dusty Hinz was a student who had his own personal struggles with swearing and verbal abuse. During the spring of 2005, he was disciplined by the school administration for verbally abusing a special education student. Most recently, he has been banned from school property and from any school sporting events for one year because he verbally abused a Richfield high school coach during a football game. With these additional facts in mind, it does not take a leap of faith to conclude that Dusty Hinz's complaints about Coach Dimick's language had absolutely nothing to do with his using profanity in front of players. His conduct both during the school year and since graduation undoubtedly demonstrates that he is no stranger to using profanity and being verbally abusive. In closing, the real reason behind Dusty Hinz's complaint to the school board is Coach Dimick's philosophy of playing the best players, and clearly, he was not one of them.

It really is that simple.

Martha Holton Dimick

Shorewood

Hinz justified in addressing board

To the editor:

A recent issue of the Richfield Sun-Current included an editorial submitted by Blaine Joerger regarding the boys basketball coaches' alleged use of foul language. He chastised Dusty Hinz and his parents for bringing this serious issue to the school board rather than go through the chain of command. I find it strange that Mr. Joerger did not fully investigate the matter before he jumped to this inaccurate conclusion and made these rash statements.

I attended both school board meetings in which this issue was on the agenda. I recognized everyone in attendance, they included Richfield's recreation director, a city councilman, a member of the clergy, youth coaches, numerous fans and supporters of our kids, parents of former players and Dusty's teammates. Their very presence reflected their feelings about the seriousness of this issue.

If Mr. Joerger had attended these meetings or contacted the Hinz family, he would have become aware of the reason for Dusty going to the school board. I understand that after going through the official chain of command and waiting several weeks for a response to a letter submitted to the superintendent, in which he requested answers to some very pertinent questions, did he then ask to be included on the school board agenda. Evidently, school administrators felt the allegations were legitimate and a reprimand was necessary because the headlines in that same issue focused on such an action.

Now that this type of demeaning and disrespectful behavior has been brought to the attention of our administrators and school board members, I trust that they will take actions required to create an environment and enforce a code of conduct in which it no longer will be tolerated. The least our young people should expect is to be treated fairly, with respect and in a professional manner by everyone involved with their school activities.

Oz Mullerleile

Richfield [49]

I sent a printed copy of my upcoming school board speech to the recreation director, Frank White. Frank's department regularly held teaching sessions promoting good sportsmanship with the Richfield youth, and Frank was African-American. Two days later he called me. He lauded me for our effort to include the African-American kids. He said that he received a telephone call from a person who told him about the incidents, and that he decided to attend the school board meeting primarily as an observer. He added that because of his past interactions with the complainers, he wasn't putting any credence into what they said. He thanked me for supplying him with the information. He finished by saying that he hoped we could all move forward in a positive direction for all of the kids in Richfield.

Richfield should be proud of Hinz

To the editor:

Letter writer Blaine Joerger, in his opinion published in the Sept. 15 issue, questioned the merits and motives of former Richfield High School athlete Dusty Hinz's recent complaint regarding profanity used by coaches with student basketball players during the 2004-2005 school year.

I would like to let Mr. Joerger and other Richfield citizens know that, as a neighbor of the Hinz family for more than nine years, I can testify to the fact that Dusty is truly a native son to be proud of in our town. His parents have spared no effort in their promotion of excellent citizenship and sportsmanship in their family. He is a young man of virtue and sincerity who is to be commended for having the courage to exercise his American right to speak up for the sake of the dignity of future student athletes.

His appearance before the school board occurred only after he had received no reply to his written complaint submitted several weeks before. The issues raised were serious, and deserved to be addressed regardless of the unrelated matter (which Dusty wrote about for his school newspaper several months ago) of the loss of game playing time for Richfield students that results from out-of-town athletes.

In sum I am proud to witness the many outstanding qualities that the Richfield community has nurtured in Dusty and many other young people in our midst. I'm sure he is grateful for the many skills that he developed through sports in Richfield, which he has now taken with him as he begins what is sure to be a successful college career, including extensive athletic involvement along with a true desire to get a high-quality education.

Thank goodness, this is the legacy he takes from our community. I'm sure that it is his desire that all constructive criticism be applied to a positive direction from here on out.

Finally, thanks to the Richfield High School administration for taking action to address Dusty's complaints. The result is part of the legacy that Dusty leaves behind, along with his stellar career in baseball and many other outstanding contributions he has already made during his young life to a rewarding community life in Richfield. I am thankful he is one of my fifth-grade sons' local role models.

Margaret Scheirman-Buckley
Richfield [50]

* * *

The first week of October I spoke at the school board meeting. I admitted to using profanity on two occasions. I told them that I swore after one game, and that I swore at a janitor in front of the team before practice one day. I then went on to tell the board how I left practice and went and found the janitor and apologized to him. I also told the board about how I sat the team down after practice, and told them what I had said to the janitor with the apology. I also explained to the board that I told the team that I had broken the rule that I had learned from my mother, that you treat all people the same. I then mentioned another rule from my mother. "My mother taught me when I was four years old, that when you tell a story, you tell the whole story. You don't just tell part of the story. Clearly, some parents don't care if their children ever learn this."

I next reminded the board that the demographics of the community had been changing, and that since I had been hired this change had accelerated. I then went on to explain what I had done, to accelerate the inclusion of the minority kids. I also told them that when a team starts winning, open enrollment kids start showing up. And when open enrollment students show up who are good athletes, they are always followed by allegations of recruiting.

The next week the *Richfield Sun-Current* contained another article written by Seth Rowe.

RHS basketball coach responds to complaints

Richfield High School basketball coach Jim Dimick responded last week to critics whose remarks in August alleging that he had used profanity prompted the Board of Education to initiate an investigation and suspend him for two games.

In a statement that Dimick read at the Oct. 3 school board meeting, he emphasized the progress he has made in promoting diversity on the team...Last summer, more than 40 out of about 90 young people at a local basketball camp were minority students. Four years ago, the district did not have any financial aid available for economically underprivileged students to play on traveling teams, Dimick said. Last winter, 12 boys received such financial assistance. He also mentioned a varsity player who was able to stay academically eligible at the high school "due in a large part" to study halls for team members. Dimick and his staff have voluntarily held sessions during the past three summers free for all students who come to work on skills and fundamentals, he said.

"The Richfield basketball...participation profile is very similar to the profile of our student population," Dimick said. "Bottom line: it's harder to make the team, it's harder to earn playing time, and some people are upset about this."...

Dimick also responded to complaints that some students from other school districts who enroll at Richfield High School are getting more playing time than some students from Richfield. Athletic Director Todd Olson said the Minnesota State High School League had conducted an investigation earlier this year after receiving a complaint. When Olson checked into the matter with the league, he was told the investigation had been closed. "They had nothing of substance," Olson said..

Dimick said,... "I coach basketball because I think I have a calling. I do it because I'm making the world a better place. And this is the thanks I get. A small group of people try to bring me down in any possible way that they can think of. This is the exact thing that drives good coaches out of coaching."

This was followed by another letter.

Dimick's defense takes low road

To the editor:

In recent weeks, Richfield High School basketball coach Jim Dimick and his supporters have resorted to two classic low-road tactics in his ongoing battle with former players, parents and boosters over his questionable conduct.

1) The obligatory "stand-by-your-man "letter of support from Dimick's spouse has been printed in the Sun-Current wherein Dusty Hinz and his family are attacked for both failing to give her unfortunate husband prior notice and failing to provide the board with "mitigating factors" to lessen his discipline.

2) In an Oct 3 statement to the Richfield school board (extensively quoted in the Oct. 13 Sun-Current) the beleaguered coach has played the race card.

Such distractions should not be permitted to obscure these facts:

Dusty Hinz's essay and statement to the Richfield school board focused on the treatment of five or six senior players. He discussed the effects of the arrival (some say recruitment) of a single senior transfer from Prior Lake on and incidents of verbal abuse toward some players.

Neither Hinz nor any of his supporters have criticized freshman transfers. These senior players were not given prior notice of coach Dimick's plan to play the senior center from Prior Lake.

These issues have nothing to do with race. The senior transfer is white and some of the very players who either lost a varsity position or opportunities to play are African-American.

Dimick's contention that these critics didn't complain when few minorities played on the basketball team is, in my opinion, a shameful attempt to, by bringing up students of color, distract from his conduct. His spouse's lengthy defense is a lot about process, about how he, like some perpetrator, should be afforded certain due process by his critics or how the fact that he said he is sorry should mitigate his admitted violations of the school's code of conduct for coaches.

These tactics; playing the race card and dwelling on process rather than the coach's admitted actions are, sadly, both desperate and irrelevant. Mr. and Mrs. Dimick should stick to the facts about his conduct for which he has been duly reprimanded and suspended.

Martin Demgen

Minneapolis [51]

I sent a letter to the administration and school board listing every open enrollment student by name who played in the program in my four years at Richfield. The list included twelve players who played on any of the four high school teams, freshman through varsity. I wrote a short paragraph on each student, stating where they attended grade school and middle school, when and where they open enrolled from, when I or any of my assistants first met them and/or their parents, and where they were currently attending school.

I also listed the names of five additional players to the letter. These were players who lived in Richfield. I explained how I recruited all five students to Richfield High School. The letter had seventeen names.

* * *

The controversy soon caught the attention of the *StarTribune* and its high school beat writer John Millea. The Tuesday October 11th issue of the *StarTribune* ran the following article:

Season of celebrations, accusations

Open enrollment issues, along with allegations of recruiting and abusive language, erupted long after the Richfield High School boys 'basketball team made a rare state tournament trip

The 2004-05 boys 'basketball season at Richfield High School was one to remember. The Spartans made their first trip to the state tournament since 1974, sparking a renewed sport fervor in the first-ring suburban community. The team was the darling of Richfield all the way through the Class 3A championship game, which ended with a loss to Shakopee.

But underneath the cheers ran a current of dissension that finally bubbled over as the school year ended. A player who had just graduated complained that coaches used abusive language during the season. The coaches countered that the player's complaint was based more on a lack of playing time than obscene language. The school board got involved, the head coach was suspended for the first two games of the 2005-06 season and a volunteer assistant was fired.

The situation at Richfield goes deeper, however. It serves as a case study of what can happen when explosive issues-recruiting allegations, open enrollment, the desire for playing time, pressures on coaches, administrators, players and families-come together in a tightly packed athletic pressure cooker.

And the root cause in this case appears to be one disgruntled player, unhappy when a senior from another community transferred in, joined the starting lineup and displaced athletes who had grown up in Richfield.

Dusty Hinz, who was a senior basketball player last season, wrote an essay for the school newspaper in June. In it, he alleged that Richfield coaches recruited players and he criticized the Minnesota State High School League's monitoring of Minnesota's open-enrollment law, which allowed incoming transfers to take roster spots and playing time from homegrown players (the Richfield roster included one player who transferred in as a senior and four who did so as freshmen; one of those four graduated last spring and the other three will be on the 2005-06 team). Hinz also wrote that coaches used language that constituted verbal abuse.

School officials ruled the essay was unfair and improper, and they stopped distribution of the school paper.

In August, Hinz asked to speak to the Richfield School Board about the language used by the coaches. He told the board of four instances when coaches allegedly used obscene language; head coach Jim Dimick and volunteer assistant Lance Berwald, he said, each did so twice. Each specific allegation by Hinz also was witnessed by Octavius Crawford and Adam Smith, who also graduated in June.

When asked by school officials, Dimick and Berwald admitted they had used such language on those four occasions.

Athletic director Todd Olson suspended Dimick for the first two games of the upcoming season, and terminated Berwald.

"Lance and I both used profanity," Dimick said last week. "I don't think it was more than two occasions for me the whole year, and the same for him. I'm not a swearer. We did use profanity four times, and we totally admitted to it."

Said Berwald: "Should I know better than to swear? Yes, we all should. But in athletics we let the moment get the best of us. And to label us habitual swearers or intimidators is an absolute fallacy."

In an interview Sunday, however, Hinz said his main motivation for going to the school board had less to do with cursing than with his concerns about the future of Richfield basketball. He said it angers him to see players who grew up in Richfield lose spots on the high school team to players who transferred in.

"People probably look at this and think I'm just this little whiner who didn't get any playing time," said Hinz, now a freshman at Augsburg College. "The fact of the matter is, nothing could change what happened to me this season. But I really have a keen interest in the future players that are coming into the Richfield basketball program that are from Richfield, that came up through the program. I don't' want to see the same stuff happen to them.

"I wish I could go after (the coaches) for recruiting; I wish I could go change the law of open enrollment, and I'm going to try to make some efforts to do that. But basically, what happened is, I wanted to get the coaches on something, and I couldn't do it, so I went to something else."

Under MSHSL bylaws, student-athletes can transfer once without penalty. If a student-athlete transfers a second time, he or she must sit out half the varsity season before becoming eligible. Open enrollment, which began in Minnesota in 1988, is one of the most volatile issues in high school athletics. It often leads to suspicions of recruiting.

Richfield officials and the MSHSL have investigated allegations that Dimick recruited players at Richfield. The result?

"Nothing illegal has been going on," Johnson said.

Johnson said if students from other school districts are interested in transferring to Richfield, "We talk academics first and athletics second."

Both Johnson and Olson said troublesome situations might be defused if handled through a chain of command, beginning with coaches and working their way through the athletic administration, the principal's office and ultimately the school board.

"If people would have simply followed procedure and protocol, some of this may never have escalated," Olson said.

In late September Dimick sent a letter to the school board. He wrote that in his four years as Richfield's coach, the number of minority youth attending his summer basketball camp has risen dramatically and the successful high school program is attracting more players interested in open enrolling at Richfield, which means more competition for playing time.

"The real issue is certain kids expecting that positions and playing time on the high school team be reserved for them, regardless of their talent level, he wrote. "A small group of residents are upset, and they are attempting to discredit me with various allegations."

Last week, Dimick spoke at the school board meeting.

"*I don't coach for the money (a coaching salary of about $5,000), I don't coach for the prestige,*" *he said.* "*I do it because I think I can make this world a better place. And this is the thanks I get. This is exactly the kind of thing that drives good coaches out of coaching.*"

The basketball season ended seven months ago, but tempers still run high in Richfield. Letters to the editor of the weekly Richfield Sun-Current continue to be printed, with some supporting the coaches and some opposing them. Olson and Johnson have received letters and e-mails from basketball parents and fans on both sides of the issue.

Olson, a former football coach at Richfield and Edina, was hired as Richfield's athletic director in April and started July 1. Dealing with the basketball situation was his first major task, he said, and lessons can be learned from it.

"*This is still about playing after school,*" *Olson said.* "*The classroom is why everybody is here; basketball and football is what everybody comes to watch. As a society, as a culture, we're a little out of whack. Maybe we need to turn down the pressure valve on the public.*"

The article displayed a team photo taken after the Section championship game, which can be viewed on the internet. The article also displayed four inserts in bold print.

"*This is a huge concept, and it's extremely complex, it's multi-headed. This is not just a boy crying wolf. This is not just coaches swearing at kids.*" *-Todd Olson*

"*The mature coach always has emotions under control, does not attack officials, never uses foul language, and always keeps in mind the responsibility he/she has to set a worth example for the player and the fan. You must always maintain the dignity and decency of the coaching profession and the institution you serve.*" *-Richfield High School's coaches code of conduct*

"*I'm OK with scrutiny. If we're not clean, we're going to get clean.*"*-Jill Johnson*

"*What's sad to me is that this overshadowed an incredibly positive experience for our school and our community.*"*-Jill Johnson* [52]

***

A week later the *StarTribune* contained Millea's editorial:
Open enrollment? Nay, they say
The controversial ruling continues to be the scourge of prep athletics, and there is little reason to foresee any changes
It also included an insert in bold print:

By the numbers. In recent years, more students change schools through open enrollment than through changing residences, according to data from the Minnesota State High School League.

2005-06 (through Oct 12)

Open-enrollment transfers: 462

Change-of-residence transfers: 332

2004-05

Open-enrollment transfers: 661

Change-of-residence transfers: 556

2003-04

Open-enrollment transfers: 667

Change-of-residence transfers 568

Two other inserts were from readers:

"Open enrollment is a bad idea because it is so very difficult to monitor. The transfer rules for eligibility are too lenient. Any player that transfers to a non-resident public school district after his/her freshman year should lose one year of eligibility, including practice time.

-Bob Jentges, North Mankato

"On recruiting, it seems to me the coaches like to play semantics. Is there really a difference between approaching a player directly vs. letting it be known that your program will welcome premier players from outside your city with open arms? I would like to see the state tournament rosters list a player's hometown/residence, just like colleges."

-Doug Degerman, Oakdale

The editorial read as follows:

Here's how high school recruiting often happens: Athletes from different schools play together on summer/offseason/all-star teams,...A coach who has a little bit of sneaky in him sits in the background...Before anybody knows it, a young athlete has changed uniforms, making enemies in his old school (where people feel betrayed) and his new school (where people don't like a newcomer waltzing in and taking a roster spot that would otherwise have gone to a homegrown player).

When I wrote a week ago about the situation with the Richfield boys' basketball team, the response from readers was powerful. There were several layers to the story, but many of the problems began when a senior transferred to Richfield and became a starter on the team. The player had every right to do so under Minnesota's open-enrollment law, of course. But the Richfield scenario shines a bright light on the spider web that open enrollment has become.

Here's Open Enrollment 101: At the urging of Gov. Rudy Perpich, it was enacted by the Legislature in 1988 as a way for students interested in math, science, languages, fine arts, athletics, etc to get the best possible education. It allows students to attend any public school they choose, no matter where they live..

.."I don't like it. And I don't think our schools like it, but we're stuck in a position, because of state law, that allows kids to move for athletic as well as academic purposes," MSHSL executive director Dave Stead said.

We have been down this road many times. I have written about open enrollment in previous years...I received dozens of e-mails about the Richfield situation, and many of them see open enrollment as the monster that won't go away. But the monster still walks among us...

...The MSHSL and school administrators have discussed a further tweaking. Stead said one possibility is this: if a student transfers without moving into the new school district, he/she will not be eligible for athletics in the new district for one year.

"The league could do that," Stead said. "Whether legislators or attorneys would jump in and say we're denying an opportunity, I don't know."

At this point, any change is good change.[53]

* * *

This was followed by more letters to the *Sun-Current*.

Coaches can learn from Hinz episode

In June, Dusty Hinz wrote an editorial in the Richfield student newspaper questioning how Bill Bauman, a lifelong resident of the upscale suburban community of Prior Lake, ended up commuting 50 miles round-trip each day to Richfield High School for his senior year.

That question may have already been answered on Feb. 18, the night seven senior Spartan players were recognized for their contributions to the basketball program.

Fans in attendance received a program featuring a photo and in-depth profile of each senior. Each informative, well-written profile contained a biography and commentary by Coach Jim Dimick, who proudly acknowledged that he had authored the program using information provided by players and parents.

Bauman's profile stated: "He played in the Prior Lake system from first through eleventh grades. He then made the decision to transfer after his junior year. He visited three other area high schools and ultimately chose Richfield, primarily because he thought it was the place where he would learn the most basketball, and also have a chance to win."

This seems inconsistent with a statement made by Richfield High School Principal Jill Johnson in the Oct. 11 issue of the StarTribune.

"We talk academics first and athletics second," Johnson said.

Was Bauman recruited? Coaches insist he was not. Bauman himself has never publicly addressed the matter. Still unanswered, though, is how a player unfamiliar with Richfield or the Classic Suburban Conference reached the conclusion that Richfield was the best place for him.

For the record, I found Bill and his parents to be friendly, passionate people who possess a great enthusiasm for life. This debate has never been about Bill, but rather about the pros and cons of the open enrollment system, along, of course, with the expected conduct of coaches.

Rather than make excuses, perhaps coaches and administrators should take a long, hard look at why an amiable, tolerant young man like Dusty would be harboring such bad feelings two months after the basketball season ended that he would feel compelled to write a lengthy editorial about it.

Was profanity a problem? Yes. Was playing time an issue? Absolutely.

Even with a logjam of talented players in front of him, there were plenty of occasions when Dusty could have been put into the game but was not. Many people do not realize that he was a talented player who would have started on several other area teams.

Coaches on all levels should learn a lesson from this episode and understand that no player is to be taken for granted. Winning is important, but not so critical that sound judgment and common decency should be lost along the way.

Jason Gabbert

Apple Valley [54]

Like Blaine Joerger, Jason Gabbert was from a small town outstate, the town of Wood Lake. The town happened to be the same little hamlet where one of our senior Richfield basketball parents was born and raised. And like Staples, I had a connection to Wood Lake. When I was a young coach at LeSueur I had an All-Conference point-guard named Jon Wolford. Jon's father Casey, at 6-4, was one of the all-time great athletes to play at Wood Lake. This Richfield father and I made the Wolford connection when we first met, and he always brought up Casey Wolford and enjoyed reminiscing about Casey, Wood Lake, District 9, and Region 3.

Wood Lake is located almost straight west of the cities about thirty miles from the South Dakota border, and as the crow flies about forty miles southwest of the largest community in the area, Willmar. Like Staples, it is a typical small prairie town, with an even shorter main street. Its population peaked in 1960 at about 500 people, and was now 400. Also like Staples, it's the kind of town where the families have been tight-knit for generations, and most of the people are the same European nationality. In little schools of this size, over the years, the same surnames tend to appear on the basketball roster, and this was true at Wood Lake.

One night before a big game the previous winter this father introduced his 'good friend' Jason Gabbert to both me and Alcindor. He eagerly pointed out that just like Casey Wolford, Jason was from Wood Lake. Alcindor and I both remember Jason saying that being from a small town, he was a big fan of high school sports, as well as an avid collector of Minnesota Twins souvenir baseballs. Gabbert backed this up by attending many of the boys and girls Richfield sporting events, oftentimes sitting with this same set of parents. Both Alcindor and I remember Gabbert standing in that Friday night gym with fans filing in behind him. We also both remember Jason with his chest puffed out and a huge grin on his face, very proudly acknowledging that as a young boy he dreamed of someday playing for the Wood Lake Warriors.

Bauman family responds to criticism

To the editor:

Much has been written about our son's decision to open enroll at Richfield for his senior year. We felt it unnecessary to dignify all of the false allegations with a response. The letter from Jason Gabbert changed that. This will be our only response.

Bill Bauman has been vilified in the school newspaper and other publications as the evil poster boy of open enrollment. It is the law, so change the law or get over it. People who know Bill will tell you he is a model son. Because of these articles his car has been vandalized more than once and he was forced to change his phone number due to very serious threats.

For the record, his alleged recruitment by Richfield coaches DID NOT HAPPEN. Bill came to Richfield, in part, because he wanted better coaching in basketball, and for several other reasons as outlined on the open enrollment form he filed with both high schools. We suggest any interested parties obtain a copy of that form for further clarification, or cease further speculation.

Regarding coaching, Coaches Dimick and Berwald are excellent coaches, and class individuals. They tried to discourage Bill from transferring for reasons related to Bill's academic and social life. There are some folks in Richfield that don't have any idea how these coaches have worked with the kids in this program, to make them better athletes and better citizens. Were they perfect? No. Who among you reading this letter is? The way these two gentlemen, especially Coach Berwald, were treated in the wake of one student's misguided vendetta is pathetic.

The same standard should be applied to the school newspaper faculty advisor, who failed to oversee the newspaper article written by the malcontented student who felt violated by the open enrollment system and by swear words from coaches in particular. The article was mean spirited, lacked objectivity, and appeared in the year's final newspaper, precluding any response from Bill, who was not even contacted for his input. Bill's only comment was that he felt saddened that students who had not gotten to know him would forever judge him on this one sided, venomous article. We have asked frequently for an apology from this faculty advisor, who failed to do his job in a professional and fair manner. We have yet to receive one. In fairness, let's apply the same standard to that individual as was applied to the coaches.

By the way, Mr. Gabbert, the round trip from Prior Lake to Richfield High School is 35 miles, not 50 miles. Perhaps it would be a good idea to check ALL your facts in the future, before assuming you know what is right and what is wrong, 'cause we all know what happens when you assume.
Todd Bauman and the entire Bauman family
Prior Lake

Bauman letter called 'off base'

To the editor:

Because Dusty Hinz's comments appeared in an editorial format, not a news story, he had no obligation to seek comment from Bill Bauman and the faculty advisor has nothing to apologize for. Hinz stated that Bill's arrival from Prior Lake had a domino-type effect on playing time for lifelong Richfield athletes. The Baumans had an immediate opportunity to respond in the StarTribune, but the story said calls seeking comment were not returned.

Todd Bauman seems to be suffering from over-sensitivity more than anything. Bill has not been portrayed as the "evil poster boy of open enrollment." In fact, he is just one of hundreds of students, athletes and non-athletes, who exercise the open enrollment option each year in Minnesota. In past weeks, the StarTribune has profiled several area boys and girls basketball teams which have benefited from open enrollment. I find it ironic, even amusing, that student-athletes-and their coaches-now seem to fear the label of "recruit' just as much as they would "child molester" or "drug dealer." Is there really much difference between a student who is encouraged to transfer and one who makes the decision on his or her own?

The fact that Bill transferred to Richfield was never a secret. From all appearances, he was quickly accepted and befriended by Richfield students and staff, enjoying a senior year not unlike anyone else's. By the time Hinz's editorial was published, Bill and the basketball season were an afterthought. Yet, Todd Bauman wants us to believe that the good citizens of Richfield, after learning of one disgruntled student's opinion, suddenly turned rabid and vandalized Bill's car?

If Bill was discouraged by coaches from transferring to Richfield for social and academic reasons, why did his parents allow him to do so anyway? Had Bill simply wanted a change of scenery, a Minnesota map reveals 13 public high schools all closer to Prior Lake than Richfield.

Bill's decision to enroll and play cast him into a public debate about open enrollment, not about him as a person. I've never heard anyone make negative or disparaging remarks about Bill or his family. (Letter writer Jason) Gabbert even complimented them, then was criticized for it.

I can't help but wonder if Todd Bauman, while typing his letter, was muttering to himself: "This will teach that Gabbert guy never to compliment my family again!"

Steven T Thompson
Edina

Parents need to let their children handle their failures

To the editor:

I have written many letters to the editor on the subject of Dusty Hinz vs Coaches Dimick and Berwald-most of them were to help me process what has gone on and how it has and will affect the Richfield Community! This is the first one that I've sent!

I have come to the conclusion that yet while I believe that parents should "stand up" for their children, I also believe we should be an example when doing this and face the problem head on, taking action when the problem occurs and running it through the chain of command. I also believe that whatever wrongs their child has done, that they too should be held accountable! (?Reason for waiting until after graduation?!!)

When I go over this situation in my mind it makes me sad for many reasons: 1-that my boys , Jordan, a player on the 2004-05 team and Jared, the water boy for the team had to deal with a player whose behavior was inappropriate to the team and the coaches numerous times throughout the season, 2-that this player is not receiving any repercussion for his actions, 3-the sadness of losing a bright spot in Richfield's Basketball history with the tarnish this has all put on their accomplishments in the State Tournament, 4-the way the transfer was treated by some players (we accept students from other countries but not nearby cities?!!!), 5-the division this has made in our small community, 6-the disappointment for Coach Dimick with his suspension, AND 7-Lance Berwald! A man, coach, and mentor who has been there for so many past and present players! I know his passion for the game of basketball and I understand his love for being with the players!

I remember after the State Tournament how everyone in the community had a smile on their face and a friendly word to the people of the community, people you might only know by a familiar face. Now, I see sadness, worry and a division between the people, avoiding each other.

The hardest thing is being around the players from the last year and hearing the disappointment in their voices when they talk about the upcoming season without Coach Berwald! Who has really won in this whole situation? Not my family, Jordan and Jared enjoyed every part of playing for and being with Coach Berwald! He will truly be missed this season, but the team will rise above the adversity and use this as incentive.

I found a quote that I thought was especially fitting for Dusty and his parents: "And one of the things we need to do as parents is to let our children handle their failures-be there to support them, but let them handle the disappointing moments. Because that's how they build the ability to go out on their own and face obstacles."-Gray Whitestone

No matter what comes out in all of this, no one can make me think other than that this was all created because of a player who thought he was all about team until he didn't play and then it became all about him! One's true character comes forth when things don't go their own way! Sad for all of us, but so great for all the other players who rose up above all of this during the season and still achieved success. Those are kids to be proud of!!!
Jean Noonan
Richfield [55]

* * *

By means of the internet and two newspapers, the controversy spread from the high school in May to the community in September to the state in October. It began with the *Spotlite* article published on the Internet, written by the student Dusty Hinz and reviewed by the faculty adviser, Bruce Wiebe. In my opinion, much of this article was not factual, and where it was factual, it only told half of the story. The end result was a community debate and a state-wide discussion. And both were based upon some pertinent facts that were assumed to be true, but were not true.

The article on the Internet stated WRITTEN BY DUSTY HINZ, WITH SHARED VIEWS OF ADAM, MIKE, NATE, AND OCTAVIUS. This gave the Internet reader the impression that five students and four of my players were endorsing the article. Millea's October article in the *StarTribune* repeated this notion, when it stated that each specific allegation...was also witnessed by Octavius Crawford and Adam Smith.

Nate definitely agreed with the article because he was cut in November. Octavius had no idea that his name would be on the article, and he was furious. The day after the paper copies were distributed at school, he slammed Dusty up against some lockers in the hallway, pinned him with one arm, pointed his finger in Dusty's faced, and berated him. Adam's only comment that I later heard was "Dusty's been my friend since grade school". Mike told me, "You know I had nothing to do with that article." And the player who was cut in mid-season, Dennis Robinson, said to me, "Coach, I never badmouthed the program."

One of the main points of the Spotlite article was that Bill's transfer had caused a bubble player to be cut. *When new talent is imported,…bubble players are cut…and that's exactly what happened in Richfield this season.* The article was written with the assistance of a friend who was the last player cut from his #1 ranked high school basketball team following the importation of a senior center who came to play for his school. –Dusty Hinz. I made sure during try-outs that Bill's presence would have absolutely no bearing on any other player being cut. I discussed this with the coaching staff, the administration, and the team. The statement that a bubble player was cut was a flat out lie. The coaching staff knew it was a lie. Jim Baker knew it was a lie. Jason Wenschlag and Jill Johnson knew it was a lie. And all of the players and Dusty knew it was a lie. In the same situation, I believe that Bruce Kugath at Shakopee did not cut a player to make room for Jarod Ewing when he open enrolled/transferred in as a senior. I also believe that Bob Vaughn at Braham did not cut a player to make room for Chris Vavra when he open enrolled/transferred in as a junior from Cambridge-Isanti. This flat out lie was an impetus for John Millea to write in the *StarTribune*, *Before anybody knows it, a young athlete has changed uniforms,…taking a roster spot that would otherwise have gone to a homegrown player. –John Millea*

When it came to profanity, once again, only half of the story was told. Both times that I threw out f-bombs, I apologized to the team the same day or the next day. Both times that Lance threw out f-bombs also included Dusty Hinz throwing out f-bombs. Lance made two mistakes; he raised his voice and he swore. There was nothing wrong with his message. Dusty Hinz heard the message before, and Dusty Hinz had said that he was on-board with it. This half-told story was followed by letters to the *Sun-Current* describing our behavior as *demeaning, disrespectful, and lacking sound judgment and common decency.* The *StarTribune* article stated that *a player who had just graduated complained that coaches used abusive language during the season.* To say that either I or

Lance treated any player unfairly, verbally abused a player, or exhibited a lack of sound judgment or common decency was a joke.

The *Spotlite* article described the 'domino effect'. Bill Bauman's transfer did cause a domino effect of playing time. Bill averaged about 24 minutes of playing time per game. Had he not been at Richfield, Adam, Octavius, and Santino who were all part of the playing rotation, would have played more minutes. When a player transfers in, there is always a domino effect of playing time. Conversely, when a player transfers out, there is a reverse domino effect. If Isaiah Goodman had not transferred to Holy Angels as a freshman, we would have had two great point guards. If I had known that Dusty was not going to be happy as a bench-warmer, we would not have cut Dennis Luke, who had a perfect attitude. Dusty's 'domino effect' deprived Dennis from being part of a state tournament team. The name of Dennis Luke wasn't mentioned one time in the *Spotlite* article.

The *Spotlite* article also stated that *Mike, Adam, Octavius, Nate, and I in varying degrees, came all the way up through the Richfield basketball program.* Mike, Adam, and Nate all came all the way up through the program. Octavius did not. Octavius and his brother Xavier moved to Richfield at the beginning of their fifth-grade year. They attended the Richfield schools in fifth, sixth, and seventh grade. Beginning in their eighth-grade year, they moved to Okinawa for two years. They moved back to Richfield at the beginning of their sophomore years. As seventh graders they played on the middle school team with its twelve-week season. In these three years in Richfield, they never attended the summer camp, and they never played on the traveling team. They played winter traveling basketball with the Urban Stars. To state that Octavius came 'all the way up through the Richfield basketball program in any degree' was literally true. In my opinion, it was also disingenuous and intentionally misleading. This untruth combined with the untruth that a bubble player had been cut, coyly deflected the question of whether or not the increased competition from the black kids had anything to do with the Dusty's frustrations and anger. Nate (black kid) *was deprived of his chance to finish his career on varsity.* Octavius (black kid) *had his minutes reduced dramatically.* Bill Bauman (white kid) was *the new talent that was imported.* Later in the *Spotlite* article the reader is assured that race cannot be an issue when the article says *when Governor Perpich devised open enrollment in 1991, his aims were education and integration...I would like our school and community as a whole to discourage upper-class transfers.* So from Dusty's perspective, clearly, race had nothing to do with any part of this controversy.

However, earlier in the *Spotlite* article Dusty Hinz wrote, *not getting any playing time would have been a whole lot easier to accept if the minutes had gone to someone who had at least come up in our program.* And Millea quoted Dusty Hinz in the *Star-Tribune* to say *it angers him to see players who grew up in Richfield lose spots on the high school team to players who transferred in.* It is self-evident that freshman transfers don't come up through the program or grow up in Richfield. During Dusty Hinz's two years on the varsity, 'minutes/spots' had gone to 11 players in four classes who <u>both</u> did not 'come up in our program' <u>and</u> who had not 'grown up' in Richfield. They were Jawaun Bowman, DeRail Moore, Bryson Scott, Chris Brinson, Ray Brown, Xavier Crawford, Octavius Crawford, Dennis Robinson, Dennis Luke, Ojullo Madho, and Bill Bauman. Bill was the only senior transfer. Bill was also the only white kid. The other 10 were all black.

In my opinion the core issue was entitlement, as evidenced by the above statements about kids who came up in the program and kids who grew up in Richfield. The concerned citizens believed in entitlement, that program kids should be granted roster spots and playing time over non-program kids. Nothing had changed from the first time that the parents and concerned citizens had tried to fire me two years earlier. And the cause of this loss of entitlement was the rapidly changing demographics and the result of me aggressively recruiting the <u>Richfield</u> black kids into the <u>Richfield</u> program. In the *Richfield Sun-Current,* writer Seth Rowe clearly sent my message to the community. Millea only forwarded a portion of this message to the state. His *StarTribune* article stated *and the root cause in this case appears to be one disgruntled player, unhappy when a senior from another community transferred in.*

The 'concerned citizens' knew that they couldn't use entitlement as their reason for demanding my termination, because lurking beneath it was the issue of race. They searched for any other possible reason. The only two that they could find were an open enrollment white student and profanity. I wanted the community to know that the concerned citizens were trying to get me fired in any possible way that they could think of. In the *Sun-Current,* Rowe quoted me to say *a small group of people try to bring me down in any possible way that they can think of.* Millea omitted this sentence in the *StarTribune,* but included the sentences that were sandwiched around it.

Because the initial source of the *StarTribune* articles was the Internet article from the *Spotlite,* other statements in Millea's article were misleading or not true. His statement that our roster *included one player who transferred in as a senior and four who did so as freshman,* was not true. Plus, it gave the reader the false impression that we had four open enrollment players who transferred in as freshman primarily to play basketball. Bill open-enrolled and transferred in as a senior. Ray and OJ open enrolled and transferred in as freshman. Octavius Crawford transferred in as a sophomore when his parents moved to Richfield. Dustin Driefke transferred in as a freshman from Bloomington Lutheran Elementary. He was born and raised in Richfield. So out of Millea's supposed five transfers, two lived in Richfield.

We actually did have two other open enrollment players on our roster, Santino and Dexter. Both were sophomores. Dexter transferred in and open enrolled from Minneapolis as a sixth grader. Santino transferred in as a second grader when his mom moved to Richfield from her hometown of Aberdeen, Mississippi. They moved back to Mississippi for a year and then back to Richfield when he was a sixth grader. When his mom moved to Bloomington for his freshman year, he open enrolled and continued his attendance in the Richfield public schools.

The Richfield school system had over 4,000 students in grades K-12. About 400 students open enrolled in, and about 400 students open enrolled out. Almost all of the students who open enrolled out lived on the west side of Richfield, and they open enrolled to Edina. Almost all of the students who open enrolled in came from south Minneapolis and the vast majority of them were minority students, via The Choice is Yours Program. Over 100 of these open enrollment students played sports.

Ironically, the *Spotlite* article never mentioned Santino, the player who caused the 'domino effect' that planted Dusty Hinz firmly on the bench. Clearly, Santino had spent most of his elementary and middle school years living in Richfield and attending the Richfield schools. He was never part of the basketball program until I recruited him into it as an eighth grader. Compared to Dusty's *nine years of Richfield basketball, eleven teams and roughly 1,500 hours of work put in,* Santino played on four Richfield basketball teams and practiced over 1,600 hours in only two years. And the 'concerned citizens' never brought the plight of kids like Santino to the attention of the school board. Yet one of their mantras was that they 'just wanted what was best for the Richfield kids'. There is no question in my mind that these self-appointed community watchdogs didn't consider Santino and other kids like him to be Richfield kids.

The distribution range of the *StarTribune* was the entire Twin City metro area, most of rural Minnesota and part of western Wisconsin. The many people who read Millea's two articles did not know the above facts. In the Richfield situation, these facts were material and significant, as evidenced by the letters to the editor in Millea's second article. Not one of the letters addressed entitlement or demographic change. All of the letters were about one issue, open enrollment.

This incident also marked what I believe was a step up in the effort of the 'concerned citizens' and disgruntled parents to undermine the program. They now had more people in their ranks feeding the community with misinformation. My sources soon reported to me that some parents of the youth players told them that some Richfield residents had been talking with some of the traveling players. These people were telling the kids that they shouldn't play traveling basketball because when they get to high school, they will lose their spots to city kids. I asked my assistants to check on this. I wanted to have two facts verified, if youth players were being told these things, and if they were indeed hearing the term 'city kids'. When my assistants got back to me, they confirmed that both facts were true, to which Alcindor responded, "I don't remember Bill Bauman ever being called a city kid."

* * *

The first week in November I found another letter in my mailbox at the high school.

11-5-05

Coach Dimick:

You did a good job, in good faith, with your basketball team. Don't let them bug you about recruiting, etc.

Dean Torgeson

Richfield

The coaching genius was ready to move on.

1974 Basketball Team

In the 12 years following the storybook 1960 season, the basketball program remained solidly in the upper half of the Lake Conference. Vance Crosby replaced Gene Farrell as the head coach in the 1963-64 season. He remained the head coach for eight years. He had two great teams that were a break or a cold shooting night away from making deep runs into the state tournament, and quite possibly winning it. And with the exception of his first season, the team was never below five hundred.

The 1964-65 team tied for the Lake Conference title with Edina with a conference record of 14-2. Crosby pulled off this title with one of the shortest teams in the Lake. The Spartans were spearheaded by Denny Bengtson, and the Bishop twins, Barry and Bob. Minnetonka finished in third place at 12-4. The first time around the conference the Spartans lost to Edina 67-64 and they defeated Minnetonka 58-41. Both games were at home. Late in the season they won at Edina 56-53, and they lost at Minnetonka 72-62. Both games had overflow crowds.

In the District 18 tournament semifinals, Minnetonka defeated Edina 63-53 and Richfield beat Hopkins 60-51 to set up the championship game at Williams Arena. The final was not close as Minnetonka jumped out to a 25-14 lead after one quarter and extended it to 45-26 at halftime. The *Richfield News* reported that

Richfield hit at a dismal 32% while Tonka hit at a devastating 57% clip... [56]

The closest that the Spartans could get in the second half was 12 points early in the fourth quarter, but it was too little too late and the Skippers finished with a 75-59 victory. Minnetonka then beat St Cloud Tech 82-60 and Willmar 65-58 to go to state. In the state tournament they won out over Franklin 76-54, Bemidji 67-57, and Faribault 71-60 to win the state championship with a final record of 22-4. Richfield's final record was 19-3.

* * *

The 1967-68 team had both height and athleticism. At about mid-season Crosby settled on a starting line-up of Jon Nicholson (5-8), Jim Thompson

(6-5), Doug Kingsriter (6-2), Gary Haugen (6-5), and Ken Anderson (6-8). Thompson was a slender pure shooter who could elevate. Nicholson's quickness created offense off of the dribble going either way. At the end of the regular season both were voted to the five man All Lake Conference first team. This was after Richfield finished second to Edina in the Lake with a record of 14-2. The Hornets won the Lake outright at 15-1. The Spartan's two losses in the Lake were both in the first round of conference play, at Edina 54-48, and at Bloomington Lincoln 56-53. Crosby's team avenged the Bloomington loss in February with an 85-65 rout at home.

This set up the rematch with Edina. It was also a state wide showdown game, as the Hornets and Spartans were ranked #1 and #2 in the state for most of the winter. Edina had been undefeated state champs two years in a row going into the season, with identical records of 26-0, and they were holding a 69-game winning streak.

Two preliminary games were played, a sophomore game and a JV game. When the sophomore game began the gym was already filled to capacity. An estimated 8,000 fans were turned away, and there was not an open parking space on the residential streets within two miles of the high school. More than a few longtime supporters sneaked in through the back door to athletic director Harold Alhbom's office.

The first half of the varsity game was the best played half of the season for the Spartans. With point guard Jon Nicholson controlling the ball they only had one turnover and they hit their open shots, while the Hornets shot poorly. When the first half buzzer sounded Richfield had a 45-25 advantage and the home town fans stood and screamed wildly. In the basement locker room below the gym coach Vance Crosby reminded his players that Edina would make adjustments, and they would not shoot cold the whole game. "We're going to have to withstand their runs, because they're gonna make a couple runs at us."

His words rang true. The Hornets switched to a 3-1-1 half court press, which resulted in two third quarter runs to narrow the score to 57-49. In the fourth quarter the margin fluctuated between 6 and 10 points. With 6 seconds to play Edina scored to cut the margin to 79-75, followed by a time out. In the huddle, Crosby shouted "who says it's over, there's still time on the clock." With four Spartan players lined up near the baseline, Jon Nicholson cut off a back pick and streaked towards mid-court. The in-bounder, Doug Kingsriter lofted a perfect arching pass. Nicholson caught it over his shoulder in front of the scorer's bench without breaking stride. As he dribbled all alone towards the basket the Spartan crowd began celebrating. He released a soft wide-open lay-up as time expired. When the ball bounced softly through the net to the floor fans swarmed the court, he was mobbed, and bedlam reigned. Richfield had halted Edina's 69 game winning streak.

Jim Thompson finished with 29 points against the tall and athletic Edina front line. The 69-game winning streak still stands as a state record today. In the post-game locker room Coach Crosby was quoted in the *Richfield News*,

"We played close to perfect basketball in the first half, but the key to the whole ballgame was the fact that we didn't collapse in the second half when they cut the lead to six points." [57]

More than one Richfield old timer told me that the 1968 Edina game was the biggest standing room only crowd in the history of the program. Bruce Hoffarber was a fifth grader at the time. Standing in the gym forty years later, Hoffarber told me, "I was sitting with my buddies in the top row right up there", as he turned and pointed to the top row of the end zone bleachers on the east end. "I remember it like it was yesterday. This place was jam packed. Nobody wanted to get up and leave their seat to get popcorn. It was one of the most exciting basketball games that I've ever seen".

When the first week of districts began, Lake coaches considered five conference teams capable of winning the state title. Richfield marched to the final with solid wins over Bloomington Kennedy 58-40, Robbinsdale 65-50, and Hopkins 80-65. This set up the rubber match with Edina at Williams Arena. Twin Cities news outlets billed the game as the 'state championship game two weeks early'.

When the teams took the floor for warm-ups, it felt like a state tournament atmosphere. With 13,640 fans, the area was filled to 75% capacity, with the only empty seats in the back rows. Soon after the opening tip, Edina jumped out to a 7-0 lead. Crosby called a quick time out and his team regrouped. Edina then maintained a 4 to 8 point lead for most of the game. The halftime score was 33-28, and after three quarters it was 45-37. With the Hornets playing a stingy man to man defense, Richfield was unable to narrow the margin. When the clock ticked below three minutes, Richfield was again down by 7, with the score 54-47. Edina coach Duane Baglien ordered his players to spread the court. The Hornets took care of the basketball, hit their free throws, and the Spartan shooters went cold. When the game ended the score was 65-51. Crosby was quoted in the *Richfield News* to say

"We didn't get the scoring spurt we needed". [58]

Richfield finished the season with an overall record of 19-3.

Edina went on to win their third consecutive state championship. They posted victories over St Cloud Tech 78-60 and Willmar 66-54 in Region 5. At state they took out unbeaten Hayfield 63-49, unbeaten Duluth Central 91-61, and Moorhead 70-45. They finished 25-1. The lone blemish on their record was to the Richfield Spartans inside the jam-packed gym at 70th and Harriet.

* * *

From 1961 until 1970, the Lake Conference had dominated both the region and the state. The 1970 tournament was the last year of the one class system in Minnesota. During these 10 winters, the region champion was a Lake team eight times. Five of the nine Lake schools had taken turns advancing to state; St. Louis Park, Bloomington, Minnetonka, Edina, and Robbinsdale. They won a combined five state championships, St. Louis Park in 1962, Minnetonka in 1965, and Edina in 1966, 1967, and 1968. The only things lacking in Crosby's tenure were a Region 5 and a state championship trophy. The program had remained stellar in what was clearly the best conference in the state.

* * *

Stu Starner was promoted from assistant to head coach in the fall of 1971, inheriting the youth program that the previous coaches had built. The feeder program for basketball was similar to the other sports. It began with a third and fourth grade skills program which was taught by the high school assistant coaches. All eight elementary schools had a fifth-grade and a sixth-grade basketball team, and all three Catholic schools had basketball teams for fifth through eighth graders. The public-school teams played 12 games, and the Catholic teams played more games. When the kids eventually entered one of the two junior highs, East or West, they competed to make the seventh, eighth and ninth grade teams. These teams played a 12-game schedule against junior highs from Bloomington, Edina, and St Louis Park. And they played each other twice. The starters from East and West lined up at the center jump circle knowing that only five of them would be starters when they were sophomores on the B squad. So out of the 100 boys who made their elementary school teams, about 15 would make the B squad at the high school.

The entire program was school based, and was administered by the high school coaching staff. The youth coaches used the same fundamental drills that the high school teams used, and all of the teams played man to man defense. There were no traveling teams, no basketball board, and no parents donating time. The teams did not spend their practice time working on zone traps. And there were no parent/coaches from outside the community trying to recruit the best players to an All-Star traveling team.

In the summer groups of boys shot baskets at the city park courts and at the driveway hoops that hung on the garages. In each neighborhood, older boys bonded with younger boys. If a neighbor was a starter at the high school, the younger kids saw his work ethic displayed on their street. Each group of boys knew the kids in their neighborhood, and their friends at their grade school. Most kids from the east side didn't know the kids from the west side, and visa-versa. But they did know that there were about ten schools at their grade level, all full of players in their grade hoping to someday play for the Spartans. And when they attended the high school games with their folks, the gym was always full. The goal for many boys was simply to make the team when they got to high school.

Starner inherited a talented class of sophomores that had come out of this program. By the time they were juniors, four of them were starters along with 6-5 senior center Paul Kottom. Sometime after Christmas, Starner made a change in the playing rotation which changed the complexion of the team and the season. He moved up sophomore point guard Bruce Hoffarber from the junior varsity. The team immediately jelled. They finished the season strong, ending up in second place in the Lake Red Conference with a record of 9-5. First place Robbinsdale Cooper was 11-3.

Then they surprised everybody by marching to the state finals. In the region tournament they won three consecutive games. They defeated Minnetonka 58-47, Bloomington Jefferson 52-38, and Hopkins Eisenhower 57-53.

They opened up the state tournament by defeating Lake Blue champion Edina West 64-49. This was followed by a dramatic come from behind semi-final victory over Rochester John Marshall 52-47. In the finals they played Anoka. With a huge lineup, Anoka was heavily favored. Richfield played one of their best games of the year and ended up losing 58-54. The following winter expectations would be high and Richfield would not surprise anyone.

* * *

Starner began the season with six solid players. Paul Meissner (6-6), Brian Denman (6-3), and Bruce Kottom (6-3) posed a tall and physical front line. Steve Bender (6-2) could play both inside and out. The guards were Bruce Hoffarber (6-0) and Joel Zilka (6-1). Like the 1960 and 1968 teams, they had great overall height and athleticism.

The team opened the season beating Minneapolis Southwest 46-43 before a sellout crowd at home. This was followed by wins over Minneapolis Central 61-51 and Hopkins Eisenhower 73-52. A tight non-conference win over Mounds View 67-60 was followed by an easier 77-60 win over Edina East. Richfield then beat Wayzata 79-42 to make it 6-0 at Christmas.

In January the winning streak continued. They ran off eight consecutive solid wins against Lake Conference foes; Minnetonka 69-47, Cooper 49-41, Bloomington Kennedy 73-52, Mound 59-49, Robbinsdale 73-61, Armstrong 64-61, St Louis Park 74-60, and Bloomington Lincoln 62-52. They were drawing full house crowds both at home and on the road and their record was 14-0.

The second Saturday in February they played Austin in a non-conference game at home. Austin was again fighting for the Big 9 title with an overall record of 12-2. Another capacity crowd included many coaches who were scouting for the tournament.

They played maybe their best game of the year to win 74-62. The following Tuesday the *Minneapolis Tribune* included a column by high school sports writer Bruce Brothers. Hopkins Lindbergh coach Ken Novak (Sr), whose team had a record of 14-1 at the time was quoted:

"Richfield is as physical a ball club as I've seen in years. That team is really impressive. Every guy shoots well. And they've got three or four guys taller than my tallest player. I was looking for a weakness, but I couldn't find any. They reminded me of the Edina teams when Bob Zender was leading them to several state championships in a row."

Austin coach Oscar Haddorff was also quoted:

"We're taller and stronger than we have been, but Richfield shut off our inside game tonight…our defense couldn't stop them. That's the best team we've seen all year."

Brothers went on to write;

Starner, the Richfield coach, whose team has won 15 straight, was all smiles in his team's dressing room after the game and abandoned his usually cautious approach to comment that it was one of his team's best games, "and it was against a good club."…

…The opinion here is that no one can stop Richfield. Like Anoka last year, the Spartans have good balance, height and depth. They also have excellent leadership from 6-footer Steve Bender, who seems to make the team click and can go underneath and rebound with the big boys…

… And it should be noted, all of the top six players on the team made important contributions last year when Richfield went to the Class AA finals before losing to Anoka by four points. The tournament experience is there.[59]

The next two games produced wins over Edina West 75-59 and Bloomington Jefferson 54-53. The last game of the regular season would be a showdown against Lake Blue champion Hopkins Lindbergh at Richfield. Coach Ken Novak's team at Lindbergh was small and quick, with a record of 16-1. The Richfield gym was full before halftime of the sophomore game, and when the fire marshals arrived to remove some of the fans, they couldn't fit through the doors. When the Richfield varsity players left the stands to head to the dressing room, fans quickly moved in to take their seats. Long time loyalists said that it was reminiscent of the 1968 Edina game, punctuated by the fact that it was 'back to the 50's day' at the high school. In what proved to be a barn burner, Lindbergh won 68-67. The two Lake Conference champions both finished the regular season at 17-1.

* * *

Beginning with the 1970-71 school year, the state tournament was expanded from one to two classes. The 68 largest schools were placed in Class AA, and were divided geographically into eight regions, with letters to denote them, A-H. A few more of the largest schools were added the next couple of years, so that by the 1973-74 season, some of the regions had 10 or 11 teams. Five of the eight Class AA regions were comprised of metropolitan schools, which were all formerly in Regions 4 and 5 in the old one class system. The outstate regions on the prairie in the western half of the state changed very little. These regions are listed with the number of schools which were moved up to Class AA; Region 2 (2 schools), Region 3 (0 schools), Region 6 (5 schools), and Region 8 (1 school).

In Class A the historical eight regions and 32 two districts were altered somewhat to balance the number of teams in each district. The districts around the metropolitan area had the most modifications. Some of the outstate districts and regions changed very little.

Richfield was in Region E. In the opening round of Friday night games, the Spartans demolished Minneapolis North 91-45 at Edina West. The Polars had finished 6-8 in the Minneapolis City Conference. In the semi-finals the following Tuesday at Bloomington Kennedy Richfield faced Edina East. The Hornets had finished in the middle of the Lake Red. Richfield won easily 82-63. The game was basically over after one quarter when the Spartans surged to a 31-10 lead. At halftime the score was 50-30.

Two days later were the finals. The Thursday night games were played at the Metropolitan Sports Center, which hosted three consecutive Region championship games in one night. The facility was the home of the Minnesota North Stars NHL hockey team. It was built to be converted to a basketball court, and it had also been the home court for the two brief years that the Twin Cities had a professional basketball team in the ABA. It was cavernous and it did not have the feel of a high school gym. Richfield played in the 5:15 game followed by the Region F and D title games. On this night it held a crowd of over 7,000 people.

The region final game would not be as easy as the first two games. Bloomington Jefferson had finished the season in the top half of the Lake Blue. The Jaguars had come within one point of defeating the Spartans at Jefferson three weeks earlier. They would come into the game knowing they could defeat Richfield.

Under the direction of Coach Jack Evens, they began the game in a stingy 2-3 zone defense, limiting the Spartans to one shot on almost every possession. The Jaguars also controlled the tempo with a patient offense and very few turn-overs. After one quarter Richfield was in the lead 13-8. At halftime Jefferson was in the lead 23-21. Richfield, which had been playing a 1-2-2 match-up zone, switched to a man-to-man defense at the half. At the end of the third quarter, it was still anybody's game. Richfield was holding on to a 36-33 lead.

With a little under two minutes to play Richfield was ahead 45-41, and Jefferson had the ball. The Jaguars were patiently working their offense against the Spartans pressure man to man defense. Then Bruce Hoffarber picked off a pass near mid court and drove in for a layup which increased the lead to 6 points. The Richfield defense shut down Jefferson in the last minute, and Brian Denman and Bruce Kottom combined to sink 4 free throws. Richfield had a hard fought 50-42 victory. They avoided a loss on a cold-shooting, 33% night from the field in the spacious sports center.

***

For the first time in many years the state tournament would not be played at Williams Arena. The city of St Paul with its new hockey/basketball arena had given the state high school league a sweet financial deal in order to get the tournament at the St Paul Civic Center. First round games in Class AA were to be played on Wednesday. Afternoon games pitted Alexander Ramsey (15-7) against Bemidji (21-2) and Rochester Mayo (16-5) against Anoka (15-6). The first evening game featured Minneapolis Washburn (20-1) and Hopkins Lindbergh (20-1). Richfield (20-1) would face Willmar (14-6). If the format of the tournament had been one class with the historical regions, Mayo would have been in Region 1 and Bemidji in Region 8. Ramsey and Anoka would both have been in Region 4, and the four schools of Washburn, Lindbergh, Willmar, and Richfield all would have been in Region 5. The enrollments of the schools ranged from Willmar with 1,070 students and Bemidji with 1,150 students, to Anoka with 2,500 students and Richfield with 2,700 students.

The week of the tournament members of the 1960 team showed up at practice and spoke to the team. They told the team that they were about to experience something unlike anything they had ever experienced before, and to enjoy it, because it would be over by Sunday.

***

Willmar had finished the season strong. They had been red hot in the regional tournament shooting over 60% from the field in their three games. With an average height of only 5-10, they were quick and used a full court press.

The game was close the entire first half, with Richfield ahead 32-28 at the break. Brian Denman opened the third quarter with consecutive three-point (and one) plays, which expanded the lead to 38-28. At the quarter's end the score was 41-35 and the Spartans coasted to a 68-52 victory. In other first round games Bemidji earned a come from behind win over Ramsey 67-53, Rochester Mayo nipped Anoka 52-51, and Washburn beat Lindbergh and Coach Novak 58-56 in overtime.

The next opponent was Washburn. The Millers had run the table in the tough Minneapolis City Conference. Their only loss was to St Paul Mechanic Arts in the annual Twin City game 55-46, on the last Saturday of the regular season. Both Washburn and Richfield had identical records of 21-1. Richfield hammered the boards with their trademark rebounding balance. Their rebounding margin of 54-34 carried them to a 68-56 win on the scoreboard.

In the first semifinal, Bemidji defeated Rochester Mayo 66-51. Like Richfield, Bemidji was big with 6-7 Steve Vogel in the middle averaging 19 points a game. Also, like Richfield, their strength was rebounding and they liked to get out and run.

The state championship game was close from start to finish. At the first quarter break Richfield lead 15-10. At halftime the Spartans were ahead 31-30, and after three quarters they led 39-38. In the fourth quarter both teams missed good shots, but a couple more shots dropped for the Lumberjacks than they did for the Spartans. Bemidji was hanging on to a 2-to-4-point margin as time became more precious.

According to an article Bruce Brothers wrote in the *Minneapolis Tribune:*

Pre-tournament favorite Richfield trailed 50-48 and gave up the ball on a traveling violation with 40 seconds left in the game, but Steve Bender brought the 13,361 spectators to their feet when he intercepted a Bemidji pass near the Richfield basket and headed toward what he hoped would be the tying points. "I got hit," Bender said of some body-bumping as he drove the lane, "but the referees didn't see it that way."

His shot caromed off the backboard and into the hands of teammate Brian Denman, who immediately went back up for a shot. As he let the ball go Bemidji center Vogel leaped high, batting it down and with it Richfield's chances.

"I don't know what happened," Vogel said. "I saw two hands on the ball and I just jumped. The ball went into my arms."

"I didn't even see him," said Denman, the 6-3 Richfield forward. "He came out of nowhere and leaped high. He's a great ballplayer and he knocked it away and there went our chances."

This was followed by two Bemidji free throws and a basket at the buzzer by Bruce Kottom. The final score was 52-50…[60]

Starner's team finished the season 22-2. Richfield High School had completed exactly 20 years since it opened in the fall of 1954. In those 20 basketball seasons, five teams had proved themselves worthy of winning the state title; 1960, 1965, 1968, 1973, and 1974. Once again, Richfield had come up short in a close game to the team that was crowned the state champion; Edgerton, Minnetonka, Edina, Anoka, and Bemidji.

For the seniors of 1974, the loss to Bemidji was a heart-breaking way to end a season that had been a fantastic ride. As juniors they had surprised everybody when they advanced just as far to the state championship game. As sixth graders, they sat together in the stands and experienced the post-game pandemonium when the 1968 team ended Edina's state record 69 game winning streak. As third graders, some walked into a packed and loud Richfield gymnasium with their parents holding their hands when the 1965 team made its memorable run. And beginning as elementary students, these seniors had most certainly heard the legend of the 1960 team from their coaches, parents, older siblings, and neighbors. As one Richfield athlete put it many years later, "they were our heroes,…they were gods."

Fifth Winter

You don't win games as a coach during games. You win games as a coach before games. Players win during games, not coaches.

—*Red Auerbach*

Before school started, I hired Omar McMillan as an assistant coach. According to the administrators, he was a hard-working teacher who would go as far in education as he chose to. As a fifth-grade teacher at the Intermediate School, he was one of those people that parents hoped their kids would get as a teacher.

Omar had a stellar basketball background. He spent the last four years as an assistant women's coach at Minneapolis Community Technical College. The Lady Marauders won the NJCAA D3 national championship in 2003-04. He grew up on the north side of Milwaukee. He attended Washington High School and played for long time renowned coach James Gordon. As a junior he helped lead the Purgolders to the Division I (largest class) state championship. In the state championship game at Kohl Arena, Omar calmly made two free throws with four seconds to go to seal a 70-67 victory over Sheboygan North. He attended Bethany College in Mankato, which at that time was a two-year school, along with his grade school buddy Bu Hayes. Bu had attended Bradley Tech High School in Milwaukee. After being recruited by a number of Division 2 universities, they stayed together and moved on to D3 St Scholastica College in Duluth. At St Scholastica they played on winning teams that defeated schools that the Saints rarely beat including Minnesota Duluth and UW-Superior. He was still as fit as when he played. He was a physical 6-2 and 190. As an old coach once told me, "It never hurts to have one coach on your staff who can beat any of your players one on one." We now had that. The coaching staff also now had a presence in the lower grades of the school district.

Another bonus of having Omar on the coaching staff was that he taught the 1st and 2nd grade winter Saturday morning skill sessions. These consisted of six Saturday mornings. The sessions were one hour, and they were held in the small gym. We rolled out the six rows of wooden bleachers on the north wall.

The parents sat in the bleachers and watched the activity. From my first year at Richfield, we usually had about thirty kids attend these sessions.

As a young coach I heard CM Newton speak at a coaching clinic about working with elementary school kids. At the time Newton was the coach at Alabama. He talked only about ball handling, explaining that it was the one skill that little kids could do as well as bigger stronger older kids. He then demonstrated a number of individual drills. We taught all of these drills at these sessions. We also did a number of fun drills, which kept all of the kids organized and in lines, and always moving. We used eight-foot baskets throughout the sessions. At the end we let them play three on three or four on four half court.

I believed that we should use the sessions to not only teach the kids, but also educate the parents on how to help teach ball handling and shooting. We talked about learning how to shoot the ball with the proper grip and mechanics. We explained to the parents that little kids develop bad habits when shooting regulation size basketballs at ten-foot baskets. They need smaller basketballs and shorter baskets. A few of the kids didn't have basketballs at home. With the money donated by the VFW and American Legion, we were able to give these kids a smaller basketball to take home and practice with.

Omar was a natural at relating to kids of this age. His teaching style was upbeat and excited, and he always had a smile. A few of the high school players assisted him. As with the summer camp, Omar used the lesson plans and parent hand-outs that I had designed, and that we had been using for the past four years. Given his impeccable reputation as a teacher, this was good for the program and it was good for the school district.

****

As the fall progressed and I worked with Todd Olson, we quickly became good friends. Todd grew up in Fridley, a second ring suburb north of Minneapolis on the east side of the Mississippi River. After graduating from Fridley High School, Todd played football at St Thomas. In 1987 he began teaching at Richfield and assisting head football coach Dick Walker. He and his wife Lisa settled into Richfield and bought a house on the east side of town. When Dick retired in 1990 Todd became the head coach. He continued the success of Walker by helping the Spartans win the Section championship four consecutive seasons. In 1995 he made the move one suburb to the west when he was hired by Edina. When he took over at Edina there were 450 kids playing football at all levels. He increased that number to over 1,200. He was the head coach from 1995 to 2004. His 2002 team finished 10-2 with losses to two state champions, Eden Prairie from Minnesota and Rockhurst High School from

Kansas City, Missouri. In the ten years that Todd spent at Edina, the family never moved. He and Lisa's three sons were now in middle school and high school. They were all football, hockey, and baseball players.

Todd's dad Warren had been the football coach at Brooklyn Center, a small inner ring suburban high school on the north side of Minneapolis. Brooklyn Center was on the west side of the river, directly across from Fridley. Warren began his career in southwest Minnesota before moving to the suburbs. He was a Minnesota Hall of Fame high school football coach and a long-time basketball official. He officiated games for me when I coached at LeSueur. He was now retired and was sometimes around the athletic offices. He was also a big-time vegetable gardener, as am I, and like gardeners do, we often talked gardening.

In terms of housing stock and demographics, Brooklyn Center and Fridley were almost mirror images to Richfield. Their high schools didn't have the history of the large enrollments and the athletic glory years that Richfield had. Yet from comments that both Todd and Warren made, I had the impression that they clearly understood the entire Richfield situation and the demographic change.

However, Todd would never be the athletic director that hired me. In addition to this, he had lived in Richfield for eighteen years. His sons all played youth sports and he coached little league baseball. He and his wife were tied into many of the parents. They sat with them in the bleachers at youth games, and they waived to them from their back-yard barbecues. These people would have his ear.

By far the best move that Todd Olson made was to hire Mike Karnas as his assistant. Mike was the younger son of the longtime legion baseball coach George. Mike was in his fifties, and retired from his career job. A few years earlier he replaced his dad as the legion baseball coach. He and his brother Jim officiated football and basketball, and were two of the best high school and small college officials in the state. Like their dad George, they had impeccable reputations. They played town team baseball with my LeSueur buddy Joe Driscoll, on the 1975 and 1976 Prior Lake state championship teams. Mike had lived his entire life in Richfield. He was a member of the back-to-back state tournament basketball teams in 1973 and 1974. He bled Richfield cardinal. One of the first things that Mike did was to begin a program where low-income kids could work in the athletic office to pay for activity fees. It was a win-win situation. These students were able to play sports, and it lightened the work load of the office. Almost all of these students were minority kids. Mike was also a member of the Optimists Club and he lived the Optimist attitude. He always saw the good in everybody and in everything. He was one of the first faces that the kids and parents saw when they entered the athletic offices. His eternal optimism was contagious.

* * *

The October traveling tryouts went well. Our sixth graders were going to be really good. There were enough good players to field two teams, and they were gym rats, and there would be height.

When the season began in November, our coaching staff had a new look. I was now in charge of both the defense and the offense. Matt Schock accepted a job as the assistant coach at Bryan College, a small NAIA school in Tennessee. Omar replaced him as the B squad coach. On game nights Alcindor coached the junior varsity, and Matt Mullenbach assisted both Alcindor and Omar. Mike Kroupa who was a junior at Hamline University, was the ninth-grade coach.

The Richfield gym also had a new look. At my urging, the basketball board paid for four state tournament banners, commemorating the 1960, 1973, 1974, and 2005 teams. They were cardinal with white letters and they hung in the northeast corner of the gym. In addition, one of my former players from Washburn called me in November. He was working for a large south metro business. This business had asked him to select a few high schools in which to hang a sponsorship banner and donate a considerable amount of money to the boys' basketball program. This banner was hanging in the southeast corner.

* * *

At tryouts we had a small number of players trying out in the top two grades. However, we had a lot of sophomores and freshman. All four returning seniors from the state tournament team tried out. When we made our cuts, we told Carl Ermisch that he did not make the team. Carl was a three-sport athlete. I told him that we had younger kids who had been in the gym all summer, and that they had passed him up. He nodded and thanked us for everything. I told him that he had been an important member of the state tournament team, and I thanked him for this.

We ended up with five seniors, Noonan, Dreifke, OJ, and the two transfers, Dwayne Hardy and Eric Gusaas. We returned two juniors, Santino Clay, and Steven Fischer. Two other gym rats, Eddie Belanger and Didier Mbilizi also made the team.

Two sophomores would play on the scout squad and also play on the junior varsity team. BJ Skoog and Chris Daly were also gym rats who totally bought in to the program and did everything that we asked of them. I projected Chris to become one of our best ever spot up shooters. BJ was another very good shooter, a great defender, and he played hard in every drill year-round. Three freshmen would also play junior varsity and varsity. DeAaron Hearn was now 5-11, still growing, and getting quicker. Chris Williams was another combo guard who was 5-9 and athletic. Renard Robinson was 5-11 and solidly built, but looked like he might be done growing. He played mostly inside with the Urban Stars. He would need to learn to play facing the basket. All three players were always in the gym and played AAU ball.

Over the summer, the state high school league changed the game format from four 8-minute quarters to two 18-minute halves. This added 4 minutes to the game, going from 32 minutes to 36 minutes. This added 20 minutes of playing time to the game (4 minutes x 5 players = 20 minutes). This basically added one player to the playing rotation. However, the previous rule regarding maximum playing time per night, was that a player could play in only five quarters on a game night. This rule was changed to three halves.

This year's depth was totally different from the previous years. We lacked depth in our playing rotation, and there was a clear line of delineation between the players in the rotation and the other players. In some ways, this was the easiest type of team to coach. The reason was because there was no player sitting on the bench, who maybe thought that he should be playing. There was a greater chance that everybody would be happy with their role. The flip side of this was that we couldn't afford any injuries.

Dustin, Jordan, Santino, and Dwayne would all have to play 28 to 32 minutes a game. Eric Gusaas (Goose) would play 24 to 28 minutes. Steven Fischer would play 18 to 24 off the bench, as well as play one half JV. OJ might play 4-8 minutes per game. We needed to find a seventh player to pick up the remaining 10 to 18 minutes. To begin with I would give these minutes to DeAaron.

Our style of play would also be different from the previous two years. On offense we would still get out and run, but we would score fewer points off of turnovers. We would pick up the ball beyond the half court line and deny the first pass to the wing. After that, we would pack our defense inside the three-point line. We would allow the ball reversal pass, but have more help on the drives to the basket. As always, we would know who the shooters were, and we would stay home on them. We would also play behind the post more, and double down off of the weakest shooters. We would use more time outs, sometimes calling a full time out, merely to rest our players. We would definitely have a different look.

*　*　*

We opened the season the second Friday in December at St Paul Harding. Because I was serving my two-game suspension, Martha and I scouted Minneapolis South. South was playing at Mounds View. Alcindor replaced me as the head coach. On the way home, Mullenbach called me. We won 95-91 in overtime.

We played South the following Saturday afternoon at their place, followed by a game at St Thomas on Tuesday. We spent the week preparing for both teams. On Saturday at two o'clock I was out cross-country skiing. When I got back and the phone rang, Mullenbach's call was not good news. We lost 66-59. The game was close from start to finish. In both games we did not shoot well.

*　*　*

St Thomas was ranked #1 in Class 3A. They returned their two D1 recruits Bryce Webster and David Hicks. Both their junior and sophomore classes were good, plus another good junior point guard had transferred in. Because we were now in Class 4A, the two teams would only meet twice. There was no rubber match looming on the horizon for a section championship. Both coaching staffs would not be saving any strategies for the tournament. We played well but lost 61-54. It was clear that we needed to either get in better shape or play more kids.

The next big game was at home against Holy Angels on Friday. They returned a good nucleus and they had a new coach. Jesse Foley resigned and was replaced by Clarence Hightower. Like myself, Clarence was not a teacher at the school. He was the chief operating officer of a local non-profit. The previous three years he was the coach at St Agnes, a small Catholic school in St Paul. He was well known and respected for both jobs. On paper the game was even.

When the game opened, we hit shots and quickly built up an 8-point lead. The teams played each other even until the nine-minute mark of the second half. They began sagging off of Eric Gusaas to help on Santino's drives and Dwayne's post ups. On three consecutive possessions Eric swished jumpers from the top of the key. He ended up drilling five in a row. As each shot went in, the student section stood and flapped their wings like geese, as he ran back down court pumping his fist in the air. He was emotional and smiling and having a blast, and he was also quickly becoming a crowd favorite. As the clock wound down it was our student section that was delivering the 'We own Richfield' chant. Goose finished with 23 points in the 89-77 victory. The next day I received a voice mail from his former coach Jeff Evens, saying that he saw that Goose had a big night, and that he and his staff were happy for him.

Our last game in December was a 68-61 win over Eau Claire Memorial at home. Our record was 3-2, but we had still not found our identity on offense.

* * *

We began January with four consecutive wins against teams that I felt we should beat. Our overall record was 7-2, but we would play three ranked teams the following week. We had home games against Tartan and Henry Sibley on Tuesday and Friday, followed by an away game at Johnson on Saturday afternoon.

Tartan's record was 11-1 and they were ranked #4 in the *StarTribune* Metro poll. As with almost every year, they had graduated some scholarship players and they reloaded with younger talent. Because they had beaten us twice the year before by a bucket, this was a game that we were pointing to. Their best player was their 6-2 senior point guard Kwadzo Ahelegbe, who had signed early with Northern Iowa, and coach Mark Klingsporn had geared the offense more to him. Both teams had players that had played summer ball in the Howard Pulley AAU system, and these kids knew each other. I was hoping that our kids would raise our play to another level.

By the end of warm-ups, the gym was mostly full. For a Tuesday night game, it was going to be a big crowd. The game was a grind from start to finish. We led 31-27 at the half. We maintained a small lead until the end, hit five out of six free throws in the last minute, and when the buzzer sounded, we had a 72-64 win. After the game Jim Noonan told me, "that's as big a win as we've had in this gym."

The kids had tired legs the next day at practice. We shortened the practice and did a lot of shooting. Our prep for Sibley was mostly a walk through. Sibley was leading the conference with a record of 5-0. Trevor Mbakwe was now a junior, and he was being recruited by the top level D1 universities. Their two talented classes were now sophomores and juniors. They were young and tall. The game was decided on the final possession. We were ahead 66-63 and they had the ball. We were in our three-point defense, staying home on their perimeter players. As time expired, Pierre Harris appeared to make a highly contested three with Santino in his face. However, Harris had one foot on the three-point line, and he was awarded only a two pointer. We won 66-65.

The next afternoon I was sitting on the bench in the gym at Johnson watching the pregame warm-ups. It felt like I had taken a catnap, woken up, and was right back on the sideline coaching. It was our first time playing at Johnson. It was an old gym similar to the old gym in Eau Claire, with steel beams and handrails. The banners of all of the St Paul City Conference teams hung on the end walls. The banners included the present high schools and the schools that had been closed. The gym gave one a feeling of St Paul sports history.

Vern Simmons' Johnson team was better than his team of the year before. They were 9-1, ranked #6 in the *StarTribune* Metro poll, and they were the heavy favorite to win the St Paul City. Vern's system of relentless full court pressure and rotating ten players was in full swing. If we couldn't get the ball inbounds and up court quickly, our point guard Dustin Dreifke would be facing two or three sets of fresh legs defending him the entire game.

The game was never close. After I called two time-outs, we were down 16-4. They were denying Dreifke the ball on the inbounds pass. They went on another run. I called time out again, another full one. The kids sat down in the folding chairs with the reserves behind them. They were leaning back in their chairs with their legs extended. I knelt in front of them, took a long breath, and said, "you guys are really tired, aren't you.?"

Dustin sighed and said, "yeah."

Then Jordan said, "coach, we're really tired."

I answered, "well, we've got two time-outs left, and we've gotta save both for the second half. Let's focus on the next five minutes. Jordan, you and Santino take turns bringing the ball up court."

At the half we were down 43-25. They outscored us 46-30 in the second half. Both teams emptied the bench the last five minutes. The final score was 89-55.

* * *

The next Tuesday we beat Mahtomedi at home 90-75. Our next game was on Saturday afternoon at Eastview. Eastview was one of the large outer ring suburban schools in our section. It was one of four high schools that were in the old Rosemount school district. Eastview was the newest school, opening in 1997. They had a young rising star coach in Mark Gerber. I knew Mark from my days at St Thomas, when he played on the junior varsity. Mark took the Lightning to the Class 4A state finals the year before, where they lost on the famous last second shot by Hopkins' Blake Hoffarber. They were rebuilding, with only one starter back. Their 6-1 senior point guard Alex White was a D2 recruit. It would be an important game for section seedings.

There was a bad cold bug going around as well as the flu. During the week Santino missed two days of school and both Dustin and Jordan caught the bug and also missed practice. On Saturday all three insisted that they could play. When the game started, it was obvious that we weren't at the top of our game. Eastview played with energy and totally outplayed us. At halftime the score was 45-24, and the final was 87-60. The game ended with them emptying their bench for the last five minutes, accentuated with a lot of cheering and high fives. I also emptied our bench.

On Tuesday we traveled to St Thomas, and the result wasn't much better. This time we were down 60-39 at half, and the final was 99-73. We had been blown out three out of the last four games, and our overall record had dropped to 10-5.

We had a light practice on Wednesday. After practice we met and talked as a coaching staff. Santino and Dwayne were both averaging about 20 points a game, and both were shooting over 50% from the field. They had developed into our two best shot creators, Dwayne posting up in the low or mid post, and Santino catching the ball 12 to 15 feet from the basket and driving into the paint. And they were creating great shots for everybody by drawing double-teams. Jordan Noonan had not shot as well as the year before. I found out early that Eric Gusaas had weak hands, and a habit of getting the ball knocked out of them. However, he was working diligently on it and he was improving. Steven Fischer was the perfect sixth man/role player with great court sense who made the others better on both ends of the floor. Although three of the younger kids were better one-on-one players, we were a better team with him on the court. He was a textbook case of Bob Knight's maxim that the best team isn't always the best five players.

We agreed that we needed to define our roles on offense more clearly. We would begin playing the freshman DeAaron Hearn one half junior varsity and two halves varsity. We also reviewed our goals for the next five weeks, until the tournament. Our defense was fine. We were doing a good job of not making dumb fouls or missing box outs. We began practicing our set plays and our out of bounds plays that we were saving for the tournament. It was also the time of the year when the kids needed to shoot free throws on their own before and after practice. It was time to regroup with a team meeting.

* * *

The next day I brought a roll of 4" blue painters' tape to practice. I taped off a trapezoid around the lane area. The corners of the bottom of the trapezoid were 8 feet from the basket on the baselines, and the corners of the top of the trapezoid were 1 foot outside and above the elbows. I told the kids that before anybody could take a shot, we had to get two touches inside the trapezoid, and the touches had to be either by Dwayne or Santino. Lance always called the center of the trapezoid the sweet spot. I said that Dwayne and Santino could shoot after the first touch, but nobody else could. I added that after the second touch, anybody could shoot. I told Goose to play mostly at the high post, except when screening for Dwayne. Because Goose could hit the open shot at the high post, they had to guard him. Jordan, Dustin, and the action of the others would not change. They would pass, cut, look to drive, and screen from everywhere on the perimeter. I explained that this didn't mean that Santino and Dwayne had to shoot, or that they were going to get more shots. We were going to run our same offense, but with this 'two touch' rule, and we were going to count passes. Instead of shooting after four or five passes, we needed more possessions with ten passes. Of course, if we got an open layup after one pass, we were going to take it. I told the kids that we were still going to get out and run, but if the shot wasn't there off of the break, we were counting passes.

On Friday we hosted North St Paul. They were in the middle of the conference with record of 5-3, and they had played us close at their place in early January. We ran our offense the best that we had run it all season. We shot a lot of lay ups on curl cuts. The final was 86-62. We shot 30-44 from the field for 68%. The following Friday we won at Hill-Murray 58-52.

The following afternoon we played at Minneapolis North. North had graduated their good senior class, but they were still talented, and they were leading the City Conference. It was a big game for Dwayne. He played his sophomore and junior years with these kids, and they were another set of his buddies.

To begin the game both teams traded baskets. We successfully got the ball inside to Dwayne and he made his first five shots on a combination of drop steps and face up moves. Santino was also scoring off of touches inside. They weren't double-teaming either player. At halftime we held a 36-31 advantage and Santino and Dwayne had combined for 33 of our points. We talked at halftime about the need to withstand a run. Their run never came. When they started helping on Dwayne and Santino, the others hit shots. With five minutes to go and an eight point lead we spread the court. Our kids ran the delay offense perfectly. When Jordan fouled out DeAaron Hearn came in and played his best floor game of the year. We won 76-65 in a gym that was not easy to win at. I told the kids after the game that if we can play at this level, we can play with anybody.

The next week we beat Simley and South St Paul. The following week we would find out if we had improved. We played at Tartan on Tuesday and at Henry Sibley on Friday. Along with us, they were chasing St Thomas for second place in the conference. John Sherman wrote in his column in the *Richfield Sun-Current*:

Cohesive unit

It has been a pleasure to watch the Richfield High boys basketball team this season because the players fit together like fingers on a hand.

I'm not shocked that Richfield has a 15-5 record, but mark me down as pleasantly surprised.

Senior Dustin Dreifke is the catalyst, a great passer at the point guard position.

Dwayne Hardy, a 6-6 power forward, and Erik Gusaas, a 6-9 center, transferred in at the start of the school year.

Hardy grew up in Richfield and has moved back to the community after playing for Minneapolis North the last two seasons. Gusaas was at Bloomington Jefferson last season and needed to get out of the shadow of all-state center Cole Aldrich.

Luckily, both Hardy and Gusaas fit in very well with their teammates. They have bought into coach Jim Dimick Jr.'s team concept.

Steady Jordan Noonan and speedy Santino Clay round out the Spartan's starting five, and how about junior guard Steven Fischer, a junior guard, who is improving every week?

The Spartans took second in the state Class 3A tournament last season and have moved up to Class 4A this year.

Theoretically, 4A is a tougher division but the Spartans will compete with anyone regardless of class, as long as they continue to play great team basketball.[61]

* * *

We expected Tartan to try to take Dwayne and Santino out of the game. Mark Klingsporn scouted us at North. At the half we trailed 31-23. With seven minutes to play we tied the game 45-45. From then on it was an even game. Dwayne scored our next 9 points in the paint. His last bucket gave us a 59-58 lead with 51 seconds remaining.

Tartan called time out. They patiently looked for an opening and finally got one when Matt Haas drove the middle and scored in the last 10 seconds. We turned the ball over on the inbounds, and we fouled their point guard

Ahelegbe. He made one of two free throws. Now we were down two. Without calling time out, we ran a full court play that we had practiced many times. The ball was quickly passed up court. Dustin found the trailing Goose for a wide open three pointer in front of our bench. He was squared up, on the arc, and shot the ball in rhythm. It hit the inside of the rim, and bounced up and out. It was the shot that we wanted, and it looked good when the ball left his hands. After the game I told him those words in front of the whole team, and I told them that we played well. We just had to keep the ship on course. We were going the right direction and the wind was at our back.

Three nights later at Sibley we trailed by 10 points most of the game. Then we hit some shots and tied the score with about eight minutes to go. After we made two stops on defense and scored two possessions in a row, they came down and missed again. We boxed out and got the ball to Dreifke who was dribbling it up court.

I turned to my assistants and said, "Should we spread it? We're up four. We haven't been ahead the whole game." They said to go for it. I stood up and spread my arms. Jordan backed the ball out to mid court. We patiently worked the ball for over two minutes, until Jordan hit Santino for a diagonal cut back door layup. Henry Sibley missed yet another open 15-foot jumper. We worked another minute off the clock. Then Dwayne caught the ball on the block, and scored on a drop step layup. The game was now under three minutes and we were up 8. We traded baskets the rest of the game. Jordan, Dustin, and Goose made 9 out of 10 free throws, and we left with an 87-77 win. I told the kids in the locker room, "that's a really big road W. We are a way better team than we were three weeks ago. We can't let up. We just have to continue getting better, and keep the ship moving."

* * *

The last week of the season we handily won at Mahtomedi and we won a close game against Hill-Murray at home. We finished the regular season with a record of 19-5. St Thomas won the conference at 15-1. We were in second place at 13-3, with Tartan and Henry Sibley behind us at 12-4 and 11-5. We won eight of our last nine games, and we had an offensive identity.

I felt good about the section tournament. Five of the eight schools in the section were members of the Lake Conference. The Lake had 11 schools and with a double round-robin schedule, all teams played 20 conference games. Eden Prairie won the conference with a record of 18-2 and an overall record of 22-2. They were ranked #2 in the *StarTribune* Metro poll behind Hopkins, and both teams were in the same section. The #1 seed in our section would be Eagan, which finished second in the Lake with a 14-6 conference record and an overall 18-8 record. Burnsville and Apple Valley, who had finished fourth and fifth in the Lake and both had overall records of 17-9, would be the #2 and #3 seeds. We would be seeded #4 or #5, along with Eastview. Eastview finished the season seventh in the Lake with an overall record of 12-14. The remaining #6 to #8 seeds would be Minneapolis South 12-14, Bloomington Kennedy 10-15, and Minneapolis Southwest 9-15.

I had seen all of the top seeds play twice, in addition to the times that my assistants had seen them. These were all typical Class 4A schools, with more height and depth than us. The bottom of the Lake Conference was unquestionably tougher than the bottom of our conference. However, the top half of our conference was just as good or better than the Lake. The big advantage that we had was that the Lake was a 'set play' league. Most of the teams relied upon set offenses to generate shots. Those types of offenses weren't going to work against a St Thomas or a Tartan or a Hill-Murray. Our conference was a motion offense conference. Also, except for Eastview, none of these teams played the same style of man-to-man defense as the top teams in our league. With our scouting reports and their set offenses, I knew that our defense could shut them down. To win the section, we would have to win three games in a row that were what I called 'coin toss' games. The odds of us winning each of the three games was fifty-fifty. The team that made one more run or made one more play would win the game. This being said, our odds of winning the section were one in eight ($\frac{1}{2}$ x $\frac{1}{2}$ x $\frac{1}{2}$ = 1/8). I figured that the toughest team for us to beat would be Eastview. The question was would we be seeded #4 or #5? The #4 team hosted the game. We had the better record. Eastview beat us by 27 points. Comparing opponents, there were arguments both ways. The home court advantage might be the difference in the game. We were seeded #4. Eastview was seeded #5. Eastview would be coming to our place the following Thursday

This was a year when we would be preparing for one opponent at a time. We had no margin for error. I believed that if we could get by Eastview, we had a good chance of running the table to the section title. The Lake teams all played against our traveling teams in grade school and middle school. Our seniors had competed well against their seniors. Our juniors (without Santino) had been trounced by their juniors. Many of their kids had memories of beating the Richfield traveling teams by thirty points. These kids would have no respect for us, although I knew that their coaches would. If we could not fall behind early, the longer each game would stay close, the more that their kids would tighten up. We had to shoot well early in each game.

* * *

Eastview brought a large contingent of student fans to the game. When the game started the gym was close to full. It was ironically a game between two schools that both lost in the state finals the year before.

We played and shot well right from the get go. It was obvious that their game plan was to wear Dustin down, as their point guard Alex White was in his face all over the court. And like Tartan, the Eastview players were denying Santino the ball. When teams did this, we focused on driving the ball towards Santino. Because his defender was in the passing lane, there was no help on the drive. These drives began pass sequences that got Jordan open and he hit three consecutive threes. At halftime we held a 38-35 advantage. In an attempt to wear out our thin rotation, they did not call a single time out.

To start the second half, we made a concerted effort to get Dwayne more touches. With Goose feeding Dwayne from the high post, Dwayne went to work. After four minutes Mark Gerber called his first time out. We were up 6. Our bench was excited and relaxed. Their bench was tightening up.

The teams began matching baskets and stops. With less than eight minutes to play, Dwayne scored to give us an 8-point lead, our biggest of the game. They came down and another good shot rimmed out. I called time out and we went to our spread offense. They used three more time-outs in the last five minutes. With 0:49 on the clock we were up 4 with Jordan at the free throw line. He missed the front end of the one and one. They hit a 15-footer and our lead was down to 68-66. With 7 seconds to play they fouled Dustin. He also missed his free throw. They rebounded the ball and called time-out. On the ensuing play they pushed the ball up the far sideline. White launched a 35-footer on the run. It clanked off the rim and down to the floor. Our student section stormed the court.

Once again, behind the leadership and decision making of Noonan and Dreifke, we had controlled the ball in the last six minutes of the game. However, for the first time all year, we did not convert free throws. When I got to the locker room, I felt like I was sitting in a canoe in calm water after running a set of rapids. The kids were all laughing. It was a feeling of having gained respect from an opponent that had no idea how good we truly were. I praised the kids. I reminded them that if we had one more, bad free throw shooting game, we would be done. I closed by telling them that we had one day to celebrate. At three o'clock tomorrow we go to work on Eagan.

* * *

Eagan was coached by Kurt Virgin. He was a great player at South St Paul near the end of that school's glory era. He was the floor general of a team that made a run to the state finals in 1970, the last year of the one school state tournament. He then played at St Cloud State, before beginning a career as a teacher and a coach. Kurt built the Eagan program from the ground up when the school opened in 1990.

Eagan had the most talent and was the best team in the section. They had a big and athletic front line of 6-6, 6-5, and 6-4. The section semi-finals would be played in a doubleheader at Prior Lake High School. We would play Eagan in the opening game, followed by #2 Burnsville against #3 Apple Valley. We had four good days of practice, and our scouts ran their offense to perfection.

As the game began, they hit shots and we didn't. They began to pull away. I used two time-outs to tell the kids that they were hot and we weren't, and to just stay focused on playing one possession at a time. At one point they were up by 12 before we got it quickly back down to 8. Then we got four consecutive stops in the last three minutes, and when the halftime buzzer sounded their lead was down to 36-31.

We were taking away all of their set plays, and they were being forced to create shots which were not from their offense. They started missing more shots. Slowly we inched back and with 12 minutes left in the half it was an even game. Then Jordan switched a set play double screen to steal a pass at the top of the key, and he dribbled down court and laid it in.

They were having a hard time guarding Santino. He repeatedly caught the ball in the trapezoid, faced up to the basket, and went to work. He took one or two big dribbles and elevated over the defender to shoot, or he drew a helper and kicked the ball to the perimeter. With eight minutes to play, Santino got another good touch on the right elbow. He took two big steps to his right and jump stopped. This time instead of passing, he went up off of two legs and one hand hammer dunked over the Eagan big man. Our student section went crazy. All of their players were looking up at the scoreboard as they ran down court. We were up 5.

A couple of possessions later, we got the ball inside to Dwayne who was double-teamed. He passed the ball out to Dreifke, hitting him perfectly in the numbers. Dustin swished the wide open and in rhythm three. With five minutes to play and a 7-point lead, we went to our spread offense. From then on, we made our free throws. And when we didn't, Goose ripped two offensive rebounds. On both he went back up strong. He scored on one and was fouled on the other. When fouled, he made his two free throws, while our students flapped their arms like geese. We had outscored them 40-24 in the second half. The final score was 71-60.

I sat in the stands with my assistants for the second game, and we scouted both teams. Parents, fans, and old friends stopped to say hello. I savored the moment. On the court, Apple Valley gained an early 10-point lead and coasted to a 68-53 win over Burnsville. The #3 and #4 seeds would meet for the section title on Friday at the University of Minnesota Sports Pavilion.

* * *

Apple Valley had a record of 18-9. They were coached by Mike Fritze. Fritze had been teaching and coaching at Apple Valley for 25 years. He was the defensive coordinator in football before becoming the head coach in 1995. These teams won two state football championships. He also served as an assistant basketball coach. He was currently the head coach of both sports. Apple Valley had an extremely quick point guard in 5-10 Jontae Koonkaew. Like the other Lake teams, they also had good size and good three-point shooters. As was my custom, I let the kids decide the match-ups. Santino would guard Koonkaew.

The game began with the ball bouncing our way. Jordan, Dustin, and Dwayne all hit open threes, and Santino was scoring inside. They countered our early run, and with three minutes to go in the half Apple Valley led 31-28. On the last possession of the half, we went for one shot and Jordan hit a three pointer. We were down 35-33. They had scored 10 points off of fast break baskets, not off of steals or turnovers, but off of fast break baskets after we missed shots. We adjusted by putting two guys back on defense.

The score was tied five times early in the second half. With 1:30 to play we were ahead 67-65. Jordan banked in a layup on a curl cut, but McGuiggan answered for them with a spinning lay-up. Dustin Dreifke was fouled and made both free throws. They missed a good shot, and with 35 seconds left, Santino made one of two free throws. The score was 72-67 and we were in our three-point defense switching all perimeter screens. They missed five contested threes in the last minute. They scored at the buzzer to make the final score 72-69.

After the game, Mike Fritze was quoted in the *StarTribune*, *"We didn't shoot well, when McGuiggan got into foul trouble, that got us out of our rotation...*

but you've got to hand it to them because they played a very good basketball game...they made shots when they had to and we didn't." I was also quoted, *"When Santino and Dwayne get touches within 12 feet of the basket, we're getting our shots."*[62]

In the *Richfield Sun-Current*, the headline to John Sherman's column read;

Lake teams watch from home as Spartans move on to Target Center

For many years the Lake Conference was the gold standard for Minnesota high school boys basketball...Richfield played in Class 3A last year and placed second in the state. The move up to Class 4A this season was a challenge for the players and head coach Jim Dimick Jr...

Three of our seniors were quoted;

Dwayne Hardy, "After the North game, we realized we can beat anyone if we play as a team."

Dustin Driefke, "We moved the ball around and played good defense."

Jordan Noonan, "We're playing well as a team, at state, we just have to do what we've been doing..."

..Regardless of what happens this week, Richfield is a team that achieved all season and overachieved in the playoffs.[63]

***

We were going to state with a record of 21-6. We would play Cooper (22-3) at noon on Thursday at the Target Center. Elk River (26-3) and Woodbury (21-8) would play before us. The other bracket featured St Paul Johnson (23-4) against Andover (21-8) at 2pm followed by Hopkins (27-2) against Lakeville North (10-19) at 4pm. Hopkins was the obvious favorite. With the exception of them I knew that we could play with all of the teams if we played well and if we didn't shoot cold. When I looked at their records, the comparative scores confirmed this. Cooper beat Minneapolis North in the section semifinals 84-79. Johnson lost at North 75-72 late in January. Woodbury beat Tartan in the section semifinals 57-52. Elk River lost to Tartan early in the season 69-57. After beginning the season with a record of 6-2, Hopkins, with their customary improvement won 21 games in a row. Their two closest games were in the section tournament. They defeated Shakopee in the semifinals 51-45, and Eden Prairie 55-54 in the finals. Their section was loaded, and many considered the Eden Prairie game to be the state championship game.

Our biggest issue would be depth, having to play three games in four days, with our seven-man rotation. All three games would be played on the Target

Center's long NBA court. If we could get to the semifinals, we would have the luxury of the TV time-outs. On the other hand, the opposing coaches might do what St Thomas' Mike Sjoberg and Eastview's Mark Gerber did, which was not call any time-outs.

***

Cooper was the less affluent of the two high schools in the Robbinsdale district, which encompassed the majority of four municipalities; Robbinsdale, Crystal, New Hope, and Plymouth. Like Hopkins, Cooper attracted many open enrollment kids from north Minneapolis. Like other inner ring suburban schools, they now had a diverse basketball team. They won the North Suburban Conference with a record of 14-0. The last two winters had been breakthrough years for them, climbing to the top of their league. Ken Novak Sr told me early in the winter that they were going to be really good.

Jermain Davis was a 6-3 shooting guard who accepted a scholarship to Iowa. Jefferson Mason at 6-6 was a slender jumping jack who signed with D2 power Minnesota State-Mankato. They had a physical post in 6-7 Dennis Williamson and freshman Rodney Williams at 6-6 was a top level D1 prospect.

As we expected, they began the game in a full court man to man press. We were getting good shots, but our shots weren't dropping. We were withstanding their perimeter size and quickness just fine. We only made 5 of 27 shots from the field in the first half. On the defensive end, we were playing well containing their quickness and limiting them to one shot. I told the kids at halftime that given how we shot, we were lucky to only be down 30-19.

They extended their lead early in the second half, and with 11 minutes to play we were down 48-29. We needed to come out of our packed in man-to-man defense and do something different. After Dwayne made two free throws we diamond (1-2-1-1) pressed. Dustin stole the ball and passed to Jordan for a layup. Our rule was that if we scored off a steal from the press, we continued pressing. Our hard trap forced another turnover. Then Santino got in a zone, hitting 5 of 6 shots to ignite a run. When their lead was down to 11, Cooper called time out.

We scored again the next two possessions. They continued to miss shots. With less than four minutes to play, Santino scored on another mid-lane jumper to tie the score. Then we got a break when Jefferson Mason fouled out.

With 1:17 to play and the score tied, I called time out. I reviewed a set play that we saved to get Dwayne the ball on the mid-post. They defended it well, and denied him the ball. We kept on running our offense and looking for an opening, but we couldn't get anybody open for a good shot. I called time out again with 16 seconds to play. We went for one shot. They were fronting Dwayne in the post and denying Santino the ball. They were also not letting Jordan get open. Dustin drove the middle, drew a help defender and passed crosscourt to DeAaron Hearn on the perimeter. He caught the pass in rhythm and had a wide-open shot. The ball rimmed in and out at the buzzer.

We won the opening tip of the overtime. We patiently worked the ball again. Then Jordan had a wide-open catch and shoot three-pointer from the left side. It hit the front rim, bounced up, hit the back rim, and bounced out. Cooper rebounded the ball. After a minute, Jermain Davis buried an NBA range three pointer from the left wing. That was the difference in the game. On our next possession, we missed another good shot. Davis hurt us again, with a slicing runner in the lane to put Cooper up 62-57 at 1:33. In the overtime we ended up being outscored 9-3, and Cooper had a 66-60 victory.

When the game was over the kid's legs were gassed. If we had won, we would have played Elk River the next afternoon. They had a solid nine-man rotation with good overall height. When I mentioned this to their coach Randy Klasen after the tournament, his response was that they were fully aware of that, and that they were pulling for us to beat Cooper.

Cooper coach Kurt Pauly was quoted in the *StarTribune* to say, "*Davis is a tough kid from Chicago that came here, I think, in eighth grade, and he plays like a tough kid.*"[64]

The *Richfield SunCurrent* covered the game with the following headline;

Spartans fly under the radar to Target Center

…not many fans expected the Spartans to wade through Lake Conference powers Eastview, Apple Valley, Burnsville and Eagan in Section 6. But that's exactly what they did, topping Apple Valley 72-69 in the finals. That's how Richfield wound up in the state field as a virtual mystery team.

John Sherman quoted me in the *SunCurrent* to say, "*The difference in the game was that their three-pointer dropped and ours didn't. It was anybody's game. Cooper is a talented, athletic team that pressures the ball very well…we had a quiet self-confidence, and we just kept improving each week. The last month of the season we played our best ball.* "[65]

* * *

Cooper went on to defeat Elk River 62-59 in the semifinals, while Hopkins beat St Paul Johnson 66-48. Hopkins defeated Cooper in the finals 69-53. In Class 3A DeLaSalle marched to their first 3A state championship since being moved up from Class 2A. Dave Thorson's senior dominated lineup won three games by an average score of 21 points. In the semifinals they took out St Thomas 63-44. Braham won Class 2A for the third year in a row in similar fashion, outscoring their three state tourney opponents by an average of 18 points. Braham benefited from two more open enrollment transfers from nearby Cambridge-Isanti, 6-3 junior Alex Thiry and 6-2 sophomore guard David Vavra. In a November season preview article in the *StarTribune* written by John Millea, Braham coach Bob Vaughn was quoted:

"This is a sensitive subject. They came here to play. I didn't go get them. They saw what it's been like here the last few years, and they wanted to be part of it. I'm still opposed to open enrollment, but there's nothing you can do. I was told by my principal, 'We do not want you to discourage these guys.' And then my union people said, 'If you ever discourage a kid from coming, you could be in trouble as a teacher because of the money (state funding that accompanies each student).' What am I supposed to do?"

In March, after the season, Millea wrote again about open enrollment in his column:

It's time to close gaping loopholes in open enrollment

…Catholic schools, Lutheran schools, private schools, public schools, charter schools, home schools, trade schools, yada yada yada. We all know that the elephant in the arena is recruiting. But the problem isn't simply recruiting. It's the open-enrollment system, which makes recruiting possible.

Under the current bylaws of the Minnesota State High School League, virtually any high school athlete can attend virtually any high school they choose. And then switch to another school for whatever reason they like.

The rules allow one transfer with no penalty. If a student transfers again, he/she must sit out the first half of a varsity season before becoming eligible at the new school. (One loophole for abuse: If a kid has an injury and knows he/she will be on the shelf for half a season, the barn door is wide open for a change of schools.)

…Open enrollment was instituted by legislative action in 1988, and the MSHSL knows that any changes to the current system are likely to prompt legal challenges. But there are strong feelings that the time has come to do what's best for high school athletics.

This is what we could see in a couple years: no more penalty-free open enrollment transfers. Kids will have to pick a school-public or private, no difference-before they begin ninth grade. Because once the bell rings to begin the first day of ninth grade, any open-enrollment transfers will result in one full school year of athletic ineligibility.

Maybe our prayers will be answered.[66]

Every high school coach that I knew was in favor of the above rule change. The two coaches with the most career wins in history were both still coaching and were very outspoken about it. Bob McDonald at Chisholm called open enrollment "the scourge of high school athletics." Bob Brink at Rocori said, "we work hard to develop our own kids, then we get to state and come to the cities, we have to play these All-Star teams." The new rule wasn't going to stop open enrollment. But now parents would have to make a decision before a student was a ninth grader, and pick a high school. It would take away some of the power of parents to shop their kids during their high school years. It would also intensify the recruiting of eighth graders, especially by the private schools. We would continue to recruit the Richfield kids hard.

***

The last week in March I received an email from Kim Niederluecke, the longtime successful RHS softball coach.

I just wanted to take a minute to say "Congratulations" on a great season. Once again, the team made the games exciting and fun to watch. I do really think that the success of your program has had a very positive influence on our WHOLE student body. It is so great to see all kids talking about the games and the team and their bus ride to the Target Center. It is really nice to hear how proud the kids are of the team...even after losing to Cooper. I had a great bus ride home with a bunch of kids that were already planning on what they will wear to next year's state tourney. How can we not be proud of that enthusiasm? All of that positive energy can only mean that we will be a better school too. Thanks for all of your hard work.

It was a season, that for me personally, atoned for the 2004 season when we should have gone to state and didn't. This was a year when we should not have gone to state, and we did. Every long-time basketball coach will look back on his career and see this, teams that lost earlier than he expected, and teams that made runs deep into the tournament that surprised him. The longer one coaches, the greater the probability that this will happen.

It was my first season working under Todd Olson as the athletic director. He stopped in to observe practice often and was always curious to learn where we had picked up some of our drills. The conversation was usually about basketball theory and evolving game strategy. I don't remember him mentioning anything related to the meeting with Craig Holje and the 'Letter of Reprimand and Suspension'. The subjects of swearing and treatment of athletes were never discussed, not one time. I was also never required to participate in any type of leadership training.

After the season I ran into Andy Berkvam, the successful Lakeview North girls' basketball coach, who at the age of 42 had already collected two state championships. He told me that one of the Lake Conference coaches told him that we had the fourth best team in the section. Then he quickly added, "And that's a helluva compliment to you, Jim. It says a lot about what you did. You won the section with the fourth best talent."

John Sherman then wrote his weekly column in the *Richfield SunCurrent*:

It's time for RHS to review Berwald situation

The remorse I felt after Richfield High's boys basketball team's 66-60 overtime loss to Cooper last week was not for the team, but for former assistant coach Lance Berwald.

Berwald, a volunteer coach under Jim Dimick Jr., was dismissed last spring because students complained that he used profanity in the locker room...Why do I think Berwald should be asked to come back?

It's my observation that the student-athletes want him back on the bench. After Richfield's 72-69 win over Apple Valley in the Section 6 finals, Berwald was standing near the entrance of the University of Minnesota Sports Pavilion. I watched as Richfield starters Dustin Dreifke, Jordan Noonan, and Erick Gusaas gathered around him and visited for more than 30 minutes. It was obvious to me that they missed him. Parents approached him, too, and there was more conversation.

If the players and parents have this much respect for Berwald, why shouldn't he get another chance?...Given the fact that he donated thousands of hours to building the program over a four year period, Berwald should have been treated better... When this issue was being discussed week after week in the Sun-Current last spring, I stayed out of it.

Now it's time to take a stand. I say bring Lance Berwald back.

The next edition of the *SunCurrent* contained the following letter:

Fan disappointed with team

To the editor:

Rather than campaign for the reinstatement of potty-mouthed basketball coach Lance Berwald, sports editor John Sherman would have better served Sun-Current readers by investigating how the Spartans dug a 19-point hole to Robbinsdale Cooper and suffered a season-ending loss to an inferior team for the third straight year.

The Spartans were fortunate to be moved to a Class 4A section, which included a bunch of Lake Conference also-rans, then wind up in the weaker state tournament bracket opposite powers Hopkins and St Paul Johnson.

Richfield was far better than Cooper and would-be semifinal opponent Elk River. Lady Luck smiled on the Spartans, then they slapped her in the face.

Rather than exploit advantage in height, skill and experience via penetration and a set offense, Richfield settled for lower percentage outside shots – and missed most. Seniors Jordan Noonan and 6-9 Erick Gusaas, contributed only 4 points each. Only a heroic 29-point effort by junior Santino Clay kept the Spartans in the game.

Berwald and Dimick may very well be reunited, but not at Richfield. The Spartans lose four starters to graduation and the girls team will have more height next season. The cupboard is bare, so don't be surprised if Dimick finds his next meal somewhere else.

That may not be such a bad thing.

William Beckett

Minneapolis[67]

When I read the letter, I wondered who this William Beckett was. I asked Todd Olson, Mike Karnas, and Jim Noonan, and all of them had no idea. I then checked the Minneapolis phone book and the name wasn't listed. I called directory assistance and was told that they did not have the name, either as a listed or an unlisted number. I had a friend who worked for a private firm which had access to a number of thorough search engines and data bases. He searched this name and only this name for me. He found a 73-year-old man living in Moorhead with this name, but nobody in Minneapolis or anywhere else in Minnesota with this name.

When I got home that night I smiled at my wife and asked the question, "what are the odds of a person existing...who lives in Minneapolis...doesn't have a phone or a driver's license...or own any property...follows both the Richfield boys and girls basketball teams, and gets the Richfield Sun Current?" She burst out laughing.

Sixth Summer & Winter

As long as there are young men with the light of adventure in their eyes and a touch of wildness in their souls, rapids will be run.

—*Sigurd Olson*

In September my middle school coaches alerted me that a talented and precocious eighth grader had enrolled in the middle school. He was 6-2, well built, athletic, and was still growing. His family recently moved to Richfield from south Minneapolis. After working him out at the middle school one day, I projected him to be in our varsity rotation as a freshman. He played traveling basketball for a team of all-star caliber players. The team was coached by one of the dads. I wanted him on our ninth-grade team. He chose to keep playing for his traveling team and he also played for our eighth-grade middle school team. I recruited him hard, meeting with his mother in Todd Olson's office. He decided to attend DeLaSalle with a couple of his teammates. Under my watch, he was the second really good student and really good player who lived in Richfield and who didn't attend the public high school.

My eighth-grade coach Greg Von Ruden told me late that winter about another talented player who enrolled at the middle school over the winter. Jay Sewer was a point guard who had attended schools in both Minneapolis and Burnsville. His mom moved into one of the apartment buildings in Richfield. He also had played for all-star traveling teams since elementary school. When the basketball season ended Greg had set up a program at the middle school that he called 'Homework & Hoops'. The kids would do homework in his room after school for an hour followed by another hour of basketball. Jay was one of the players who attended every day. At Greg's suggestion, I went to the middle school one afternoon to meet Jay. He was 5-9, well-built and he had potential top level explosive D1 quicks. He was probably done growing, but he wouldn't have to grow any more. Some of the coaches from the city conference were recruiting him. He had a great attitude and work ethic when I helped him with his shooting form and footwork.

* * *

Early in May my brother John, and our buddies Dale Pippin, Steve Madson, and Reid Nelson camped four nights on Kekekabic Lake, in the heart of the BWCAW. Kekekabic is one of the jewel lakes of the area, located at the top of the watershed. It runs about five miles from southwest to northeast. Looking at it on the map, it lays midway between Ely to the west and the end of the Gunflint Trail to the east. The southwest end is a bowl, and the northeast end is a tail. The tail has dark gray granite cliffs on both sides, and the entire lake is studded with small islands. The islands and cliffs are adorned with aspen, cedar, white pine, and jack pine. We arrived four days after ice-out, and there were rivulets of snow melt water flowing down the cliffs, which glistened in the sun. The aspen trees were budding, the white throated sparrows were singing, and the lake trout were feeding in the shallows. There are sixteen campsites on the lake, and we were one of three parties occupying them. To get to Kekekabic it is eight lakes and portages from Ely, and twelve lakes and portages from the Gunflint. We arrived from the Gunflint.

It is sometimes customary to use adjectives of profanity to describe canoes, Duluth packs, and other portage objects, when arriving at or leaving a portage. I had trained myself the previous fall to not swear, ever. I don't think that I swore one time the entire winter at home or at my office. At these portages I made up for it. I swore loud and clear with my head high in the air. I used strings of blasphemous adjectives with perfect enunciation, and I gave the swear words slightly more volume than the other words. I stretched the vowels and hammered the consonants. It was very gratifying. Unless there were some parents of bench warmer players hiding in the cedar trees, nobody but Dale, John, Steve, Reid, and the white throated sparrows heard me.

* * *

One day after working the basketball camp I stopped into a store in the shopping center in the center of Richfield. I made a purchase and was walking back to my car when I heard someone screaming. I turned around and on the other side of the parking lot I saw one of the players that I had cut a few years earlier. He was standing and facing me and screaming over and over again as loud as he could "FUUUUUCK... YOOOOOUUUUU...DIMICK" at the top of his lungs. He had both hands held high in the air flipping me a double bird. When I realized what was happening, I felt no anger. I just felt sorry for him. He was a good kid.

We took the varsity team to northern Minnesota to play games at Bemidji and Cass Lake. Once again, the kids bonded, and we won most of our games against the outstate teams. Santino was again playing in the Howard Pulley program and he was establishing himself as one of the best juniors in the state.

* * *

In June the Minnesota State High School League voted to form an ad hoc committee for the purpose of reviewing the open enrollment process. The monthly edition of *The Minnesota Prep Coach* displayed a front-page editorial on its September issue written by the executive director of the Minnesota State High School Coaches Association, John Erickson.

Open Enrollment was put into law by the Minnesota State Legislature and is defined by the Minnesota Department of Education: All public school students in Minnesota are eligible to choose to attend any public school in the state... Families may make the choice to use open enrollment for any reason important to them and their student.

Erickson, then went on to write:

It is my belief that the initial intention of the Open Enrollment Law was to provide enhanced educational opportunities for students. The law is written to provide this opportunity. The problem that has developed is that there has been increased use of the Open Enrollment Law to make transfers for athletic purposes. There has been considerable documentation by the media regarding the transfer of some of the elite athletes from one high school program to another. These transfers have resulted in a lot of finger pointing and blame. From my point of view I would make the following observations. This is not a public vs. private school problem as some would have you believe...

I believe that a lot of the pressure to transfer results from the summer traveling teams and exposure to coaches not connected with the high school programs. I think there is a lot of misinformation out there and promises made that cannot be kept. The unfortunate losers in this process are those student athletes who go to their home school districts, put in their time in the youth programs leading up to varsity athletics only to find that they are replaced by transfer students in their high school years. The ramifications of this problem are far reaching in terms of community support for youth programs and volunteers that make the school programs go... The instances of abuse and the finger pointing are growing in number... High school athletic programs were never started for the purpose of developing all-star teams to secure athletic scholarships for their participants and a resume of state championships.[68]

* * *

In July the middle school hired its first African-American principal, Stephen West. He had been in the Burnsville school system since 1994, and he had been an associate high school principal at Burnsville High School since 2003. After growing up in Memphis, Tennessee, he came to Minnesota to attend Saint Mary's University in Winona. According to an article in the *Richfield Sun-Current*,

The Burnsville School District has transitioned from serving primarily Caucasian students to having an ethnically diverse population, prompting some in the district to "wish things could be the way they used to be," West said.

"That's been the biggest challenge is watching staff deal with that transition, that switchover, something I expect Richfield is going through," he said. "I think that's probably been the biggest challenge in my career; coming on board as a teacher and administrator and watching that happen."[69]

I knew a couple of coaches who had worked with Stephen and both of them said nothing but great things about him.

* * *

The last week in October I received a voicemail from Todd Olson saying that there had been an allegation from a parent that my assistant coaches had paid for kids' fees for camps and for Howard Pulley tryouts. He asked Matt Mullenbach, and Matt said that he had no knowledge of us every paying for a camp, but that he paid the fee for the Howard Pulley tryouts and that I had reimbursed him.

When I saw Todd at his office later in the week, I told him that I received an anonymous donation to pay for the tryouts, the total of which was $80. He quickly responded that the football coaches received anonymous donations for underprivileged kids in the past, and that he totally understood. He then said that these same parents also complained that we provide transportation for kids. I told Todd that we make transportation available for any kids that request it, or we help them carpool with other kids, and that the kids take advantage of this. I added that some of our players were from one parent families that had one car or no car. His response was that he totally understood. I told him that I had seen the Pulfords, the Noonans, and other parents pull up to the high school many times with a carload of players. It was usually the same parents giving rides to the same kids. I then asked him if these same complainer parents wanted us to use lack of transportation as a way of eliminating kids from the basketball program.

* * *

When tryouts began in November, we knew that it was going to be a rebuilding year. We returned three players from our playing rotation in Santino, Steven, and DeAaron Hearn. Santino was the only one who had played major minutes. Three other seniors were in the mix, Dexter Jones, Didier Mbilizi, and Eddie Belanger. All were gym rats with great work ethic and attitudes. When I told Didier after tryouts that he wasn't going to get any playing time, he chose to not be on the team. He then shook my hand and thanked me and all of my assistants for working with him. Eddie began the year in the playing rotation. When I told him in late January that I was taking him out of the rotation, he also chose to not be on the team.

Our junior class was made up of a core of kids who had been in the program since first grade. They had always won more than they lost as a traveling team. The original group of nine or ten was now down to half a dozen. Chris Daly, BJ Skoog, and Garret Wallstein had all continued to get to the gym, and get bigger and stronger since middle school. Wallstein had sprouted to 6-3. They had emerged as the three best players in the class. A new player was Dylan Olson. Dylan was 6-8 and played hockey since grade school. He was Todd's second son, and he was growing into his body. He would spend the year playing junior varsity. We all saw two other juniors as a long shot to ever play varsity minutes, but my assistants felt that they could both help the JV. We kept both.

The sophomore class won a lot of games as they had come up through the program. DeAaron was 6-1, slender and growing. Renard Robinson had stopped growing, was getting buffed, and starting to get his hops. He had effectively made the transition to playing outside. He was a certain scholarship prospect in football. Both would start and play major minutes. Two other guards; Chris Williams and Phillip Freeman would play JV and possibly push for playing time. Michael Jones was over 6-2, and would also play JV, and possibly varsity. Another sophomore guard who had moved in from Kansas City also made the team. This was the class that we had seen as our next exceptional class, if they grew to the heights of 6-2 and 6-4. However, I was seeing signs that most of them were going to reach only 5-9 and 6-0. The freshman guard Jay Sewer would also play JV and maybe varsity.

This team was going to be a work in process. Unlike the prior winter, it was not clear who would play and who would not play. The playing rotation would evolve and it would take time. While this happened, my goal was to keep our record above five hundred.

***

An article in the December issue of *The Minnesota Prep Coach* appeared with the results of the Minnesota State High School League three ad hoc committee meetings regarding transfer eligibility:

The committee voted to continue to allow transfers to another school in the following instances; 1. They are entering the 9th grade for the first time, 2. The parents move from one school district attendance area to another school district attendance area, 3. There is a court order under a child protection area...A student who does not meet any of the criteria for eligibility shall be determined to be ineligible at the varsity level in all activities for one (1) full calendar year (365 days) from the date of the transfer.[70]

This rule change effectively would stop most of the transfers of players during their high school years. A student could open enroll to any school as a freshman. Once he attended a high school for one day as a freshman, he was locked into that school unless his family moved to a different school district, or he/she met one of the exceptions listed above. Every high school coach that I knew was strongly in favor of this rule, including me and all of my assistants.

***

At the Christmas break we were 0-4. We had opened the season at home losing to Minneapolis South by 2, followed by 12-point losses at Bloomington Kennedy and Mahtomedi.

The Friday night before the break, we played the annual Holy Angels game in front of a near capacity crowd at their place. We played a great game from start to finish and lost a heart breaker. With less than two minutes to go in the game we had the ball and a two point lead and we were in our spread offense. The ball went out of bounds off the leg of a Holy Angels defender in front of our bench and the referee who was out of position gave the ball to Holy Angels. They went down and scored to tie the game. We missed two good shots in the last minute, and they hit one shot and three free throws to win 85-82. The first four games of January were a tough four game stretch with maybe two winnable games. Although our morale was good, we needed a win for our confidence.

We again played well but lost to Eastview 70-62 at home the first Tuesday. On Friday we traveled to Hill-Murray. Hill-Murray began the game in a zone. Early in the half Chris Williams and DeAaron Hearn hit four consecutive threes to open up an 8-point lead. We lead the rest of the game and Renard Robinson made 5 of 5 free throws at the end to seal a 63-59 win. The win returned some of the confidence to our underclassmen.

The next week we hosted Henry Sibley on Tuesday and went to St Thomas on Friday. Along with Tartan, they were picked to fight for the conference title. Sibley pounded us on the boards and left with a 91-61 win. St Thomas then beat us 83-64 to drop our record to 1-7.

The next morning after practice I and my assistants talked to Santino. I shared with him what an old coach had once shared with me. If an athlete can play on one great team in one sport throughout his playing career, he is lucky. Santino had already been lucky to play on the great team that we had his sophomore year and the really good team that we had his junior year. Those classes both had a lot of really good players. His class was weak. And both classes behind him were nowhere near as talented as those two classes. This year was going to be different. Every time that he got the ball, he was going to have two defenders on him. As a sophomore he had the opponent's third or fourth best player guarding him. We had to be realistic and just keep improving. I also told him that next year he would be playing with 6-8 and 6-9 D1 posts, and shooting 'in and out' threes.

Santino had already verbally accepted a scholarship to San Jacinto Community College in Pasadena Texas. 'San Jac' as it was called was one of the top D1 JUCO programs in the country. They were coached by Scott Jernander who had been there since 1987. Jernander was a native of Duluth and a friend of Bob and Denise Pulford. Bob sought me out to tell me about Coach Jernander and San Jacinto, thinking that it would be a great fit for Santino. San Jacinto was a perennial national power in NCAA junior college D1. They had three or four players sign with D1 major universities almost every year. In his eighteen years as the head coach, Jernander averaged over twenty wins per season and took the Gators to the NJCAA D1 national tournament nine times. They were a big deal in the media in the Houston area, with newspaper and radio coverage and a big fan base.

Santino always bought-in to what we told him, and this was no exception. Alcindor then spoke up saying, "come on Tino, basketball is supposed to be fun. You've gotta get back to having fun. You've always worked hard. That's you. But you gotta forget about our record and get that smile back on your face."

The same week I received an anonymous email from an untraceable address at my office. It contained two paragraphs and was very well written. The first paragraph criticized a couple aspects of my allocation of playing time. The second paragraph suggested that I play one of the marginal junior varsity players. It was the first email that I had ever received from a fan. After practice the next day I showed it to the girls coach Lee Ann Wise. After reading it one time, she said, "oh I know who wrote that", and then she named a person by name. She then said "that person does that all the time. I know who it is. I can tell by the writing. That person's done that to me and the volleyball coaches too. And it's always a different email address and a fake name. The real name is never signed." I didn't respond to the email, deleted it, and put a block on receiving any more emails from the same address.

* * *

We then had two consecutive weeks of Tuesday, Friday, and Saturday games. We won four of the six. We were becoming efficient offensively. Like the year before, I had taped off an area around the lane in the shape of a trapezoid, and instituted the rule that before we shot Santino had to touch the ball in this area. He was averaging over 20 points per game and shooting over 55%. He was creating well over half the shots that we were taking, by drawing a double-team and passing to a teammate. This teammate could then shoot, shot fake and drive, or quickly pass to another teammate who could do the same. The others, and in particular junior Chris Daley were beginning to get more open threes. Except for Santino, our scoring was very balanced. And amazingly, Santino was steadily improving.

Our team defense had been strong since the first week of practice. Except for our lack of size, we were a very good defensive team, with good quickness on the perimeter. Dexter Jones, BJ Skoog, and Garret Wallstein were all excellent if undersized post defenders. DeAaron Hearn and Renard Robinson drew the toughest defensive assignments. We started each game with them guarding the opponent's best players, which kept Santino out of foul trouble. Late in the game I could put Santino on their best player. Santino learned as a young player to not make stupid 'out of position' fouls, and had never been prone to fouling. Chris Williams and Jay Sewer were used to applying instant ball pressure on the point guard.

Our overall record was now 5-9, but we were in need of a signature win. We had a chance for that win the next Tuesday against Tartan. We again played well and with confidence, and came within one possession of beating them, losing in the last minute 74-69. On Friday we avenged the loss to Mahtomedi with a 105-60 win. Santino drilled five of six threes, and had 42 points with three dunks. We emptied the bench.

The next week we split games against Hill-Murray and Henry Sibley. The following Tuesday St Thomas came to our place. We played our best game of the season in front of a big crowd. With three minutes to go in the game the score was tied 62-62. They scored two possessions in a row and hit free throws to leave with a 75-64 win. Three days later we beat North St Paul.

We had two weeks and four games remaining before the tournament. We were most likely going to be the #7 seed and play either Apple Valley or Burnsville. Both teams were currently in the top half of the Lake Conference. By March I would have seen both teams play two times, and my assistants had also seen both teams. Like most 4A teams, both were much bigger than us, but I liked our match up and our chances, if we could play at our highest level. Without telling the kids, we geared our defensive drills toward both of these teams the last two weeks. We also put in a couple of simple set plays that both of these teams ran, and used them in our last four games. If we ran these plays ourselves, we would know how to stop them.

We defeated Simley 79-77. Our next game was against St Paul Johnson at home. Johnson was ranked #7 in Class 4A with a record of 19-4. It would be another chance for the big win that we needed. After leading the entire game, we lost in the last two minutes 70-66. We then split games against South St Paul and Tartan to finish the regular season 10-14, and 8-8 in the conference.

* * *

As expected, we were seeded #7 and opened the section tournament at #2 Burnsville. Apple Valley was seeded #1 with a 20-5 record. I saw all six of the teams seeded above us as beatable. There was no team like Henry Sibley or St Thomas, who were near impossible match ups for us.

Burnsville was coached by Doug Boe. After winning back-to-back state championships as the girl's coach in 1991 and 1992, he took the Burnsville boys to the state finals in 2004. They owned an 18-6 record. Burnsville was a fourth ring suburb on the south side of the Minnesota River. We had scrimmaged them the past three years. Doug shared with me that Burnsville was going through the same demographic changes as Richfield. His varsity team was now almost half African-American. Three years prior, his state runner-up team had only had two black kids out of 18 players.

On this year's team Burnsville was inside oriented with four big posts all between 6'5" and 6'9" who rotated at two positions, and they had an athletic 6'3" All-Conference wing. I decided to play behind their posts, double down hard when they got the ball, and hope that they were missing their outside shots. We weren't big and athletic enough to ball pressure on the perimeter. Plus, if we tried to front, they would kill us on the boards. Like all of the teams in their conference, they were a team that ran a lot of set plays. From our scouting, we knew all of their set plays, and we knew that we could stop their sets. On offense we would spread the court and drive on them. It would be the kind of game where we would need to hit some shots early, and not let them make a run. If they made one ten-point run, it could be difficult for us to match it and get back in the game. The longer that we could stay in the game, the more we would play with confidence, and the smaller the rim would get for them.

The game couldn't have started better for us. They missed shots and we got the ball to Santino. He made his first two field goals, and his first four free throws. They built up a 6-point lead midway through the half and we quickly closed it. At the half we were down 31-27.

The second half was similar to the first. When they switched to a 2-3 zone, we penetrated and made good hard cuts to the openings. We continued to get good shots and hit enough to stay in the game. Every time that we needed a basket the ball seemed to end up in Santino's hands. He was now drawing double teams and the others were getting wide open looks. As the minutes clicked down, they couldn't pull away. We had our defense packed into the paint, and we were limiting them to one shot. DeAaron Hearn, BJ Skoog, Chris Daly, and Renard Robinson, all hit clutch shots in the last ten minutes.

With a little over one minute to play we had the ball trailing by one point. I called time out. I diagrammed a set play that we had saved and practiced to get Santino the ball 10-12 feet from the basket. I told them that if Burnsville was denying him the ball to not force it. Then we would just run offense and try to penetrate hard, jump stop, and kick out for an open jumper. I reminded them that we had a minute and a half. If we miss, we foul immediately. If we make, we match up and three-quarter court press. No long passes. This was all review.

They were all over Santino. He couldn't get the ball. With under fifteen seconds to go DeAaron Hearn drove to the paint from the left wing and drew a double-team. Two passes later Jay Sewer was squared up on the right side of the arc for a wide open three pointer. He swished it and the crowd was screaming and on its feet. A Burnsville player quickly inbounded the ball and their point guard Max Van Ostrand faced our press. After hesitating for a couple of dribbles, he pushed the ball and launched a shot from just over half court. It went in, hitting the back inside of the rim as it went down. Their bench swarmed the court. We had lost on a buzzer beater 70-68.

I couldn't have been prouder of the team, and in the locker room I told them this. They had improved constantly, they had pulled together, and they had fun. Once again, we just couldn't quite get a big upset win. We had played our best game of the year. It was a very bitter-sweet ending to the season.

* * *

Looking back on it, after a rough first half of the season, it had been a very fun second half of the season. In a way the last game was a fitting summary of the year, a year of near misses, and a year without a signature win. Our final overall record was 10-15. We lost four games in the last two minutes to top ten teams. The kids never got to experience an on the court, after the game, pandemonium style celebration.

After dominating the conference with a 16-0 record, St Thomas went on to win the Class 3A state championship. With the exception of a buzzer beater 54-51 win over Rocori in the state semifinals, every one of their tournament victories was by more than ten points.

The Class 4A tournament was made a wide-open affair when #1 ranked Hopkins lost to Minnetonka in the section semifinals when a shot at the buzzer bounced out. After defeating Hopkins, Minnetonka lost to Bloomington Jefferson and Kansas bound Cole Aldrich 84-76 in overtime. After defeating us, Burnsville lost a close game to Eastview. Apple Valley then beat Eastview 70-62 in overtime in the section finals. Apple Valley defeated Jefferson the first game of state 68-66, before losing to Armstrong 70-67 in the semifinals. Greg Miller's team then lost a heartbreaker in the finals to Buffalo 67-65.

The girls' team under first year coach Lee Ann Wise finished 9-16. Our lack of height was an obstacle all season, and the girl's team indeed did have more height than us. On one point, the ghostwriter William Beckett had been right.

Open Enrollment

In 1987 Minnesota was the first state to adopt statewide open enrollment, allowing students to attend public schools across district lines. This bill was passed when Rudy Perpich was Governor. Perpich was a Democrat who was born and raised in the heart of the Iron Range in Hibbing, the son of native-born Croatian parents. The Mesabi Iron Range is located in northeastern Minnesota. Along with some Scandinavians, it is a melting pot of many Eastern and Southern European nationalities which are not common in other parts of the state. It also has a history of being strongly aligned with the Democrat-Farmer-Labor Party, and a history of labor unrest, some of it violent. His Iron Range upbringing no doubt had some influence on his views on open enrollment and equity in education for all.

According to *'Strange Brew: Minnesota's Motley Mix of School Reforms'* written by Mitchell B. Pearlstein in 2000, (Perpich)

was deeply bothered by the fact that poor families enjoyed far fewer educational choices than did more affluent families. As a result, he has been credited with nothing less than redefining the very idea of school choice to include the public sector. Joe Nathan, a St. Paul educator...had argued for public school choice in a 1983 book...One would allow students to cross district lines-long the Berlin Walls of public education-to attend the public school of their choice...

Due in part to Nathan's influence, Perpich agreed with the idea, and he announced his plans at a Citizens League speech. Pearlstein wrote,

Compared to public schools in Hibbing, Perpich was very disappointed by what he saw as the inferior quality of public schools in St. Paul after moving there, early in his political career, with his wife and two children. Unable to afford private education for his son and daughter, he relocated his family to a suburb where he found public schools more to his liking.

A 'Governors' Discussion Group' was formed. It was made up of people who were both for and against open enrollment. By the end of 1986 the group agreed on endorsing open enrollment, if it was voluntary two ways. It had to be voluntary by the open enrolling families, and it also had to be voluntary by the school districts. This resulted in a state wide discussion in the editorial sections of newspapers. Some opponents to open enrollment argued that school choice already did exist with private schools, and that private schools had scholarships for low-income families.

According to Pearlstein...*it didn't take long for open-enrollment proponents to control the moral high ground on the equity issue. Opponents...found it increasingly difficult to argue against the proposition that choice already did exist-but only for families who could buy their way to better schools for their children.*[71]

With a liberal Democratic controlled legislature, the open enrollment bill passed in 1987. In the 1989-90 school year, open enrollment became mandatory for school districts with more than 1,000 students. The next year, open enrollment became mandatory for all school districts across the state. In 1989-90 it was estimated that about 3,000 Minnesota students chose open enrollment. By the 2000s, the estimated number was ten times that amount at 30,000 students.

***

In 1994 the State Board of Education drafted a statewide desegregation rule which was to be considered by the Legislature, but the rule was never implemented. In 1998 an attempt was made to establish a 'diversity rule' to again address segregation in schools. This was killed by another state board. Behind both of these failed efforts was Arne Carlson, a Republican who followed Perpich as governor, after defeating Perpich in the 1990 election. Carlson was the son of native-born Swedish parents and was raised in New York City. He attended public schools in the Bronx before earning a scholarship to a private college-prep high school in Connecticut. After graduating from Williams College in Massachusetts he came to Minnesota to attend law school at the University.

Again, according to 'Strange Brew: Minnesota's Motley Mix of School Reforms' written by Mitchell B. Pearlstein in 2000;

...so much of the inspiration for school choice on the part of Governor Carlson and others was rooted in what it can accomplish for low-income, inner-city children...

...In early 1994, the State Board of Education was getting ready to adopt a new desegregation plan, mainly for the Twin Cities metropolitan area...(it) would break new ground not only by requiring, in effect, massive busing between the central cities of Minneapolis and St. Paul and their suburbs and exurbs, but also by requiring districts with more than thirty minority students to ensure that these youngsters performed at essentially the same levels as white students

in the district. *Four measures were called for: academic performance, dropout rates, rates of suspension and expulsion, and rates of participation in remedial and honors classes.*

According to one story in the *Star Tribune*, the '*push to bring the suburbs' into the process had come from the NAACP and other groups that maintained that 'racial segregation in schools prevents equal educational opportunity and leads to segregation in the broader society.' The article quoted Matthew Little, retired president of the Minneapolis NAACP, who warned that if the Legislature didn't approve the plan and adequately fund it, 'that is going to set the grounds' for a lawsuit.*[72]

In March of 1994 an editorial on the topic appeared in the *StarTribune*, written by Katherine Kersten, who was a resident of Edina.

Again, according to Pearlstein,

Here are a few of her main points...even though Minneapolis and St. Paul had been busing students for more than twenty years, 'they have little to show for it but large tax bills.'...

...Kersten concluded by suggesting several more promising ways of improving the academic performance of poor children, including giving greater weight to 'neighborhood schools,' which she said could 'provide stability, contribute to a sense of community, and make it easier for parents to become involved in their children's education.'[73]

The desegregation plan was soon a hot topic on talk show radio. A short time later the African-American mayor of Minneapolis, Sharon Sayles Belton came out in support of neighborhood schools, and a majority of the members of the Minneapolis school board agreed with her. The desegregation rule was defeated.

In 1995 the Minneapolis NAACP (National Association for the Advancement of Colored People) sued the state of Minnesota. The lawsuit was based upon the premise that racially isolated schools did not provide students with the adequate education they are promised under Minnesota's Constitution and that segregated schools discriminate in violation of the state's Human Rights Act.

Two years later state officials were working on the 'diversity rule'.

On this Pearlstein wrote,

Under the new rule, public schools would have an enforceable obligation to 'reduce or eliminate' gaps in performance among demographic groups...racial and ethnic, male and female, poor and middle class, 'abled' and disabled. Gaps were defined as 'any measurable disparity in student performance, attendance rates, graduation rates, suspension rates, and rates of participation patterns in course offerings and extracurricular activities.'...

...Writing once more to the Star Tribune, in late 1997 Kersten alerted Minnesotans to some of the ramifications of the proposed 'diversity' plan that would go into effect two weeks later if at least twenty-five citizens didn't contact the Department of Children, Families and Learning (CFL) to request a hearing... Opposition to the diversity rule burst open soon after Kersten's piece ran in the Minneapolis paper.[74]

The hearing requested by at least twenty-five people included two hundred people and lasted two days. Norman Draper of the *StarTribune* reported that hundreds more, called, e-mailed, or wrote CFL with their opposition. Talk show radio debated the issue with many people ridiculing the rule's faults.

***

In March of 2000, after a bitter legal battle, a settlement was reached between the Minneapolis NAACP and the state of Minnesota. The result was a voluntary school integration program which included Minneapolis and the surrounding suburbs. Suburban school districts where less than 50% of the students were on reduced or free school lunch were required to participate in the program. The settlement was greatly influenced by the 1996 'Sheff vs. O'Neill' case in Hartford, Connecticut.

The Minnesota settlement agreement required eight suburban school districts to reserve 500 seats for K-12, low-income, Minneapolis city students each year for the next four years. The lawsuit also stipulated that the state would pay for busing, and also communicate with families about school options. The eight suburban districts that began in the program were Columbia Heights, Edina, Hopkins, Richfield, St. Louis Park, St. Anthony, Robbinsdale, and Wayzata. These eight districts comprised seven of the eight inner ring school districts which were contiguous with the city of Minneapolis. Brooklyn Center high school and its feeder schools were not included in the program, most likely because over 50% of its students were on reduced or free school lunch. Wayzata was the only second ring suburb in the program. The third ring suburb Eden Prairie was not involved in the original lawsuit, but was voluntarily admitted in 2005.

In the Minneapolis schools during the first decade of the twenty first century roughly 70% of the K-12 students were on reduced or free school lunch. This amounted to an average of about 31,000 out of the 45,000 total students each school year. According to 'The Choice is Yours After Two Years': An

Evaluation", by Elisabeth A. Palmer PH.D. of ASPEN Associates, most parents of participating students listed reasons for enrolling in the program as academic quality, high standards, high achievement, and curriculum offerings.

The description of the program on the *website of the Minneapolis Public Schools* reads as follows:

"The Choice is Yours" Minnesota Program

"The Choice is Yours" is an open enrollment program that give low-income Minneapolis families more options to attend suburban schools. Students who qualify for free or reduced lunch may apply to attend school in another school district and may be eligible for transportation to and from school. Students who live on the north side of Minneapolis may apply to schools in Columbia Heights, Hopkins, Robbinsdale, St. Anthony/New Brighton, St. Louis Park, or Wayzata. Students who live on the south side of Minneapolis may apply to schools in Eden Prairie, Edina, Richfield, or St. Louis Park. The program is administered by the Minnesota Department of Education in partnership with Minneapolis Public Schools and the West Metro Education Program (WMEP).

Applications for open enrollment must be submitted to the district of the school the student is applying. For more information about "The Choice is Yours", call the school you are interested in attending or visit the WMEP website.[75]

According to a multi-year *State Department of Education* report, the first year of the program saw 472 Minneapolis students participate, and that the number tripled the first seven years.

On April 29, 2006 the following editorial appeared in the *StarTribune*.

Choice program benefits students
Income diversity makes a difference for low-income kids

A recent evaluation of a program that sends Minneapolis public students to suburban schools reiterates this reality: When it comes to education, family income matters.

The state-sponsored assessment of the five-year-old Choice Is Yours program found that low-income students who were bused to the suburbs made three times the academic progress of their peers who remained in city schools. Clearly, when students are exposed to middle-income peers, attitudes toward learning rub off on them.

That is a strong argument for finding ways to break up high concentrations of poverty in schools. Although other efforts are important-including teacher training, good curricula, and parental involvement-changing the income mix appears to move the academic bar more quickly...

...Ultimately, school and metro leaders might have to consider major boundary changes or consolidations.

This is not an indictment of poor kids and their families; low-income students are as capable of learning as any child. But when schools are overwhelmed by poverty-related issues, academics can and do suffer.

To help close the achievement gap faster, society must get serious about addressing poverty. And it must do a better job of integrating schools and neighborhoods by income.[76]

In terms of athletic prowess, open enrollment and the Choice Program eventually took their toll on both the Minneapolis and St Paul City Conferences. According to Charles Hallman, in a December 14, 2011 article in the *Minnesota Spokesman-Recorder,*

Longtime observers cite two reasons: open enrollment, which erased the old "neighborhood schools" rules, and the demise of middle-school athletics. Both factors occurred almost simultaneously two decades ago. Minneapolis Roosevelt Athletic Director Al Frost, a graduate of old Minneapolis Central High School in the 1960s, vividly remembers the conference's glory days. "We had 11 schools in our conference," he recalls. "We were all very competitive."...

The "togetherness" once seen in the city league seems to have gone as well, Frost believes. He fondly remembers when the entire community attended city football and basketball games. "I don't think we have that community feeling in Minneapolis (anymore). Things have changed."...

Add those city parents who Frost calls "very manipulative-they seize on everything if they can," using open enrollment to better promote their child's athletic prowess. He suggests a modification of the rules: "You can go to any school you want, but you compete (athletically) in your attendance area. That would give us equity."[77]

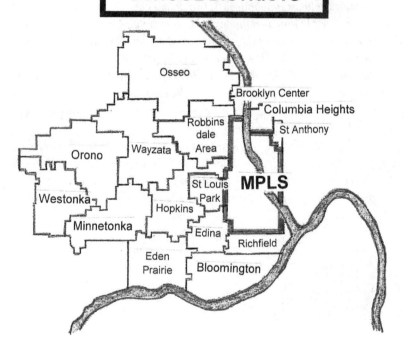

MINNEAPOLIS AREA &
THE CHOICE IS YOURS
SCHOOL DISTRICTS

Osseo

Brooklyn Center

Columbia Heights

Robbins
dale
Area

St Anthony

Orono

Wayzata

MPLS

St Louis
Park

Westonka

Hopkins

Minnetonka

Edina

Richfield

Eden
Prairie

Bloomington

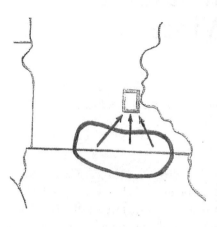

EUROPEAN-AMERICAN MIGRATION TO RICHFIELD
1940-1960

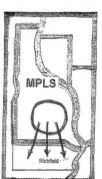

MPLS

Richfield

AFRICAN-AMERICAN MIGRATION TO RICHFIELD
1990-2010

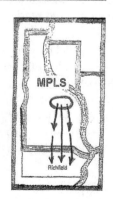

MPLS

Richfield

Chicago

Kansas City

Memphis

273

Seventh Summer
& Winter

Some of my favorite teams were my five hundred teams.
Sometimes those teams are the most fun to coach.
—Augie Schmidt

During the 2007 Minnesota legislative session a bill was enacted 'Notice of nonrenewal, opportunity to respond'. The bill was authored by Dean Urdahl, a Republican who represented a rural district west of the Twin Cities. After teaching history and coaching track and cross country for twenty-nine years, he moved back to his home town of Litchfield and he entered politics. He was elected to the state house of representatives in 2002.

The bill read as follows:

Before a district terminates the coaching duties of an employee who is...an athletic coach..., the district must notify the employee in writing and state its reason for the proposed termination...The employee may request...a hearing... before the board...Within ten days after the hearing, the board must issue a written decision regarding the termination...The hearing may be opened or closed at the election of the coach.

Fired coaches now had a chance to respond to administrators and school boards in an open public setting. After a number of great coaches had been fired in recent years, the firing of Rich Decker in Rochester spurred the bill to be passed. Rich never had a chance to respond to the Lourdes administration. Nobody expected any firings to be reversed. But it would give fired coaches a chance to be heard.

***

There was significant turnover on the basketball board. In July the president resigned, but he remained on the board as a director-at-large. He was the president for four years after his son had not tried out as a junior. His son was a typical program player who had participated in all facets of the program beginning as a 1st grader. Then he was outworked and passed up by other kids in middle school and high school. He never attended one open gym. Another member resigned when her son was cut as a junior.

A father with three sons joined the board. His oldest son was a senior my first year at Richfield, and he would not have been good enough to make the varsity in any of the following years. His middle son was a program kid through eighth grade, before not trying out as a freshman. His youngest son was going to be a ninth grader. He had been the starting point guard on his traveling team since fifth grade, in a very weak class. He had not been in the gym one time all summer, and there were at least ten eighth graders who were gym rats who were clearly better than him.

A woman without a son in the program joined the board. She had been a loyal and enthusiastic fan of the entire program since my first year. She worked in the school system and the kids loved her. When I was at the Intermediate School recruiting kids for the basketball camp, she was always in the cafeteria surrounded by many kids, and kids of all colors. She raised the question of 'how do we get the Hispanic kids into the program'. The smaller houses on the east side of Richfield were being bought by Hispanics, and their children were attending the grade schools. The board voted to have all future basketball advertising flyer's to be translated to Spanish and distributed to these kids. This woman was always upbeat and excited about everything that she did, and she was a champion of the underdog. She was a great addition.

The only board member who had a son who was in middle school or high school, and who was a good basketball player was Jim Noonan. Jim's son Jared was one of the many good eighth graders. And Jared and his buddies were always at the gym bouncing a basketball.

* * *

In September one of the parents told me that Todd Olson told him that he would allow Lance back as an assistant. This parent called Lance to tell him this. I immediately met with Todd and asked him if this was true. Todd's answer was that yes, he gave it some thought, and he decided that it was OK for me to bring Lance back as a volunteer.

I told Todd that there was no way that I could do this. All of the young assistants had stepped up and grown into their jobs. Every coach was happy with their role, and we worked together well. I now had three young assistants who all understood our defense and how to teach it. Mullenbach was the lead scout. Alcindor and Omar were both ready to be head coaches. They were all equally my top assistant. If I brought back Lance, he would have to be my top assistant. As great as it would be to have Lance back, it wouldn't be fair to the other three. I told Todd all of this. I asked him why he hadn't come to me to discuss this before he announced it to a parent. He didn't have an answer.

I then explained all of this to the parent, who said that he totally understood. I did not contact Lance to meet with him and tell him all of this. I have regretted not doing this ever since, and our friendship has never been the same.

In October I and one of my assistants once again had the tryouts for the traveling teams. The overall number of kids who tried out gradually decreased over the years. Specifically, the number of white kids who tried out decreased. The number of black kids trying out increased. We were averaging about a dozen kids on financial aid each year, almost always all African Americans.

There was a pattern here. The fifth and sixth grade teams usually had at most one or two kids of color. As these players progressed up through the grades each year, more and more black kids would make the team. The new kids were from families that moved into the apartment buildings. These were kids who first showed up in the summer program. They were gym rats who improved dramatically by working on fundamentals and playing with older players. They hung out at the gym with the other kids in their grade, both black and white, who were also gym rats. They passed up the remaining program kids, many of which were doing something other than practicing basketball fundamentals every day. The good players and their parents saw this as a positive improvement in the program. This wasn't always the case with the parents of the other players.

* * *

I did not see one instance of overt racism in my time at Richfield. Earlier in the fall, a friend of mine did. He was a Minneapolis guy who attended a Minneapolis high school. He and his wife bought a modest home in Edina to raise their family. His son was in middle school, and my friend often gave his son rides home from sports practices. Sometimes his son's friends needed rides and he gave these kids rides, too.

One day this spring he pulled into the parking lot at the school to pick up his son after practice. He was standing outside his car as half a dozen kids were talking and piling into his car. The friends were 'The Choice is Yours' open enrollment kids from Minneapolis and they were black.

A brand-new sports utility vehicle pulled up behind him and a well-dressed woman quickly got out. As her son was getting into her vehicle, she walked directly towards my friend and began speaking, "those kids don't live in Edina, do they?"

My friend looked at her with a questioning expression on his face and said, "no, they live in Minneapolis."

The woman answered immediately and loudly, "well their mothers should have thought about giving them rides before they open enrolled them. You shouldn't be giving them rides home."

My friend responded "did you just say that? I can't believe you just said that." The mother repeated herself and walked back to her SUV, got in, shut the door and drove away.

During the summer one of the high school kids who attended the open gyms shared an experience with me. He was African-American and he never played in the basketball program. He was standing at a bus stop on the south side of Minneapolis on his way to a summer job early one morning. He was dressed 'office casual' with khaki pants, a short-sleeved polo shirt, and a small backpack over his shoulder. He was not wearing gang colors. Suddenly a police car screeched to a halt in front of him, and two white officers hopped out. He did everything that the officers told him to do. He never reached into a pocket or his backpack and he never raised his voice. The officers rifled through his backpack and took his id. Within a minute they had him up against a cyclone fence with a gun to his head. He was handcuffed. One officer returned to the squad car and spoke on the phone. Ten minutes elapsed. After the officers spoke to each other out of earshot of the young man, they approached him again. One officer took off the handcuffs, and told him that he was free to go, explaining that he looked like a gang member who had a warrant out for an arrest. The officers walked away. They did not apologize. The young man then yelled at them, telling them that he missed his bus, and that now he was going to be late for work. One officer looked back and laughed and said "that's not my problem, that's your problem." He continued to laugh loudly as he got back into the squad car.

* * *

Tryouts began in November with an upbeat group of players. We returned seven players with experience. All seven were in the gym or played on AAU teams all summer. They would have to learn how to play without Santino.

I took a look at the talent in the pipeline of the program. The sophomore class had two players about 6-4, but neither one was ready for varsity. The one with the most athletic ability was afraid of contact and played timid. The other was a plodder and could not shoot. Since they were in grade school, we had been telling both to get to the open gyms. Both had never done this.

The freshman class was historically thin and never won very many games. Jared Etienne was going to be at least 6-4, had great hands, and could pass and shoot, but had slow feet and no lift. Daron Garvis was a 5-8 combo guard who would maybe be ready for varsity as a sophomore. His dad graduated from Richfield about 20 years earlier. Daron attended grade school in south Minneapolis, and also attended our summer camp. He open-enrolled as a freshman. John Johnson was an African American who moved to Richfield during his eighth-grade year. The remaining program players were all no shows all summer. The eighth graders were continuing their growth and improvement. There was always at least half a dozen of them at the open gyms.

When it came time for cuts, there were no difficult decisions. A week after we had made our cuts, my sources informed me that two sets of parents whose sons had been cut, had met with the athletic director and then the principal to air some complaints. My sources also said that these sets of parents did this together, not separately. Later Jill Johnson confirmed this to me. One set of parents was white and one set of parents was black. The only thing that I and my staff found puzzling was the fact that the African American parents had complained at all. We had known that the white parents were not happy. However, the black parents had always been very appreciative of the coaching staff, going out of their way multiple times to thank me and my assistants "for everything that we had done" for their son/grandson.

Once again, my goal for the varsity was to win more than we lose, and with steady improvement, be tough by tournament time. We would be stingy on defense, and we would have good shooters. In terms of basketball talent, we were in the middle of a down period, but it was going to be a smart team that was well schooled in our system. We would hopefully win some close games, and in the process knock off a couple of ranked teams.

* * *

We split our first two games, before hosting Minneapolis South on the second Saturday night. We lost 89-86. The Friday before Christmas we played the annual Holy Angels game at home. Holy Angels had their best team in five years. We played well and lost 91-76 in a game that was closer than the score. We won our next game and then traveled to St Paul Johnson for a Saturday afternoon game. The Governors were ranked #8 in Class 3A. We played our best game of the season, in front of a big crowd and intense atmosphere. With the score tied 74-74 and the clock ticking down they scored on a jump shot that bounced on the rim as the buzzer sounded, and then rolled around and in. We were 2-4, with conference favorites Henry Sibley and St Thomas up next.

Henry Sibley was ranked #8 in Class 4A. Their talented classes were now in high school. And they had added a transfer student who was to be the best player in the conference in Mike Bruesewitz. Bruesewitz was a muscular 6-7, and was being recruited hard by Wisconsin. He grew up in Litchfield, and then played AAU ball with a couple of the Sibley kids. When his parents had moved to the metropolitan area over the summer, he chose to attend Sibley. They easily beat us 82-58. St Thomas then came to our place on Friday. They returned three starters from their state championship team. We played them tough until late in the game and lost 80-58. We were now 2-6, with a string of winnable games ahead of us.

We defeated North St Paul and St Michael-Albertville at home, and Simley on the road. St Michael-Albertville was 9-1 and ranked #6 in Class 3A. We shot well and they couldn't buy a basket. Phil Freeman had a break out game for us hitting 5 of 5 threes. We ended up with a 92-78 victory.

Our rotation had settled into eight players. Juniors Phil Freeman, DeAaron Hearn, Chris Williams, senior Chris Daly, and sophomore Jay Sewer played on the perimeter. Seniors Garret Wallstein and BJ Skoog along with junior Renard Robinson played up front. Senior Dylan Olson also played limited minutes in the post. Dylan got the ball knocked out of his hands one time, and after we talked about this, it never happened again. We were beginning to play at a higher level. We would need to. The next Tuesday we hosted Hopkins.

* * *

Hopkins was the defending Class 4A state champions, undefeated, and ranked #1 in Minnesota in Class 4A. Three of their starters were juniors who had already been offered D1 scholarships; 6-8 Mike Broghammer, 6-4 Trent Lockett, and 6-4 Raymond Cowels. Their junior point guard Marcus Williams was a D1 football recruit. They were coached by Ken Novak Jr and assisted by his dad Ken Novak Sr.

Ken Jr was in his nineteenth year as the head coach at Hopkins. After playing for his dad in high school, Ken Jr returned to Hopkins as the head coach in the fall of 1988. As the open enrollment and The Choice is Yours program had grown, many of the African-American kids from North Minneapolis began choosing Hopkins as their high school. Because the east side of the Hopkins school district abuts the west side of North Minneapolis, Hopkins is the logical choice for many north side kids if they decide to opt into The Choice is Yours program. A handful of other kids from other suburbs had also open enrolled at Hopkins over the years. Rick Majerus once said of Ken, "Offense is spacing, spacing is offense, and yet it seems to be the least-taught thing at every level. I've been in 150 high school gyms in the past five years and I've heard two coaches talking about spacing, and one was the guy up there at Hopkins, Ken Novak Jr." When a north side kid has scholarship potential and the word spreads that Coach Novak is a great coach, it makes the high school choice a lot easier. One sportswriter called Hopkins the 'Duke' of Minnesota high school basketball. Along with all of this came the inescapable accusations of recruiting.

Ken Sr was one of the coaching icons of his generation in Minnesota high school basketball. He grew up in the small town of Crosby on the Cuyuna Iron Range in north central Minnesota. The combined population of Crosby and Ironton was 3,400. Under the one class system Crosby-Ironton was the eleventh biggest town in Region 6, and they won 11 region titles over 40 years. The two biggest towns in the region of Moorhead and Brainerd with populations of 23,000 and 12,900 combined to win 12. Crosby-Ironton and Brainerd were District 24 rivals and they faced off in the district finals many times during this span. Ken played for celebrated coach Herman Wook. Wook took the Rangers to state 7 times in his 21 years as the coach in the 1930s and 1940s.

Wook also administered one of the first feeder programs in the era before summer camps. He simply picked a couple of his high school players from each ethnic group, and these kids organized and refereed basketball games in their home neighborhoods. Crosby and Ironton were settled at the turn of the century by European immigrants who came to work in the mines. When Ken Sr was a boy, he spent his summers playing basketball games with the other Slovenian kids in his neighborhood, while the Serbian, Finnish, and Croatian kids played with each other in their neighborhoods. Ken Sr was a walking history book of Minnesota high school basketball. After playing and coaching at St Cloud State, he spent two years assisting legendary coach Butsie Maetzold at Hopkins. He then replaced Maetzold as the head coach in the fall of 1956. He continued Butsies's winning tradition for 25 years until his last year in 1982. When Ken Jr returned to his home town as the head coach at Hopkins in 1989, Ken Sr came back as his assistant.

We played our best game of the year. It was one of those nights where we as the underdog were playing with a high level of energy and they as the favorites just couldn't get going. We spread them out on offense and we were very patient. When they overplayed too aggressively, we back cut for layups. On defense we packed our man-to-man defense into the paint. Garret Walstein,

BJ Skoog, and Dylan Olson worked relentlessly playing post defense. They missed a lot of open outside shots, and we didn't have one missed box out. We had four possessions in the game where we held the ball for over two minutes and then Chris Daley or Phil Freeman buried a wide open three. At halftime we were down 4. With four minutes to go in the game, they got their lead up to 6. We missed a good shot, and couldn't close the gap. We ended up losing 88-75, which was their closest game of the season to date.

After the game both Novaks were very complimentary. Ken Sr emphatically told us what a great job that we were doing and that we were getting everything that we could out of our kids. We had known that neither Ken Jr nor Ken Sr had scouted us, although we had seen their assistants at our games. Before the game Ken Sr told me that many teams schedule them for a non-conference game at the opponent's home gym, and then they back out of the return game the following year at Hopkins. I knew that both Novaks would be scouting us the following year, and that we were going to honor the contract and play them at their place. The mood in our locker room after the game was one of realization. The kids now realized that on any given night, we could play with anybody. I have never been prouder of a team, after a loss.

* * *

In January, the girls' basketball coach LeeAnn Wise asked me to help her with their man-to-man defense. For the next few weeks, Alcindor and I spent half an hour each day at her practices setting up and teaching our defensive drills. And she and her coaching staff were constantly picking the brains of me and my assistants.

LeeAnn was hired as the girls coach the previous winter. She replaced Kim Burns, who resigned after 17 years. LeeAnn was the principal at Centennial Elementary. She was originally from Michigan and played at Lake Superior State in Sault Ste Marie. When I asked Todd Olson about her, he was very excited and he described her as a fighter whose style is very much 'in your face'. To her credit, Kim left LeeAnn with a talented group of sophomores, who had dominated at every level. They were now juniors, and the team had an overall record of 12-3.

In the seven years that I was at Richfield, the girls' varsity roster was always entirely juniors and seniors, and program kids. The girls traveling teams had a policy of no financial aid, and the varsity team and traveling program was almost entirely white girls. One of the parents of the good players confided in me that if I had been the girls' coach, her daughter would have played

varsity as a freshman. There was a dichotomy between the boys and girls' programs. The two programs had completely different philosophies on how to
distribute roster spots and playing time. In the girls' program, if you were a
senior, you probably started. The two programs also had completely different
racial make-ups and win loss records. LeeAnn was going to change this.

LeeAnn shared with me the previous winter that she faced a lot of criticism and outrage when she began the season playing these sophomores on the
varsity. She was experiencing what I experienced four years earlier. This didn't
bother her a bit. As she told me, "It's simple. I'm playing the best players." She
reduced the fee of the summer camp to $20. She implemented the same after
school study hall system that Mullenbach was running. And she was committed to playing pressure man to man defense. As her team began dominating
with this style, it was fun to watch.

***

We closed out January winning three out of four games, and losing another
one possession game to Tartan 68-67. The next three games were going to be
tough, with games against Henry Sibley and St Thomas sandwiched around a
game at Rocori. We played well and lost to both conference schools.

The Rocori game was our out-state Saturday game with a coach bus. The
school was a consolidated district made up of three towns, Rockville, Cold
Spring, and Richmond, in the heart of the German Catholic section of central Minnesota. They were coached by Bob Brink, who had been there over 30
years. His career record of 876-292 ranked second in total wins behind Bob
McDonald of Chisholm. He took Rocori to the state tournament 12 times, and
his 1988 his team won the big school state tournament, when there were only
two classes, and Rocori was one of the smallest schools in the bigger class. The
most amazing thing about his coaching record was that in over 30 years, he
only had one season under five hundred. His teams ran a modified flex offense,
played tough zone defense, and they always had shooters. We again played
well and lost 86-78.

***

As we entered into February, we began gearing up for the section tournament. Although our enrollment had decreased, we had opted up to Class 4A.
The sections had been realigned as they were every two years, and we were
now with Prior Lake, Shakopee, Edina, Bloomington Jefferson, Bloomington

Kennedy, Eden Prairie, and Chaska. We would most likely be seeded #7 and draw Eden Prairie or Shakopee.

We would close out the season with seven games in four weeks. We won three of the first four games, including a 73-71 loss at Minneapolis North. In a Friday game at Tartan, we played our best game yet and held on for a 66-58 victory. With less than 30 seconds to go in the game I walked down the bench and told the kids to not celebrate it like it was the NCAA finals. "Celebrate it like a normal win. Then when we get to the locker room, we celebrate." I also sent the message to the kids on the court. After the game Mark and his players were complimentary and gracious in defeat. When I got to the locker room the kids were going crazy. I told them "We've never won here. Even when we had Ray and Travis and all those guys, we never won here. You guys accomplished something that no other Richfield team has ever done. Savor it over the weekend. You deserve it."

The last week of the season we split games against Mahtomedi and Hill-Murray at home to finish the regular season 13-13.

***

The next day we began getting ready for Shakopee. Bruce Kugath had another good team. They won the Missota Conference and finished with an overall record of 23-4. After defeating us for the state title in 2005, they were moved up to Class 4A, and they were in the same section as either powerhouse Hopkins, or the outer ring mega school of Eden Prairie. They had not been back to state. Eden Prairie was seeded #1. I felt that we could play with either of these teams, in spite of being undersized.

The first round of the section games was played as double-headers at the home court of the highest seed. We arrived late in the first half of the first game, and the gym was already mostly full. The Shakopee school district had built a new state of the art high school on the outskirts of the town with a beautiful gym. Their fans were eager for a tournament run.

To begin with the game was close. Then in the middle of the half, Shakopee's best shooter Jake Ewing, an open enrollment student from Prior Lake, got loose in transition and hit three consecutive threes to open up a 10-point lead. Just before the half we turned the ball over on two consecutive possessions which led to lay-ups. At halftime we had 12 turnovers. I wasn't happy and the kids were disgusted with themselves.

In the second half we settled down. They didn't shoot as well and we took care of the ball and made shots, with BJ Skoog swishing three consecutive three pointers. With less than nine minutes to play, the lead was down to 8. Shakopee called time-out. Their lead then remained between 6 and 10 as the minutes ticked off. Then we made another run to narrow the gap to 4 with just under four minutes to play. Bruce called time out again and had his kids spread the court. We couldn't force a turnover and they burned time off of the clock. They made their free throws down the stretch to build their lead back up and earn a 77-64 victory.

***

Shakopee then defeated Edina before losing to #4 seed Bloomington Kennedy 74-62 in the finals. Kennedy had also beaten favored Eden Prairie in the semifinals 74-71. Kennedy then lost to Minnetonka 66-59 the first game of state. Minnetonka went on to win it, beating Henry Sibley 68-59 in the championship game. The closest game of the tournament for Minnetonka was in the section finals when they took out Hopkins 74-71 in overtime. Hopkins finished the season 27-2, with both losses to Minnetonka. In Class 3A, St Thomas marched to the state finals for the third year in a row where they lost to Benilde-St Margaret's, another metro Catholic school 58-52. St Michael-Albertville also went to state in Class 3A, finishing the year 26-4.

We had completed the season with a record of 13-14. Our junior varsity finished 15-11 and our sophomore squad finished 16-9. In the conference we ended up in fourth place at 10-6. Our non-conference record of 3-8 included five losses to ranked teams, four of which were close games. Renard Robinson and DeAaron Hearn both made the All-Conference team. It was one of the most fun seasons that I could remember, due to a large degree to the great leadership of our four seniors, Chris Daly, Garret Wallstein, BJ Skoog, and Dylan Olson. They executed our team defense, and they ran our offense as good as any group of seniors that we had coached. It was extremely disappointing to drop the last two games of the year, after having played much better in the game's leading up to them. As the old St Louis Park coach Augie Schmidt once told me, "some of my favorite teams were my five hundred teams, sometimes those teams are the most fun to coach." For me this was one of those teams.

The first week in March I received another handwritten note from my friend Dean Torgeson:

3-5-08

It's a thrill to watch Daly, Wallstein, Sewer, Freeman, Hearn, Robinson, Williams, and Skoog. A great winning season, CPA.

Dean Torgeson

7439 Lyndale
-a fan since 1970

That letter put a little more bounce in my step all spring.

Eighth Summer & Winter

The most we can hope for is to create the best possible conditions for success, then let go of the outcome. The ride is a lot more fun that way.

—*Phil Jackson*

One morning in the spring I got a call from Mullenbach. "DeAaron transferred to Washburn. He wasn't in school the last two days, and the kids confirmed that he's gone." I wasn't surprised. With an eight-man rotation of four, point guards, a shooting guard, and three small forwards, no one point guard was going to have the ball in his hands the majority of the game.

DeAaron attended my camps in Minneapolis when I was at Washburn. When he was a third grader, I taught him how to grip the ball on his shot, and the ball handling moves and footwork. He grew to over 6-1 and he was as good a defender as any we ever had, having played varsity since his freshman year. He was a great student, a great kid, and he had an infectious laugh. He would be missed.

Reggie Perkins was in his fourth year as the head coach at Washburn. He played high school ball in Milwaukee, before attending St Cloud State and playing for coach Butch Raymond. While at St Cloud, he and Barry Wohler formed one of the best pair of guards to ever play D2 basketball in Minnesota. Years later Reggie got into coaching with the Howard Pulley Panthers AAU team, and he became an assistant at North under Bret McNeal.

When the Washburn job opened up in the spring of 2004, Reggie was hired to replace Jason Moore. Jason, who was hand-picked to be the coach by the same parents who had gotten me fired, didn't last any longer at Washburn than I had. His overall record for three years was 15-56. Reggie continued coaching for Pulley, and began attracting the young talented Minneapolis kids to Washburn. This was the sure-fire way to win in the City Conference. It was all about recruiting the best seventh and eighth graders to your high school. It wasn't about developing the best fourth through sixth graders in your school's home area. The best way to recruit college bound talent was to coach junior high kids in the summer before they were choosing their high school. And the best place to do this was in Rene Pulley's program.

The other way to coach in the city was to take the kids who showed up at tryouts and coach the heck out of them over the winter. A coach in this situation has to simplify his system. It's difficult to play the good team man to man defense or a motion offense which takes at least a year to learn. You have to play more zones, run more set plays, and keep things simple. You have to spend more time teaching fundamentals that the kids never learned in the summer. It is similar to coaching a junior college team or an 8th grade Spring AAU team. You only had most of your kids for two or three years. Many of them had played only a year or two of lower-level AAU ball, or had only played at the YMCA and the playgrounds. Some would be kids who had been ineligible due to grades until they were a junior or a senior. Rewarding these kids with a junior and/or senior year of varsity basketball was a very good thing.

Joe Hyser at South, Dennis Stockmo at Roosevelt, and Rick Robel at Edison had done an excellent job of coaching in this way. They always got the most that they could out of the revolving door of talent that they had, and they did it by stressing the fundamentals and concepts that would pay off in the short term. However, one night of facing DeLaSalle with a full team schooled in four years of team man to man defense would be an uphill battle. Looking back on my experience at Washburn, I had spent three years trying to get my system in at Washburn, only to discover that half of my roster was new kids every year. In terms of getting my system in, I never got past year one. This had been a mistake.

Reggie's first really good class was now going to be seniors, and DeAaron would join them. For a player of DeAaron's abilities, Washburn and Reggie was the obvious choice. Like his old teammate Barry, Reggie was establishing a reputation as a great coach who was fun to play for. DeAaron would go from being one of the tallest kids on his team to one of the shortest.

* * *

At the end of the school year the superintendent Barb Devlin retired. In July she was replaced by Bob Slotterback. Slotterback started his career in central Iowa as an art teacher and a basketball coach. In 1995 he completed his doctorate and became the superintendent in Wauwatosa, Wisconsin. Wauwatosa is a large inner ring suburb on the west side of Milwaukee. In terms of demographics and housing stock, parts of it are similar to Richfield and parts of it are similar to Edina. Wauwatosa has two high schools, East and West. Slotterback was 57 years old, nearing the end of his career, and this would probably be his last job.

I felt good about the fact that a former basketball coach was now occupying the top office in the school district. The next winter he would see my teams play. He'd probably attend quite a few games and some practices, become a fan, and have my back. The next week I heard something that I didn't feel good about. One of his sons played basketball at East. As a senior this son got beat out by a freshman or a sophomore. This underclassman was an open enrollment student from Milwaukee. One of my sources soon informed me that two disgruntled parents of a player from one of my previous teams, dropped in at his office his first day on the job, and that the meeting lasted more than a couple of minutes.

***

The last week in July we traveled to western Minnesota for our annual summer trip. We played all of the kids in varying combinations, finishing with a record of 7-1, but most of the wins were against Class 2A teams. We were guard heavy, small, and quick. My hope was that two bigger young kids would step up and give us a solid inside presence. We knew that if we could get one of them to not play scared, he could be good. He had a bad habit of getting the ball knocked out of his hands, and he avoided any and all physical contact when going for rebounds. The next week an old coach and Richfield resident stopped by an open gym. He asked how this player was doing. "I have to get him to stop playing soft. He's afraid of contact. My high school coach would have called him a candy ass." He quickly answered, "Some kids you can break of this, others you can't."

***

In September I got a call from Sabrina Freeman, the mother of Phillip. Phillip had gotten into trouble with the Richfield police and had an upcoming appearance in court. Sabrina and Phillip needed a short, written statement from me, as a character reference. Also, they wanted me to hear the story from Phillip, and not from someone else. A couple of days later I, Omar, and Matt met with Sabrina and Phillip at the high school.

According to Phillip, who I trusted, the incident occurred after school one day in September. Phillip was on his way home and driving his mother's car. He was alone and heading south on one of the wide Richfield residential streets. He stopped next to a parked car to talk to a friend who was in another car. With his passenger's window open and the motor running, they were talking. Because the streets are wide, there was plenty of room for another car to get around his car. Also, at three or four in the afternoon, there was hardly any traffic on these streets.

A police car quickly pulled up behind him with its lights flashing. Two young white cops walked up and ordered Phillip out of the car. He got out. They asked for his license and he showed it to them. They asked him if they could search the car. He answered, "no." He asked them why they stopped him and why they needed to search his car. The cops answered that he was double-parked. He responded that his car was in drive, and he had just stopped to talk to a friend for a minute. The police then answered "well, we heard shots fired in the neighborhood." Phillip then lost his cool, raised his voice, and said "what's that got to do with me? Why are you stopping me because you heard shots?" The police then began using words like 'uncooperative and resisting arrest'. Ten minutes later, Phillip was sitting on the curb wearing handcuffs, and his car was being towed to the impound lot. He was issued two tickets, a misdemeanor for double-parking and a gross misdemeanor for resisting arrest.

When we heard this story, we were also surprised for another reason. We always had a great relationship with the police officers who were on duty at the high school basketball games. They made it a point to interact with all of the players, and they were huge fans of the team. I guessed that both of them would be shaking their heads and not happy if they heard the story.

Phillip was now going to court to contest the ticket. He was an exemplary student and citizen in the hallways of the high school. He would do well in front of a judge. I prepared a short statement for the judge, stating his B average, discussing his character and behavior, and listing the area colleges that were recruiting him including UW-River Falls, St John's, and Southwest State. The judge dismissed the tickets.

***

When the season started, we knew that a big key to our success would be to find out which young players would step up to compliment the four players that returned from our rotation. Renard Robinson was a 6-1 small forward and Chris Williams, Phillip Freeman, and Jay Sewer were all point guards at 5-9, 5-10, and 5-9. Because these four could all create their own shot against most teams, there was an opening for guys who could shoot off the pass, post up, and of course guys who could rebound. Besides Jay, six juniors made the team, and four of them were program kids. Four sophomores made the team.

We opened the season with close wins against Rochester Century and South. The last Friday before Christmas break was the annual Holy Angels game in their gym. We had a full week to get ready. After compiling a three-year record of 55-29, Clarence Hightower had resigned. He was replaced by Larry McKenzie, the former Patrick Henry coach. Larry left his position at Minneapolis Patrick Henry to coach the Minneapolis Ripknees, a semipro professional team based out of St Paul. After the Ripknees folded, Holy Angels hired him. As the junior varsity game wound down, the gym filled up. This would be our first game with a big crowd atmosphere. I could see the intensity on the faces of the seniors prior to the game. We went on a small run midway through the first half to build up an 8-point lead, and we were in control of the game from then on. The final score was 65-56. It was a boisterous locker room full of high fives, screams, and laughs. The seniors, who had won a lot of games as they rose through the feeder program, were getting their swagger back.

The next Tuesday we hosted Minneapolis North in an afternoon game. North was now guided by second year coach Broderick (Bo) Powell, a former DeLaSalle assistant. North brought their usual big following. We played our best game yet, hit shots early, and when the buzzer sounded, we had a 77-73 victory. The following week we traveled to Owatonna for a four team Holiday tournament. We won our first game before losing to Owatonna 66-64. This was followed by an 85-83 loss at St Michael-Albertville. We were 5-2 heading into the conference season.

* * *

We won our first two January games before defeating Tartan at home 55-52. They were ranked #7 in Class 4A and it was another signature win. Our record was 8-2, but we had the toughest part of our schedule ahead of us.

After experimenting with ten different players, our rotation settled into a top seven. We were starting the three-point guards and Renard Robinson as an undersized power forward. Corey Fitzgerald was a shooting guard coming off of the bench, and senior Michael Jones and sophomore Jared Etienne were our posts. On defense, our perimeter quickness and ball pressure were exceptional. We were all over the ball from end line to end line. In the half court, we were pressuring on the perimeter to disrupt the inside feed. We were dead fronting the post and taking our chances on the box out. Our weakness was clear, our lack of size. The problem was that our best players, and our best rebounders, were our smaller players. Except for Renard, when we did get the ball inside, the shot was usually blocked, or we got no shot at all. We were very proficient at getting good outside shots off of the pass. If we were hitting them, we could beat anybody. If they weren't dropping, we could lose to anybody.

Given the fact that we were off to such a great start, I was surprised at our small crowds. The previous two years, we had played five hundred basketball. Our crowds had dwindled, and except for when we hosted the ranked teams, the gym often felt more empty than full. During our three consecutive twenty-win seasons, it was the opposite. Opposing coaches had often made comments about the crowd atmosphere, and how well we drew the townspeople. The Richfield adult section, which was behind the Richfield bench, was usually full. The Richfield student section on the opposite side had typically been full from free throw line to free throw line. By early January, I expected these big crowds again. This wasn't the case. The gym was surprisingly not full. I was also surprised that the new superintendent, Bob Slotterback, hadn't been to a game.

* * *

Next up was the return match of the two-year home and home contract with Hopkins. During the off season I had received many compliments about how we had played Hopkins tough the year before. My standard reply was, "yeah, but we're going to have to play them at their place next year, and this time they're going to be ready for us." Ken Novak and his dad had both personally scouted us at two separate games.

Besides the four starters that they returned from last year, they had also picked up Royce White, whose parents had moved to Hopkins, effectively transferring him from DeLaSalle. At 6-7, Royce was the best player in the state. At DeLaSalle Royce had been schooled by Dave Thorson for three years, and he had signed in November to attend Minnesota and play for Tubby Smith. He was listed by Rivals.com as a five-star recruit and the No.19 player in the nation among seniors. The three other Royal starters had also signed early in November; 6-8 Mike Broghammer with Notre Dame, 6-4 Trent Lockett with Arizona State, and 6-4 Raymond Cowels with Santa Clara. At point guard they had Marcus Williams, who would later sign a football scholarship with North Dakota State as a defensive back. As with every year, their bench was also loaded with younger future scholarship players and very good upperclassmen.

On the first possession of the game, I could see the fire in the eyes of the Hopkins players. They hit four of their first five shots to open up an 8-0 lead. I called time-out. Three minutes later the lead was 18-2, and I called time out again. They were picking us up full court, pressuring us hard, and dominating us at our own strength. They were attacking the boards with a vengeance. At the half we were down 30, and the score at the end of the game was 87-45. The game was one continuous run. This game was clearly one that they had circled on the calendar over the summer. After the game the Novaks were gracious and encouraging. We had gotten our butts kicked. More ominously, we had lost part of our swagger.

After the game I told the team, "that might be the best team in the history of the state. They're ranked in the top five in the country. When they're on, they can do that to anybody. They were on. We have to learn from it and move on."

* * *

The following Tuesday we played at #2 ranked Henry Sibley and were drubbed again 82-47. Although not as talented as Hopkins, they were bigger. They rotated four players at 6-7, 6-8, 6-8, and 7-0 in a three-man front line, and they were an incredibly difficult match up for us. With a lighter schedule, we won five of our next six games. In the middle of this stretch we played at Hill-Murray. Hill-Murray was now coached by Dick Ghizoni. After building St Agnes into a small school power in St Paul, the school had fallen on hard financial times, and had closed. Dick was a Washburn and St Thomas alum, and he could coach with anybody.

Since Christmas, all three of my assistants were telling me that Darrien Johnson was the best rebounder in our program. Darrien was a 6-2 freshman who had open-enrolled from Bloomington after attending grade school in North Minneapolis. He played both junior varsity and B squad, and he improved steadily at learning our defense. Against Hill-Murray, I put him in the rotation. In less than 20 minutes, he had 7 rebounds. He was aggressive, tough, and he was one of those kids who just went after the ball. He didn't back down from anybody or any contact. This was going to change the complexion of the team for the remainder of the season. Having tried all of our other options, we had found what we were missing up front.

In the next game on Friday, Darrien hurt his finger early in the game. The trainer taped it up and he played the rest of the game. The next morning, he showed up at practice with the finger in a cast. An x-ray had revealed a broken finger. After two varsity games, he was done for the season.

We lost two close games followed by a 62-44 loss at Tartan. The next week we had a bye which would give us four straight days of practice, and the tournament was three weeks away. We met as a coaching staff, and set our goals as to fundamentals and strategies that we had to improve on. We also mapped out the remaining scouting of the teams in our section. We were going to most likely be seeded #4 or #5, with Bloomington Jefferson as our opening opponent. On Friday night we hosted Henry Sibley. We took the air out of the ball to start the game, played well, and we hung with them for eight minutes, trailing 16-12. Then they went on a ten-point run. The final was 75-49. We closed out the regular season winning three out of four games. Against Sibley, the new superintendent attended his first and only game of the season.

* * *

As expected, we were seeded #5 in the section and would open the tournament at Jefferson. The top three seeds were Edina, Eden Prairie, and Shakopee. After the meeting we practiced. After the practice I told the team that there was no reason why we couldn't win the section. We would have to play well, shoot well, and win three close games. There was no team in our section that was an impossible height match-up such as Henry Sibley.

Jefferson was led by the two Alipate brothers, Moses and Marcus, whose father Tuineau had played linebacker for the Minnesota Vikings. Moses was a 6-5 senior inside player and Marcus was a 6-0 sophomore guard. Jeff Evens was in his thirteenth year as the head coach. I knew that they would be well prepared for us and not beat themselves.

The game was everything I expected. During the first half both teams flirted with 4 to 6 point leads before the other team closed the gap. Neither team could take control of the game. Every possession felt enormous. Our defensive game plan was working perfectly. Jefferson was used to running a large number of set plays, and we were taking the sets away. Similarly, they were playing tough man to man defense against us, and forcing us to be patient and work hard for our shots. The second half was no different than the first. As the clock ticked down from twelve to eight to six minutes, once again, neither team could get more than a 4-point lead. With about three minutes on the clock and the score tied, Jefferson had the ball. They patiently worked the ball, got a good shot and missed. Renard Robinson got the rebound, and I signaled for a time out. Phillip Freeman dribbled the ball to the other end of the court in front of the Jefferson bench and called it.

After the strategic time-out I told the kids, "this is why we go to open gyms all summer, to be able to play in a game like this. This is fun. This is why we play basketball. This is our game to win." We worked the ball for 40 seconds before Renard put up an open 12-foot jumper. The ball rimmed in and out. As the

Jefferson guard dribbled the ball up court, I looked up at the clock and saw 1:35. After half a dozen passes Marcus Alipate got the ball on the left wing. He drove the baseline and went up for a 10-foot jumper over an outstretched hand. The ball hit nothing but net. We had the ball again, in what was now a must score possession. This time Phillip lofted up another beautiful open jumper. The ball rimmed in and out again, and they got the rebound. We had to foul. They hit two free throws. We pushed the ball up court and missed another good shot. We fouled one last time, and they made two more free throws. The final score was 63-57 and our season was over.

It was a somber heart wrenching locker room. Everyone knew how close we had been to having the victory in our grasp. I reminded them what my old college football coach Tom Porter had always taught us, "one play doesn't win or lose a game." I told them that "everyone can look back at the entire game and think of at least one play where they could have done something different which would have changed the outcome of the game. The game wasn't won or lost only in the last few possessions." I then told them "you guys played a great game. I couldn't ask you to play any better."

After the game, my assistants reiterated my thoughts to me. I remember Omar saying "no matter how you look at it, that's a tough one to take." Mullenbach added "the only thing that would have made it worse would have been to lose on a last second shot." Alcindor stressed that "we have to keep telling the kids how proud we were of them."

***

Jefferson then defeated Edina 74-65 and Eden Prairie 51-46 to advance to the state tournament. The anticipated state final showdown between #1 Hopkins and #2 Henry Sibley was derailed when Jefferson upset Henry Sibley 60-56 the first game of state. The Jaguars then lost to Osseo in the semifinals 59-51. Osseo fell to Hopkins in the finals 69-59. The Royals finished the season 31-0 and ranked #6 in the country by USA today. In Class 3A the Washburn Millers won the title with DeAaron Hearn as a starter and major contributor. Hopkins fourth state championship in the last eight years did not come without controversy.

The first week in March the *StarTribune* had ran a story which covered three fourths of the first page and a full second page. The article was co-authored by John Millea and David LaVaque. It was about the Hopkins basketball program. It gave a short profile of their four D1 recruits listing when they first began attending school in Hopkins; one went to kindergarten in

Hopkins, one open enrolled from Minneapolis in eighth grade, one open enrolled from Mound-Westonka in ninth grade, and one moved to Hopkins from Minneapolis as a senior. Three of the prominent metro area coaches were quoted.

Can't lose. Can't win

Hopkins is undefeated, nationally ranked and well on its way to another state championship...But the perception is that the team is only as good as the players it gets from other districts

Bruce Kugath, Shakopee: "My first statement when you talk about Hopkins is, what's the point? They bring in players to create this super team. ...I refuse to play them because they don't play by the same rules. The more teams that do it, the more of these elite teams we'll have, and it's going to destroy high school sports."

Greg Miller, Armstrong: "The last straw was when the dominant player in the state went to Hopkins. This year, everyone I've talked to seems to think that it's really exposed itself, that it's almost making a mockery of the high school system."

Mark Klingsporn, Tartan: "There's something not right about community-based athletics when you have so many kids from outside the community. It's how you define it. A lot of people have different opinions. We do have open enrollment, and we do have kids making choices nowadays on schools they want to go to based on athletics."

The article went on to state that *of the current high school enrollment of 1,965 at Hopkins–a school actually located in Minnetonka and one that is part of a sprawling west metro district–nearly 20 percent are open enrolled from other districts. Twenty five percent of the senior class is open-enrolled. Some of the open enrolled students came to Hopkins through a program called The Choice is Yours. It allows students who live in north Minneapolis and qualify for free or reduced-price lunch to apply for enrollment at Hopkins and have school transportation provided at no charge...Even those critical of the program say Hopkins is one of the best-coached teams in the state.* [78]

Three weeks later when the dust had settled from the state tournament, Hopkins coach Ken Novak was quoted in the *StarTribune* by a different writer.

"It's been a hard year...because people kind of have come after us. And, I think, very unjustly. So we're living in a different society. Every school all over the place has got kids coming in. I don't think people like to admit the ones that have transferred in. Our kids, besides Royce, have all come in the normal way. We only have two starters that are open-enrolled in. They both came in like eighth grade, so they've been in there as long as a lot of students in private schools, like a Benilde-St Margaret's or a Cretin-Derham Hall. They've been here a long time. They came in before anybody knew who they were. Mike Broghammer came in,

and he'll tell you himself that he was just a very OK player that really developed...
But you've got to take criticism. I'm amazed at the hostility, though, that some
people do have about the topic."[79]

* * *

We ended the season 16-11, and 10-6 in the conference, which was our seventh consecutive first division finish. Renard Robinson, Phillip Freeman, and Jay Sewer were All-conference. For the second year in a row, a large part of our success was due to the leadership of four seniors; Renard, Phillip, Michael Jones, and Chris Williams. They were as fine a group of defenders as we had ever had in the program, and they shot a combined 52% on two pointers and 34% on three pointers. With many of our freshman playing up with the older players, our junior varsity finished 16-10, our B squad 22-4, and our ninth grade 22-4.

* * *

In the latter half of April, I was in Todd Olson's office for my coaching performance review. Todd had revised the review to four grades; unsatisfactory, basic, proficient, and dynamic. Except for a grade of basic in the category of 'compliance with MSHSL rules, regulations, and deadlines' for missing a state high school league rules meeting and having to then complete an on-line test, I received grades of proficient and dynamic. Since Todd became the AD, this meeting was as much a discussion of how we could improve the basketball program, all programs, and the school, as it was a review of my performance. Since the swearing incident of four years ago, I always felt that Todd and I saw things the same way, and that he had my back. More than once I remember leaving office with him looking me in the eye and nodding and saying, "I get it, Jim, I get it."

Near the end of the discussion, I brought up the fact that our home crowds were small, given our great start and winning record. I explained to him how big the home crowds were when we started winning late in my second year at Richfield. I used the term 'undercurrent'. I told him that I felt an 'undercurrent of unrest' from people who were not happy with the program. I said that I couldn't really put my finger on it, but my sources reported to me that the primary complaint was that it wasn't a Richfield team, because "the players don't live in Richfield."

In fact, all four of our senior starters did not live in Richfield. Phillip Freeman lived in Farmington, Michael Jones lived in south Minneapolis, and both Chris Williams and Renard Robinson lived in Bloomington. However, there was a story behind each of them. Renard grew up in south Minneapolis until his mom moved to Bloomington for his seventh-grade year. From fifth through eighth grade, he played for his uncle, who was his coach in the Urban Stars program. He open-enrolled at Richfield as a freshman, following his cousin and his uncle, who had recently bought a house in Richfield. The other three all lived in and attended the Richfield public schools beginning in grade school. Chris' family moved to Richfield from Lansing, Michigan when he was in second grade, Michael's family came from Memphis when he was in second grade, and Phillip's family came from Chicago when he was in kindergarten. All three families open enrolled their sons when they moved out of the district after middle school. All three attended the summer program and played on the traveling and spring AAU teams. These three had unquestionably come all of the way up through our system.

After discussing all of this, Todd said something that I had heard him say before, "when a student open enrolls as a freshman, that student becomes a Richfield kid." He added, "these are Richfield kids, and we tell people that."

I told him that I saw some irony here. I pointed out that when two sons of the basketball board president played for Greg Miller, nobody ever said it wasn't a Richfield team. They both open enrolled from Bloomington as freshman. They were products of the feeder system, having been eligible for the traveling teams because they attended Blessed Trinity in Richfield. Unlike my three seniors, they never once lived in Richfield. In addition, the point guard Dwayne Starr was an open enrollment student from Minneapolis. I also pointed out to him that I had been told by a couple of faculty members that Dwayne wasn't exactly welcomed in Richfield. Yet these same disgruntled people considered the other two boys Richfield kids right from the get go. We both knew that the two kids from Bloomington were white and Dwayne Starr was black. He nodded with a serious look on his face, and I remember him saying that he didn't disagree with me on anything. He then steered the discussion to the validity of my sources, adding that he wasn't saying what I was saying wasn't true, but that rumors do grow and change and circulate.

"Todd, I know rumors circulate. I also know how small towns are, and Richfield is a small town. I've seen the change in the size of the crowds."

He brought up the idea of the term undercurrent again, saying that it was a great word to describe it. He asked, "well, what do you do about it?" My answer was that I ignore it, and without telling him where the quote came from, I quoted what Jim Baker had told me "They have to get used to how I'm going to run the program, because I'm going to run it the way that I think is right."

Declining Enrollment

The size of the graduating senior classes peaked at over 900 students in the late 1960s and early 1970s, which was the largest in the state. According to Frederick L. Johnson in his book *'Richfield, Minnesota's Oldest Suburb'*,

The Richfield High senior class of 1970 numbered 867, a student legion larger in size than the entire student body of typical Minnesota school districts of the time...And the student tide did recede from 827 seniors in the class of 1975 to 626 in 1980, 447 in 1985, 328 in 1990, and 305 in 2000. Non-whites made up just 4.5 percent of all Richfield public school students in 1980, but by 2003, students of color were 44.6 percent of the total.[80]

In the early 1990s the Lake Conference added a few more fourth ring schools to its two divisions of Red and Blue. The inner ring suburban schools were now the small kids on the block. Beginning in the 1993-94 school year, Edina, Hopkins, Minnetonka, St Louis Park, Richfield, Robbinsdale Cooper, Robbinsdale Armstrong, and Wayzata left to form the Classic Lake Conference. This was essentially the Lake Conference of the 1960s, minus Bloomington and Mound. Even without the huge third and fourth ring suburban schools, Richfield's enrollment was the smallest of these eight schools.

As the enrollment decreased the dominance in athletics decreased. The last football team to go undefeated in the conference was in the fall of 1986. Todd Olson replaced Dick Walker as head coach in the fall of 1990. The next four years Richfield finished 6-2, 4-4, 6-2, and 5-3 in the conference, but they won the section and reached the round of eight in the state playoffs every year. One reason for this was that they were the only Lake team in a section of Minneapolis City Conference schools, and compared to the Lake, the City was now weak in football. Then when the Edina district contracted back to one high school and offered Todd the football job in the spring of 1994, he took it. He was replaced by Dan Fogelson. The next four years the team finished 1-8, 1-8, 0-9, and 4-5. The conference football records reflected the enrollments, and this had become the new norm. Hockey and baseball, although competitive, were also struggling to win half of their games.

In basketball, Stu Starner left in the spring of 1978 to become an assistant to Jim Dutcher at Minnesota. A few years later he was the head coach at

Montana State. In the next 17 years, Richfield had three basketball coaches; Mike Plinske from 1978-79 to 1984-85, Cliff Peterson from 1985-86 to 1988-89, and Jeff Etienne from 1989-90 to 1994-95. As the enrollment declined, the team fell to the middle of the conference in the 1980s. In the 1990s the Spartans were firmly planted on the bottom of the Lake. In Etienne's six years, his teams averaged 5 wins per year. When his last two teams finished 4-19 and 2-21, the program had bottomed out.

***

Greg Miller began the long process of rebuilding the program in the fall of 1995, when Richfield was still in the Classic Lake. The Classic Lake was a great basketball conference, and the hill to climb was steep. The other seven schools were all in Class 4A, and they had veteran coaches and established programs. And the conference included Hopkins, which was growing into the perennial state-wide power. Slowly the fruits of his labor were evident, as the record improved every year. In the winter of 1998-99 the team finished 10-12, and the Spartans were solidly back in the middle of the conference.

After four years in the Classic Lake, it was evident that competing even in this conference was not a level playing field. In the fall of 1999 Richfield dropped out to join the Missota Conference, which was made up of schools in the outer ring suburbs and smaller towns south of the cities. The enrollments would now be equal. Richfield was soon to find out that these towns were football towns. The football team never won a game in the Missota, with the only wins being non-conference over Minneapolis Southwest. The Spartans got beat up on the gridiron again, and they were taking long bus rides to do it. In basketball the team finished in the bottom half of the Missota with overall records of 9-14 and 6-18. In spite of this, the program was again on stable ground, and the talented kids in the middle school had more potential than any of the kids walking the halls of the high school.

***

In the late 1990s and early 2000s, some of the best Richfield athletes began to attend Holy Angels rather than Richfield. The Academy of Holy Angels was founded in 1932 as a small Catholic high school for girls. For many years it remained a small high school educating girls from the south side of Minneapolis and the southern suburbs. It was located four blocks north of Richfield High School next to St Peter's Catholic Church. In 1972 the school became co-educational and the enrollment began to grow. As the enrollment grew both the boys and girls' teams began to experience athletic success. Eventually a first-class football field, ice arena, and gymnasium were added.

Historically, the Catholic schools had competed for their own state championships at the end of each season. For basketball, like the public schools, they had a one class state tournament and eight geographical regions. Because there were only about 25 Catholic schools in the state, teams needed to win only one or two games to advance to state. The tournament was played at the St Paul Auditorium. The finals usually drew about 3,000 fans. The semi-final and final games were often rematch games between the larger schools from the metropolitan area or large outstate cities. In regular season games between top ranked public schools and top ranked Catholic schools, the Catholic schools held their own. In the 1974-75 school year the Catholic and all of the other private schools joined the Minnesota State High School League. Like the public schools, they were placed in a region based upon geography, and they were placed in a class based upon enrollment.

Parents almost always cite academics as to why their children pick one high school over another. This is true, but it is also true that athletics and coaches oftentimes have a lot to do with it. Kids want to go where they think they can win. Some of the best players to come out of the Richfield youth hockey program began opting for Holy Angels. They probably saw it as their best chance to play in the storied state high school hockey tournament. Members of the Holy Angels coaching staffs began attending some Richfield traveling basketball and youth hockey games.

One of the most notable home-grown Richfield athletes to go to Holy Angels was John Stocco. Stocco graduated in 2002 and was drafted by the Minnesota Twins but instead accepted a football scholarship at Wisconsin. He went on to become a three-year starter at quarterback for the Badgers. The last Big Ten quarterback to graduate from Richfield High School was Bob Sadek in 1960. In the Bob Collison or Dick Walker era, a great junior high football prospect choosing to not play for the home town Spartans would have been unthinkable.

* * *

By the time I was hired as the basketball coach in the summer of 2001, the school district was down to five schools; the high school, the middle school for grades 6-8, the intermediate school for grades 3-5, and two K-2 schools, Centennial on the east side and Sheridan Hills on the west side. About 300 seniors were graduating every year. Richfield was now an aging community of grandparents. Some of the 10,000 houses had families of the twenty first century, with two or three kids. Many of the 5,000 apartments had families with kids, and included many minorities.

The new athletic director, Jim Baker moved Richfield to the Classic Suburban Conference. This conference was made up of the smaller schools bordering St Paul. In terms of enrollment, it was a perfect fit, and there would be no long bus rides on country roads. The conference included North St Paul, South St Paul, Henry Sibley, Tartan, Mahtomedi, and Simley which were all public schools. The two private schools were St Thomas Academy and Hill-Murray. Richfield was the lone school on the west side of the Mississippi. It was a good football conference and its top half was a great basketball conference. Jim also hired a new football coach named Kyle Inforzato. The football team immediately won more games than it lost.

The racial makeup of Richfield had also changed. By 2000, the city was roughly 80% white, 7% African American, 6% Hispanic, and 5% Asian. The school district served 4,200 students in grades K-12. The students were no longer all kids who lived in the 10,000 rambler homes. Many of the minority students lived in the 5,000 apartments. And many of the Hispanics lived in the little homes on the east side of town, and were now property owners. Their children were now a majority at Centennial Elementary.

People were still migrating to the community like spokes on a wheel. When I meet people, I have a habit of asking them where they are from or where they went to high school. Many of the answers to this question were South, Southwest, Roosevelt, or Washburn, the public high schools on the south side of Minneapolis. A parent who was from north or northeast Minneapolis and attended North or Henry or Edison was a rarity.

The other answers that I most often heard were the small towns of southern Minnesota. If one named some of these small towns and plotted them on a map of Minnesota, they would look like a pattern of buckshot on the wall of an old barn. The pattern of buckshot would extend from Winona to Willmar, with many towns in-between, towns like Rochester, Belle Plaine, New Ulm, Slayton, Magnolia, Waconia, and Clara City. A parent who grew up in northern Minnesota like Duluth or Two Harbors was a rarity.

The exception to this was the African-American parents. Some attended the Minneapolis south side public high schools including Central which closed in 1982. Many others were from the states of the old confederacy straight to the south; Louisiana, Arkansas, Mississippi, and Tennessee. These people from the south had rural or small-town roots. Oftentimes I heard cities named such as Memphis, Kansas City, Chicago, and Gary, Indiana. These city people also had family histories which went back to the same rural areas of the same states. The most commonly named state was Mississippi.

***

One local person told me that if you could pick up the city of Richfield and place it a hundred miles to the west, that it would be no different from any of the neighboring small towns. This may have been true in many ways, but it was not true when it came to European ethnicity. It was also not true regarding long-time athletic tradition.

Most of the small towns of outstate Minnesota have roots that go back to two or three countries in Europe, and to when the state was settled by Europeans after the Civil War. The southern and western part of the state is mostly Northern European. The northeast portion, including the Iron Ranges and Duluth also has many Southern Europeans. The author Bill Holm was born and raised near the tiny village of Minneota. He wrote about the humorous clash of cultures between the Belgian Catholics, the Irish Catholics, the Norwegian Lutherans, and the Icelandic Lutherans. Most of the towns of the lower Minnesota River Valley were German Catholic and Irish Catholic. My mentor and the long-time football coach at LeSueur, Bruce Frank, finished his career coaching many of the sons of his former players. Many had German or Irish last names, and many were part Irish and part German. When recalling stories of some of his great teams, I would often hear comments like, 'my uncle played on that team', or 'my neighbor from the next farm was on that team'. At football games, former players walked the sidelines, cheered for the current players, and interacted with other former players. There was a connection that all of the kids felt to the football legacy of the town, and it was strong.

In the suburbs, the white people were a complete mixture of many European nationalities. Only a handful of players who tried out for my basketball teams had parents or uncles who played for Richfield during the glory years. The baby boomer children of the World War II vets had moved on. If they were still in the Twin City area, they had migrated further to the south to the third and fourth ring suburbs. We sometimes competed against children of Richfield alums when we played these schools.

Probably by the 1990s, and certainly by the 2000s, the student body of Richfield felt no connection to the glory years. And it was clear that those glory years would never return. The 20-year period when almost all of the houses were full of school age kids was a one-time phenomenon. It would never happen again.

Some of the parents from southern Minnesota or the Minneapolis high schools knew the Richfield sports history. If they were former high school athletes, they had followed it in the Twin City newspapers. They had seen Richfield's name in the statewide rankings and they had followed the Spartans at the state tournaments. The parents who were from the Deep South had no idea of this history. And they'd never heard of Edgerton. But they'd seen the movie 'Hoosiers'.

Ninth Summer & Winter

The kids all know who the best players are.
—Butsy Maetzold

T he summer program was as strong as ever, except for the number of boys attending the camp. The total enrollment in the camp decreased by about 10 players every year and now was holding steady at 40 campers. The number of boys who pre-registered with the Community Education office was actually less than this, as many of the black kids didn't pre-register, but showed up the first day of camp. The enrollment was now about two thirds black and one third white. With fewer kids, our student teacher ratio increased, and the kids who did attend received more individual attention. Jordan Noonan and Santino Clay, who were back from college, supervised the 3 on 3 league.

Omar taught the 1st and 2nd grade program every winter, and we changed it very little. He was always assisted by some junior and senior players. Both the basketball board and I paid Omar. As with the camp, the numbers decreased. In the early years we had between 40 and 50 students. We were now down to between 30 and 40.

Our spring AAU team was a success every year, and we eventually began including seventh graders on the team. As with the camp, the demographics changed. Fewer white kids chose to play, and all of the black kids played. Greg Von Ruden did a great job communicating with the middle school faculty regarding the team. When two players lagged academically, they sat on the bench for a weekend tournament. One day a middle school teacher stopped me in the hallway and thanked me for all of this, adding to thank both Greg and Omar.

The open gyms were the one segment of the program that I never delegated to my assistants. It was gratifying to be in the gym and watch the kids stream in. It was not uncommon for a kid who I had never seen before, to approach me and ask for help with his shot. It brought me back to high school when my coach Jed Dommeyer had tweaked my shot and I started seeing the ball going in the basket more. I was passing on what Jed had passed on to me. The same demographic change had occurred with the open gyms. They were attended by probably three fourths African-American kids. These were kids who played basketball year-round.

The second week of June Todd forwarded an email from a mother of one of the returning senior parents. The email said "We were told that the communication within the basketball program was going to improve. However, it's Saturday night and we just now found out that open gym starts next week. The coaches may want to get the word out to all the other players that they are expecting to attend." I reminded Todd I didn't communicate with parents via email, and I called the mother and left a message on the home phone. The next time that I saw Todd, I told him that I found it really ironic, because this was the mother of a player who we had been trying to get to the open gyms since he was in fifth grade, and he never showed up until after his freshman year, and he didn't start attending regularly until after his sophomore year. "I remember standing in the hallway telling the boy and his dad how much we'd love to have him at the open gyms and how much he'd improve. This was when he was in grade school. And now she's complaining about not knowing about the open gyms."

This was not the first sign that the senior parents were not happy. The previous spring Todd had said to me, "the feeling among the junior parents is that you pay your dues before you play on the varsity." My answer to Todd was, "I went through all this six years ago. I'm playing the best kids. They all know this."

* * *

We changed our man-to-man defense somewhat the past winter, and we met as a staff to discuss more changes for the following winter. The game was changing. Most teams were now much better at back cutting and driving and dishing. Basketball was becoming more like soccer. Teams would simply space the court, and drive the ball to the paint. The game was more about match-ups, and about which offensive player could drive on which defensive player. Offenses were not predicated as much upon screening action away from the ball. There were more screens on the ball, and screen the screener action on or near the ball. The goal of the screening action wasn't always to get a shot, but sometimes to get the defense to switch a screen, which gave the offense a desired match-up.

To return to Bob Knight's maxim, the offense was now picking the match-ups by running specific screens to dictate specific switches. I remember former Gustavus coach Bob Erdman speaking once at a coaching clinic and stating that it is easy to devise a game plan to stop an offense, and it is easy to devise a game plan to stop individuals, but it is difficult to do both. The offenses were evolving, and defensive coaches were now being forced to do some of both. The challenge to the defensive coach was to devise the best strategy to counter all of this, and to keep it as simple as possible for the players.

The successful coaches are always on the cutting edge of the strategy changes as the game progresses. Thirty years ago, Keith Erickson and I were at Macalester trying to figure out how to stop the flex offense. Now I and my young assistants were contemplating the ball screen and dribble drive game. This was fun. I was looking forward to the challenge of improving our defense to stay on the cutting edge. And after one more winter, we would once again have good overall quickness and size, which always makes it easier for any strategy to be successful.

The million-dollar question was going to be whether to keep or cut the two board members sons. They were both average outstate Class 2A players. If they were playing major minutes in our 3A/4A conference, we would be in trouble. If they had exceptional attitudes and leadership skills, they could play on the scout squad and help the team. If not, they would have to be cut. I asked my assistants more than once if either one should be playing for us, and if I was missing the boat in my evaluation of them. The answer that I always got was that they we had better players. Should I make an exception for the countless hours that their dads had contributed to the program? I certainly couldn't cut a player who was better than them, simply because of this. This was high school basketball. If I kept these two, it would have to be similar to five years earlier when Bill Bauman made the team. I was not going to cut two other players to make room for them. We would pick the varsity team, and then add two extra spots for them.

One father administered the house league for at least five years. He was at one of the elementary schools two nights every week. This was an enormous time commitment. The other father was the board president, and had volunteered many hours in all facets of the program. To compound this, he and his wife had opened up their home to Jay Sewer. Saul Phillips at North Dakota State was recruiting Jay hard, dependent on the continual improvement of his ACT score. Jays' mom had died of cancer during his junior year, and his father lived out of state. Jay moved in with this family. They were housing him and feeding him. You were not going to find two greater guys than these two fathers.

In October I ran into a retired coach who asked how our team would be. I answered, "we'll be about five hundred again." Then I went on, "I don't know what I'm going to do. We've got some really good sophomores and our seniors aren't very good. And two of the senior's dads are basketball board members who have worked really hard for the program, and are great guys. And their sons aren't very good. And one of them has my starting point guard living in their basement. And I've gotta decide whether to keep or cut these kids."

He rolled his eyes and started chuckling and shaking his head, "You're damned if you do and damned if you don't."

* * *

When tryouts began in November, we knew that the team would be our most inexperienced team in a number of years. Our two 5-9 point-guards Jay Sewer and Daron Garvis would play major minutes. Sophomore Darrien Johnson was now over 6-2 and ready to pick up where he left off prior to his season ending injury.

One senior who surprised us and made the team was Hillary Luke. Hillary was part of a large extended family that was originally from Uganda and had settled in Richfield nine years ago. He and his older brothers never missed an open gym. They had impeccable attitudes and work ethic, and always thanked me for working with them. Hillary had been one of the last kids cut his freshman, sophomore, and junior years. He had grown four inches over the summer and suddenly was 6-3 and playing above the rim, and he played great post defense.

Two more junior guards made the team. John Johnson who moved to Richfield as an eighth grader, and open enrolled when his mother moved back to Minneapolis. He was staying with another player's family. Like the board member and Jay, this family was going beyond the call of duty. Jordan Stefan was another African immigrant who was in the gym all summer.

I decided to keep both board members' sons. I explained to them that they would both be scout team players and leaders. They both asked if there was a chance to break into the playing rotation. My answer was yes, but they would have to prove it in practice and I couldn't promise them anything. They both said that they understood and wanted to be on the team.

* * *

We began the season with 10 players in the rotation. Jared Etienne, Darrien Johnson, and our 6-6 senior split two positions in the front line. Another senior played a lot of minutes as a shooting guard. The remaining minutes were split between four players; junior John Johnson, and sophomores Lorenzo Evans,

Jared Noonan, and Erick Jimson. These four were playing both junior varsity and varsity.

I had deliberately softened up our non-conference schedule, fully aware that we were going to need wins. I knew that if we played our usual non-conference schedule of five or six top ranked teams, and were beaten badly a number of times, it wouldn't be good for our morale or our progress.

We opened up the season with a 69-60 home victory over Mound. We lost the next two games at South and North, 71-58 and 58-52. We then had a full week to practice in preparation for Holy Angels.

On paper the game with Holy Angels appeared to be an even game. Like us, their talent level was down from what it had usually been. Nevertheless, as the preliminary games came to an end, the Richfield gym was two thirds full. Over our first three games our two point-guards, Jay Sewer and Daron Garvis had very proficiently averaged 13 and 18 points. They were also averaging a combined 12 assists a game. Against Holy Angels they combined for 42 points on 68% shooting from the field and we won 61-53.

* * *

Over the fall and into December, my sources informed me that a succession of past and current boys basketball parents had been making their way to the superintendent's office, and meeting with the superintendent. In December these sets of parents had all requested and been granted meetings with Bob Slotterback, who was now in his second year. The list of known names included a few of the mediocre players from this year's senior class, both who had sons who were either on the team or not on the team. The list also included program players who had been cut in previous years.

I brought this up with Todd Olson the next time that I was at the high school. I told him what I had heard, naming the known sets of parents. I then asked him, "so the protocol of first meeting with the coach, then meeting with the AD, and then meeting with the principal has been thrown out? I thought that if parents went to the superintendent, the superintendent was supposed to direct the parents back to the coach, or at least ask them if they had met with coach, AD, and principal."

Todd looked at me, sighed, and told me that the first thing that Bob says when someone complains to him is "come on in to my office and we'll talk about it." He then added that the next thing that the parents do is call the superintendent's office and set up the appointment. I asked Todd if he had ever confronted Slotterback about this. Knowing Todd like I did, I knew that he would have done this immediately. His answer was that yes, he had, and that it hadn't changed anything. My response was that now the complainers pretty much know that Bob has an open door. I made a phone call the next day to schedule my own meeting with the superintendent.

The same month an article ran in *The Minnesota Prep Coach*. Once again, it was authored by John Erickson, the executive director of the MSHSCA.

Due Process Continues to Elude Coaches

In the September Prep Coach I addressed the challenges of coaching in the 21st century...The attempt to provide more opportunities for our young athletes, in most cases, has been made with the best interest of the young athletes in mind. The problem that has been generated from the development of these opportunities is that they have taken the place of many of the more tightly controlled school programs. They also come with a price tag. This same price tag forced schools to cut many of the programs that were in place for youth teams. The cost of these programs is most often paid for by the parents of the participants on the non-school youth teams and by their booster clubs. One of the results of the parents paying the bills is that a sense of ownership is developed and in many cases a sense of entitlement to management.

The problem that has started to become more difficult to deal with is that once the athlete moves on from the non-school youth teams the unwillingness of parents to relinquish control of the teams and the coaches to the schools and the Activities Administrators. The failure to transition to the next level of athletics has helped evolve the profession into a new challenge. More and more parents are demanding and being allowed to micromanage coaches and teams. There appears to be a belief, in some instances, where the high school team is not the schools team

The problems that this new mentality has caused have become more and more common. Four years ago the MSHSCA worked hard to get some sort of a process in place that would allow the coaches who were under fire and facing nonrenewal to address their accusers. Thanks to the legislative efforts of Dean Urdahl (R-New London-Spicer) a state law was put into effect that required school districts and their administrators to provide coaches with the reasons for their nonrenewal in writing and that the coach is given the right to an open hearing. We have seen two approaches to this legislation. The first reaction was noncompliance. This approach seems to have gone away but the second approach is equally disturbing.

During the past two years there have been numerous cases where a coach has been facing nonrenewal and has requested their right to the reasons and a hearing. In more than one case the hearing has been a travesty of the coaches' rights. More often than not the presiding administrator has directed the school board members in attendance to remain silent and not to enter into discussion or answer questions. The decision to take away the coaches position has been made well in advance of the open hearing. There is documentation of two hearings this year where the coaches had never received a negative evaluation prior to the nonrenewal and yet after an open hearing during which several people testified to the ability and quality of the coach they were still removed from the coaching position. One of the hearings has resulted in a brief being filed with Minnesota Appellate Court charging a violation of due process.[81]

***

Over the Christmas break we traveled to Albert Lea in southern Minnesota and won two games. Heading into January our record was 4-2, but three of our wins were against teams that in previous years would not have been on our schedule.

The next day before practice the senior guard and son of the board member approached me. He was in his street clothes and holding his practice jersey in his hands. He told me that he no longer wanted to be on the team. When I asked him why he was quitting, he said that he thought he should be playing, and that he didn't think he should be riding the bench. I told him that I respected his honesty, but the entire coaching staff disagreed with him.

We then defeated three more mediocre teams. We had no team chemistry or senior leadership. The feeling of the seniors helping the underclassmen had disappeared, and the underclassmen were competing with each other for limited minutes in the rotation. The next three weeks resulted in six losses to good teams sandwiched around a win at South St Paul.

Offensively, we were very dependent on our two guards. We were getting outplayed game after game inside. Hillary Luke was improving rapidly, and he had no fear of going after the ball in traffic. After sixteen games our three leading rebounders were the sophomore Darrien Johnson, followed by our two point-guards.

After shooting well in December, our senior wing was slumping. The three sophomore wings, Lorenzo Evans, Jared Noonan and Erik Jimson were all increasing their productivity playing limited minutes. They were also playing junior varsity, and the junior varsity was winning big. The sophomore team was also dominating, led by two freshmen, Tory Mason and Deshawn Jones. They were improving weekly, and they looked taller every month.

The first week in February the remaining board member's son approached me before practice and asked if he could play in the junior varsity games. Some of the schools in our conference played bench riding seniors in their JV games. In the past we had never done this, and we had scout squad seniors who never asked this question. I thought it over during practice and asked my assistants for their opinions. After practice, I told the player he could play junior varsity. During practice I approached Hillary Luke and asked him if he wanted to play JV. He said "yes", and both seniors played JV for the remainder of the season.

* * *

The next week we had two home games on Friday and Saturday. After losing to Simley 69-64, our record in the last eight games was 1-7, and our overall record was 8-9. Our senior wing continued his shooting slump going 0-6 from the field. Our 6-6 senior had another 3-rebound game, which was his season average.

On the drive home from the game, I told my wife. "I'm making some changes tomorrow. The seniors have had their chance. I'm playing the sophomores." I called all of my assistants. Omar was excited, "I'm all for it. The sophomores are better. They get better every week. We got your back, Jim." Alcindor was just as excited, "Go for it. The sophomores are the best players. In December it wasn't as obvious. Now it is." Another assistant added, "The seniors had their chance. The kids all know who the best players are."

The next morning the coaching staff met at the high school at 10am. I told them that I was going to take two seniors out of the rotation. We would now be playing eight kids; senior Jay Sewer, three juniors and four sophomores.

When the two seniors arrived, I met with them and one of my assistants. I told them that they were no longer in the rotation, and they would be on the scout squad. I also told them that if they wanted to prove me wrong and get back in the rotation, they needed to show me in practice. I then told them that I was going to tell the team before the game. I wanted to tell them first, because I didn't want them sitting on the bench during the game wondering why they weren't getting in the game. They both nodded and accepted it and didn't say much.

New Ulm was no match for our quickness and we won 84-41. The four sophomores combined for 38 points, 18 rebounds, and shot 59% from the field. When a coach makes a change like this, the team often plays with more energy. The sophomores played hard and with emotion, which proved to be contagious.

* * *

The next Tuesday we beat North St Paul at home 63-55. Friday night we played at Tartan. We matched them blow for blow. We trailed by 8 with 3:30 to play. Then they missed shots on six consecutive possessions and we hit four shots in a row. With less than minute to play we had the ball trailing 60-58. Jay dribbled the ball to in front of our bench and called time-out. I diagrammed a play that we had practiced many times for this situation. We knew that they would be all-over Jay. He caught the inbounds pass, dribbled hard to the elbow, forcing Daron's defender to help. Daron was on the opposite wing squared to the basket with his hands at his chest as a target. Jay jump stopped and hit the target with a perfect pass. Daron went up, and released the wide-open shot. The gym was silent. It caromed twice on the inside of the rim and bounced up and out. We fouled immediately, they hit two free throws, and the final score was 62-58. At our place a month earlier, they had beaten us by 27 points.

We again played well the next Tuesday at home against St Thomas. Sophomores Jared Noonan, Lorenzo Evans, and Erik Jimson, all hit shots to open the game. At halftime we were ahead 27-15. We maintained the lead the entire second half. With four minutes to go we went to our spread offense, hit free throws and had a 64-50 victory. The two juniors stepped up. John Johnson had his most effective offensive game to date scoring 13 points and Jared Etienne had 12 rebounds. Four weeks earlier they had defeated us by 21 points. We had our first signature win of the season.

* * *

The next day at 2pm I was sitting in the superintendent's office. This was six weeks after I had first called to schedule the meeting. He greeted me very cordially, shaking my hand, smiling and calling me "Coach."

After a minute of small talk, I got right to the point. I told him that I heard that there were a number of basketball parents who had met with him, and that I wanted to make sure that he heard both sides of the story. I told him that I was under the impression that parents were supposed to first go to the coach, then the AD, and then the principal before meeting with the superintendent.

He said that his first day on the job in the middle of the summer, a couple walked into his office without scheduling a meeting. He had no idea why they wanted to meet with him. He was smiling as he spoke. He said that they sat down where I was sitting, introduced themselves, and the first thing that the husband said was "are you aware of <u>the problem with the boys' basketball program?</u>" He then smiled again and said "and this is my first day on the job."

He told me that all of these parents were telling him the same thing, that "Richfield kids come all of the way up through the program, and then never play for the varsity, losing their spots to kids who don't live in Richfield." He added that he told every set of parents that unless there was verbal abuse, mistreatment of players, or something similar, he saw no reason to terminate a coach.

I spoke next. I explained everything that I had done in my nine years. I explained how the racial makeup of the school and the team began to change in Greg Miller's last few years as the coach. I told him about this change accelerating during my nine years as the coach. I told him about the changes that I made to make sure that low-income kids weren't excluded because of money. I explained the financial aid in the traveling program, the reduced fee for the summer camp, the 8th grade spring AAU team, the grade reports and study halls, and the free 3 on 3 league and open gyms. I also told him that "I was going to play the best kids regardless of grade or what team they played on in 6th grade." I told him that the sons of the complaining parents were losing their spots to mostly black kids who lived in Richfield and not open enrollment kids.

He spoke next, saying that he knew this better than anybody. He told me the story of his son who as a senior at Wauwatosa East lost his spot to an open enrollment freshman from Milwaukee. He grinned and added that the player from Milwaukee was Devin Harris, who later starred for the Badgers and went on to the NBA. He told me that he had explained to his son, that "the best kids play." He then kept on grinning and said, "I know this better than anybody, coach."

He went on, saying that he knew that many parents didn't get this. He elaborated about one mother of a program player. He said that he first met her on a committee that they both served on, and that she repeatedly complained to him about me. Then he said some nice things about the guard play of Jay and Daron. A minute later he brought up our senior center, stating that in the one game that he saw, the kid got the ball knocked out of his hands twice, adding "I understand why you don't play him, coach, he can't even hold onto the ball."

At the end I told him what I told everybody. I said, "there are many points and counter-points to both sides, but underneath it all, it's about one thing, it's about black kids who live in apartment buildings beating out white kids whose parents own houses." I added, "they can argue until they're blue in the face that race has nothing to do with it, but if I run the program the way that the complainers want me to run it, almost all of the black kids will be systematically excluded." He then emphatically said, "coach, I know it's about race, because they always use the term 'city kids', they never say 'black kids.'"

As I was about to leave his secretary interrupted us, saying that he had a phone call and she named the person. It was the mother of a program player. He looked at me and said, "see, there she is again."

As I left the office and walked down the hall, I started laughing to myself. I was laughing because I knew that he was telling me everything that he thought I wanted to hear. My mind kept going. I began thinking that maybe it's time to give this up. One of my favorite sayings is "life's too short to have a boss." This was the only area of my life where I had a boss.

The telltale sign was that he never once complimented me as a coach. He was an ex-basketball coach. Every other ex-basketball coach always complimented me. Retired coaches like Bob Erdman and Dean Verdoes would say things like "I love the way your kids play defense," or "I know your kids will play hard, they always do," or "It's always fun to watch your teams play. You do a great job." He didn't offer one compliment. Bob Erdman and Dean Verdoes were great coaches. Maybe Slotterback had been a poor coach, and he simply didn't see this. The more that I thought about it, I knew then that he wanted me gone.

***

After playing the second and third place teams in the conference, next up was the fourth-place team Mahtomedi at home. We were beaten 71-55. The next day we played at St Paul Johnson. Vern Simmons team was undefeated and ranked #1 in Class 3A. We were blown out 100-41. We recovered to defeat South St Paul at home 70-52 the following week.

With two weeks to go in the season, we had begun gearing up for the section tournament. We were back in Class 3A for the first time in four years. We would probably be seeded #4 or #5 and open up with Holy Family, a Catholic school from the far western suburbs. Benilde-St Margaret's would be the #1 seed, having won the North Suburban Conference and ranked in the top ten in Class 3A.

Our last two games of the regular season were at home against Henry Sibley and Hill-Murray. Sibley had already clinched the conference title with a 13-1 record. We played well, but lost 85-73. We closed the regular season at home again against Hill-Murray. We played well again and lost again 74-72. When the regular season ended, we finished 6-10 in the conference and 12-14 overall.

* * *

Over the winter Lee Herman resigned as the head football coach. Todd Olson then named himself to replace Lee. The next time that I saw Todd, we discussed this. He was excited and animated. I remember him talking about the offense and the fact that they would have quick kids as the receivers and defensive backs. He planned on opening up the offense and attacking the entire field. Before the conversation ended, he looked me in the eye and emphatically said, "and we are going to adopt your study hall system for the football team." At this time only the boys and girls' basketball teams were doing study halls.

* * *

Holy Family was a Catholic school that was established in 2001. After spending nine years in Class 2A, their enrollment had grown and they were now in their initial year in Class 3A. They had finished the season with a winning record, but they played in the Minnesota River Conference with mostly 2A teams. They were bigger than us, but not as quick. Because I and my coaching staff saw the game as even, we were happy to have the #4 seed and home court advantage.

As expected, they opened the game playing zone. We moved the ball well and our shots dropped. After Daron hit three consecutive threes, they called time out and went man to man. The game went our way, and the final score was 81-72. We had played well and beaten a team that was our equal at home.

Our semi-final game would be at Benilde-St Margaret's, who had defeated Chanhassen 78-36. John Moore was in his seventeenth year as the coach, and he had amassed an impressive record, with nine 20-win seasons in the past 12 years. He had developed point guard Jordan Taylor who went on to star at Wisconsin, and who had led his 2008 team to the Class 3A state title. He had also had four great years when his team lost in the section finals to the eventual state champion Patrick Henry. The school was located in St Louis Park, the inner ring suburb north of Edina and west of Minneapolis. The school attracted good players from both Minneapolis and the western suburbs with its strong academics and athletics. John always made it a point to schedule the stiffest competition that he could find. This was one of his best teams, with a record of 22-5. He had a very good senior class, and a better junior class, both with size and talent. His best class was his sophomores with three D1 recruits, 6-2 Isaiah Zierden, 6-4 Sanjay Lumpkin, and 6-7 Kyle Washington. We had scouted them thoroughly. With a great inside game and big outside shooters, it would be a difficult match-up. We would have to hit shots early, not give them a run, and keep the game close for as long as possible.

Unlike Tuesday night, the game did not begin well for us. We pressured the ball on the three-point line and packed our other perimeter defenders into the lane. We were playing behind their posts and doubling down off of two of their perimeter players. When we doubled, they passed the ball back out and made threes. We were quickly down by ten. When we didn't double team their posts, they scored inside. By halftime they had opened up a 61-39 lead and the pace of the game was much quicker than I wanted. In the second half, we played them closer, but it was too little too late. The final score was 98-71.

***

Benilde-St Margaret's defeated Holy Angels in the section finals 77-70, before falling in the first game of state to Grand Rapids 70-61. Grand Rapids followed that up with a two-overtime victory over DeLaSalle 57-53. In another close game in the finals St Paul Johnson edged Grand Rapids 59-55. Coach Dan Elhard's Grand Rapids team had come within one play of accomplishing what had never been done, a northern Minnesota team winning the Class 3A state title. And his team had done it by beating two of the metro private school powerhouses back-to-back before falling to the St Paul City champion. After five trips to the state tournament in the past seven years, coach Vern Simmons' Governors won their first state title with a 31-0 record.

In Class 4A, with no better talent than the other teams, Hopkins repeated as state champions with an overall record of 30-2. Their closest game was a semifinal victory over Henry Sibley 90-82 in two overtimes.

***

When the season was over, the coaching staff took a big collective sigh of relief. It had been a year of transition, and at times it had been trying. We lacked senior leadership, and a few of the senior parents had not been on-board. Jay Sewer was being recruited by the top level D1 junior colleges in the area. He ended up going to perennial power Iowa Central Community College. The Tritons were coached by Dennis Pilcher, who had been there 32 years. More importantly, Pilcher's program had a track record of helping students, who were first time college students in their families to succeed academically.

The All-Conference team was selected by a blind vote of the coaches. Coaches did not nominate their own players, and coaches could not vote for their own players. If a player received more than one vote, he was named Honorable Mention. There were nine schools in the conference and each coach voted for 15 players. Jay Sewer was a unanimous selection. Junior Daron Garvis and sophomore Darrien Johnson both were named Honorable Mention. These were the only three players from Richfield who received votes.

We were looking forward eagerly to the spring and summer. The talent in the pipeline was on the upswing. The junior varsity and B squad teams had finished 17-7 and 14-9 with most of the kids playing up a grade. Four of our sophomores were playing on upper-level AAU teams. Freshmen Tory Mason and Deshawn Jones had grown to 6-4 and 6-2, and they weren't done growing. Both were playing on the Howard Pulley 16 and under squad. Eighth grader Lewis Williams was pushing 6-0 and would also be a D1 prospect. We were going to be loaded once again with some scholarship players surrounded by really good players, and we would have size to go with the quick perimeter players that we always had. I once again filled up our non-conference schedule with top-level ranked teams. After getting through four seasons of winning half our games, I saw us as putting together another three year stretch of 20-win seasons, and hopefully getting back to the state tournament at least once. We would be in the toughest 3A section in the state. My goal was to get back to state, resign, and turn the program over to one of my assistants, who would have a talented, seasoned team to coach in his first year.

Tenth Summer

One year some fathers raised hell and tried to get me fired. There sons weren't very good. In my opinion the only problem was a weak administration.

—*Jed Dommeyer*

The day after the banquet I called Todd Olson and told him that we needed to meet. Because of the parade of senior parents and 'concerned citizens' to the superintendent's office, I wanted to make sure that Todd had all of the facts to counter their complaints.

As the season wound down, a number of other things occurred. In early January one mother emailed me with a litany of complaints. I sent her back an email stating that "I do not receive and/or respond to emails from parents." Another parent sent me an email stating that "I know you favor quickness in your program." Both parents declined my offer to meet face-to-face.

Late in February Todd told me that there were complaints that I was not honest with some of the seniors when they made the team and then sat on the bench. He also said that there had been complaints to the superintendent that I was not holding the players accountable enough for their academics. I told him that these complaints were ridiculous and laughable. He answered, "I know that."

Todd and I met again the first week in April in his office. I had prepared an excel spreadsheet with seven columns. The seven titles of the columns were; name of player, grade, 1st year in Richfield basketball program, lives in, parents own home or rent, race, and comment. For example; Erik Jimson, 10th grader, 1st year in program was 2nd grade, lived in Richfield, parents rented, was African American, and the comment was 'moved from Minneapolis to Richfield in 2nd grade. At the bottom of the page were totals. There were 32 current players on the list. I also prepared a similar spreadsheet which encompassed all of the players that had been in the basketball program during my nine years. After showing both of the one-page documents to Todd and discussing them with him, he looked at them, nodded, and said, "this is great stuff, Jim. This is great." I emphatically requested a meeting with him, the superintendent, the principal, and Tom Flood the chairman of the school board. He quickly answered, "No, I can handle it."

"They need to be shown the entire picture here, Todd. I want to be able to explain the entire situation to them face to face, so they totally know the history and what has been going on."

"No, Jim, I can handle it."

* * *

When we had our first practice for our spring eighth grade AAU team, the team was entirely African-American. With the exception of one spring, we always had at least half a dozen white program kids. This year we didn't have any.

The first week in April Jim Noonan resigned from the basketball board. He told me late in the winter that he thought the board might attempt to get me fired. At first, I didn't believe this. When he told me this again, and said that he was resigning for this exact reason, I believed him.

The April board meeting was the next week. At the board meeting I was asked if the basketball program needed the basketball board. I knew that this question was coming. I said that the number of program kids on the varsity was usually one or two players in each class each year. I told them that most of the varsity players had moved into Richfield in middle school or moved in or open enrolled in high school, especially in ninth grade. I added that they come to the open gyms, improve dramatically, and then pass up the program kids. I said that maybe we should focus more on the spring AAU teams, adding that I and my assistants could coach sixth and seventh grade teams in addition to the eighth-grade team. I told them that we could use the high school gym, and the high school coaching staff. I added that developing varsity players wasn't the only purpose of the traveling program. I told them that many program kids would never play varsity basketball, and that we needed to give them a positive experience so that they could enjoy basketball for the rest of their lives.

* * *

Later in the spring Jill Johnson announced her resignation. She was leaving to become an assistant principal at Wayzata. She was replaced by the middle school principal Stephen West. Jill had been the high school principal for seven years. She was forceful, sincere, direct, and a great leader. I knew that she had totally believed in our program, and that she had had my back. I knew that her leaving the district wasn't good for me.

* * *

The last week in April, I met with Todd Olson for my annual review. I was surprised when he gave me four grades of dynamic, ten grades of proficient, seven grades of basic, and two grades of unsatisfactory. During my previous four reviews with Todd and my previous four reviews with Jim Baker, almost all of my grades were in the top category, with a few grades in the second-best category, and no grades in the middle or bottom category.

In addition to this, for the first time, Todd had given similar forms to the parents to fill out, evaluating me as a coach and evaluating the basketball program. At the end of the meeting, he gave me a copy of all of these forms and told me to read them.

I said to him, "why would I want to read these?" I don't specifically remember his answer. I then said, "if everybody likes me, I'm not doing my job. If they don't like who I play, that's their problem, not mine." He answered that he decided that for this year he wanted parental input in writing for all sports. I answered that in my opinion, this just gave them a platform to complain, and the chance to do it without a face-to-face discussion. He answered that he and I were not going to discuss the evaluations, but that he wanted me to read them.

As I drove back to my office from the high school, I gave it more thought. I decided that I wasn't going to read the parent evaluations. They would just piss me off. I remembered Jim Baker's pamphlets that he distributed to the parents listing subjects that they could and could not complain about. Todd was giving the parents the freedom to complain about subjects that Baker considered off limits. When I got to my office, I threw them in the wastebasket.

* * *

The boys' basketball camp wasn't the only program that experienced a severe drop in numbers. The same thing had happened with the girls' basketball and volleyball camps. The volleyball camp was canceled.

LeeAnn Wise experienced great success with the girls' varsity program. Both the 2007-08 and 2008-09 teams finished with overall records of 24-4. Because they were in the Class 4A tournament, they lost out to large school powers Bloomington Kennedy and Chaska in the section semi-finals. After being hit hard by graduation, her team had finished 18-7 the past winter with a young roster.

In her four years as the coach, the program continued to go through the same demographic changes that the boys' program had gone through five years earlier. As the team changed from a white team to a mostly black team, they won more games and there was the expected parent controversy. She and her assistants shared much of this with my staff. She told us that if she heard it once, she heard it a thousand times, "these kids have played together since third grade." Unlike me, she responded to emails. Her response was one sentence and it was always the same, "thank you for supporting the Richfield girls' basketball program."

*　*　*

Two weeks later I was in the BWCAW on our annual spring trip. The following week I met again with Todd to finalize my review. The meeting was brief. He asked me if I had read the parent evaluation forms and I answered, "no, I threw them away." He answered "OK".

I met again with him the second week in June. He placed a one-page letter on the table in front of us and asked me to read it. Before I began reading it, he said "I don't' know if you can recover from this."

The letter was from the basketball board.

Athletic Department

C/O Mr. Todd Olson

Dear Todd,

Per our conversations, the following synopsis is submitted. Please find attached our current status of rewritten by-laws that go into effect 1 May 2010. While these are not 100% completed they are reflective of our situation and direction for next basketball season.

The participants of this Board change, the constant should be a working relationship between the high school athletic department, boys basketball coaches and volunteer parents who try to provide avenues for kids to participate in boys basketball from kindergarten through high school.

We all know changes happen, we as a board have seen the ever decreasing involvement by the Boys Varsity Head Coach (BVHC) over the years, more so in the last few. While we have provided financial support and avenues for boys, it has become apparent that our current BVHC has found either the board and/ or direction to be lacking in his vision. To date he has not submitted anything to the board requesting changes or specifics to enhance boys basketball through the board or in our youth programs. We as a board would expect our High School Coach to be present at specific functions that have group settings of youth and promote his desires to teach, but he has spent the last few years avoiding this. We deem this unacceptable.

The BVHC has been critical of our traveling program, even though we have retained coaches, who specifically taught his coaching ways, who have been through his high school program and been major contributors during their high school days. He has even gone to the aspect of recommending not having traveling basketball as an option. The board finds this contradictory to his evaluation of the traveling, when it has been directed by him.

His recommendation of AAU over a community based traveling program reflects this, while others may wish to pursue this route for boys basketball, we as a board question the results this may bring and whether or not it would be promoting a sense of community which this board has always tried to accomplish.

While our board is removing the Varsity Head Coach from it's membership, we have created a position that does reflect involvement with the High School. This was created to hopefully keep an avenue/option open to the BVHC to either attend and discuss items, or appoint someone either within the coaching staff or possibly a parent that the BVHC could entrust to express his desires/recommendations, with the understanding that this all reflects back upon the BVHC!

The board has been a volunteer organization since its inception, the board has worked within the community to promote boys basketball and support the Boys Varsity Head Coach, but as of late, the board has the feeling that the BVHC does NOT support the board.

Our current board is comprised mostly of younger boys' parents and if this is the perception now, what could the perception be later on as time moves forward and these boys/parents prepare to enter the high school?

The letter was not signed. There were no signatures. It wasn't even signed 'Richfield Basketball Board'. After I read it, I said, "what do you mean, I can't recover from this? Why do I need the approval of the basketball board to be the coach? So, the basketball board now has the power to fire the coach?"

"No, it doesn't."

"Then what is there to recover from?"

"Well, this isn't good. The head coach in any sport needs to work with his board. How are you going to respond to it?"

I answered, "Well, I've got three choices, number one I can resign, I've got nothing to prove as a coach."

He instantly interjected, "you're right. You have nothing to prove as a coach. Everyone knows you can coach, Jim. You have absolutely nothing to prove as a coach." When he said this, his body language perked up, his voice was louder, and my intuition told me that he seemed a little relieved.

I then said that my second choice was to respond to the letter and meet with the board, and that my third choice was to ignore the letter, and let the board members resign.

His answer was again, that he didn't think that I could recover from it. He then pointed out that the number of students in the summer camp decreased, and that there were less than five students pre-registered for the upcoming camp which was to begin the next week. This was an aberration from previous years when we normally had at least 20 kids pre-registered at this time of the year. I responded that we would have at least 30 black kids walk in the door and register the first day of camp. I told him that this had happened every year for the past six summers. I also told him that we would have over 30 kids attend the 3 on 3 league, just as we had for the past six summers. They just wouldn't be white kids whose parents pre-registered them with the community education office.

He then told me that as the new football coach, he was holding meetings with the parents of the youth players in grades three through eight. He pointed out that I had never done this, and he added that he was building the football program by building community support from the bottom up. He closed by saying, "well, you need to decide what you're going to do. Think about it over the weekend, and we'll meet next week." I asked if I could have a copy of the letter, and he answered "sure."

***

In the afternoon I called Jim Noonan and told him that Todd was going to fire me. There was a long pause.

"No. I can't believe that."

"No. He's gonna fire me."

"Well, I can't believe that the basketball board got to him. There has to be more to it than just that."

He then told me that Todd was going to hear from him, that he wanted his last son Jared to play for me, and all of Jared's buddies wanted to play for me.

He called Todd and they spoke the next day. The conversation lasted about forty-five minutes. Jim told me that Todd listened to him, but was noncommittal with his responses. When Jim brought up the issue of homeowners versus renters and the change in the racial makeup of the team, Todd's response was that this had nothing to do with it, and he wouldn't discuss it.

Next, I called Sabrina Freeman. Sabrina was the mother of Phillip, and the aunt of Tory Mason. Like Noonan, she had been a huge supporter of the program at all levels during my entire nine years at Richfield. She called Todd. She told me that Todd listened to her for about ten minutes before he cut off the conversation. Sabrina was African-American. She was not a homeowner.

I called Dave Thorson. His initial reaction was also disbelief. Dave had student taught at Richfield when Todd was a teacher. Dave knew Todd. I told him about the letter from the basketball board.

"What the hell do they want? Do they want to go back to winning five games a year?" His conclusion was that if the basketball board had the power to fire the coach, he was glad he was coaching at a private school.

Next, I called Mark Klingsporn. After the period of disbelief, he told me to throw a copy of my contract in front of Todd.

"Here's what you say to him Jim, 'Show me where it says in my contract that I have to run the feeder program. Show me where it says in this contract what I have to do with the traveling program. Show me where it says anything about the traveling program or the basketball board. Show me in this contract. I want to see where it says this in my contract." When I got back to my office, I looked at my contract. There was no mention of the feeder program, traveling program, or basketball board.

That night I told my wife. Her response was quick.

"I'm not surprised. Jill Johnson resigns and there's a new principal. Now the principal doesn't have your back. You know the superintendent wants you fired. They see this. They know they have an opening."

Then she repeated what she had told me many times, that being she had never felt welcomed by many of the board members, in particular the ones whose sons were poor players. "You know I have a strong intuition, Jim. My intuition is never wrong. Some of those people never liked you right from the start."

* * *

The following Wednesday I was back in Todd's office. I began the meeting by setting the basketball board letter in front of him. I pointed to the paragraph stating that I had been avoiding group settings of youth. I told him that I had been delegating the presence of the coaching staff at most of the group settings to Omar for a couple of years. I told him that Omar had been running the 1st and 2nd grade program for five years with my lesson plans. I also said that I ran the traveling tryouts, and that many of the young traveling players attended the open gyms. Why am I hearing this complaint now?" He didn't say anything.

I then pointed to the paragraphs saying that I was critical of the traveling program, recommended not having traveling basketball, and recommended instead AAU basketball over a community-based program. I told Todd what I said at the board meeting two months earlier. I said, "how is a team of Richfield kids coached by the Richfield high school coaching staff not a Richfield based program?" He was silent again.

Then I pointed at the paragraph stating that I didn't support the board. "In the past eight years I've personally raised over $18,000 for financial aid so that low-income kids could play traveling basketball. How is this not supporting the basketball board?

I went on. I asked why he didn't consider the source of the letter. I pointed out that the board was made up of two groups of parents, parents of young kids, and parents of below average players who weren't good enough to ever play on the varsity. I added that these kids came all of the way up through the program, but came to very few open gyms, adding that two of the board members had sons who never came to one open gym. "Their sons choose not to come to one open gym, where they can get free one-on-one instruction directly from me, and then they say that I don't support them."

Then I threw the contract in front of him. "And show me where it says in this contract that I am required to do anything with the traveling program, or the basketball board. Show me." I was pointing at the contract.

"Well…well…but…it…well…well, it doesn't."

I went on. "And Jim Noonan doesn't sign the letter and resigns from the board, the one parent whose son is good enough to play on the varsity. Todd, this letter doesn't pass the smell test."

The room was silent again. We looked at each other. I then said, "well Todd, it's obvious that you're gonna fire me."

He quickly answered, "you're right, I'm firing you." He then quickly sat up straighter and blurted out louder, "and it's my decision and nobody else's."

"Well then at least tell me why. I don't believe it's because of this letter."

He answered that I kept three seniors on the varsity and they played no minutes on both the varsity and the JV. "You kept three seniors, Jim and they never had a chance to play. I can't back you up on that one Jim."

"But I've been doing that since I've been coaching here, and I was always backed up on it."

"I never backed you up on that."

"And until now you never told me that you disagreed with it."

There was another silence. He then opened up, and his body language changed. "Jim, I'm tired of the split in the community. I'm tired of it. You've burned too many bridges. I'm tired of the controversy. I want somebody who can come in and unite the community."

I knew that he would bring up the split in the community because we had talked about it twice in the past two years, both times when I had brought it up. I looked Todd again in the eyes, leaned forward over the table, and spoke slowly. "Todd, you're talking about the split in the Richfield white community. There is a split in the white community over me. I know that. But there's no split in the Richfield black community over me. They're all for me and my coaching staff. You're only concerned about the split in the Richfield white community. You have no concern about the Richfield black community. They have had no say in this."

"Well, we have to listen to the voice of our tax paying constituents."

"So, the voice of the white parents who own the houses count more than the black parents who rent."

"No...no...but...ah...ah...no."

"Well then why didn't you call up any of the black parents and talk to them? How many black parents did you talk to? Did you talk to one set of black parents?"

"Well......ah......no."

"The high school teams are three fourths black, and you didn't seek the input of one black parent."

Same answer, "ah...no...ah...well...well...no."

Then I said, "are there any other reasons I was fired?"

"No."

I stood up, and gave him my set of keys. "Todd, I would like to have those reasons in writing. Can you send them to me in writing?"

"I will do that."

* * *

That night I began my last open gym by gathering 25 players in a circle at mid-court. Mullenbach was with me. I told them that I met with Todd Olson that morning and that he fired me. I then said dead seriously, "I'm not kidding."

I could see the hurt and the shock in their eyes. I said that "the people that were behind this all thought that they were doing the right thing, and that getting me fired was what was best for Richfield basketball. You've got a lot of people on both sides, people for me and people against me, and they're all good people."

I then told them that I loved working with them, and that I was going to miss them. I felt myself getting teary eyed, which was unusual for me. I told them that I believed in them, and to "never give up. Stick together and work harder than ever. I will be cheering for every one of you next winter. Don't ever give up."

I then went around the circle and asked every one of them individually if they got it. They all nodded and said yes. This was followed by a lot of hand-shakes and "thanks Coach Dimick." By now they were in lines doing drive and dish drills with Matt yelling instructions "big first step…give a target…pass to the target…don't pass to the body, pass to the target…" As I walked toward the doors I stopped, folded my arms, and looked up at the state tournament banners, 1960, 1973, 1974, 2005, and 2006. I imagined the gym packed with people. I looked to my left and saw the door to our locker room. I pictured Alex Tilman and Kris Pulford leading the team out of the door, snaking a path through the overflow crowd and the crowd exploding in a roar. It was a sad feeling but a good feeling, a really good feeling. I walked down the hall and out into the enduring light of the June evening. I was on the way to my swimming hole on Lake Minnetonka.

***

Growing up African-American in Milwaukee in the sixties, my wife's hero was Angela Davis. When I talked to her that night, she was furious. Then I heard the answer that was vintage Martha.

"You need to request a hearing, and you need to throw the race issue right in their face. You throw that right in their face, Jim. That's what this is about, and that's all that this is about, and they need to hear that, and they need to hear that from you." Thanks to Rich Decker and Dean Urdahl, I had that option, and there was nothing that they could do to stop me.

The other person that I knew would take it really hard was my Dad. I had to tell him before he heard it from anybody else. I called him the next day. I wasn't going to tell him over the phone. I was overdue to spend a morning helping him weed his garden. The weather report for Friday was clear skies and no wind. It had rained earlier in the week. The soil would be perfect for pulling weeds. When I told him that I wanted to come down to Northfield to help him weed his garden he quickly answered, "that would be great."

***

The sun rose Friday to a glorious June day. One of my paternal grandfather's sayings was 'nothing prettier than a June morning', and the day fit the saying. I picked up my Dad at his place and we drove north of town to his garden. My Dad share-cropped a garden plot with a farmer named Dave Legvold a few miles north of town. Legvold had about 800 acres, and my Dad's plot was about the size of a basketball court. They had the sharecropping arrangement for over 10 years. What produce my Dad, the Legvolds, and my brother's families didn't eat, he gave away and he sometimes bartered his squash with the local co-op.

Well before 7am I was on my hands and knees working my way down my third row of plants. The sun was now well over the tree line to the northeast, beginning its elliptical midsummer path across the sky. After circling to the south, it would set 14 hours later in the northwest. There were no clouds and not a ripple of a breeze. The birds were singing and the insects were buzzing. The black loam soil of the Minnesota prairie was on my forearms and under my fingernails. All of my senses were full of the moment. It was the kind of moment that I dreamed about during the winter. My Dad's father Richard was a tenth-generation American farmer, the Dimick line having pushed west from Massachusetts to Connecticut to upstate New York to Wisconsin every couple generations. We were doing together what other sets of fathers and sons in this line had been doing together for almost four hundred years on this continent. My Dad was alternating between hand weeding and running the tiller in the open spaces between the rows. When the tiller wasn't running, we would talk. At one point my Dad was also on his knees, bent over, and pulling weeds 20 feet away from me. There was a lull in the conversation.

I broke the silence by leaning back on my heels, looking at my Dad, and saying, "Dad, I'm gonna tell you something, and I 'm not kidding. I'm not joking."

He answered with a short "yeah" and kept on weeding. He was on all fours with his head down.

"Todd Olson fired me."

A couple seconds later, he sat up, looked at me with an expression of disbelief and said "What?"

"Yeah, he fired me. Two days ago."

"He fired you. He fired you?' Now he was standing up and looking at me, his hands and knees full of dirt. "I can't believe that. Why? Why on earth would he fire you? Let's go get a drink of water."

As we walked towards the shade of some trees and my car, he went on. "Jim, I just can't believe it. Todd always had your back."

We sat in the grass and leaned back against the tires. The cooler of ice water rested between us in the shade. I told him about the two meetings, the reasons Todd had given me, and my responses. More silence.

Then I heard the answer that was vintage Dimick. "Well, I'm really pissed off."

"Well, I'm going to have a hearing. I will have my say."

We went back to weeding. The discussion over the next two hours was mostly a monologue, with my Dad doing the talking. The topic went from out of line parents, to proper chain of command, to analyzing who made the call, to Todd not listening to Noonan, to what Karnas did or did not know, to what Baker would have told Slotterback, to northern racism, to weak administrators. The portion of the monologue on weak administrators was greatest in both length of time and tone of voice.

At one point, he stopped weeding, sat up and said, "Jim, look at me."

"You were going to have another great team next year."

"I know. And they knew that. And that's why they did this now. They knew that if they didn't do it now, they couldn't do it next year."

* * *

As word of the firing spread through Richfield, the African-American parents of the players were outraged. They called Todd Olson and other administrators. They all asked why they were not asked for their opinions. They were livid because they thought they had been marginalized. One of them told me that it was a 'coup'. It was done behind the scenes, and nobody knew about it until it was over. They echoed what Noonan had told Todd a couple of weeks earlier, "Why would you not ask for the opinions of the parents of the players?"

There were also many white parents who were outraged. And there were many white retired community members who were outraged. These were people who had raised their families in Richfield, followed their kids through the high school, and continued to attend school events. Many of them loved high school sports and high school basketball. The oldest ones had witnessed the glory years, as well as the lean years that followed. These people told me that they were in total support of what I and my staff had done, and that they couldn't believe that I had been fired.

On Monday I made a short list of my close friends and called them to tell them that I had been fired. The list included coaches, clients, canoe buddies, and relatives. After the first two calls, it was fun. I would tell them that I wasn't joking and that I had been fired. This was always followed by a long silence and a statement of disbelief. Then I would start laughing and say "I'm not kidding."

As the news of the firing hit the streets, the phone started ringing at my office. One of my good friends, who I called earlier, called me back a couple of days later. He told me that he got a dozen phone calls from buddies asking him to confirm if it was true or just a rumor. "Jim, these are the words that I hear when I tell them that it's true, 'ridiculous, crazy, incredulous.'" Tom Critchley, the chairman of the Coach's All-Star Game and a Hall of Fame coach used the word 'bizarre'. Both Hopkins coaches, Brian Cosgriff and Ken Novak called. Willie Braziel called. One young coach called me and said, "This has all of the young coaches talking. If you can get fired, anybody can get fired." Unlike the time that I had been fired at Washburn, this was no blow to my ego. It was the exact opposite.

***

Seventeen days after I had met with Todd, on July 9th I received a *'Notice of Non-Renewal of Coaching Contract'* signed by Craig Holje, Director of Personnel and Administrative Service and Todd Olson. The notice stated that "The non-renewal is based on overall performance concerns, especially concerns regarding communications, leadership, and program development."

Three days later I mailed a letter to all of the administrators and school board members. I also sent copies to John Erickson, the executive director of the MSHSCA, and Minnesota House of Representatives representative Paul Thissen.

Shown below is the conclusion of the letter:

Minn. Stat. Sec. 122A.33, Subd. 3 states as follows:

"A school board that declines to renew the coaching contract of a licensed or nonlicensed head varsity coach must notify the coach within 14 days of that decision. If the coach requests reasons for not renewing the coaching contract, the board must give the coach its reasons in writing within ten days of receiving the request. Upon request the board must provide the coach with a reasonable opportunity to respond to the reasons at a board meeting. The hearing may be opened or closed at the election of the coach unless the board closes the meeting under section 13D.05, subdivision 2, to discuss private data."

Todd Olson's decision not to renew my coaching contract was done unilaterally absent approval from the Richfield School Board. The statute mandates that it is the Richfield School Board that makes the final decision not to renew a coaching contract. Todd Olson's unilateral decision not to renew my coaching contract violates Minn. Stat. Sec. 122A.33, Subd. 3. Therefore, until the school board ratifies his decision, the decision is invalid. It is the school board's responsibility to accept Todd Olson's recommendation of non-renewal and to make a sufficient record after a hearing to prove the decision was justified.

If the school board accepts Todd Olson's recommendation not to renew my coaching contract, I am exercising my statutory right to an **open** *hearing. Alternatively, if the school to board does not accept Todd Olson's recommendation not to renew my coaching contract, I am willing to forgo any further action and continue coaching. Please notify me as soon as possible of your decision.*[82]

* * *

I attended the next school board meeting on the second Monday in July. All of my assistant coaches were with me. Two of the 'concerned citizens' who were outspoken in the community about my use of profanity were also there.

When the open microphone portion of the meeting began, two people addressed the board in support of me and to question why I had been fired. Mary Ross was the mother of three players in the program; Chris, Taronn, and Jawan. She and her husband Sam had been regulars at games and events for my entire nine years. They lived in Richfield and all three sons plus their daughter Destinee attended the Richfield schools during this time. She spoke without a written statement and she spoke from the heart. She talked a little less than five minutes.

She was followed by Dave Boie. Dave was the head baseball coach, and assistant football coach, and had been my ninth-grade coach in 2004-05. He grew up in Richfield and was a long-time faculty member. He read a short statement, and he gave me a copy.

I speak to you here tonight in regard to the dismissal of Jim Dimick as the Basketball Coach at Richfield High School...As a Science teacher at the high school, a baseball, football, and former basketball coach, I serve and have served many roles within this district...No staff at the high school does as much monitoring and intervention with students' grades and their behavior than that of our Boys Basketball Program...They do way more than just react to poor grades; they are more proactive in dealing with these issues than it is probably their responsibility to be...If Jim Dimick is not what we value in our coaches here in Richfield, then I do not know what it is we value.

Fifteen minutes later I was driving home with Martha. Our conversation was interrupted by my cell phone ringing. It was Omar.

"Jim. You've got to hear this. I've got a friend who's at the Richfield Legion baseball game. He just called me. He said that two guys just showed up at the game. They were telling everybody in the crowd that they had just been at the school board meeting. They were saying that they heard a bunch of bullshit in support of Dimick, and that Dimick didn't care about the Richfield kids, and that Dimick just wanted to bring in city kids."

* * *

The next day I called an attorney from my home town of Northfield. David Hvistendahl was four years older than me and a graduate of St Olaf. He was originally from Brookings, South Dakota. During the sixties he was one of the students who led the anti-war protests on campus. Ten years later he and his friend Ron Moersch opened up a law firm, and it grew into a solid mid-sized small-town firm. He wore a pony tail down his back, and was brilliant, aggressive, and an unabashed liberal. He also owned a bar and restaurant on the Cannon River in town and had some other business interests. I was the accountant for his businesses and I referred him legal work. I had been confiding the Richfield situation to him and his partner Ron for years. He eagerly accepted the job, and added, "Jim, this is going to be fun." Two days later he sent a letter to Craig Holje, stating that he would be representing me. He later contacted Holje to find out if the district had a lawyer for him to communicate through. Holje told him that the district hires different attorneys based on the type of situation, and that the district had hired a local attorney named Sara Ruff.

I began writing the speech for my hearing. After one morning, I realized that it was going to take 15 to 20 hours to prepare. I wasn't going to make any statements that I could not back up, and I needed statistics to back up my statements. I needed definitions of both institutional/systemic racism and tokenism. When I found them, it was an 'a-hah' moment. The more that I worked, the more energized I became. When I was finished, I forwarded it to Dave Hvistendahl. He told me that he liked the fact that everything that I said was backed up with statistics, and that I wasn't just complaining. He kept using the word 'educational'. "It's bullet proof, and above all, it's educational. It's going to force the school board members to think about things that they haven't given much thought to."

* * *

My hearing was in late August, over a month away. This gave me and my inner circle of supporters, time to analyze how it had transpired. I would never know all of the dynamics, but there were some that I would be willing to bet money on.

Tom Flood was the chairman of the school board. He was a Richfield native, and we cut his son as a sophomore in my first or second year. He was very complimentary to me during our three-year run of twenty-win seasons. Dave Lamberger and Sandy Belkengren attended many games in both the up years and the five hundred years. I believed that the other members were ambivalent, and did not follow athletics. Even though Todd Olson told me that the decision had been 'only his decision', there had to have been discussions among Todd, Slotterback, and Flood. Todd's position had flipped. There was no doubt in my mind that Slotterback wanted me fired. And my intuition told me that Flood also believed that it was time for me to go, but I would never know this. My sources told me that the new principal, David West withdrew himself from the discussions regarding my job status.

There had to have been at least one conversation between Todd and a basketball board member, which preceded the letter of non-endorsement. I believed that this leaked out to the disgruntled parents.

I also believed that there was an organized boycott of both the Spring AAU team and the basketball camp. This answered the question why there wasn't one white traveling kid on the AAU team, or enrolled for the camp.

During the school year, school district employees went door to door up and down the streets of Richfield. They rang every doorbell. They carried clipboards and took notes. If the homeowners had children, they were asked questions about the children, where they were attending grade school, where they were going to attend high school, and why. They covered every house in the suburb. I do not know if they went to the apartment buildings. I believe that my detractors spread the word to tell these young parents to complain about the boys' basketball program. I also believe that this message trickled back to the administration. My sources confirmed this.

There was no doubt in my mind that they knew I would hire an attorney, and that I would throw the race issue in their face at the hearing. They had to have discussed the influence of my wife, her 'stand up-in your face-militant' personality, and her legal background. There will never be any doubt in my mind that they knew what was coming.

As the weeks passed by, one of my sources informed me that a school board member confided to him that the school board members felt that they had no choice but to back up Todd, because of the large number of phone calls they received that were against me. There had been an organized telephone campaign.

*　*　*

The second week in August, Dave Hvistendahl called me. The attorney Sara Ruff called him twice. She called the first time on Monday, August 9th to say that the school district wanted the hearing to be a closed hearing, in other words closed to the public. He pointed out to her the literature in Dean Urdahl's bill that said that it was up to the fired coach to decide if the hearing was open or closed.

"I then told her that Coach Dimick requests an open hearing, and I also forwarded the appropriate documentation to her." I could almost see the smile on his face over the phone.

A week later she called Dave again. She called to say that she thought the hearing should be closed due to privacy laws. The school district was concerned that I would mention names of players or parents in my speech.

Dave told me that he had said to her, "oh no, oh no, Coach Dimick won't mention any names. Coach Dimick and I have already discussed this and he is aware that he can't mention any names. You can be assured that no names will be mentioned." He then told her that I would call no witnesses and that I would not get personal with anybody. He stressed to her that it would be educational, that I was going to educate the board about the situation and the problem.

Richfield Boys Basketball
Feeder Progams

Winter	Grade	Summer
Saturday morn	1	
Saturday morn	2	
House league	3	Camp
House league	4	Camp
House league/Traveling teams	5	Camp/3on3 league
House league/Traveling teams	6	Camp/3on3 league
RMS teams/Traveling teams	7	AAU team/Camp/3on3/Open gyms
RMS teams/Traveling teams	8	AAU team/Camp/3on3/Open gyms
RHS teams	9	Open gyms
RHS teams	10	Open gyms
RHS teams	11	Open gyms
RHS teams	12	Open gyms

Richfield Boys Basketball
Funnel

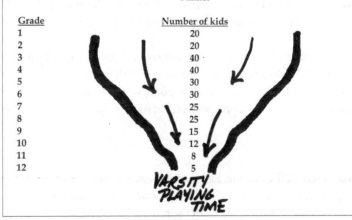

Grade	Number of kids
1	20
2	20
3	40
4	40
5	30
6	30
7	25
8	25
9	15
10	12
11	8
12	5

VARSITY PLAYING TIME

School Board Hearing

Illegitimi non carborundum.

—*General Joseph Stilwell*

I called a few members of my small inner circle of family and friends. One of the best words of advice was from my brother Dan. He told me to write my entire speech, and then read it to the school board. He said "Then they can't misquote you. They can't say that you said something that you didn't say, or say that you never said something that you did say. You will have exactly what you said in writing." It was great advice.

I called the veteran sports writer at the St Paul Pioneer Press Charley Walters. I told him that I was fired, and he answered that he knew this. I explained the school board hearing, and that I thought the paper should cover it. He confirmed that they would be covering the hearing.

I called a lead high school sports writer at the *StarTribune*. I told the writer that I had been fired, and he answered that he knew that. He answered that the paper was aware of the upcoming hearing, and that the paper was choosing not to cover it.

I said to him, "so five years ago, when there is a community debate about whether or not I should be the coach, you cover it, with big headlines. And now when I get fired and I have a chance to respond, you don't cover it."

"At this time, we are choosing not to cover it."

***

On the night of the hearing, I arrived at the administration offices half an hour early. I brought one foot by three-foot placards with quotes, statistics, and pie charts. I set them up in the front of the room so that I could page through them as I spoke. By the time the hearing was to begin there were about thirty people sitting in the folding chairs in the audience. The school board members and superintendent sat in front of me at a table. The school board members were Tom Flood, Sandy Belkengren, John Easterwood, David Lamberger, Todd

Nollenberger, and Peter Toensing. As I scanned the crowd, I noted that all of the people were in support of me.

Tom Flood opened the meeting with a brief description of the procedure. He then immediately asked the school board to vote on whether or not to reinstate me as the coach. The vote was unanimous to support Todd Olson's decision to fire me. Flood, the administrators, and the school board members turned and looked at me. I looked back at all of them.

"Well, it's clear that you are not going to reinstate me as the coach. However, I am going to give my speech anyway. I have it written down and I will read it. Shown below is my, Monday August 23, 2010 speech to the school board, edited for the reader.

I met with Todd Olson on Tuesday, June 29, 2010 in his office and he informed me that he was not going to renew my contract as the head boys' basketball coach at Richfield High School for the 2010-2011 seasons. Before that conversation ended, I requested that he tell me the specific reasons why the contract was not going to be renewed, and he stated the following reasons:

An unsigned undated letter entitled Athletic Department C/O Mr. Todd Olson

The fact that I chose to keep three seniors on the varsity roster whom played limited minutes

My inability to unite the entire Richfield basketball community

I then requested that this list of reasons be provided in writing. I received a Notice of Non-Renewal of Coaching Contract signed by Craig Holje on July 9, 2010 stating that "the nonrenewal is based on overall performance concerns, especially concerns regarding communications, leadership, and program development." The reasons provided in the notice are contrary to the reasons stated at the June 29th meeting.

I am going to respond to the nonrenewal of my contract by explaining three parts of the program; academics, varsity basketball, and program development. Criticizing my communication or leadership skills is nothing more than an attempt to state vague reasons to support my dismissal. The real reason for my dismissal is the split in the community, which I also will discuss. This has been an extremely difficult situation for everyone involved; students, parents, administrators, and coaches. I also hope to make you aware of the huge amount of misinformation that has circulated around the community regarding this emotional subject.

Academics

Matt Mullenbach is the assistant coach and a math teacher at the high school to whom I delegated the academic program. The kids are informed that they are expected to do four things:

Be to class on time.

Hand in all assignments.

Study for tests.

Be a good citizen in the hallways.

Matt utilizes the school district's Internet grade report system to constantly monitor the grades of the students. If a student is failing in a class, the student immediately begins staying after school to work with the teacher, the student reports to practice late, and the student does not play in games until he raises the grade. I believe that removing the student from the team is not a good option, so we keep him on the team, monitor his progress, and sit him on the bench during games. In addition to this, we have study halls for all of the players on some of the days when we begin practice at 5 o'clock. If a student misbehaves in class, the teacher emails Matt, who then forwards the email to me and the other two coaches. If a student gets kicked out of class, he does not play in the next game, a situation that Dave Boie shared with you a month ago. Dave Boie also told you that we are proactive in setting up meetings for players, their parents, teachers, and the entire coaching staff when a student is academically at risk. You also need to know that the student he told you about was a marginal 9th grade player. We don't just do this for the best players. In November after we have chosen our rosters for grades 9 through 12, Matt emails the entire faculty with a list of our players and a list of our rules, encouraging the faculty to communicate their concerns to us at any time.

Mike Karnas has told me on more than one occasion, that "all sports should be required to do academically what the boys basketball team does". After Todd Olson was named the head football coach this spring, he said to me, "we are going to adopt your academic system for the football team." In my first eight years at Richfield, 35 out of 40 seniors who have graduated from RHS have graduated from college or are attending college on track to graduate. Of these 35 young men, 12 are first time college students in their families.

In terms of academics, or educationally speaking, do any school board members see any possible concerns regarding communication or leadership?

Varsity basketball

I'm not going to talk in depth on this. I'm not going to bring in other coaches to speak on my behalf. Our record in the last nine years speaks for itself. Richfield has qualified for the state tournament two times during my watch, and I've been selected coach of the year twice. When we made our run to the state finals five years ago, that team ended a thirty-one year drought in boys basketball state tournament appearances for the community. We've averaged 16 wins per year in the nine years that I have been the coach at Richfield.

My two predecessors, Greg Miller and Jeff Etienne, combined to average 6 **wins per year** in the nine years before I was hired, and Greg had most of the wins, especially in his last few years. The number of wins per year increased every year that Greg was the coach, with less talent than my teams had.

A big reason for our success has been our summer program of open gyms which stresses individual and small group skill development including our trinity of individual skills, shooting form, ball-handling, and offensive footwork; both on the perimeter and in the post.

In the **Classic Suburban Conference our winning percentage** is 66% in the last seven years, which is considerably higher that other similar team sports during the same period.

Another reason for our success is that every player always knows his role on the team, and I make sure that every player feels important. Some kids are told that they are part of the playing rotation. Some are told that they will only play mop up minutes, and that their role is to be a member of the scout squad in practice. They are constantly reminded that they are important contributors to the team in this role. When roles change, the players whose minutes are reduced are informed first. One mother of a senior scout squad member told me at the end of season banquet "you made my son's senior year".

Eleven young men that I have coached at Richfield have gone on to play college basketball.

I've spoken at a number of coaching clinics sharing my drills for teaching team defense with other coaches, sometimes with over 500 coaches in attendance. I've also worked with Coach Leanne Wise and the Richfield girls' basketball team on court at their practices teaching her team the same drills in order to help them to improve their team defense. My athletic director has told me in the past that my game preparation and halftime adjustments during games are unsurpassed.

After one player graduated in 2005 and went on to attend the University of Northern Iowa, his head coach Ben Jacobson told me that "your kid knew our team defense after one week of practice, and it takes most kids a year to a year and a half to learn it." That same year Bo Ryan from the University of Wisconsin told me, "your teams are as well schooled in the fundamentals and how to play the game as any high school teams that we see." And our former principal told me this on more than one occasion, "thank you for what you have done for this school."

In terms of coaching the varsity basketball team, do any school board members see any possible concerns regarding communication or leadership?

Funnel concept

Before discussing program development, I need to explain to you the funnel concept. The feeder program that extends from 1st grade through 8th grade, and which develops student athletes whom enter the high school program as 9th graders, can best be described as a "funnel." The number of kids playing a sport in each grade is unlimited in elementary school. The number of kids playing a sport in each grade decreases each year as they get older. Different sports have different sizes of "funnels". Football has the widest funnel, as many varsity teams have 30 kids that get regular playing time in games. Basketball has the narrowest funnel, because most varsity teams have 7 to 8 kids that get regular playing time.

The feeder program in place in Richfield has a number of winter and summer programs. The programs administered by the youth board are the 1st & 2nd grade Saturday mornings during six weeks in the winter, the winter house league for students in grades 3 through 6, and the traveling teams for grades 5 through 8. The programs administered by the high school coaching staff are; the middle school 7th and 8th grade teams, the summer camp and 3 on 3 league for grades 5-8, the spring AAU team for 7th and 8th graders, and the summer open gyms for kids entering middle school or high school.

Let's superimpose a funnel over these programs.

In an out-state town, the size of Richfield, for example a Grand Rapids, or a Willmar, this model of a feeder program works quite well. A group of kids in each grade advances year by year through the program. Each year as the funnel narrows, the kids in the group that are the most talented and that have the best work ethic improve more than the other kids. As the funnel becomes narrower each year, the best kids make it through the funnel, and the best kids play. The same group of kids advances from grade to grade up through their senior year. There are **three demographic premises** on which this model is based.

1) **Limited** or no **movement of families** into and out of the school district from grades K-12

2) **Apartment building** dwellers are mostly young singles without **kids** or parents of kids who **don't play basketball**

3) **Open enrollment** is **not utilized** because of distances between schools, and equality of schools and programs

These demographic factors make it easy for the same group of kids to advance year by year through the program until they are seniors.

Now let's change the picture of the funnel to fit the demographics of an inner ring suburb. You now see **three additional inflows** of students into the funnel; students moving into the community in middle school, students open enrolling in 9th grade, and students moving into the community in high school. These three inflow valves accurately represent the demographics of an inner ring suburb of the twin cities today. Now, these are the **demographics** that exist **in Richfield.**

1) **A lot of movement of families** into and out of the school district from K-12
2) **Apartment building** dwellers are parents of **kids** who **play basketball**
3) **Open enrollment** is **utilized** because of close proximity of schools, and inequality of schools and programs.

The "narrower the funnel", the more disruptive these factors become. In other words, these factors are very disruptive in basketball, but not nearly as disruptive in football. Each November we as a coaching staff are greeted with a group of kids trying out for the high school basketball team in grades nine through twelve. Based on this funnel, we can classify these kids into three groups; the kids who have been in the program since their elementary school years, who I will call "traveling kids", the kids who with their parents move into the district after 6th grade, and the kids who open enroll as 9th graders.

Given this situation, many parents of traveling kids become frustrated with the program and the coach. They expect that their child's group will move up through the feeder program all the way to the senior year. The bottom line is that many traveling kids are displaced by kids who move into the community or open enroll, or when they get to high school, they are passed up by younger traveling kids.

Now we could **close** these **three intake valves,** and I will draw red lines in front of them. Here is how we do this.

1) Have **expensive** traveling **fees** and summer camp fees **with no financial aid**
2) **Eliminate** grade monitoring and **study halls**
3) **No** free **open gyms**
4) **Play the senior traveling kids** every year even if the juniors, sophomores, or freshman are better players

The expensive fees will encourage kids from low-income families to play for other traveling teams and attend other camps, where they will become friends with kids from other schools. Eliminating study halls will increase the number of students that will be academically ineligible, and then can't try out for the team. No open gyms will help prevent younger kids that play every day from passing up older kids that don't play every day. And playing the senior traveling kids will broadcast the message to gifted and talented freshman and potential open enrollment kids that if they come to Richfield, they will sit on the bench. The combination of these four red lines, will decrease the competition as the funnel narrows, and will reinforce parental expectations of entitlement.

You then would have in place a system of institutional racism. **Institutional (or systemic) racism is defined as "societal patterns that have the net effect of imposing oppressive or otherwise negative conditions against identifiable groups of people on the basis of race or identity...often practiced by governmental entities or other community-based organizations."** The basketball program would be excluding the African-Americans without creating the appearance of being discriminatory.

You have recently received a lot of messages from concerned citizens urging you to not bring me back as the coach. These people will be the first to emphatically tell you that this issue has nothing to do with class or race

These people will name two Black traveling kids who were cut as seniors. They will name two White kids who open enrolled as seniors, when you could still do that. **These charts** and **pie diagrams** show the demographics of the eight-year totals of traveling kids who were cut, and of kids who entered the program after 6th grade. As you can see, 96% of the traveling kids who have not made it through the funnel have been White kids, and 92% of the kids who have entered the program after 6th grade have been Black kids. To say that this is not about class or race is a textbook example of tokenism. **Tokenism is defined as "a policy or practice of including limited members of a minority group, in order to create a false appearance of inclusive practices."**

Does the school board want a basketball feeder program of institutionalized racism, backed up with an argument of tokenism? This type of program with the red lines in front of the three intake valves, would effectively exclude these kids, 92% of whom are African-American, and most of whom live in Richfield. This is the feeder program that this group of people, led by some of last winter's traveling parents, want to have.

During the past two years my sources informed me that three sets of senior parents and a number of past boys' basketball parents had met with Dr. Slotterback to discuss the basketball program. I then scheduled a meeting with Dr. Slotterback. On that day I asked him what the concerns of the parents were. He told me that the concern of all of these parents was the fact that "traveling kids who had come all of the way up through the program, ended up never playing for the varsity." This was the only answer that he gave me to my question. And now that you understand this, we can discuss program development.

Program development

I have been blamed for the fact that the numbers in four parts of the feeder program have declined, even though the numbers in other comparable sports have declined in a similar fashion. No other sport in Richfield has a varsity coach who volunteers his time in the off season to coach a junior high spring AAU team, which is open to all kids who want to be included, and which is certainly a community-based program.

I donate three nights a week in June and July to coach the open gyms, which would more accurately be called skill sessions. They are open to kids entering middle school or high school. We average between twenty and thirty kids a night. At these sessions, we have developed and encouraged a culture in which older kids mentor younger kids. The kids learn individual drills that they can work on when they are alone, or with their friends. We have seen kids improve 100% over a summer due to their improved footwork and ball-handling.

I have been told that I don't support the youth board because I am not present at some of their activities. When I am not present, my assistant Omar McMillan is present. As you are all aware, Omar is a star teacher in the school system, and he represents the high school staff very well.

"The best leadership quality of Ulysses S Grant was his ability to delegate." -Virginia Historical Society

Each year I have donated a portion of my salary back to the program, part of which goes to pay Omar and my other assistants when they work with the Richfield youth. When I am paying them out of my own pocket to be present at activities instead of me, I am criticized by the youth board for not supporting the youth of Richfield.

In the past 8 years I have personally raised over $18,000 to provide financial aid to middle school students who are on reduced and free school lunch so that they can play traveling basketball. How can this not be considered supporting the youth of Richfield?

In my nine years, the program has evolved from a program where some kids would hardly touch a basketball all summer, and still make it through the funnel to the varsity, to a program where if a kid doesn't play basketball year-round, he probably won't make the varsity team. What we have is a smaller number of kids, who are playing basketball every day, and they are surpassing all of the other kids who aren't as talented, or who don't want to work as hard.

We have a large number of kids for whom basketball is their favorite sport, and they are outworking and out "fundamentalling" the kids who spend their free time doing other activities. This is a gifted and talented program, where the bar has been raised.

We have a great group of unselfish hard working talented kids returning to the varsity next year. Other coaches remark at what great shooters they are. At the open gyms and summer camp I have worked with every one of them on their shooting form, many of them beginning when they were in elementary school. So now, with the program poised to once again make multiple runs at a state title, because of talent that I and my assistants have developed with our program, I am told that I am deficient in program development.

Perception gap

There is this huge perception gap that the past few years, the varsity team is not made up of Richfield kids, but that it is made up of "city kids," and I believe that this idea has been actively promoted by a small group of vocal citizens. I am now going to show you some statistics regarding the makeup of the varsity team, which shows that the message of these detractors simply isn't true. I have six charts that I am going to supply to the school board members, and I am going to utilize pie graphs to illustrate their trends to everyone else.

These diagrams show the breakdown of the varsity team by when was their **first year in the feeder program.** As you can see, in my first year 72% of the team was traveling kids. The last four years which are 2007 to 2010, their numbers have been basically cut in half to about 40%. The number of kids who enter the program in 7th and 8th grade has increased from 0% to about 30%. This is because kids who move into Richfield with their parents in middle school are displacing traveling kids. We have two such young men who played varsity minutes as sophomores last winter. One moved into Richfield with his family during 7th grade, and the other moved in prior to his 8th grade year. These are two of the kids who passed up last winter's seniors.

If you look at the chart titled **"where they have lived",** you will also see that on the average, we have had 20%, or three open enrollment kids on the varsity team almost every year. If you have a winning program in the metro area, you are going to have that. Kids want to be a part of a successful program. In 2002, 14% of the roster was kids who had never lived in Richfield, and if you look at the returning players who will try out for next year's team in grades 9 through 12, only 11% haver never lived in Richfield. The reason why I use the term "have lived in Richfield" instead of "live in Richfield", is because we have had a number of kids who began their school years in Richfield, and their parents don't own property. When their family moved out of the community, they chose to keep their kids in the Richfield school system.

The fourth chart shows the breakdown of the varsity team by whether their parents are **homeowners or renters,** and the fifth and sixth charges show the breakdown of the varsity team by **race.** As you can see from these pie diagrams, the makeup of the team has completely changed in these aspects in the past nine years. In fact, the transformation has almost been reciprocal, basically going from 75% homeowner and 25% renter to the opposite. In terms of race, the same thing has happened, going from 70% white and 30% kids of color; to 30% white and 70% kids of color.

What do these statistics tell us? They tell us that **the percent of kids who live in Richfield has not changed, but the racial makeup of the team has changed dramatically.** Yet there is this huge perception gap, actively promoted by certain citizens, that the varsity team is no longer a Richfield team, and that I don't care about the Richfield kids. These people have even gone to the parents of the elementary school kids, and they have spread this lie. Many of these young parents hear this lie, and they believe it. These closet racists have persistently spread the word that it is a team of **"city kids",** and this is what is causing the split in the community.

Race

I am now going to share some things that I have witnessed that I think you as school board members need to be aware of.

Here are the demographics of our starting lineup from 2008-2009. My sources informed me that there was a lot of criticism of the team that winter because of the fact that not one starter lived in Richfield. However, four of these young men who were black, had lived in Richfield, then moved out of Richfield and open enrolled at Richfield. Two of them attended Richfield schools K through twelve. One moved into Richfield in 5th grade, and one moved into Richfield in 8th grade. Three of these kids came all of the way up through the program. Because of financial aid, they were traveling kids. I know what my detractors are saying. They are saying if those kids move out of Richfield, they aren't Richfield kids anymore and they shouldn't be on the Richfield team.

You now see the demographics of the starting lineup from 1998-1999. Two of these starters who were white, lived in Bloomington from K through 12. Because they attended the Catholic grade school in Richfield, they were eligible for and played on the traveling team. They came all of the way up through the program. Did any concerned citizens approach any school board members at that time, complaining about the fact these two young men from Bloomington were displacing Richfield kids? Were they labeled "city kids?"

What are the traits that help these people to distinguish between the Richfield kids and the city kids? It certainly isn't whether or not they came all of the way up through the program, because all five of these kids came all of the way up through the program. It certainly isn't whether or not they live in Richfield, because all five young men didn't live in Richfield during their senior years. Yet three of them as seniors are considered "city kids", and two others are considered "Richfield kids" from beginning when they were in grade school.

We had a senior on the team this past winter who is African-American. He moved to Richfield with his mother during his 8th grade year. During his sophomore year, his mother was diagnosed with cancer, and during his junior year they moved to his grandmother's apartment in Minneapolis. She died that May. A set of traveling parents opened their home to this young man, and he lived with them during his senior year. Other traveling parents had also reached out to him and he had stayed over and eaten meals in their homes. These traveling parents bent over backwards to make this young man welcome in Richfield. He is now attending college.

Last November we had nine kids show up for 9th grade tryouts who were new to the program. Their basketball abilities varied from very good to below average. Eight of these young men were African-American. One of our traveling kids, who is European-American quit after two days of practice. When his father stopped by the athletic office to collect his activity fee refund, he told the secretary that "his son was intimidated by the city kids." Eight out of nine of these young men whom were new to the program lived in Richfield.

We had a young man who attended the Richfield schools beginning in the 3rd grade. He was not able to be included in the traveling program and summer camps because of family income, until I instituted a program of financial aid during his 8th grade year. He began playing basketball every day and attended the summer camp, the 3on3 league, and every open gym. During his sophomore year, his family moved to Bloomington. He learned study skills from Matt Mullenbach. He would come late to varsity practice, so that he could get extra help from teachers. As a sophomore, he beat out a senior, and he was the 6th man on our state tournament team. That senior and his parents addressed the school board the next spring, complaining among other things, that "Richfield kids who come all of the way up through the program, were losing their spots to outside kids." However, they didn't tell you that the kid who beat out their son had been in the Richfield schools since 3rd grade, and that he was excluded from the program. This same young man will be a senior in college next year on a basketball scholarship. He will be the first person in his family to graduate from college. These same parents of the senior are urging many people to contact you and tell you to not reinstate me as the coach. If I had ran the basketball program to conform to their wishes, their son would have played, and the other young man would not be in college today.

I was leaving the VFW one winter morning two years ago after our team had eaten breakfast there. I had stayed late and had talked with my seniors. All four young men were African American and all four were wearing Richfield letterman jackets. We were stopped at a table by the door, by a man in his eighties, obviously a World War II vet. He asked if I was the coach and if these were players, and he asked about the team. Before we left, he shook my hand and said "you got some fine-looking young men". I believe that the majority of the Richfield citizens see it his way.

When I met with the superintendent, he told me that he knew that there was a race issue, because concerned parents always used the term "city kids" instead of calling them black kids. When I discussed this with the athletic director, he told me that he didn't' see a race problem in Richfield, and that he felt that the black kids had always been welcomed.

Split in the community

When the administrators talk about their concern about the split in the community, they are only concerned about the split in one sector of the community, the homeowners, or as they like to call them the "taxpaying constituents who make their voices heard". 20 out of 28 parents of the returning high school players are renters. 25 of these parents live in Richfield and they pay rent to their landlord, and twice a year their landlord pays property taxes. They are also taxpaying constituents. 21 out of 28 parents of the returning high school players are African-American. There is no split in their part of the community over the issue of the high school basketball team.

When the administration talks about this problem of the split in the community, they give no thought to the black part of the community in Richfield, even though 75% of the varsity team is African-American. The administrators have only been concerned with healing the split in the white part of the community. These African-American parents have had no chance to make their voice heard regarding this issue, and the administration made zero effort to communicate with any of them.

Closing

This is an incredibly difficult situation for everybody involved. You have parents who are passionate about their kids on all sides of the issue, and you will have kids who will be cut. It is difficult for kids, parents, coaches and administrators.

How did the administrators deal with this difficult situation? The superintendent opened his door and listened to the complaints of a small group of traveling parents whose sons got passed up by younger kids.

When the youth board asked the coach at a meeting in April if the varsity team needed the traveling program, the coach responded by discussing the historical numbers, which was the truth, and which they didn't want to hear. The youth board then contacted the AD, because they were upset. The AD then communicated with the youth board more than once which led to the unsigned undated letter. When the coach showed the athletic director his description of the funnel problem, the AD told the coach to not show it to the youth board, because in his words "they aren't going to like it", even thought he admitted it was the truth. In June the AD then showed the coach the unsigned undated letter, which in my opinion, distorted what I had said at the April meeting.

At the request of the coach, the AD then contacted Jim Noonan who had resigned from the youth board because he did not agree with the unsigned undated letter. Their entire discussion was about the unsigned letter and the split in the community. Four days later the AD fired the coach, telling him that it was because of:

1-the unsigned undated letter, which deals with a non-school program which is mentioned nowhere in the coaching contract

2-because he kept 3 seniors as members of the scout squad, even though the AD supported the coach on this decision when it was made

3-and because of the split in the community.

In the end the solution of the administration was to communicate with a small group of traveling parents, make no attempt to communicate with the African-American parents of the high school players, avoid confronting the closet racists, and avoid discussing the issue of institutional (systemic) racism. Instead, quiet the complainers by firing the coach, and sweep the entire issue under the carpet, so that no one would have to talk about it. Then fabricate a sub-par performance review for the coach which is inconsistent with the excellent performance reviews of the previous eight years, and then tell the coach that he is the one lacking in the areas of leadership and communication.

In closing, the real issue here isn't about whether or not you reinstate me as the basketball coach. As I have been telling the AD for the last year, I was only going to coach one or two more years. If you stand behind his decision, I will be in the stands cheering these kids and another great Richfield basketball team.

You have four choices.

You can reinstate me as the coach. I realize that you will probably see this as being difficult, after all that I have said tonight, because I and the AD would have to agree to disagree and to work together.

You can hire a new coach and you can tell him;

"Coach, we want you to play the best kids, and if you win and if you send kids on to college, and if in five years there's a long line of people who want you fired because their kids never played, we'll fire you."

Or you can tell the next coach;

"Coach, we want you to play the traveling kids, and mostly seniors every year, even if they aren't the best players, and even if there are more talented kids who are enrolled in our public high school, and who out outwork these seniors. However, if you don't win, we may have to fire you in five years for not winning."

Or you can tell the next coach:

"Coach, we want you to play the best kids. And we know that there are a lot of people out there saying that the team is not made up of Richfield kids, and if they tell us this, we're going to confront them. And we know that there are a lot of parents demanding that you play the traveling kids, and we'll tell them that to do so would be endorsing a program of systemic racism. And if anyone uses the term "city kid" as a racist label in front of us, we are going to challenge them. And if you win and if you send kids on to college, and if in five years there's a long line of people who want you fired because their kids never played, don't worry coach, we got your back, because loyalty goes both ways."

The real issue here is about how this community chooses to respond to demographic change. All across the northern tier states of our country, suburbs are experiencing integration for the first time. This is the age that we live in. The first place where European-American kids get displaced by African-American kids is on the rosters of the high school basketball teams. Its' happening at Tartan, and it's happening at Columbia Heights, and it's happening at a lot of places.

This suburb has two choices. It can put up the walls and send the subtle but clear message to the African-American community that their kids aren't welcome here. Unless of course they buy a house and move in when their kids are in grade school, and you can welcome them with open arms and proclaim to everyone that Richfield welcomes diversity. Or the community can welcome diversity, and with it the increased competition that it brings to all of your programs.

This isn't about individuals being overtly racist. This is about people collectively behind the scenes promoting a program of **systemic racism.** There are many valid points and counterpoints, on both sides of this issue, but underneath it all, it is about one thing. It is about Black kids who live in buildings taking away spots from White kids whose parents own houses.

History will judge you.

* * *

The next morning edition of the *St Paul Pioneer Press* paper ran an article in the bottom left-hand corner of the first page. It included a photo of the Columbia Heights coach Willie Braziel and me shaking hands after the meeting.

Dimick's long shot rejected
School board upholds ex-coach's dismissal

Former Richfield High School boys basketball coach Jim Dimick Jr. took one last shot to get his job back Monday night, but it might as well have been an air ball. Unknown to him, his shot was doomed from the start.

Dimick's passionate, 45-minute presentation filled with graphs and pie charts to defend his job performance and illustrate race issues in the western first-ring suburb apparently fell on deaf ears as the school board voted before the special hearing to approve his dismissal.

"I knew it was a long shot to get reinstated," said Dimick, who averaged 16 victories per season in his nine years as the Spartan's head coach. "It's pretty disappointing to hear that they already had their minds made up. Hopefully, I had a chance to educate them on some issues they are facing."

Superintendent Robert Slotterback confirmed after the meeting that a vote to approve Dimick's firing already had been taken. He said Dimick's presentation didn't require more discussion or a re-vote by the board.

"I'm very disappointed that coach brought the race issue into this," Slotterback said.

Dimick, son of legendary St Olaf College baseball coach Jim Dimick, said he is considering a legal appeal.

"Even with all of the opposition, I still want to coach these guys," said Dimick, who led Richfield to two state tournament berths, including a runner-up finish in Class AAA in 2005. "I have a group of kids that I've been coaching since fourth grade. I'd like to see them through to their senior year."

On June 29, Dimick was told by Richfield activities director Todd Olson that his contract would not be renewed. According to Dimick, Olson said one of the reasons cited was his inability to unite the entire Richfield basketball community," Dimick said. "He told me I've burned too many bridges."

Olson attended the meeting but left quickly and was unavailable for comment.

Ten days later, when Dimick received his letter of nonrenewal of his coaching contract, it cited overall performance concerns, including communication, leadership and program development. Prior to his arrival, the two previous coaches averaged six victories a season.

In his presentation-which was attended by about 30 supporters, half of them African-American-Dimick demonstrated the changing demographics of an inner -ring suburb as it relates to student athletes and basketball.

With the rampant open enrollment of the past decade, not just in Richfield but throughout Minnesota, kids who played in the community traveling leagues were getting displaced by students moving into districts.

According to Dimick, from 2003-10, 92 percent of the boys playing basketball in the Richfield community who moved into the city after sixth grade or open enrolled as ninth graders, were students of color. In that same period, 96 percent of the participants in the Richfield boys basketball traveling program did not make the varsity team as seniors.

From 2007 to 2010, 64 percent of Richfield's boys basketball varsity roster were students of color. In 2002, 71 percent of the varsity roster was white.

"You've got a small group of traveling (basketball) parents that don't consider themselves racists, but are pretty good people, yet they want a program of institutional racism," said Dimick who is a certified public accountant in Minneapolis. "Then you have a group that you can call closet racists that don't want to see black kids wearing Richfield uniforms. It is a difficult situation. Nobody wants to talk about it."

Richfield resident Jim Noonan, who is white, was so disgusted with the racial divide that he resigned from the traveling board. He attended the meeting in support of Dimick.

"I've been on the (traveling) board longer than anyone here," Noonan said. "The demographics in the community have changed, period. Jim has provided a lot of money to the program for scholarships for all kids-white, black, green, or yellow. He always did what was asked of him by the traveling board."

Tartan boys basketball coach Mark Klingsporn attended the meeting in support of Dimick. Richfield plays in the Classic Suburban Conference along with Tartan and many other east metro schools.

"Jim had a very well thought-out and organized presentation on why he should not be fired," Klingsporn said. "I agree with him 100 percent on all of the issues and the situations he shared. I am concerned about quality coaches getting fired for the wrong reasons."

Dimick said he plans to attend Richfield basketball games this coming season.

"I've got a lot invested in these young men," he said. "I've seen them grow, and I want to see them excel."[83]

* * *

The next day WCCO radio interviewed me. I was on the air for about fifteen minutes. I briefly explained what I had said in my speech. The interviewer made the point that if all of the kids who had open-enrolled from Minneapolis had been white kids, we would have had the same problem, adding that this was a good point to make that my firing wasn't about race. I countered that almost all of the black kids who were labeled city kids, actually lived in Richfield. But the complainers assumed that they were open-enrollment kids. And I added that when these Richfield black kids are blamed for the problem, it is about race. He countered that I had no proof that they had been labeled city kids. Two or three callers then called in. The first two callers were very civil and reiterated some of the many points and counterpoints of both sides. The last woman was a caller who was irate and ripped me, saying that it was obvious that race had absolutely nothing to do with it. She closed by saying that she was really glad that her son never played for me. I could hear and feel the rage in her voice.

* * *

That afternoon I was driving home from work in the afternoon when my cell phone rang. It was one of my buddies.

"Hey, turn on your radio to KFAN. You are the subject of discussion and you gotta hear it. Just turn it on, and I'll let you go."

I turned on the radio. I caught the last twenty minutes of the program. The commentators were taking phone calls, and responding to the article in the St. Paul Pioneer Press. It was a strange feeling. Here I was driving my car on Theodore Wirth Parkway listening to people alternately praise me and condemn me. At the time of finishing this book, I tried to get a taped or transcribed copy of the show so that I could quote these callers verbatim. The show was not saved or archived. I am going to paraphrase what I can remember as best I can.

Predictably, the Richfield callers jumped on the two black kids who I cut as seniors, and the two white kids who had transferred in as seniors. One caller said that the whole problem with me started in my second year when I cut the leading rebounder. He named the player (who was black) by name. Another caller named a black kid who had come all of the way up through the program who I had cut as a senior. Another caller said that the community has been split down the middle ever since I brought in the kid from Prior Lake.

My former assistant Lance Berwald even called in, stating that he didn't think my firing had anything to do with race. He noted the fact that we had cut the two black program kids as seniors. He went on to explain that although he didn't totally agree with the decision to cut one of them, the player was cut. This was the exact opposite of my clear memory. And during the spring of 2005 controversy, I remember him emphatically saying that race was an issue. I was surprised that his opinion had changed 180 degrees. When I pointed this out to him at a later date, and without answering my question, he made it clear that he didn't want to discuss it.

A woman said that many black families don't have the money to pay for traveling team fees, so they don't get to wear fancy uniforms and play on these teams, so why should they be cut from high school teams because they didn't have the money when they were younger.

A man said that I bring in a black kid from Minneapolis who beats out his son, and then I pull out the race card.

A Richfield woman was outraged that I brought race into the discussion. She talked passionately about Richfield people who did everything that they could to make minority kids feel welcome in both the schools and the sports programs.

A man stated that he was a Richfield resident and that he had been going to Richfield games for years. And he had never seen any individual do anything racist at a game, and he had never heard one racist word at a game.

Another man called in to say that his sons had played against Richfield, and that he could say one thing, that I was as good coach, a really good coach. The commentator Dan Barreiro then added that I was a great defensive coach.

An elderly man called in to saying that he was a long time Richfield resident and that he knew me well, and that if Jim Dimick said it was about race, it was about race.

When the show ended, I was parked in the lot near the old growth forest of Wirth Park. I felt like I had just canoed across a lake into a headwind of three-foot waves. I felt battered, stable, and full of adrenaline.

***

The following day one of my sources informed me that the administration placed a gag order on Todd Olson. This source also told me that the entire athletic department staff was told that they couldn't say anything about the firing or share their opinion with anybody. These facts proved to be true. Bob Slotterback was the only one who would address the press regarding the issue.

Later in the week I was interviewed by WCCO television. On the television interview I said, "These parents are passionate about their kids…they're homeowners…the vast majority of them are white and they believe their kids should be entitled to playing time and roster spots even if they aren't the best players. And the kids that are displacing them are overwhelmingly African-American…I was told I was let go because of my failure to bring together a divided basketball community…If we ran the program the way these parents want us to run it, it would be a program that would systematically exclude the kids of color, and it would be a program of institutional or systemic racism."

This was followed by an interview of Bob Slotterback who said, "I think he has a perception there is a division…the district is 65 percent children of color and its sports teams reflect that. I cannot go into reasons why Dimick's contract was not renewed, be I can say it's not about race…He has said a lot about what other people are thinking. I don't know how he knows what other people are thinking, but I have not been approached with those issues. We were surprised that he went down the path that it's a racial issue."

***

Friday morning, I emailed Dan Barreiro and Patrick Reusse. The email stated that I wrote my speech and then read it to the school board verbatim. I attached a complete copy of the speech and the visuals to the email. I added that if they read the speech, they would have the whole story.

Two days later the Richfield controversy was one of the subjects on the *Sunday Sermons* radio show. Barreiro and Reusse were on the air. I had no idea that the story would be on the show and I did not hear the show. I had friends that heard it. All of them said that the commentators were very complimentary of me and the stand that I had taken.

***

The next edition of the *Richfield Sun-Current* included an article written by Mike Hands with the following headline running across the top of the sports section.

Richfield basketball coach criticizes motives behind dismissal; cites 'closet racists'

Questioning the community's ability to adapt to ethnic changes and citing a pattern of institutional racism, former Richfield boys basketball head coach Jim Dimick Jr. spent 45 minutes Monday firing his parting shots at the school district where he coached for nine years.

Dimick's tenure as boys basketball coach included two state tournament berths-ending a 31-year drought-and an average of 16 wins per season. It also included criticism of his rosters, specifically the residency of his players, criticism that he countered in his presentation to the Richfield Board of Education at a special meeting Aug. 23.

Noting one of the district's options was to re-hire him, Dimick's monologue was less about retaining his job and more about deflating arguments made against his tenure and coaching style.

He told board members in his closing argument that they could listen to the constituents who were critical of his tenure or they "can really welcome diversity and with it the increased competition it brings to all your programs."

Dimick's salvo included pie charts and statistics to support his defense against arguments about his program. Dimick is an accountant who works outside the district, but his presentation was reminiscent of lectures his players may hear in history or science classes.

He spoke passionately about his academic requirements of students who play varsity basketball, citing academic successes of students who excelled after playing varsity basketball in Richfield, both on and off the court. He quoted Division I college basketball coaches and former Principal Jill Johnson as evidence that his program has been a success.

Using a funnel as his primary metaphor for varsity basketball, Dimick explained that "the best kids make it through the funnel and the best kids play." Basketball has the narrowest funnel of all the sports because seven or eight students end up with the primary playing time at the varsity level, he said. Although the students who work the hardest end up playing varsity basketball, "players are attracted to a successful program," he noted. The funnel may begin with Richfield youth basketball programs, but there are other inflows along the way, including players who move to Richfield during their high school years. Open enrollment also allows students to attend Richfield High School without living in the city, Dimick explained. When students are attracted to Dimick's basketball programs through channels outside the city's youth basketball program, it leads to an assumption of recruiting, he said. The city's traveling youth basketball program is commonly viewed as a feeder program for the high school team.

Dimick said Superintendent Bob Slotterback informed him this past season that parents expressed concerns about students who played on the traveling youth team not receiving opportunities to play on the school's varsity team. The argument was that those varsity roster slots were going to students outside the district, he added.

Noting his contract with the district did not require him to bolster the traveling basketball program, Dimick acknowledged participation in the traveling team had decreased, but argued that he has supported the program throughout his tenure. He raised more than $18,000 during his tenure to help sponsor participation in the traveling basket all program for children who otherwise couldn't afford to, he told the board.

Dimick's pie charts illustrated how the varsity team now comprises more non-white students and fewer students whose families were homeowners in the Richfield district. He explained that some players come from families who cannot afford to own a home, and because their family rents a house or apartment, the student might end up moving outside the district. Of the returning varsity players in 2011, 89 percent either live in Richfield or have lived in Richfield and chose to continue their education in the school district. Saying there is a negative stereotype of his team's black players as "city kids", he blamed the stereotype on "closet racists spreading misinformation" and "traveling parents trying to protect their kids."

Dimick called his recent sub-par performance review fabricated, noting his past performance reviews were contrary to his most recent review. He also defended his program development skills, saying the varsity team is poised to contend for a state tournament berth in the next four years.

Dimick said the district's decision was an effort to appease his vocal critics, but also thinks most residents view the varsity basketball team as not black or white players, but as a team of successful players and students. "I believe that the majority of Richfield citizens see it that way."

The board unanimously approved Athletic Director Todd Olson's recommendation of non-renewal for Dimick's contract. Board members said little prior to their motion and Dimick's presentation, and said nothing following it.[84]

* * *

The next week the African-American parents began calling the athletic department demanding that Omar McMillan be the next head coach. One of them shared with me that after having no voice in my firing, they were going to make sure that they had a voice in picking the next coach. Omar was very outspoken in backing me, and he made it known that he was going to make very few changes in the program. The administration hired him and he retained Matt Mullenbach as his top assistant. When school started the next fall, Tory Mason was not in school. He moved to Milwaukee to live with his father. Darrien Johnson transferred to Kennedy. Two of the returning best players and prospects were gone.

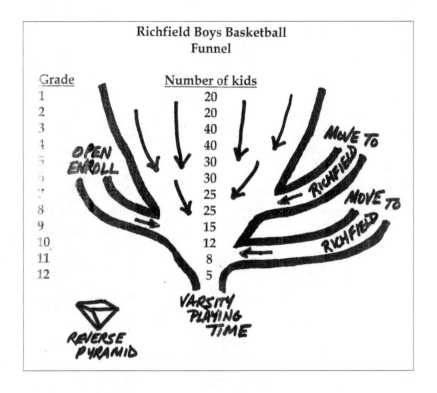

Varsity Players				
Where they have lived		Four year average	Four year average	Returning players
	2002	2003-06	2007-10	2011
have lived in Richfield	86%	82%	78%	89%
have never lived in Richfield	14%	18%	22%	11%
Total	100%	100%	100%	100%

Homeowner or renter	2002	Four year average 2003-06	Four year average 2007-10	Returning players 2011
homeowner	79%	62%	37%	29%
renter	21%	38%	63%	71%
Total	100%	100%	100%	100%

Race	2002	Four year average 2003-06	Four year average 2007-10	Returning players 2011
European American	71%	48%	36%	25%
African American	14%	44%	59%	64%
Native/African American	7%	5%	2%	4%
Asian/European American	0%	0%	2%	7%
African	7%	3%	2%	0%
Total	100%	100%	100%	100%

Race	2002	Four year average 2003-06	Four year average 2007-10	Returning players 2011
Students of color	29%	52%	64%	75%
White students	71%	48%	36%	25%
Total	100%	100%	100%	100%

Traveling kids who did not make the varsity team as seniors Eight year total		
Race	2003-2010	Pct
Students of color	3	4%
White students	64	96%
Total	67	100%

Kids who moved into Richfield after 6th grade or open enrolled as 9th graders Eight year total		
Race	2003-2010	Pct
Students of color	24	92%
White students	2	8%
Total	26	100%

Varsity Players				
Where they have lived	2002	Four year average 2003-06	Four year average 2007-10	Returning players 2011
have lived in Richfield	86%	82%	78%	89%
have never lived in Richfield	14%	18%	22%	11%
Total	100%	100%	100%	100%

Homeowner or renter	2002	Four year average 2003-06	Four year average 2007-10	Returning players 2011
homeowner	79%	62%	37%	29%
renter	21%	38%	63%	71%
Total	100%	100%	100%	100%

Race	2002	Four year average 2003-06	Four year average 2007-10	Returning players 2011
European American	71%	48%	36%	25%
African American	14%	44%	59%	64%
Native/African American	7%	5%	2%	4%
Asian/European American	0%	0%	2%	7%
African	7%	3%	2%	0%
Total	100%	100%	100%	100%

Race	2002	Four year average 2003-06	Four year average 2007-10	Returning players 2011
Students of color	29%	52%	64%	75%
White students	71%	48%	36%	25%
Total	100%	100%	100%	100%

Traveling kids who did not make the varsity team as seniors Eight year total		
Race	2003-2010	Pct
Students of color	3	4%
White students	64	96%
Total	67	100%

Kids who moved into Richfield after 6th grade or open enrolled as 9th graders Eight year total		
Race	2003-2010	Pct
Students of color	24	92%
White students	2	8%
Total	26	100%

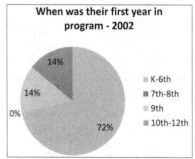

When was their first year in program - 2002

- K-6th
- 7th-8th
- 9th
- 10th-12th

14%
14%
0%
72%

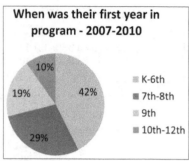

When was their first year in program - 2007-2010

- K-6th
- 7th-8th
- 9th
- 10th-12th

10%
19%
42%
29%

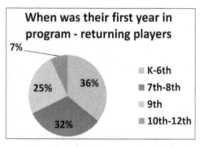

When was their first year in program - returning players

- K-6th
- 7th-8th
- 9th
- 10th-12th

7%
25%
36%
32%

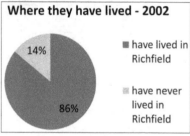

Where they have lived - 2002

- have lived in Richfield
- have never lived in Richfield

14%
86%

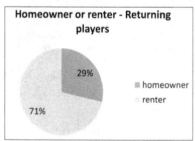

Homeowner or renter - Returning players

- homeowner
- renter

29%
71%

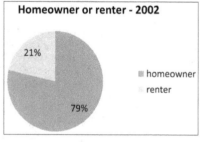

Homeowner or renter - 2002

- homeowner
- renter

21%
79%

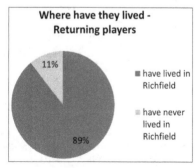

Where have they lived - Returning players

- have lived in Richfield
- have never lived in Richfield

11%
89%

The Last Word

Many a trip continues long after movement in time and space have ceased.

—John Steinbeck

T he week after the hearing my Dad called me to tell me that he wanted to write a letter to the superintendent and the school board. I said no. The next week he called me to ask again. Again, I said no.

In mid-September I was back on the Legvold farm north of my home town with my Dad. We were filling buckets with late season garden produce. At one point, he stood up, and gave me the same look that he had given me three months earlier in the same garden.

"Jim, you need to let me write that letter. I need to do it for my own peace of mind."

"OK."

The letter was dated September 25, 2010. Here is an excerpt from the letter.

...Regarding the hearing of August 23, did not the chair on that evening announce that the board, prior to the hearing, had voted not to reinstate Jim as coach? If so, I ask you, is this ethical-to vote prior to even listening to Jim's presentation?

Were well-informed people, close to the basketball situation, ever consulted on the controversial issue? Examples of such people include assistant coaches in the boys basketball program, the head girls basketball coach, coaches in other boys team sports programs (hockey, football, and baseball), Mike Karnas, a highly respected person in the Richfield school district, former administrators at Richfield High School, basketball coaches from other Classic Suburban Conference schools, loyal fans (those in attendance at the majority of games over the past decade, not short-term fans in attendance while their sons were in uniform), former players, parents of all players-not just the disgruntled few.

On the issue of "city kids" versus Richfield kids, how does the percentage in basketball compare to football? If this is a problem in basketball, why is it not a problem in football?

Regarding playing time, do any or all of you sincerely believe the disgruntled players deserved more playing time?

After the athletic director spent an hour discussing the split in the community with Jim, and after the superintendent admitted to Jim that race was an issue, how can the superintendent go on television and say that race is not an issue and that he is not aware of any split in the community? Is this honest and ethical leadership?...

Epilogue

At the suggestion of my wife who happens to be a judge, the overall format of this book is similar to the manner in which an attorney presents a case in court to the judge/jury. The attorney has the freedom to say whatever he/she wants in the opening statement. The bulk of the trial is the attorney asking questions and witnesses stating answers. During this time the attorney does not theorize or editorialize at all. The answers to the questions tell the story which is heard by the judge and jury. Then at the end of the trial the attorney once again has the freedom to say whatever he/she wants in the closing statement.

This book is the telling/documenting of a story. I was a part of the story, as were others. Most of the book consists of me documenting what happened, similar to an attorney interviewing witnesses. I only editorialized four times in the book; once briefly in the prologue, twice at length in the chapters entitled Fifth Summer, and School Board Hearing, and once briefly in the epilogue. It is not the intent of this book to judge anybody. It isn't about judging individuals, or a school, or a community. It's the story about an incredibly difficult situation, and how people dealt with it in different ways.

In the past few years, I have often been asked if I miss coaching. This question is almost always followed by a comment that I probably don't miss a lot of it, and especially the parents. My answer is always that 99% of my experience at Richfield was great, and that there were many great parents. There were also many many great community members who were staunch fans, and wonderful supporters. The faculty was fantastic to work with, and always treated me with the utmost respect. And except for the final month before I was fired, the administration was also excellent to work with. I loved coaching at Richfield.

***

Less than a year after I was fired, on May 10, 2011, an article was posted on the *Richfield Patch*, a community information website. Superintendent Robert Slotterback and high school principal Stephen West were both interviewed.

Richfield Public Schools Embrace Demographic Shifts, Diversity

While West and Slotterback see the change in the community and the schools as being a good thing, they also said the rapid changes have caused racial tensions. However, these tensions aren't among the students, but rather expressed by adults and parents. Though the reason for the increase is unclear, West sees issues like open enrollment as a source of racial tension in the community and said many of the concerns surrounding the district's rapidly changing student body stem more from parents that students. "My concern is the community, the parents. That's where I hear a lot of angst (about students open-enrolling)," said West. "That's when I fear for my students because parents set the agenda for their kids."

Slotterback concurred with West and said while many may anticipate racial conflicts to arise at the school as a result of such diversity, but that just isn't the case. "I've said this many times, in many situations. I've worked in very wealthy districts (and) in very diverse districts, with mixtures of cultures and races, and I think our kids here get along better than any place I've ever worked," Slotterback said. "We have fewer fights and fewer expulsions here, and if you spend any time in our high school, it's remarkable how well our students get along with each other."[85]

***

In March of 2012 the girls' basketball team under the coaching of LeeAnn Wise advanced to the state tournament. It was the first girls' basketball team in the history of the high school to make it to state.

When he retired in August of 2015 *Richfield Sun-Current* sportswriter Greg Kleven wrote,

One of my greatest memories was covering Richfield's girls basketball teams that competed at state...The Richfield community has always supported its athletic teams. That support was on display during the Spartans' state girls basketball quarterfinal game in 2012. Richfield supporters crammed 22 school buses as they headed for that state contest at Williams Arena.[86]

The roster of 16 players included 11 African-Americans and 5 European-Americans. The starting five included 4 black girls and 7 of the 9 girls in the playing rotation were black. The majority of the girls who played did not come up through the program, and did not grow up in Richfield.

Richfield defeated Red Wing 78-75 in the first round, and Hutchinson 45-28 in the semifinals. They were overpowered in the finals by a deep and talented DeLaSalle team 65-45. At halftime of the state championship game, I ran into one of the long-time school board members who vigorously shook my hand and smiled. This person quickly told me that the team was really fun to watch because they played my defense, and that they told this to a lot of people.

The following August LeeAnn resigned. She was the head coach for six years. She raised the overall GPA of her team to over 3.2. This was partly because her program and the boys basketball program were the only two sports that had after school study halls before 5pm practices. She continued to retain her position as the principal at Centennial Elementary. She was quoted in a *Richfield SunCurrent* Article.

"I wanted to turn the basketball program around and we did that. And we excelled in academics as well."

Todd Olson was also quoted. *"LeeAnn took over a program and turned it into a strong one...she never forgets about what is best for the kids and provided great leadership."*[87]

* * *

Two years later, Slotterback retired. A July 3, 2014 article published by the *Richfield Sun-Current* reads as follows:

"I have always been a champion of the underdog, and I felt like Richfield was kind of the underdog...There were other communities that kind of looked down on Richfield," Slotterback remembers, "and the test scores weren't very good. People were leaving the schools. The enrollment was declining, so it looked like a good challenge."

...number one on Slotterback's to-do list was to stop the bleeding regarding enrollment. Administrators figured they weren't going to attract many students who had already left and landed in happy situations in other districts, but they could try to grab more students as they entered the system in kindergarten.[88]

* * *

A year later, Todd Olson retired. The August 19, 2015 issue of the *Richfield Sun-Current* contained an article written by John Sherman.

Former Richfield athletic director looks back on Spartan career

...In 2005, Olson returned to Richfield High School to become the school's athletic director. Richfield was still his home, as the Olson family did not move once Olson took the head coaching job at Edina. In the end, Richfield is just where Olson wanted to be. "I always tell people Richfield is the best kept secret in the

metro because it never brags about itself," Olson said. "There are great teachers there. There are great coaches there, and they're all very kid-centered." Olson's primary goal when he returned to Richfield was to fix the eligibility issues that had been plaguing the school's athletic programs. Students were unable to play sports because of their grades, and Olson knew he needed to fix that issue. Olson went on to create study hall programs that were coach-monitored prior to team practices, and Richfield students, after a period of time were able to raise the average GPA to just under 3.2. "Our eligibility issues went from being a major issue to not being an issue at all," Olson said. "The kids were doing their work."... [89]

Listed below are the varsity football records for the autumns of 2013 to 2018. Also listed are the grades that the seniors of each of these teams were in, during the spring of 2010. This was the spring that Todd explained to me that he was holding meetings with the parents of all of the youth football players, in order to build the program from the bottom up with parental and community support. And he questioned why I wasn't doing the same for basketball.

Grade in 2010	Fall of senior year	Football record
8th	2013	0-9
7th	2014	0-9
6th	2015	2-7
5th	2016	3-6
4th	2017	0-9
3rd	2018	0-9

The next athletic director was Dave Boie.

***

The Sunday morning January 31, 2016 edition of the *StarTribune* included a multi-page story in the sport's section. The bottom right-hand quadrant of the first page had a headline.

The horn sounds on one of metro area's most storied programs

On another page the story was continued where it filled the top half of the page. Across the top of the page there was another headline.

'IT'S STILL SINKING IN'

The story was continued on a third page, and it again covered half of the page, the entire left half from top to bottom, with another headline.

ONE MAN'S REACTION: 'GEEZ, I DIDN'T DO MUCH TO HELP'

I have included quotes from the article earlier in this book. I didn't include these excerpts from the article:

...The death of hockey in Richfield once would have been unimaginable... (A student) said a number of players he skated with as a youngster moved, or open-enrolled at schools like Bloomington Jefferson or opted for the city's private school, Holy Angels...As late as 2000, Richfield's population was 81.2 percent white, according to census statistics. Now, minorities make up two-thirds of the senior high school population. Greater diversity does not bring with it childhood dreams of playing hockey.

Three of the former head coaches were quoted.

Mike Thomas-*I don't know if we could have done anything to stop it, because of the socioeconomics. Hockey has become a very expensive sport.*

Larry Hendrickson-*Hockey had changed. It's become a business...Richfield is a changing community, and most of the kids just can't afford to play.*

Jake McCoy-*We just ran out of kids.*[90]

* * *

As I was in the final stages of writing this book, I was reviewing the letters to the editor in the *Richfield Sun-Current*. I reread the spring of 2006 letter by the ghost writer William Beckett of Minneapolis. Then I looked back at the summer of 2005 letters by Steven T Thompson of Edina and Martin Demgen of Minneapolis. It occurred to me that Thompson and Demgen also could have also been ghost writers.

I had my friend of a friend who worked at the private firm do a data check on both of these names. He used only search engines that were open to the public. One search engine listed all previous addresses of the person for which one was searching, sometimes going back more than 15 years. Five people with the exact name Steven T Thompson were found who had lived in Minnesota. They all listed multiple previous addresses. One of them listed 16 previous addresses. Not one of them listed Edina as a previous address. Granted, it was 10 years later that we did the search. However, as in the case of William Becket of Minneapolis, on the search engines that we used, the search for a Steven T Thompson of Edina came up empty.

The same search for a Martin Demgen did not come up empty. One name was listed as a resident of Minneapolis. And actually, two Martin Demgens were shown who lived in Minnesota. A second Martin Demgen who was about 30 years older lived in the town of Willmar, in the western part of the state.

* * *

In 2010, five years after he was fired at Lourdes High School in Rochester, Rich Decker was hired as the head girls' coach at Mayo, the large public high school on the south side of the city. The Spartans advanced to state his first year. By 2018, after being at Mayo eight seasons, his teams won more games than they lost every year, and made three trips to the state tournament.

After being fired at Centennial, Dave DeWitt went on to become the head women's coach at Anoka-Ramsey Community College in the northern suburb of Coon Rapids. In his first nine years his teams compiled a record of 221-56. His teams advanced to the NJCAAD3 national tournament six times, and the Golden Rams were NCAAA Division 3 national champions in both 2010 and 2012.

Lance Berwald continued to give private basketball lessons to big kids at all levels in the twin city area. He also worked as a realtor, and helped many young men buy homes. Many of these young men were African-American and were first time home buyers in their family history.

In the spring of 2017, Dave Thorson resigned as the basketball coach at DeLaSalle, after winning six consecutive Class 3A state championships. In 23 years at the school his teams won nine state championships and he compiled an overall record of 527-130. He was hired as the top assistant and defensive coach at Drake University in Des Moines Iowa. A couple of months earlier Drake had hired Niko Medved away from Furman University where Medved put together four successful seasons. Medved and Thorson knew each other from their University of Minnesota days, when Thorson was an assistant coach and Medved was a student manager. A year later they both moved on to Colorado State. Dave's goal was to eventually be a head coach and to play the pressure man to man defense that he used at DeLaSalle at the collegiate level. Almost all D1 programs played behind the post. Dave believed that with the right talent, his teams could dead front the post, overplay the perimeter passing lanes to slow down ball reversal, switch some predetermined screens, and take teams out of their offense. He wanted to play this defense at the D1 level, and he believed that it would work.

* * *

The winter of 2015-16 was the twentieth year of the four-class state tournament system in Minnesota. The two-class system lasted 20 years, from 1970-71 to 1993-94. This was followed by two years of a 16-team state tourney made up of eight large schools and eight small schools.

Since the winter of 1996-97, four schools were crowned state champions every year. Thirty-two Section champions participated in four days of state tournament games at two sites. No sessions sold out, and for the 16 opening round games, there were always more empty seats than people. In Class 4A, 50 of the 64 teams were in the Twin City metro area. In Class 3A, 25 of the 64 teams were also metro schools.

In these 20 years, the number of small family farms on the southern and western prairie of the state continued to decrease, and the size of the farms continued to increase. As many farmers switched from sustainable farming to extractive farming, many main street businesses in the nearby small towns also disappeared. Many baby-boomers from the western half of the state migrated to the larger nearby towns, and the western suburbs of the Twin Cities. By 2019, the 250 high schools of old Regions 2, 3, 6, and 8 had consolidated to 120 high schools. Except for 13 schools, all were in Class 2A and 1A.

The high-grade iron ore of the Mesabi Iron Range was exhausted by the 1950s. After this happened, the lesser grade iron ore of taconite was mined. Beginning in the 1970s, the overall population of the Iron Range began its decline. Many Rangers moved to the northern suburbs of the Twin Cities. By 2020, the 16 high schools of the Mesabi Iron Range had consolidated to 8 schools, without one school in Class 4A. When Eveleth-Gilbert, formerly Eveleth, merged with Virginia, the 'four-peat' state championship hockey trophies from the 1950s no longer had an Eveleth high school. The populations of the port cities on Lake Superior also declined, and by 2019, the four public high schools of Duluth had contracted to two. One of the casualties was Duluth Central, with its four state championship basketball trophies.

In Class 1A, Rushford-Peterson dominated Section 1A in the southeast corner of the state. Coach Tom Vix took the Trojans to state 14 times in 20 years, and won a state championship. In the 40 years of the one class system, Rushford and Peterson were both in District 1, where the biggest town had a population of 2,600, and the district champion never made it out of Region 1.

Also, in Class 1A, the Ojibwa reservation schools of Red Lake and Cass Lake ruled Section 8A in the northwest corner of Minnesota. They combined to make 16 trips to state in 20 years. Under the one class system both schools were in District 29, along with Bemidji. Red Lake is 25 miles north of Bemidji and Cass Lake is 15 miles east of Bemidji.

Chisholm coach Bob McDonald retired in 2014 as the all-time leader in career victories with 1,012 and 11 state tournament teams. In second place was

Bob Brink of Rocori who retired in 2012 with 936 wins and 13 trips to state. In third and fourth place and still coaching were Ken Novak Jr at Hopkins with 871 wins and 15 state tourney teams and Dave Galovich at Crosby-Ironton with 744 wins and 9 trips to state. When the one class system ended in 1970, under legendary coaches of previous generations, Chisholm, Hopkins, and Crosby-Ironton had been to state 8 times, 7 times, and 12 times. In what was to be the Rocori school district, Rockville, Cold Spring, and Richmond never made it to state.

In 1985 the meat packers of Hormel Foods in Austin went on strike, which made national news. The strike ended 10 months later with the union broken. The former union workers were eventually replaced by immigrants. In 2012 the Packers went to state for the first time in 30 years. Under coach Kris Fadness, Austin won six of the next eight section championships, advancing to the state finals three times. The majority of the players on these teams were first generation Sudanese-Americans, who fathers were meat cutters. Four of the five starters on the 2019 team were Sudanese-Americans.

From 2005 to 2020, the migration of African-Americans to Minnesota from the South continued. By 2019, there were about 30 basketball teams that were majority black teams. This included all of the city schools of Minneapolis and St Paul, and all of the inner ring suburbs with the exception of Edina. It also included many schools in the second ring suburbs, and some schools in the third ring. At Tartan, Coach Mark Klingsporn's team won over 20 games, with a roster that was almost all African-American. His first team, 27 years earlier, had no African-Americans.

* * *

In the summer of 2018 Richfield's incumbent mayor Pat Elliott announced that he would not seek re-election. City council member Maria Regan Gonzalez ran unopposed and received 96% of the vote. The Latino population of the city was estimated to be 20%, with the high school over 40% Hispanic. Her victory established her as the first Latina mayor in the history of the state. When asked about Regan Gonzalez, Elliott stated "she's extremely intelligent and a hard worker and she has her heart in the right place." Fifty-five years earlier, Elliott had worn number 42 for the 1963 mythical state championship football team. When asked about the 1963 Spartans of the gridiron, he smiled and said, "there was nothing mythical about it."

In the winter of 2019-2020 the Richfield Spartans finished with a record of 20-6 and were crowned Section 3 champions. Two days after defeating Holy

Angels 67-53 for the section title, the state tournament was canceled due to the corona virus pandemic. Head coach Omar McMillan was also a fourth-grade teacher. In basketball, he was chosen Section 3 Coach of the Year, and in the classroom, he was one of 10 finalists for Minnesota Teacher of the Year. Omar and his wife Laurie own a rambler north of the high school with a basket hanging on the garage.

* * *

The March 24, 2010 edition of the *StarTribune* ran an article which filled three fourths of the first page of the sports section, and another entire page. The headline was,

1960 Edgerton Dutchmen Improbable flight
Minnesota's classic version of "Hoosiers" turns 50 this year, still resonating with tournament fans

Dean Verdoes (Edgerton player) is quoted-*Most people don't understand how big the state basketball tournament was back then. The high school basketball tournament was a big deal. The Richfield victory was the game. We had no idea how good that team was. We got a couple of fortunate breaks, and won. I don't know how many times out of five we would have beaten them, but we only had to do it once.*[91]

The superbly written book **Edgerton A Basketball Legend** by Tom Tomashek and Ken Kielty was published in 2008 to chronicle this 'Hoosiers' story of Minnesota. Some of the players were quoted:

Bill Davis (Richfield player)–*I was the captain of the team and led us out of the locker room and up the stairs into the arena. My first impression was the size of the crowd...the place was packed. The second was that, for the first and only time in my athletic career, we got booed...right out of the chute. Once the game began, it took on a life of its own.*

Dean Veenhof (Edgerton player)-*I've even wondered for nearly fifty years if he committed the (lane) violation, and second, whether it should have been called.*

Dean Verdoes (Edgerton player)-*We were very, very fortunate to have won. They were a very good team. They were bigger than us. They were faster than us. They were stronger than us. But we managed to make enough free throws in the last quarter and overtime.*

Gene Farrell (Richfield coach)-*You know, Olson has done a great job with that team, and the team's poise is simply unbelievable.*

Bob Sadek (Richfield player)- *Mac, who was setting a screen for Bill, had a 13- or 14- size shoe and his foot may have been on the line, so technically he was in the lane. You'd see guys camping out in the middle many times and it wasn't called, so why would it be called in that situation? We enjoyed playing them, and the game created some memories for us and certainly them. But it still hurts. We would have loved to have won that game.* [92]

As a coach, I can relate to what both Gene Farrell and Bob Sadek said. I am certain that Stu Starner and Steve Bender feel the same way. The 2005 state final loss to Shakopee still hurts. We would have loved to have won that game.

About the Author

J im Dimick and his wife Martha Holton Dimick live in a century-old brick farmhouse that they restored on the north side of Minneapolis. Jim is retired from his position as a CPA principal with an accounting firm. Martha is retired from her final job as a Hennepin county judge presiding in criminal court.

They practice permaculture on their city lot, with a large vegetable garden, eight types of fruit bearing bushes and trees, and three egg laying hens. They burn three cords of wood to heat their home every winter. Jim takes two canoe trips every year deep into the wilderness of North America. Jim and Martha are very involved in the lives of their daughter Joslyn and her husband John and grandsons Jason and William.

In retirement they hope to explore the most challenging canoe routes on the continent, and to spend two months every winter in a foreign country. Jim will also embark on a career as a watercolor and oil artist. Martha will dedicate her retirement to service and activism in the African-American community.

Acknowledgments

A number of people have contributed valuable information, and shared ideas for the completion of this book. To acknowledge all of them personally, while desirable, is virtually impossible. However, I am going to acknowledge the following people:

Jim Klobuchar-my writer mentor-encouraged me from the beginning that this was a story that needed to be told

Mark Babin, Sam Donatelle, Keith Erickson, Dave Finholt, Paul Glanton, John Hegelmeyer, Steve Hill, Doug Holton, Doug Johnson, Duke Lehto, Ed Manuel, Dale Pippin, Art Skenandore, and Tom Wavrin-coaches, teammates, and friends-reviewed what I had written and offered constructive criticism that improved the book dramatically

Gary Neubauer-another friend-reviewed the writing and researched Minnesota basketball history

Four Richfield alums from the glory years-contributed vivid memories and anecdotes

My dad Jim and my uncle Dave-coaches who mentored me throughout my coaching career

My mother Nancy-enough said

My wife Martha Holton Dimick-who always had my back

1961 Rice Lake (Wisconsin) Warriors-my first memory of sitting in a packed gym and watching a powerhouse high school basketball team-and my dad complained until his dying day about the famous no call that cost them the state title

Bibliography

Newspapers
Austin *Herald*
Bemidji *Pioneer*
Eau Claire *Leader-Telegram*
Faribault *Daily News*
Grand Rapids *Herald-Review*
Minneapolis *StarTribune*
Minneapolis *Tribune*
Minnesota *Prep Coach*
Minnesota *Spokesman-Recorder*
Northwest Suburban Newspapers
Richfield *News*
Richfield *Spartan Spotlite*
Richfield *Sun Current*
St Paul *Pioneer Press*

Books & Published Documents
Auerbach, Red & Feinstein, John, *Let Me Tell You a Story; A Lifetime in the Game*, New York NY, 2004
Johnson, Frederick L, *Richfield Minnesota's Oldest Suburb*, Richfield, Mn 2008
Kielty, Ken & Tomashek, Tom, *Edgerton A Basketball Legend*, St Cloud, Mn, 2008
Pearlstein, Mitchell B., "Strange Brew: Minnesota's Motley Mix of School Reforms," The Thomas B. Fordham Institute, Washington DC, 2003-2006
Ramsay, Jack, *Dr. Jack on Winning Basketball*, Indianapolis, In, 2011

Internet
Richfield Patch, patch.com/minnesota/richfield
http://by107fd.bay107.hotmail.msn.com
Wikipedia, en.wikipedia.org
Minneapolis Public Schools, mpls.k12.mn.us
Minnesota Legislature, www.revisor.mn.gov

Endnotes

1   Minneapolis *Tribune,* Minneapolis, Mn
2   Richfield *Sun Current,* Richfield, Mn
3   Ramsay, Jack, *Dr. Jack on Winning Basketball*, Indianapolis, In, 2011
4   Minneapolis *Tribune,* Minneapolis, Mn
5   Minneapolis *Tribune,* Minneapolis, Mn
6   Richfield *Sun Current,* Richfield, Mn
7   Minneapolis *Tribune,* Minneapolis, Mn
8   Eau Claire *Leader-Telegram*, Eau Claire, Wi
9   Johnson, Frederick L, *Richfield Minnesota's Oldest Suburb*, Richfield, Mn 2008
10 Minneapolis *Tribune,* Minneapolis, Mn
11 Minneapolis *Tribune,* Minneapolis, Mn
12 Minneapolis *Tribune,* Minneapolis, Mn
13 Minneapolis *Tribune,* Minneapolis, Mn
14 Minneapolis *Tribune,* Minneapolis, Mn
15 Johnson, Frederick L, *Richfield Minnesota's Oldest Suburb*, Richfield, Mn 2008
16 Minneapolis *Tribune,* Minneapolis, Mn
17 Minneapolis *Tribune,* Minneapolis, Mn
18 Auerbach, Red & Feinstein, John, *Let Me Tell You a Story; A Lifetime in the Game*, New York NY, 2004
19 Faribault *Daily News,* Faribault, Mn
20 Faribault *Daily News,* Faribault, Mn
21 Minneapolis *StarTribune,* Minneapolis, Mn
22 Austin *Herald*, Austin, Mn
23 Minneapolis *StarTribune,* Minneapolis, Mn
24 Minneapolis *StarTribune,* Minneapolis, Mn
25 Richfield *News,* Richfield, Mn
26 Richfield *News,* Richfield, Mn
27 Richfield *News,* Richfield, Mn
28 Richfield *News,* Richfield, Mn
29 Richfield *Spartan Spotlite,* Richfield, Mn
30 Richfield *News,* Richfield, Mn

31 Minneapolis *Tribune,* Minneapolis, Mn
32 Minneapolis *Tribune,* Minneapolis, Mn
33 Richfield *News,* Richfield, Mn
34 Minneapolis *StarTribune,* Minneapolis, Mn
35 Minneapolis *StarTribune,* Minneapolis, Mn
36 Minneapolis *StarTribune,* Minneapolis, Mn
37 Minneapolis *StarTribune,* Minneapolis, Mn
38 Minneapolis *StarTribune,* Minneapolis, Mn
39 Grand Rapids *Herald-Review,* Grand Rapids, Mn
40 Minneapolis *StarTribune,* Minneapolis, Mn
41 Richfield *Sun Current,* Richfield, Mn
42 Richfield *Sun Current,* Richfield, Mn
43 Richfield *Spartan Spotlite,* Richfield, Mn
44 Richfield *Spartan Spotlite,* Richfield, Mn
45 Minneapolis *StarTribune,* Minneapolis, Mn
46 Richfield *Sun Current,* Richfield, Mn
47 Richfield *Sun Current,* Richfield, Mn
48 Richfield *Sun Current,* Richfield, Mn
49 Richfield *Sun Current,* Richfield, Mn
50 Richfield *Sun Current,* Richfield, Mn
51 Richfield *Sun Current,* Richfield, Mn
52 Minneapolis *StarTribune,* Minneapolis, Mn
53 Minneapolis *StarTribune,* Minneapolis, Mn
54 Richfield *Sun Current,* Richfield, Mn
55 Richfield *Sun Current,* Richfield, Mn
56 Richfield *News,* Richfield, Mn
57 Richfield *News,* Richfield, Mn
58 Richfield *News,* Richfield, Mn
59 Minneapolis *Tribune,* Minneapolis, Mn
60 Minneapolis *StarTribune,* Minneapolis, Mn
61 Richfield *Sun Current,* Richfield, Mn
62 Minneapolis *Tribune,* Minneapolis, Mn
63 Richfield *Sun Current,* Richfield, Mn
64 Minneapolis *Tribune,* Minneapolis, Mn
65 Richfield *Sun Current,* Richfield, Mn
66 Minneapolis *Tribune,* Minneapolis, Mn
67 Richfield *Sun Current,* Richfield, Mn
68 Minnesota *Prep Coach,* Brooklyn Center, Mn
69 Richfield *Sun Current,* Richfield, Mn
70 Minnesota *Prep Coach,* Brooklyn Center, Mn

71 Pearlstein, Mitchell B., "Strange Brew: Minnesota's Motley Mix of School Reforms," The Thomas B. Fordham Institute, Washington DC, 2003-2006

72 Pearlstein, Mitchell B., "Strange Brew: Minnesota's Motley Mix of School Reforms," The Thomas B. Fordham Institute, Washington DC, 2003-2006

73 Pearlstein, Mitchell B., "Strange Brew: Minnesota's Motley Mix of School Reforms," The Thomas B. Fordham Institute, Washington DC, 2003-2006

74 Pearlstein, Mitchell B., "Strange Brew: Minnesota's Motley Mix of School Reforms," The Thomas B. Fordham Institute, Washington DC, 2003-2006

75 Minneapolis Public Schools, mpls.k12.mn.us

76 Minneapolis *StarTribune*, Minneapolis, Mn

77 Minnesota *Spokesman-Recorder*, Minneapolis, Mn

78 Minneapolis *StarTribune*, Minneapolis, Mn

79 Minneapolis *StarTribune*, Minneapolis, Mn

80 Johnson, Frederick L, *Richfield Minnesota's Oldest Suburb*, Richfield, Mn 2008

81 Minnesota *Prep Coach*, Brooklyn Center, Mn

82 Minnesota Legislature, www.revisor.mn.gov

83 St Paul *Pioneer Press*, St Paul, Mn

84 Richfield *Sun Current*, Richfield, Mn

85 Richfield Patch, patch.com/minnesota/richfield

86 Richfield *Sun Current*, Richfield, Mn

87 Richfield *Sun Current*, Richfield, Mn

88 Richfield *Sun Current*, Richfield, Mn

89 Richfield *Sun Current*, Richfield, Mn

90 Minneapolis *StarTribune*, Minneapolis, Mn

91 Minneapolis *StarTribune*, Minneapolis, Mn

92 Kielty, Ken & Tomashek, Tom, *Edgerton A Basketball Legend*, St Cloud, Mn, 2008

CPSIA information can be obtained
at www.ICGtesting.com
Printed in the USA
LVHW051921240821
696015LV00009B/105